MEDIEVAL
ENGLAND

DISCARD

MEDIEVAL ENGLAND

A Social History 1250–1550

P.J.P. Goldberg
Centre for Medieval Studies
University of York

A member of the Hodder Headline Group
LONDON
Distributed in the United States of America by
Oxford University Press Inc., New York

First published in Great Britain in 2004 by
Hodder Arnold, a member of the Hodder Headline Group,
338 Euston Road, London NW1 3BH

http://www.arnoldpublishers.com

Distributed in the United States of America by
Oxford University Press Inc.
198 Madison Avenue, New York, NY10016

The advice and information in this book are believed to be true and
accurate at the date of going to press, but neither the author nor the publisher
can accept any legal responsibility or liability for any errors or omissions.

British Library Cataloguing in Publication Data
A catalogue record for this book is available from the British Library

Library of Congress Cataloging-in-Publication Data
A catalog record for this book is available from the Library of Congress

ISBN 0 340 58531 5 (hb)
ISBN 0 340 57745 2 (pb)

1 2 3 4 5 6 7 8 9 10

Typeset in 10/12pt Adobe Garamond by Servis Filmsetting Ltd, Manchester
Printed and bound in Malta

What do you think about this book? Or any other Arnold title?
Please send your comments to feedback.arnold@hodder.co.uk

CONTENTS

PREFACE

Much of the inspiration for what follows stems from my years of teaching at the University of York and my experience of helping students come to grips with an essentially alien world. In my writing I have tried to keep firmly in mind the needs of just such readers; I do not assume prior knowledge, but I do assume a critical intelligence and a desire to know more. I have tried in a number of places to foreground the primary sources that necessarily underpin our understanding of the past and I have not been shy of showing the reader my reasoning or pointing up the ambiguities of the evidence. In compiling a social history, moreover, I have tried always to consider the experience of ordinary folk, even though their social superiors tend to be so much better documented. I have also consciously refrained from writing a chapter on 'the female experience', but have tried to integrate writing about women into the main body of my text.

Any such general survey must necessarily be full of gaps, of impressionistic remarks that do scant justice to specific historical events and, I am sure, of dubious, outmoded or even wrongheaded observations. I can only hope these last are few and of little significance. I have, however, seen it as my task to provide impressions, to offer overviews and not to overload the reader with the sort of detail that is only really useful – certainly only really comprehensible – within a broader framework. If on further study my readers find some of my arguments unconvincing, then I should like to hope that is because I have provided the framework from which they are able to construct their own ideas and understanding. The past is neither dead nor finite, but rather a living, changing entity that thrives on debate and interpretation, is refreshed by challenges to the orthodox and only stifled by dogmatism and certainty.

Although parts of this book derive from or reflect my own research – and in this sense this is not simply a work of synthesis – my understanding and writing has been informed by the scholarship of numerous other individuals (including some who are essentially anonymous since judicious use of the Internet represents one of my resources). I am also grateful to various of my current and former research students, from whom I have learnt so much. To them I owe a real debt of gratitude. I wish to acknowledge the helpful comments of my anonymous reader. This book has been some time in the making. That it was undertaken at all owes much to the patience of my first editor, Christopher Wheeler, who belongs to an earlier, gentler era in publishing. I should also like to acknowledge the support of colleagues at York, particularly Mark Ormrod and Sarah Rees Jones, and my continuing gratitude to Sandra Raban, Barrie Dobson and Richard Smith, who have done so much to make me a medieval historian. To my wife, whose knowledge of the era is always sharper than my own, and my daughter, who helps keep me sane, I am especially indebted. I dedicate this book to the memory of my father.

P.J.P. Goldberg
University of York
2004

A NOTE ON MONEY

The present currency based on pounds (£) and pence (p) represents the 1971 reform (decimalization) of an earlier currency that had its roots in the medieval era. Prior to 1971 there were three different denominations: pounds (£), shillings (s) and pence (d for the Latin *denarius*). Rather than being divided into 100 (new) pence, the pound was divided into 20 shillings, each shilling being worth 12 pence. There were thus 240 pence (d) in the pre-decimal pound. The penny was the basic unit of currency in the medieval era, its silver content underpinning its monetary worth at least until the Henrician debasements. From the later fourteenth century, numbers of higher-denomination coins were minted, including the half groat (2d), the groat (4d) and some high-denomination gold coins, notably the quarter noble (20d), half noble (or angel, 3s 4d) and noble (6s 8d). A shilling coin was not produced until the end of our period.

Although the system of £/s/d was commonly used for accounting purposes, the mark (13s 4d) served as a convenient unit of reckoning. (The mark was never issued as a unit of currency.) The logic is that 13s 4d represents two-thirds of a pound; it is also 160d, a sum readily divisible by two, four, five, eight and ten. The higher-value coins – the quarter, angel and noble – all represent simple divisions of this larger unit. When examining a medieval inventory or some other source listing prices or values, it is common to find large sums expressed as marks or represented as multiples of marks, e.g. £6 13s 4d = 10 marks. Smaller values often appear as 6s 8d or 3s 4d. This principle is found, for example, in the schedule for the 1379 poll tax returns.

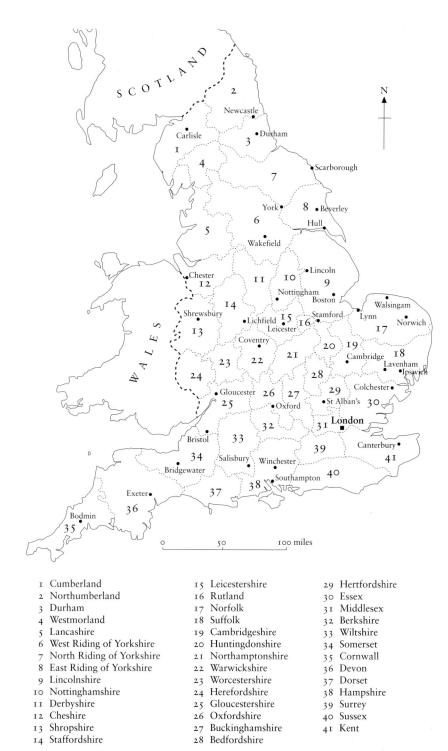

SCOTLAND

N

Newcastle

Carlisle
1

● Durham
3

4

7

Scarborough

York ●
6
8 ● Beverley

5
Hull

Wakefield

WALES

Chester
12
11
10
● Lincoln

Nottingham
9

Boston

14
Shrewsbury
15
Stamford
Walsingam

13
● Lichfield
Leicester
16
Lynn
17
Norwich

Coventry
23
22
21
20
19

Cambridge
18

24
28
Lavenham
● Ipswich

25
26
27
29
Colchester

● Gloucester
● Oxford
St Alban's
30

Bristol
33
32
31 **London**

34
Salisbury
39
● Canterbury

Bridgewater
Winchester
41

37
38
40

Exeter
36
Southampton

Bodmin
35

0   50   100 miles

1 Cumberland	15 Leicestershire	29 Hertfordshire
2 Northumberland	16 Rutland	30 Essex
3 Durham	17 Norfolk	31 Middlesex
4 Westmorland	18 Suffolk	32 Berkshire
5 Lancashire	19 Cambridgeshire	33 Wiltshire
6 West Riding of Yorkshire	20 Huntingdonshire	34 Somerset
7 North Riding of Yorkshire	21 Northamptonshire	35 Cornwall
8 East Riding of Yorkshire	22 Warwickshire	36 Devon
9 Lincolnshire	23 Worcestershire	37 Dorset
10 Nottinghamshire	24 Herefordshire	38 Hampshire
11 Derbyshire	25 Gloucestershire	39 Surrey
12 Cheshire	26 Oxfordshire	40 Sussex
13 Shropshire	27 Buckinghamshire	41 Kent
14 Staffordshire	28 Bedfordshire	

Map of England in the Later Middle Ages

PART 1
The Structures of Society

1 GENDER AND HIERARCHY

'When Adam delved and Eve span, who was then the gentleman?' So runs the question posed not just by the peasant rebels of 1381, but also by rather more conservative preachers. The question challenges the social hierarchy of this world – for the preacher, to remind his audience of the spiritual equality of the next world, and for the rebel, to urge a utopian egalitarianism. The implicit status quo is of an ordered social structure in which some command, but others labour. What remains unchallenged, however, even by the peasants who used this as a radical slogan, is the notion that males and females have very different roles and carry out very different tasks. In order to understand medieval society, we have to understand these two givens.

Medieval people wanted to live in an ordered society, and hierarchy was integral to the way they thought about order. Often these hierarchies were understood to be 'natural' or divinely ordained. Thus the hierarchy of gender could be explained by reference to the Genesis account of the Creation and Fall – the allusion made by our initial quotation – and justified by reference to these and other scriptural and patristic texts. According to the Genesis account, Eve was created from Adam's rib as his (implicitly subordinate) companion. Being the weaker sex, she was tempted by the Serpent to eat the fruit of the forbidden tree and then tempted Adam. As punishment, the couple were expelled from Eden; Adam was to live by the sweat of his brow, Eve to suffer pain in childbearing. Adam is regularly represented in medieval art digging with his spade, while Eve spins and simultaneously cares for a baby. Ordinary folk may have had but the flimsiest understanding of this scriptural tradition, but it is unlikely that they did not respect and replicate a gender hierarchy in their own family and social relations. Likewise, they accepted hierarchies variously associated with social rank, with legal status, with age, with household and marital status or with ethnic identity. They were, moreover, adept at negotiating between these differing and overlapping hierarchies in ways that some modern scholars find difficult. A medieval person would never have imagined that an aristocratic lady was inferior to a male of lower social rank because female. Nor would they have assumed that a (live-in) servant was of lower social standing than his or her employer by reason of being a servant, but would immediately have been aware of the differences in age, household status and, perhaps, gender that would have shaped their relationship.

Because medieval men and women were socialized to regard hierarchies of status, age and gender as the norm, they were concerned always to position themselves within these hierarchies. This was especially true where their positions were otherwise ambiguous or contested. Thus medieval monks, who so far as we can discern tended to be of peasant stock, came to mimic many of the trappings of aristocratic society in terms of diet and recreation. Likewise priests, as we shall see, sometimes engaged in particularly 'masculine' forms of behaviour lest their clerical estate be seen to compromise their gender identity. On the other hand, the pride of the Pastons, a fifteenth-century Norfolk gentry family with particularly aggressive social ambitions, was severely slighted when a rival drew attention to their servile origins. The late medieval aristocratic cult of genealogy and pedigree specifically came about because the ranks of the established aristocracy were seen to be diluted by the elevation of men of more humble birth.

Hierarchies were demarcated in a variety of ways, such as the manner in which people were addressed, how they behaved or the clothes they wore. The modern scholar can only hope to recapture some of these, since such crucial indicators as gesture or speech are but imperfectly recorded. One of the places we can look is conduct literature, but here we need to be especially cautious. Works such as *The Book of the Knight of the Tower*, ostensibly an aristocratic text originally written in French in the 1370s, or the bourgeois verse texts, 'How the Wise Man Taught his Son' and 'What the Goodwife Taught her Daughter', were written and circulated in order to socialize young people into particular modes of behaviour. They are not mirrors of how people actually behaved, and we need a clear sense of the agenda behind them in order to use them effectively. Depictions of people in manuscript illuminations or sepulchral monuments probably provide our best evidence for dress since so little actually survives, but again these visual representations may be idealized, or may follow aesthetic, iconographic or other normative agendas. Thus the famous and much reproduced peasants in the Luttrell Psalter appear to be dressed in clothes tastefully dyed in lilac and apricot hues, as if just kitted out by the BBC drama department. Likewise, unmarried women are invariably shown with long, uncovered hair, whereas married women wear wimples, but we cannot be sure that women who never married despite achieving adult years always left their hair uncovered.

Despite these caveats, certain observations may still be made. Social rank was clearly demarcated by dress: the wearing of the highest-quality imported cloth (notably at the beginning of our period), silk and fur was primarily an aristocratic privilege; a statute of 1337 had attempted to restrict the wearing of furs to persons with an income of more than £100. The display of jewellery also signalled aristocratic status and was part of an aristocratic culture of conspicuous consumption. The peasantry wore locally produced cloth, the cheapest of which would be undyed, and hence would be of the browns and russets of natural wool, although the use of natural dyes may often have made their clothing more colourful than we tend to suppose. Townsfolk, particularly the better-off, wore higher-quality cloth and linen in ways that would have distinguished them from the aristocracy. Bourgeois women, for example, continued to wear simple wimples to cover their heads after aristocratic ladies had begun to adopt more elaborate head-dresses. As we shall see, such fundamental differences in the dress codes of different social groups underpin the rare attempts at legislation in the form of sumptuary laws.

Gender difference was clearly signalled regardless of social rank, women's garments regularly reaching to their ankles and hair routinely being covered, other than in the case of younger, unmarried women and girls. (Here loose, uncovered hair was an indicator of youth, marital status and innocence.) What is not so apparent is the point at which young boys and girls came to be dressed differently. By the early modern period, aristocratic children wore skirts with little indication of gender for their first years (after being swaddled as babies), but we know too little about children's clothing to say how far back this tradition might extend. Skirts would, however, have been practical for all children until they were toilet-trained.

Age difference for the more well-to-do was probably represented by the degree of fashionableness of the clothing worn. Young adults would tend to wear, or at least be depicted in, fashionable clothes; older adults wore less fashionable dress of more sober colours. Widows, especially, tended to dress in dark colours and covered their hair and neck more thoroughly than their married sisters. Servants, particularly women servants, might also be distinguished by slightly old-fashioned dress since it was common for their mistresses to pass their clothes on to them. The same would also be true of some poorer persons who relied on the apparently extensive market in refurbished second-hand clothing, so here too fashionableness was also a marker of status.

We are in fact most aware of these hierarchies precisely at the moments that they appear to be undermined or challenged. This is particularly true of the decades following the Black Death, both because (as will be explained at greater length in Chapter 12) the advent of plague itself was seen as divine punishment for sin and because the economic implications of the plague tended to favour the lower echelons of society at the expense of the higher. The consequence of persons of lower rank being better off was that they could afford to indulge in the same, or similar, patterns of consumption – whether in terms of diet, dress or possessions – as those previously restricted to their social superiors. The result was moral outrage on the part of the ruling elite. We see this most immediately in a London sumptuary ordinance of 1351, designed to proscribe the wearing of furs or silks, that is 'the manner of dress of good and noble dames and damsels of this realm', by 'common lewd women'. The concern here, however, is not solely with status, but also with gender and even ethnicity. By wearing clothes inappropriate to their rank, some women, including foreign women, posed a threat to the reputation of 'good and noble dames and damsels'. Conversely, women who dressed beyond their station might be thought of as no better than common prostitutes.

Such outrage is again found in the sumptuary ordinance of 1363, two years after the second plague pandemic. Little attempt seems to have been made to enforce the law and it was repealed the next year; its importance lies in what it says about the perspective of the ruling classes, but it also reflects the way in which dress was such an important marker of social rank. The legislation set out to regulate appropriate dress and also diet for differing levels of society from peasant to magnate, silks and furs being the exclusive prerogative of the latter, but russets and simple fare being deemed appropriate for the former. The 1363 ordinance is reflective of a broader concern to regulate and demarcate hierarchy in the wake of the plague. This is seen more fully in the unusually detailed ranking of social groups in the schedule for the poll tax of 1379. Here the landed esquire is distinguished from the landless esquire, the 'sufficient' merchant from the 'lesser' merchant, the married man from the single. It is seen also in Langland's famous poem, *Piers Plowman*, which comments adversely on the dress of the lower orders and on labourers demanding from their employers white (i.e. wheaten) bread, hot meat or fish. Elsewhere, Langland hankers after a properly ordered society where husbands chastise disobedient wives and parents beat naughty children. The proliferation of conduct literature from the later fourteenth century is no less a reflection of the sense of instability produced by the impact of plague.

We can regard such literature in two ways. On the one hand, it can be seen as an attempt to recover stability by returning to or reasserting earlier value systems. This is to read these as essentially conservative texts that hark back to an idealized rather than a historic past. On the other hand, the texts may have served to lend an identity, and hence a position within the hierarchy, to persons who otherwise did not fit (or know how to fit) existing conceptions of the social order. This last is perhaps particularly true of artisans and merchants, who could not be accommodated within an increasingly anachronistic understanding of the threefold division of society into those who worked (peasants), those who fought (the aristocracy) and those who prayed (the clergy). The same was also true of a growing number of families who aspired to aristocratic rank as a consequence of successful careers in the law, or the acquisition of lands through marriage or as reward for administrative or legal service, but whose identity owed little either to birth or to breeding. Conduct literature could serve to socialize such newly arrived families in manners and values not specifically tied to warfare and military service. As a consequence they could also help an established military aristocracy adapt to the needs of a society in which warfare was no longer an adjunct of effective government.

In fact, it was with the socialization of the young, unmarried members of these families that these texts were primarily concerned. (Parents could also use the texts to help them socialize their own children, and so learn themselves in the process.) The reason for addressing the young is twofold. First, the young were considered the most responsive to such socialization because they were not yet set in their ways. Second, youngsters were in a position to marry into established families and so consolidate their families' entry into bourgeois or aristocratic society. Conduct literature thus helped shape social hierarchies and taught gendered identities.

The ideals espoused by those texts addressed to young women are depressingly similar. Women are urged to stay within the house whenever possible. The virtues of chastity, modesty, piety and obedience to fathers and husbands are much reiterated. Women's speech, on the other hand, is regarded with suspicion and silence is held up as a virtue. Texts addressed to men, on the other hand, assume that their responsibilities will regularly take them outside the home and merely urge a degree of circumspection when talking. The virtues of chastity and piety are again urged, but in more muted form.

The gender hierarchy was underpinned by scriptural, legal, philosophical and scientific thought. These underpinnings did not necessarily vary greatly through our period, but there is every reason to think that in social practice the ways in which men and women interacted varied significantly between different levels of society and over time. In particular it appears that peasant society tended to be more conservative than urban, and that more conservative values generally tended to prevail from the second half of the fifteenth century. It is likely, too, that conservative values – the tendency to see women as the weaker sex (physically, morally and intellectually) or as wives, mothers and homemakers, but men as workers, fighters and authority figures – were the norm before the Black Death. Evidence for social practice is, however, hard to find. Even civic and guild ordinances were essentially ideological and we cannot assume that, because particular kinds of regulation were made, these were necessarily followed, even by those who framed the legislation. Practice will be explored in subsequent chapters; our immediate concern here is with ideology.

Scripture provided some powerful ideas that helped shape the gender ideologies of the period. The Genesis account of the Fall presents Eve as easily beguiled by the Serpent's words, disobedient of God's commandment and the temptress of her husband. *The Knight of the Tower*, in a brilliant passage that must derive from clerical teaching, uses this account to show how women should avoid the company of men other than their husbands, guard their speech and be wary of being seduced by sensory pleasures. St Paul's Epistles were read as providing further justification for the authority of husbands over wives and the distrust of women's words. The Book of Proverbs provides contrasting images of, on the one hand, the Good Wife, who stays at home, manages the household and cares for her spouse and children, and, on the other, the Harlot, who is a loud, unruly temptress. The lives of saints, whose stories might be told by the priest on their festival days and, from at least the later fourteenth century, by guilds in the form of drama, also propagated particular gender values. The lives of virgin martyrs, such as Katherine or Margaret, emphasized their devotion from a young age and upheld the virtue of virginity, which, in the context of the lives of ordinary women who would normally marry, stood for chastity. The lives of male saints, in contrast, rarely placed such emphasis on virginity, but rather (in England at least) on their status as kings, bishops and the like.

The subordinate position of women – and specifically the authority of husbands over wives that is rooted in the teachings of St Paul – was reflected in the different legal traditions found in later medieval England, with the possible exception of canon law, the legal system that prevailed in the church courts. This last was rooted in a Roman law tradition and appears to have been fairly egalitarian. Women could initiate actions within the church courts in respect of disputed marriages, wills, breach of promise or defamation in much the same way as men, though women had to prove excessive violence or cruelty to gain legal separation from a husband, whereas men needed only to prove a wife's adultery. The royal courts, which reserved jurisdiction over all felonies (more serious crimes were punishable by death), denied access to those of servile status and largely limited the actions women could bring to the murder of a husband (and then only if he died in her arms), the killing of a child still in her womb and rape. An early fourteenth-century legal source justified this curtailment of the legal capacity of women by noting that 'women are changeable by nature'.

A married woman was liable to be exonerated from participating in felonies if it could be shown that she had acted on her husband's instruction, since her duty of obedience to her husband was paramount. Conversely, the murder of a husband by a wife was held in law to be a form of treason ('petty' treason as distinct from the treason of a subject against their monarch) and punishable by burning. In common law a husband was held responsible for his wife's debts, though borough law sometimes provided for married women to trade as *'femmes soles'* and so take full responsibility for their financial transactions. Such provision was probably designed as much to protect husbands as to empower wives. Common law held that all property a wife brought to a marriage came under her husband's control, though in theory he was debarred from alienating (selling) any land without her consent. Indeed the strict legal position was that a wife had no property rights beyond the ornaments of her head; common lawyers, unlike canon lawyers, were consequently hostile to the idea of wives making wills since they ought not to have possessed anything to bequeath. In practice we find that fewer and fewer wives made wills over our period, but it is implicit that wives were often given more practical control over possessions (if not land) than the common law sanctioned.

Customary law – that is, law based on local custom and that characterized manorial courts, but is also found in borough courts – likewise operated in gender-specific ways. Women, but very rarely men, could be presented (brought to the attention of the court) for scolding, the nature of which is not entirely clear, but could well have involved verbally challenging authority. A 1486 ordinance from Hereford specifically understood 'scolds' to be female and represented their actions as a serious threat to the good order of the city. The city governors instituted a form of punishment that was itself specifically designed to humiliate the offenders as women: they were to be stood in a special cucking-stool in a public place, their feet bare and the hair hanging loose and uncovered. Manor courts would impose fines for permission for a woman of villein or servile status to marry (the merchet fine) and in cases where an unmarried woman of like status had committed fornication (the leyrwite fine). In both instances, the concern of the lord was to augment his revenue from the court and to assert his lordship over his servile peasantry, since merchet and leyrwite were marks of servility. The implications of these in gender terms, however, could not have been lost on the peasant community.

Academic medical thought understood men and women to be constitutionally different. According to the Galenic theory of the four humours, men were composed of a greater balance of hot and dry humours, whereas women were characterized by the cold and moist humours. Men, because they possessed greater heat, tended to grow tall and to drive a greater amount of matter to the upper parts of their bodies, hence broad shoulders, but comparatively narrow waists. Women, lacking heat, tended to be shorter and wider in the hips. Likewise the extra heat of the male was able to convert waste matter into body and facial hair, whereas women were only able to lose this waste matter through menstruation. Implicit in this schema is the notion that the male constitution is the superior, indeed the norm, and that women constituted 'the other'. This is still more apparent in the understanding that the female reproductive organs represented an inverted version of the male. Thus, for example, the vagina was seen as an inverted penis, restricted by the lack of heat characteristic of woman from growing outwards.

This tendency to see parallels between male and female genitalia helps explain the belief that both females and males produced seed, and that for conception to occur, both partners needed to be sexually aroused. Here medical thought impinged upon legal practice in one particularly cruel way. Because conception was thought to depend on both sexual partners getting pleasure from intercourse, a woman was deemed incapable of conceiving as a consequence of rape. Rape suits could consequently be thrown out where the woman had conceived following the attack. When in 1314 one Joan brought a charge of rape against her attacker, she was asked who was the father of the child she was carrying in her arms. On her naming her assailant 'it was said that this was a wonder because a child could not be engendered without the will of both', hence the court ruled there was no rape.[1]

Philosophical ideas about the sexes during the later Middle Ages were largely dependent on ideas derived from the writings of Aristotle that circulated in Latin

---

1. P.J.P. Goldberg, ed. and trans., *Women in England*, c.*1275–1525* (Manchester, 1995), p. 256.

translation from the thirteenth century. Aristotelian thought saw the female very much as the man manqué, an imperfect version of the male. These ideas achieved a wide circulation from the beginning of our period through such writings as Bartholomew de Glanville's *De Proprietatibus Rerum* (On the Properties of Things). 'The male', he writes, 'surpasses the female in perfect complexion, in working, in wit, in sensory discrimination, in might and in lordship.'[2] The effects of these different, but intermeshed systems of thought relating to the power relationship between males and females are difficult to assess. Though they were used to justify gender inequalities, they do not necessarily explain these as historical facts. An important point is that women and men alike tended to accept the gender hierarchy as a given. That Adam was created before Eve, and that Eve was made out of the side of Adam to be his companion, was perhaps a sufficiently widely disseminated myth to assure people that the authority of men over women, and of husbands over wives, was part of the divine order of things.

Women neither expected nor were allowed to hold office or to be in positions of authority in their own right. The dowager lady Nicolaa de la Haye may have exercised authority as co-sheriff of Lincoln in the early years of the thirteenth century, but this sort of anomaly seems to have disappeared in a more bureaucratic era. To offer a rather different example, when in 1422 John of Ely was presented by a London jury for allowing women to subcontract his position as keeper of the assay of oysters, it was sufficient for the jury to pronounce that it was contrary to the worship (good name) of the city. We do find the odd female churchwarden and even the occasional widow who has assumed a role formerly belonging to her husband, and women must regularly have exercised authority as agents for their husbands, but this pattern does not significantly modify the broader picture. Men, on the other hand, exercised authority over their wives and their households. Guilds, towns, governments were run by men. Offices, from ale taster or reeve in manorial society to alderman, Justice of the Peace, coroner or escheator were exclusively the prerogative of men. Juries, whether to make inquest into manorial custom, an accidental death or homicide, or to determine the guilt or otherwise of a felon, were always composed of men.

The exercise of power and authority was thus a particularly masculine attribute, though wives and widows were in fact invariably seen as competent to substitute for absent husbands in the running of the household or family estate. Violence, or the threat of violence, was a corollary of male authority. A man might lawfully strike his wife for disobedience. Masters would beat insubordinate servants: John Lorymer of Nottingham justified striking his servant, Joan Potter, on the head with a staff, asserting that she had 'given him a contrary reply'. The carrying of knives by men was commonplace, as was the resort to violence. In 1303, for example, Adam de Bury is said to have stabbed his wife Mabel in the stomach and so caused her death. Adolescent males in particular seem regularly to have engaged in a degree of brawling, judging by records of assault and wounding, but males generally might resort to physical violence. To cite a couple of early fourteenth-century examples, Maud le Chesewouman claimed that Alan Kynge had assaulted her in the bread market of Bishop's (now King's) Lynn and punched her on the nose, and Simon de Refham claimed that Geoffrey Curteys had beaten him up at Holbeach (Lincs.). Sexual violence is also frequently recorded, though (all-male)

2. J. Caddern, *Meanings of Sex Difference in the Middle Ages* (Cambridge, 1993), pp. 183–4.

juries invariably acquitted alleged rapists. Rape, or the fear of rape, however, was used to discourage women, particularly young women, from going about on their own.

Two other facets of the rather aggressive masculinity reflected in legal records – and hence weighted towards extremes of behaviour – are drinking and sex. Women were strongly discouraged from excessive drinking and drunken women are rarely noted. Men were also urged not to frequent taverns, but male inebriation seems not to have been such an issue. A number of cases from the port of Bishop's Lynn at the very beginning of the fourteenth century reflect a culture of heavy drinking at the weekend (including Monday night): several men drowned falling into the harbour while drunk; a man was stabbed to death by his drinking partner when he invited him to test the toughness of the padded tunic he was wearing; a male servant was stabbed to death when he disturbed another man in a brothel with three women. This last alerts us to the fact that commercial sex is widely found in an urban context. Numbers of men used the services of women who sold their bodies, whether in informal, private brothels, on the street or in alehouses. The male apprentice was forbidden by his contract from visiting brothels, which may suggest that unmarried males were seen as particularly likely to resort to prostitutes.

Those males who purchased sex outside the household were attempting to assert a masculine identity that was otherwise (and legitimately) only available to married men as householders. During the course of our period, indeed, it seems that the right to have sexual relations within the household came to be the monopoly of the married head of household and his spouse. Apprenticeship contracts prohibited male apprentices from having sex with any women of the house; in the 1417 case concerning John Waryngton, a York apprentice who had seduced a fellow female servant, it was repeatedly stressed that the transgression had taken place *within* his master's home. This double violation – of the woman servant and of his master's authority – was sufficient to explain his employer's actions in allegedly forcing John to marry the woman he had seduced. It also reveals, on the one hand, the centrality of sexual relations to male identity and, on the other, how control over women's bodies was integral to male authority.

As Patricia Cullum has shown, for the clergy, who were debarred from marriage and sexual activity, and from spilling blood, and who were generally supposed to lead lives of pious sobriety more akin to models of femininity, their clerical identity may sometimes have appeared emasculating and a cause of anxiety.[3] Lesser clergy sometimes indulged in aggressively, perhaps exaggeratedly, 'masculine' conduct by way of compensation. The chaplain Hugh de Weston, for example, was killed in a drunken brawl over a group of women on Christmas Day 1287. In an extraordinary case from 1389, Roger de Mampton, a Nottingham chaplain presented for conducting an affair with the plaintiff's wife in the plaintiff's own home, brazenly defended himself, claiming that he was merely undertaking his pastoral responsibility to go through the parish distributing holy water! Such examples reinforce one particular variety of masculinity, but at the same time hint that many clergy found alternative models of masculinity that placed less emphasis on a boisterous heterosexuality. Moreover, we must see gender ideologies not as closed and fixed, but as changing and evolving over time.

---

3. P.H. Cullum, 'Clergy, Masculinity and Transgression in Late Medieval England', in D.M. Hadley, ed., *Masculinity in Medieval Europe* (London, 1999), pp. 178–96.

Painting with a broad brush, people seem to have been more conservative within peasant society – or at least among the more well-to-do in peasant society – than may generally have been true of urban society, though here again we must differentiate between differing levels of society and different moments in time. There is, for example, quite a lot of evidence to suggest that, from the later fifteenth century, civic elites in particular were adopting more conservative positions. The Coventry ordinances of 1492, designed to debar most adult women from living on their own (which meant they were not subject to male authority) are perhaps the most striking indicator of this, but patriarchal values were also articulated in more subtle ways, as in the text of the earlier sixteenth-century Chester Corpus Christi Play, and notably the character of Mulier (Woman) in the pageant of the Harrowing of Hell. Here Mulier first confesses to a whole litany of trading offences relating to the brewing and retail of ale and wine before being welcomed into hell by three devils for promoting drunkenness, lechery and illicit gaming.

The inherent conservatism of the upper levels of peasant society is reflected in a number of ways. We have already seen that fathers might take a rather cavalier attitude to the marriage of their daughters. Fines for fornication, levied (as noted above) solely on villein women, effectively constructed a double standard of sexual conduct, while at the same time helping guard the chastity of unmarried daughters. As we shall see, there was a rather more marked gender division of labour in the countryside than tended to be true of towns, at least before the later fifteenth century: certain activities – notably ploughing and mowing – were reserved to men and commanded both respect and, where undertaken as waged work, high rates of remuneration; women's work, such as spinning, carding and weeding, in contrast, tended to be little valued and poorly remunerated. Primary childcare, however, was women's work in both town and country.

There are other indicators of the way peasants valued men above women, even from a very young age. The evidence of accidental death from coroners' rolls for the decades before the Black Death could be read to suggest variously that girl babies were less desired than boy babies – hence the disproportionate number of girls dying in cradle fires – that boy toddlers were more important than their sisters, since their deaths were rather more likely to be reported to the coroner, and similarly that adult males were deemed more important than adult females, since there is an otherwise inexplicable imbalance in favour of males in the numbers of reported accidental deaths of males occurring in the home while the victim was sleeping. These priorities operated even at the level of individual families, since it appears that whereas both parents would search for missing sons, mothers alone were likely to search for missing daughters.

A further oblique source of peasant gender ideology is provided by the witnesses in disputed marriage cases from the fourteenth and fifteenth centuries (drawing on evidence for the diocese of York). Although both peasant and bourgeois litigants seem to have preferred to call upon male witnesses in the church courts, this preference was rather more marked amongst peasant litigants. Whether this indicates a patriarchal reluctance to allow women to travel to the city to give their testimony or a sense that women's words were of little worth is difficult to assess, but it is a telling observation. Similarly, though women initiated a majority of marriage cases in both urban and rural society, the proportion of women to men was nevertheless smaller in the latter instance. Close reading of these actions shows that rather more of the rural female litigants were clearly acting with their fathers' support than would be true of urban cases. Even within the context of the church courts, employing the essentially egalitarian principles of canon law, peasant women enjoyed much less autonomy than was true of some bourgeois women, at least before the later fifteenth century.

Peasant society seems also to have been more conservative in respect of a gender division of labour. A particular model is suggested from the tools assigned to Adam (a spade) and to Eve (a distaff for spinning). Men tend to be associated with labour in the fields and the demands of an arable economy. Women, on the other hand, are associated with the domestic, with spinning and, by extension, textiles, and with pastoral agriculture. Washing and shearing sheep, for example, appears in medieval culture to have been women's work, no doubt in part because women were associated with the care of smaller livestock and also because the wool women span was a product of the sheep. Even in the immediate aftermath of the expulsion from Eden, before the first couple have a physical dwelling to their name, but are represented both in the open air, we have hints of Eve's association with the home. A depiction in the *Holkham Bible Picture Book* appears to show Eve sitting within a hollow or cave. In other manuscript depictions, Eve seems to shelter under a tree while Adam works out in the open.

Eve, of course, is not the only model. The Good Wife of the Book of Proverbs, a paragon of domestic virtue and industry, is another obvious cultural reference. In a late fifteenth-century poem, dubbed 'The Ballad of the Tyrannical Husband' by its nineteenth-century editors, a ploughman spends the day ploughing in the fields while his wife gets on with a variety of household tasks, from caring for their children, to weaving cloth and caring for livestock. In fact her tasks regularly take her outside the home, but as this text is supposedly designed to draw attention to the importance of the role of wives, ultimately its message is conservative: in a well-ordered household there is a clear gender division of labour. So much of women's work, even within the more diverse economy of the medieval town, can be understood as an extension of the domestic. This was true of the laundress, the huckster supplying foodstuffs and household essentials such as candles, the upholder or vendor of second-hand clothing, the tapster (loosely translated as barmaid), the seamstress, the spinster, the midwife, the nurse and even the sex worker.

2 FAMILY AND HOUSEHOLD

Family, with its implications of sentiment and kinship, is one of those useful colloquial words whose meaning is readily understood, but which defies simple definition. On the other hand, household can immediately be recognized as a technical (even clinical) and historical term, the meaning of which is less accessible. The social historian, instinctively, would prefer to use the former term, but so much of the existing scholarship in this area is the product of the sub-discipline of historical demography, which favours the term 'household'. The picture is complicated further by the nature of the sources available to us. Domesday Book (1086) and the poll taxes (1377, 1379, 1380–81) aside, the period is characterized by a demographic twilight illuminated only at the end of our period with the advent of parish registration from 1538. Evidence is scarce and often very localized; these are little pools of light that may variously guide the traveller or lure the unwary from the path. They sometimes tell us about who lived together under the same roof, but have little to say about how they interacted with one another, and are still more reticent, or indeed altogether silent, on the matter of sentiment – a silence that some have mistaken for an actual want of affective relationships. As so often, we need to be able to distinguish silences created by the lack of pertinent evidence and 'significant' silences, where the absence is not accidental, but real. Our discussion will begin by attempting to understand how medieval people understood ties of kinship and co-residence, before going on to explore evidence for the composition of the household.

To return to definitions, household represents the co-resident unit. It may be defined narrowly in terms of those who eat together or sleep under the same roof. Normally we expect such households to be comparatively small, but this need not have been the case, at least in some regions in the earlier part of our period, and aristocratic households or the royal household could comprise some tens of persons and even sometimes numbers expressed in three figures. Clearly such large groups comprised persons who were not related by blood or marriage, even people who felt little or no affective ties to other members of the same household. On the other hand, the focus on the co-resident group ignores such affective ties or ties of kinship that may have extended beyond the physical entity of the household. To focus on households, therefore, is to risk overlooking other important social relationships that bound people together even where they did not share the same living space.

Family is a more difficult term because it is more enigmatic. It can mean members of the same kin group, but this begs questions as to where boundaries are drawn and how far medieval people were indeed aware of their relatives. In modern usage, we regularly distinguish between family in a general sense and 'close' family. This last can coincide with the co-resident group or household, but need not. There is no precise equivalent Middle English or medieval Latin word for family. The earliest English usage of 'family' belongs to the earlier sixteenth century and merely translates the Latin term *familia,* which itself denotes household. Middle English words like 'friend', 'kith' and 'kin' do offer overlapping terms within a wider web of meaning. Thus 'friend' can denote in different contexts variously friend, comrade, father, parent, husband or close relative, whereas 'kin' may encompass relatives more generally or imply family in the wider sense of clan or lineage.

Medieval men and women were thus able to deploy language that distinguished the co-resident group or household – which might partly comprise close kin – from kin relations, and that distinguished close kin ('friends') from the wider kin group ('kin'). In particular, the term 'friend' has resonances of intimacy or affection, which may (consciously or unconsciously) be implied when used to describe close kin. This much we may tease out from a study of language, but we have further clues from other sources. Of particular value here are church court depositions, though much can also be discerned from wills.

When people gave testimony in the church courts, they were required to acknowledge whether they were related to either of the parties bringing the litigation since this could have a bearing on the credibility of their evidence. Although reported relationships were invariably translated into the canonical convention of degrees of affinity (a relationship created by marriage) or consanguinity (blood relationship) where each degree represents distance from a common ancestor, this still provides evidence for how readily people could identify their relatives. Close relatives are always identified, but it would seem that people – even clergy who tend to be more informed about such matters – were not always clear about exact relationships much beyond the immediate family. Thus, in 1458, the priest John Collom was recorded as being a blood relative of Agnes Cosyn in the third or fourth degree. In 1439, on the other hand, the servant Joan Yarm was precisely identified as blood relative in the fourth degree to her employer, William Wright. More distant relationships are almost never noticed and many others stated merely that they were related, but did not know how closely. Wills, especially of the more well-to-do, may likewise mention cousins (in the general sense of blood relations) and 'affines' (relatives by marriage), but only specify in terms of precise relationship parents, children and siblings (including children- and siblings-in-law – no terminological distinction is made). The most substantial bequests, moreover, are invariably limited to this narrow group of close relatives.

In disputed marriage cases, issues of relationship and common ancestry sometimes arise since canon law disallowed unions of couples who were too closely related or where one party had previously slept with a close relative of the other. Such cases are, contrary to popular belief, uncommon and mostly arise in rural society. They again suggest a good general awareness of kin relationships, but – if only because these cases are contested – a tendency not to remember them in the same precise terms of 'degrees of kinship' deployed by canon lawyers. It is also striking that in the immediate aftermath of the Black Death peasant holdings often went vacant for want of heirs, suggesting that families were ignorant of more distant kin relationships. On the other hand, the shameless way in which some aristocratic marriage alliances were made between close kin for which retrospective dispensations were subsequently sought – allegedly because kinship that rendered the marriage uncanonical had been 'discovered' – cannot constitute evidence for actual ignorance of kinship relationships at this lineage-conscious level of society. Rather, as presumably in the case of the marriage of Sir Geoffrey Luttrell (of Luttrell Psalter fame) to Agnes Sutton, it was known that though the Church may not have allowed a dispensation were it to have been sought before the union, it would invariably prefer an established union to be retrospectively sanctioned than to break such a union by means of an annulment.

Another window into the nature of kin ties is provided by the (rare) evidence regarding provision for orphaned relatives. A telling marriage case from the York court relates to one William Aunger of Reedness (Yorks., WR), whose father had died by the time he was born, around 1343. During the Black Death six years later the child was to lose both his mother and maternal grandfather. His stepfather clearly felt limited responsibility for him since he entrusted him to a male relative of the child's mother (an uncle?). We are told of the grandfather's death probably by way of explaining why the child was not sent to him instead. The customary (manorial) courts sometimes made provision for orphans (in the narrower medieval sense of lacking a father) by granting guardianship to a close male relative, though actual custody might reside with the mother. Thus, in 1279, William son of John Steinulf of Halesowen (Worcs.) was assigned to his uncle's guardianship. Though he was to live with his mother, the uncle was to provide food, clothing and shoes. In other instances neighbours would take in orphans. Both responses are found, for example, at Brandon (Suffolk).

A consideration of the nature of kinship ties must take us to an exploration of the household since the co-resident group often comprised numbers of kin. Our starting point is the size and form of the co-resident group: how far households were small and nuclear or larger and extended. Our argument will be that a variety of forms existed during the course of the era as a whole, though small nuclear households increasingly became the norm from at least the later fourteenth century. Larger, extended households, perhaps of the stem-family variety, may have been common earlier, especially in rural Midland England. Nuclear households, on the other hand, emerged precociously in an urban context and in the more economically developed regions of East Anglia and the south-east. Our analysis begins, however, in the later thirteenth century.

Hallam, in a well-known and much cited article, used some documents relating to the servile populations of Spalding Priory (Lincs.) and datable to the 1260s as 'some thirteenth-century censuses'. His conclusion is that these 'censuses' permit a fairly precise calculation of average (mean) household size, precisely the sort of information that, for example, would be invaluable in order to move from numbers of tenants in Domesday Book to total population. His finding, namely that households contained on average some 4.75 persons, carried authority not only because they appeared to be rooted in an impeccable primary source, namely a census, but also because the average calculated appeared plausible. Indeed it was given added credence by the subsequent work of Laslett, who attempted to show that such an average was a universal norm across time and space. As scholars, including Laslett, moved away from this somewhat polemical position, so more searching questions began to be asked of the sources on which they were based. Returning to the Spalding 'censuses', Smith found that they were not censuses in any modern sense; rather they were servile genealogies that neither clearly distinguished between the dead and those currently living nor permitted patterns of co-residence to be determined with any confidence.

The Spalding serf lists, a more accurate designation, thus tell us more about lordship and the ways in which, given that servility was hereditary, a monastic landlord chose to keep a record of its villein population by means of recording genealogical information, than they do about demography. The problem here was that Hallam let his question – how big were medieval households? – get in the way of his evaluation of the source. The question was itself driven by a wider concern about counting numbers and the quest for the then Holy Grail of medieval demography, the household multiplier. As always, we need to appreciate the source in its own terms, and to ask why it was constructed, before we demand answers of it. If we see the serf lists as concerned with recording the names and potential availability to the lord of children of servile descent, we may be struck by several observations, notably the numbers of children recorded, the numbers of children described as having left the manor, particularly to live in Spalding or Moulton, and the numbers of children noted as having no fixed abode (the Latin text describes them as *vacabundus* or *vacabunda*, i.e. 'wandering'). We thus have evidence of a growing population, but also a comparatively mobile one. If we interpret 'wandering' as a consequence of a lack of access to land or regular employment then we also have evidence of hardship. Finally we may observe that, essentially, only nuclear relationships (father, mother, son, daughter) are recorded.

George Homans in 1941 argued for the existence of a stem-family system among the thirteenth-century peasantry. Within a stem system, one of the sons born to a couple is allowed to bring his wife into the natal home on marriage and so raise a third generation before the first has necessarily died off. The stem-family household will thus tend to be larger, sometimes extending over three generations and containing grandparents or grandchildren. His observations owe more to unsubstantiated analogy with nineteenth-century Luneburg in northern Germany than to hard evidence. His views, nevertheless, have been influential because a stem-family system is often thought of as predating a nuclear system and because we have little to test his ideas against. We have much better evidence by the later fourteenth century in the form of the poll tax returns.

The poll tax evidence for co-resident kin beyond the 'nuclear' family (that is, parents and children) is comparatively slight. As we shall see, 'nuclear' household forms appear very much the norm, but we do find (presumably widowed) mothers co-residing with married sons. At Langham (Rutland) no less than three families included widowed mothers according to the 1377 returns. Other kin appear hardly ever to be found, though the 1379 returns for Asmunderby with Bondgate (Yorks., WR), for example, list one Elizabeth del Chambre living with her 'blood relative' Elizabeth de Snayth. On the other hand, the apparent predominance of nuclear households may partly be an optical illusion created by the way the poll tax returns are compiled. This is suggested by the frequency with which in some regions we encounter clusters of taxpayers bearing a common surname. One such cluster is found in the 1379 returns for Muston (Leics.), thus:

William Baldwyn and his wife
John Funteyns and his wife
John Baldewyn and his wife
Adam Simond and his wife

John Baldewyn and his wife
Robert Baldewyn and his wife

We can identify six distinct units, but we can be less sure that we have here six distinct households. We may even have evidence here for a group of brothers sharing – what is termed a frérèche. At the very least we have close kin who live in equally close proximity to one another. Zvi Razi has argued for a pattern like this last using court roll evidence for Halesowen (Worcs.) before the plague.[1] We may thus be seeing the relic of a pattern that was more common at the beginning of our period.

If we turn from the kin group or family to the household, we shift the focus to a potentially much wider group of persons. Within the medieval understanding of *familia* or household is a hierarchical notion of headship and 'meine', that is, dependants. These dependants comprised not only co-resident kin, and hence invariably wives and children, but also servants and possibly other employees. Clearly, where households might vary enormously in size between different levels of society, the relationships between the different members of the household will be equally variable. We will consider non-aristocratic households first. We have good, but not unproblematic, evidence for such households in the form of the nominative listings (that is, those containing actual names) from the later fourteenth-century poll taxes, especially those for the first poll tax of 1377. Before that date the evidence is much more fragile. Even after that date, the earliest equivalent sources to the poll tax are the Coventry listing of 1523 and the parish listing for Ealing in 1599. It necessarily follows that the poll tax evidence will feature disproportionately in our discussion.

The first poll tax was levied on persons aged 14 and over, so it offers no information about numbers or distribution of children. Being assessed at a flat rate of 4d per person, moreover, detailed lists of names seem not generally to have been compiled (or, if they were, not returned to the exchequer and archived). We do, however, have detailed listings for a small number of towns and cities, for the county of Rutland, for one part of Northumberland (Coquetdale), and a small number of fragments for some other counties. In different ways, these returns record what Cordelia Beattie has dubbed 'fiscal units'.[2] These probably coincide largely with households, but we cannot always know for sure. This is especially true of instances where we find such 'units' associated, as we saw previously, with persons bearing the same surname adjacent to one another. By and large, members of fiscal units are identified relationally to the person presented as the head. Thus from the Hull returns we find:

Marjory Freman for herself .... 4d.
John de Waghen Wright [carpenter] for himself, his wife and Thomas his servant ..... 12d.
Adam Broune for himself and his wife .... 8d.
Joan de Upsale for herself, William de Upsale, Richard de Upsale and Katherine Berwik, the children of the said Joan and a servant .... 20d.

---

1. Z. Razi, 'The Myth of the Immutable English Family', *Past and Present* 140 (1993), pp. 3–44.

2. C. Beattie, 'A Room of One's Own? The Legal Evidence for the Residential Arrangements of Women Without Husbands in Late Fourteenth- and Early Fifteenth-Century York', in N.J. Menuge, ed., *Medieval Women and the Law* (Woodbridge, 2000), p. 45.

This tiny sample does not claim to be representative, but it does reflect the way in which fiscal unit and household (comprising head and dependants) invariably coincide. It also suggests the range of household forms regularly encountered in towns and in many rural areas at this date. We have the married couple, the couple with children and/or servants, the household headed by a single person (presumably in this instance a widow) and, finally, the solitary household – that is, the person who lives on their own. We have, however, already noted an example akin to a frérèche from the 1379 poll tax returns for Leicestershire. Other entries from the same Leicestershire returns where units sharing a common name are found alongside one another suggest other possible forms where households may be extended vertically (that is, over three generations) or horizontally (where siblings co-reside). These are speculative readings, but it is striking that such patterns are much harder to find in, for example, the equivalent source for Essex in 1381. Razi indeed contrasts a nuclear household pattern found precociously in East Anglia (including Essex) – a region associated with an active peasant land market and a more diverse and dynamic economy – with non-nuclear patterns often found in Midland England before the later fourteenth century. It could be added that nuclear households also emerged precociously within a wider urban context.

There is indeed growing consensus for Razi's model of regional difference, but wide debate as to its origins or rationale. In the peasant society of the 'champian' country of Midland England, a region associated with open fields, arable agriculture and heavy seasonal labour demands, the obligations of villein tenants to their lords tended to be more burdensome than in upland districts or regions associated with a more diverse economy. Peasants seem to have relied to a greater degree on the transmission of family land from father to son and on the support of the kin group. Lords also seem to have discouraged the subdivision of peasant holdings and hence curtailed the development of the sort of active land market found, for example, in parts of East Anglia. Something akin to a stem-family system thus prevailed. Here land is transmitted from father to male heir, who alone is allowed to marry and remain on the family holding, although non-inheriting siblings still have a claim on the livelihood provided by the family holding so long as they do not marry.

Elsewhere, different patterns of householding can be found from at least the time of the poll taxes, but probably from rather earlier. We can speak with most authority for East Anglia since much recent scholarship has focused in particular on Cambridgeshire, Norfolk and Essex. Here the nuclear household was the norm and, as we shall see, 'life-cycle' servants were probably a more conspicuous element within peasant society. The manor tended to be a more fragmented structure and it weighed less heavily on the tenant population. The prevalence of partible inheritance and the greater range of economic activities associated with wool and flax production, weaving, tanning and carpentry, or even more specialized activities such as rabbit farming and gravel extraction as in the Breckland, or fishing in coastal settlements, meant that family land (and its transmission) was less central to the livelihood of the kin group. Indeed we find an active land market alongside markets in labour and in goods and services. In this context nuclear households prevailed: sons were less dependent on inheriting family land to make their way in the world; a more diversified economy actually encouraged children to learn new skills outside the natal household.

The poll tax evidence appears broadly to support the hypothesis that at least outside of Midland England a nuclear household system widely prevailed. Some caveats must, however, be noted. Of the many apparently solitary households recorded, we cannot know whether we are dealing with a widow(er) or someone who has yet to marry, nor can we know if they are actually supporting children below the age of taxation. Where several solitaries are found in adjacent entries, they may be lodging in different rooms within the same building, but again we cannot know how far they may in fact have shared facilities. In towns, especially, we often find numbers of solitary women listed together in the returns, a phenomenon that is (not entirely helpfully) termed 'spinster clustering'. It may well be that such groups of women thus enjoyed not only a greater sense of security and social solidarity, but also co-operated in terms of sharing cooking facilities and helping one another out in times of need. Sometimes two women appear to have shared a household together.

The poll tax evidence is revealing as much for what is not to be found as what is. As has already been remarked, widowed mothers aside, we very rarely see kin other than sons and daughters specifically listed as household members. Fiscal units, which, as we have seen, may or may not equate to households, normally comprise no more than two generations. We do not find two or more conjugal units (married couples) in any given unit. Where units do indeed correspond to households, the implication is that we only find household types that correspond to a nuclear household system. Because the poll tax returns provide a snapshot of a single moment in time, we need to locate our observations within a dynamic model. Thus we may find solitaries, representing adolescents and young adults who have left home, but have yet to marry, but also perhaps adults who have not married. We find married couples that may yet have children, whose children may be below the age of taxation or whose children have left home. We also find couples with adolescent and young adult children living with them. These last are much more common in the countryside than the town. Finally, we find widows and widowers who may have dependent children of taxation age, below taxation age (hence invisible) or who have left home (and hence are indistinguishable from other solitaries). All the household types just outlined may or may not also contain servants, though servant-keeping households are much more common in towns than in the countryside.

Intrinsic to the structures just outlined is the tendency of people to leave home when or before they marry. Consequently, we find young adult solitaries and parents whose children have all left home. We do not normally find parents co-residing with married children or households comprising more than one conjugal unit. It is this process of fission that defines the householding system as nuclear. By the early modern era we know that the nuclear household system was the norm. It is very well documented, as at Coventry in 1523 or at Ealing in 1599. It is, moreover, a system that is historically specific to some regions of Europe (notably north-western Europe), but not others (particularly Mediterranean and eastern Europe). The implication is that the poll tax returns thus provide strong evidence for the prevalence of a culturally specific householding system, known to have existed at later periods; a nuclear householding system was the norm as far back as the later fourteenth century.

The foregoing discussion has suggested a rather monolithic pattern, but this needs to be qualified. There are real differences within the broader nuclear household structure between town and country. There are also more subtle differences within and between one rural district and another. The principal point of difference concerns the presence or otherwise of adolescent and young adult children and of servants. The urban listings for 1377 are remarkable for the extreme paucity of recorded children, but the relative abundance of servants. Thus, at York, the incomplete listing suggests that a third or more of all households contained one or more servants, the average being about two servants for each household maintaining servants. In the much smaller urban communities of Carlisle and Dartmouth the equivalent proportions were just under a quarter and just under a third respectively. Both had a mean of one and a half servants to each servant-keeping household. If we may extrapolate from the 1523 Coventry listing, much the same proportion of servant-keeping households still prevailed at that later date in larger English towns. For rural settlements, however, the equivalent proportion was nearer one household in ten or less.

Unlike servants, children of sufficient age to be assessed for the poll tax are but rarely recorded in towns; they are comparatively common in rural settlements. The Dartmouth returns, for example, record only four children. The paucity of adolescent children and the ubiquity of servants as dependent members of households at this date seems a very marked characteristic of urban society. As we shall see, by the later fourteenth century the normal urban pattern is for adolescent children to go into service in other people's households; there is simply a transfer and redistribution of young people between households. In rural society at this date, however, a much smaller proportion of adolescents went into service in their neighbours' households, though some may have gone into service in nearby towns. Numbers of servants are, nevertheless, found. Some are associated with peasant agriculturalists, but many others are found in the households of rural craft workers.

Some groups were more likely than others to retain adolescent children within their households. In general, more prosperous households were more likely to contain children than poorer households. Widows and widowers were particularly likely to retain children and often children of the same gender. Using evidence for the Strafforth wapentake (administrative district) of the West Riding of Yorkshire in 1379 – and hence using evidence relating only to children aged 16 or over – rather more than a third of all such children were associated with households headed by a widowed parent. Widows especially were disposed to retaining adolescent and young adult daughters, presumably to work and help provide their material needs. Like patterns, albeit on a much more modest scale, are found again in urban communities. In rural settlements we also find that artisans often retained daughters even where they also employed male servants. Indeed, rural servants tended to be male, whereas urban servants were more mixed.

To recapitulate, the poll tax evidence indicates that a generation after the Black Death the nuclear household system was the norm (so far as we can see) throughout the realm, though relics of a stem-family system are to be found in parts of Midland England. It also indicates that the inclusion of servants as part of the household is a phenomenon particularly associated with craft manufacture and consequently with urban settlements. Evidence from the Coventry listing of 1523 or the Ealing listing of 1599 would tend broadly to reinforce that picture for the last part of our era. The nature of servants or the propensity of households to employ servants did not only vary spatially or in respect of social or economic considerations. There is also a historical dimension. All these will now be considered in greater depth.

SERVANTS

Servants performed a variety of functions. They were a comparatively inexpensive, dependable, but also flexible source of labour, particularly at such times when other forms of labour were scarce and hence expensive. Service provided a mechanism for training and socializing adolescents. Service also provided a source of security to youngsters at the very ages they were most likely to lose their parents. In contemporary usage, a servant was anyone employed by another. Consequently 'servant' encompasses both those who lived as part of their employer's household and those with a home of their own or who belonged to other households. These last we would tend to label generally as 'labourers' or, in an urban context, 'journeymen'. They would invariably have been adult and might have been married. The servant who lived in, however, can usually be shown to have been rather younger and almost always single. Evidence for the ages of servants and former servants giving testimony in the consistory court of York shows that most were in their teens or early twenties. The evidence is consistent with the possibility that children might first go into service when (following canon-legal conventions) they were deemed to have reached the age of discretion – 12 in the case of girls and 14 in the case of boys. It is also consistent with their finally leaving service at marriageable age.

None of the servants or former servants who gave testimony were or had been married. Similarly, hardly any of the innumerable servants listed in the poll tax returns are recorded with a spouse. From surviving apprenticeship indentures we know that apprentices, a distinctive sub-group of servants, were debarred from marriage during the time of their apprenticeship. The same was presumably true of other servants. We can, however, find examples of employers assisting their servants in their marriage plans. Nicholas Min, for example, asked his master, John Burnett, to accompany him when he went to discuss dowry terms with his prospective mother-in-law. Older female servants in particular were sometimes given beds, bedding, cooking utensils and suchlike against their setting up house, presumably as a new bride. Thus in 1405 the York sauce maker, Thomas Catour, left his servant, Maud Pykeryng, a variety of cooking pots, pewter and silverware and bedding. Joan Buckland of Edgcote (Northants), in her will made in 1450, likewise asked that her servants be provided with bedding, napery and pewter vessels at her death.

Servants, in this live-in sense, were teenagers and young adults who occupied a liminal position between childhood and adulthood. The youngest servants were indeed little more than children, but older servants would have been actively contemplating marriage and becoming householders in their own right. They were dependants of their employers so long as their contract bound them, but were free to negotiate new terms with a new employer at the end of their term. They were subject to the authority of the employer and could be disciplined if they displeased him or her. Equally they could challenge their employer's actions if they considered these to go beyond the customary bounds of their (usually verbal) contract. When the London goldsmith's apprentice John in the Lane was instructed to thresh corn, he successfully obtained a court order restraining his master. Employers were obliged to provide food, clothing and a bed. Usually, servants ate with their employers and, before the later fifteenth century, probably slept in the same room. Employers and servants were thus obliged to develop a working relationship. It is likely that enforced intimacy at times crossed into respect, even real affection. In a sense, servants were more than just adolescent household lodgers, but an integral part of the *familia*. Servants were sometimes even related to their employers. John, one of the York merchant William Scoreburgh's three servants, for example, was named as a cousin at his master's death in 1432 and Isabel de Syggeston was described as her master's niece in his will of 1390.

The position of the servant in the household remains, however, ambiguous. Though by the later Middle Ages and beyond, the apprentice regularly served for a continuous period of seven years, the servant was usually contracted by the year or sometimes the half-year. There would thus have been a regular turnover of servants from one year to the next in many servant-keeping households, but especially around particular dates that were already established by the later fourteenth century as customary: Martinmas (11 November) in the north of England and Michaelmas (29 September) in the Midlands and south are the two most important and long-standing, representing brief moments of slack in the agrarian calendar. Roger Sayot, an Essex man, recalled how he had been in service in 1345, but had left at Michaelmas. In 1410 Agnes Kyrkeby and Isabella Nesswyk, both aged 20, testified that they had, respectively, left and joined the service of one William Pountfret of York the previous Martinmas. Alternative hiring dates are also common; Pentecost seems to have been well established in the north. The rationale for this relentless turnover is central to the whole phenomenon of live-in servants.

Demographic historians describe the tendency for adolescents to leave their natal homes to work and live in the households of others prior to getting married – or at least achieving marriageable age – as life-cycle service. The term 'life-cycle' marks this as a particular and specific phase in the life course. In late medieval Tuscany, by way of contrast, we find, variously, very young girls, married women, widows and men of varying ages working as servants. Life-cycle service fulfilled a number of needs. From the perspective of employers, it offered a comparatively inexpensive and flexible supply of labour. From the servants' perspective it provided access to training, the development of social skills, the opportunity to extend friendship and support networks and, for older servants, the chance to engage in courtship and look for marriage partners. For parents, however, service provided a comparatively secure framework into which to place children who (in the case of poorer parents) may otherwise have become difficult to support. This was a way of ensuring that adolescent children were properly disciplined and for them to enhance their future prospects. The reply 'that their children might learn better manners', supposedly given by a father to a visiting Venetian writing at the end of the fifteenth century as to why he sent his children into service, may not be so wide of the mark.

The movement of servants, other than apprentices, every year or two was dictated both by the needs of employers and those of their employees. The kind of errand-running and menial tasks that could usefully be asked of a young teenager would be an inappropriate and costly use of an older servant. Similarly, the youngster who had served their time running errands would rebel against continuing these tasks over several years and would look instead to negotiate increasingly advantageous terms for each extra year's experience, skill and strength. A sixteenth-century commentator made the same point more cynically: servants 'change their masters yearly, hunting after more wages and less labour'. On a more fundamental level, the very institution of life-cycle service was predicated on the existence of, to use anthropological jargon, a 'complex' society where craft production and commerce existed alongside agriculture. In a culture where a single type of agriculture represented the sole significant form of livelihood, there was little parents could not teach their children. In a complex society, such as we find in many parts of later medieval England, there were many skills in which individual parents would not have been able to train their children. Service as a mechanism for expanding the options open to children and for accommodating fluctuations in demand for particular skills and services thus had its own logic.

This last observation correlates very precisely with our earlier finding that (at the time of the poll taxes) servants were most conspicuous in rural and, more especially urban, craft and mercantile households. There are reasons for thinking that service developed precociously within an urban context. Certainly it would have done much to help socialize children born in the surrounding countryside in the ways of the town. Servants would always have been most in demand when the cost of hired (day) labour was most expensive, because scarce, since they were remunerated primarily in terms of bed, board and clothing. (Probably only older servants were given any kind of money sum at the end of their term.) The demand for servants ought to have risen sharply after the Black Death as wage labour became more expensive; the snapshot from the poll tax may very much reflect post-plague conditions.

It would seem that servants remained integral to town life for the rest of our period, despite the increasing availability (and hence decreasing expense) of hired labour from the latter part of the fifteenth century. It is likely, however, that whereas at the time of the poll tax servants were drawn from all social ranks – this must certainly have been true of urban society – children, especially daughters, of the more well-to-do would have been less likely to enter service. It would also seem that in towns artisans increasingly looked to employ only male servants (and apprentices). The corollary was that service for women became more focused on the households of the mercantile elite, for whom the possession of a number of female servants became a mark of status. Thus Thomas Astlyn, one of Coventry's most prosperous inhabitants in 1523, employed two 'lads', but five women servants. We may conclude that for these women service became more 'domestic'. This is graphically illustrated by a case from later fifteenth-century London where the apprentice, William Taylbos, sitting in the workshop and physically separate from the living quarters of the house, was able to report that when he briefly went into the house proper he had seen Rose Langtoft, his fellow servant, washing clothes and she had told him that she was intending afterwards to prepare food.

Service cannot be understood solely in economic terms. It also acted as a safety net for young people in so far as many would lose one or both parents while adolescents. After her father's death in 1409, for example, Joan Billinggey, the daughter of a London citizen, was apprenticed to Richard and Joan Osborne to learn Joan's craft – probably embroidery or silkwork. Such provision is recorded because the City of London took formal responsibility for the orphans of citizens. Like concern for the orphan heirs of villein tenants was exercised by the customary court. In the rural manor of Halesowen, for example, on the death of Thomas le Fremon in 1279, his teenage son Henry was placed in service with John Borri and William le Fremon, presumably a relative, until he came of age. In later medieval towns, however, many children would already have been in service when they lost their father or indeed both their parents. In a rural context orphans were perhaps more likely to be taken in by kin, as indeed was partly the case with Henry le Fremon. We have already noticed William Aunger, who was born after his father's death and, whilst still a small boy, lost his mother and maternal grandfather in the Black Death and was then taken in by a kinsman of his mother. Such informal arrangements were probably fairly common, but from a documentary perspective are largely invisible other than by chance, as here.

By the end of our period it would appear that hiring fairs, focused around Martinmas, Michaelmas, Pentecost and other traditional hiring dates, had become an established means by which employers and servants were paired. At earlier dates more informal information networks probably prevailed, variously based on ties of neighbourhood, trade or kinship. Ellen Swyne, noted in a York will of 1460, was a kinswoman of her mistress, and Thomas Hornby, tanner, was uncle to his servant of the same name. Similarly, Joan Amgill, the servant of John Smith of York (d. 1463) probably owed her position to John Amgill, probably her brother, who was Smith's apprentice.

Servants, including apprentices, were thus an integral part of many, particularly urban, households. Servants were also very much a feature of the aristocratic household, though here we may perhaps distinguish between servants from lower-status backgrounds, who would have been largely male and essentially subordinates, and those from like backgrounds, including young ladies in the service of the mistress of the household, who would have been using service as a way to gain experience, but also to win patronage and even secure marriage partners. By and large we may assume that the relationship between employer and servant was moderately harmonious. Employers could chastise servants, but not abuse them. Where this occurred, servants were quite capable of asserting their rights. Joan Potter, a Nottingham servant, sued her master for assault when he struck her with a club supposedly for answering him back, and Thomas and William Sewale were released by a London court from their apprenticeships as a consequence of their master having 'cruelly beaten' the brothers. Female servants would still have been at risk of sexual abuse. Aristocratic employers may sometimes have coerced peasant women servants into sexual relationships. Somewhat different circumstances are suggested by the financial provision made by the York draper and widower, John Stranton, for his servant Maud More and the child still in her womb at the time he made his will. Most servants, however, would have aspired to marriage rather than concubinage. It is to the subject of marriage that we turn next.

MARRIAGE, REPRODUCTION, BAPTISM

Marriage represents one of the central cultural institutions of later medieval society. From 1215 it was recognized as one of the sacraments of the Church. Women were normally expected to marry as adults and were socialized with this end in mind. For men, too, marriage represented a form of social adulthood. The married couple, the conjugal unit, was also central to the nuclear household. In studying marriage in this period we know much about the law respecting what constituted a valid marriage; we know something of marriages that were disputed and hence resulted in litigation; but as a generality we know little of how young people met and why they eventually married. Indeed, it is this absence of evidence that has led some to suppose that medieval marriages were essentially business arrangements devoid of emotional content. Certainly a reading of aristocratic marriage contracts or of petitions to circumscribe canon-legal impediments to marriage might lend weight to such a view, but records of payments of merchet, the marriage fine, in respect of villein women within peasant society, for example, ultimately tell us more about manorialism than the process of marriage. In attempting to explore marriage, therefore, we need to acknowledge the limitations of what we can know, but we need also to be sensitive to real differences between different levels of society and over time. We must also recognize that marriage constitutes a process. Couples do not suddenly wed. There is always a period of negotiation, of planning and often of courtship prior to a marriage. Each marriage thus has its own history. Our task here is thus to unravel something of these histories.

In any culture more than just the couple contracting are involved in the process of marriage. Even if marriages are not 'arranged' as such, a variety of individuals and collectivities will influence the process. Parents and close kin, employers, lords, all might have an interest, whether emotional or material. So, too, might the Church through the intermediary of the local clergy, although the interest here might be moral and legal. Peers, and indeed the wider community, might also exercise a degree of influence in so far as they would articulate views as to which relationships were acceptable, or indeed to be encouraged, and which were socially aberrant and to be discouraged. Thus parents or employers could support or oppose a particular courtship relationship by their willingness or otherwise to allow couples to see one another. The priest could warn of the sinfulness of sexual relations outside of marriage and indeed of the ways in which a marriage might be contracted. Peers could show disapproval of couples perceived to be ill-matched in terms of age or wealth, but equally could encourage relationships of which they approved. It is, however, easier to make these assertions than to document them. We must also recognize that popular notions of what made a marriage probably changed over the period.

In writing a history of marriage in the medieval era it is conventional to start with canon law and the Church's teaching on what constituted a valid marriage. There are two reasons for this. The first is that this is particularly extensively documented. The second is that canon law provided a framework within which most marriages operated. Throughout the period covered by this book, moreover, the authority of the Church to determine what constituted a valid marriage, and hence to intervene in the case of dispute, went largely unchallenged. We must not, however, read what the Church taught as a simple model for what people actually did. Canon law permitted a whole variety of marriage customs and we can find evidence for considerable diversity of social practice between different groups and over time.

During the course of the later twelfth century the papacy had come to consolidate its teaching on what made a lawful marriage. This was both in response to appeals from well-to-do laity to rule on the validity or otherwise of their contracts and as part of a broader clerical concern to differentiate a celibate clergy from a non-celibate laity. The Church's position, formally ratified by the Fourth Lateran Council in 1215 and reiterated by subsequent provincial councils, was that it was consent alone that made a marriage. Thus a couple could lawfully be wed if they exchanged words that demonstrated their agreement to be married to one another. However, consent is not the same as freedom of choice, and no contemporary churchman would have imagined such consent operated outside of a social context in which parents, other kin and the wider community exercised some influence or even control over marriage. The Church was instead primarily concerned to curb perceived abuses of parental authority seen principally in the marriage of underage children, but also in forced marriages.

Canon law elaborated on this basic principal. Consent, expressed verbally, could be understood as 'present' or as 'future'. Thus a couple who exchanged words like 'I take you Agnes to be my wife' and 'I take you John to be my husband' were contracting by words of present consent and, as in modern marriage ceremonies, were lawfully married from the moment they spoke those words. However, a couple could instead exchange words of future consent by intimating an intention or desire to be married at some future date, a position akin to engagement in contemporary society. In canon law such a contract was held to make a binding marriage if the couple subsequently initiated a sexual relationship; this was understood to indicate the couple's intention to make immediately binding what had previously been only a future intention. Sex of itself did not make a marriage, nor in canon law was it strictly necessary: Joseph's marriage to the Virgin Mary was chaste, but necessarily valid. Couples could marry only if they were old enough to have an understanding of their actions. Girls below the age of 12 and boys below the age of 14 were said to be below the age of consent or canonical majority. These ages reflect as much contemporary understanding of the advent of sexual maturity derived from an academic medical discourse as they do emotional maturity, but canon law did thus protect against child marriages by insisting that children below canonical majority (and aged seven years or over) might only enter into contracts to marry. Such a contract would only become binding if the child ratified it on reaching their majority. Children under seven could not, in canon law at least, even enter into a contract to marry. This was, however, only modest protection since few 12 or 14 year olds would have had the means to oppose marriages made for them. Indeed in one disputed marriage case involving a minor gentry family from late fourteenth-century Yorkshire, the child-bride Alice de Rouclif seems to have so absorbed aristocratic notions of honour that she wished to be married to the man who had effectively raped her rather than be considered his mistress.

The Church imposed other conditions on what made a valid marriage. Couples contracting were not supposed to be closely related by blood ties (consanguinity), by marriage or sexual relations (affinity) or indeed by ties created by acting as a godparent (spiritual affinity). Because people supposedly lived all their lives in the same introverted communities and had their marriages arranged, it used to be argued that such 'impediments' were frequently disregarded but subsequently remembered if the marriage did not work out so as to engineer a de facto divorce. In fact, the assumptions upon which this view was based do not stand up to scrutiny. As noted earlier, some marriages, particularly within the higher echelons of society, were made between persons who were related within 'forbidden degrees', yet this knowledge was rarely used subsequently to undo the marriage. Marriage was also impossible if one party had a spouse still living, had taken holy orders or had entered into a vow of chastity.

It is likely that most young people expected their parents to take an interest in their marriages, but that only parents from the aristocracy and perhaps the uppermost echelons of peasant society actually arranged marriages – particularly, but not only, the marriages of daughters. The example of William Crane of Bingham (Notts.), noted in a marriage case of 1333, represents one pole in a spectrum of marriage practice. He was allegedly forced into agreeing a marriage while not yet in his teens and under threat of having his ear cut off. The other pole is perhaps represented by Thomas Fox of Snaith (Yorks., WR) who willingly exchanged words of matrimony with Isabel Wakfeld, a York seamstress's apprentice in order to spend several nights of passion with her in a York lodging house. Young people, particularly those in service and living away from their parents, probably enjoyed the greatest freedom to engage in courtship and hence make their own marriages, but this was only conspicuously so in respect of urban society in the century after the Black Death. Even here the pattern suggested by disputed marriage cases may disguise a more general picture that allowed young people only modest autonomy. The same source suggests that from about the middle of the fifteenth century daughters at least were socialized not to consent to proposals of marriage unless approved by their fathers or other close kin. In a London case of 1472 one Walter Isaak recalled that his sister Elizabeth had agreed to John Bolde's proposal of marriage only after asking his consent. By the end of our period parents and families appear even more conspicuous in the making of marriages, such that most marriages probably represented a complex negotiation between individual initiative and family influence. Thus a key stage in the making of the marriage of Clement and Joanna Weldish of Kenardington (Kent), noted in a case dated 1549, was a meeting of numbers of kin of either party to agree matching sums of money to be given in support of the couple setting up home together.

This last alerts us to the fact that marriage making was routinely accompanied by numbers of ritual stages. Solemnization, customarily held at the church door, represented only one such stage, albeit one that increasingly became the norm over the course of the period as a whole. Such a solemnization was often preceded by a formal contract made at the house of the parents or employers of one of the parties. Thus John Bedeman and Agnes Nicholas were present in Agnes's parents' house in London in 1469 where negotiations were made about their possible union. The couple were then asked if they were agreeable and everyone went into the garden. John and Agnes, posing beneath a vine and holding hands, then formally agreed to marry one another. Finally, they kissed and shared ale together. At a still earlier stage, a couple might exchange words of matrimony, or at least of intention to marry, with few if any witnesses present. They might also exchange gifts: rings, gloves or sometimes coins were the most usual tokens of intent. Solemnization was sometimes followed by a marriage feast. Ceremonial actions involving the couple's first night also followed. The vicar of Scalby (Yorks., ER), testifying in 1333, remembered the guests at the wedding feast afterwards riding to see the bride's entrance to her new home. He also recalled blessing the marriage bed for another couple on their wedding night. Some century and a half later, a London man recalled how he and his wife saw the newly wed couple naked in bed since 'his wife had made certain preparations in the said chamber' before the couple retired for the night.

Marriage was the point at which couples might legitimately engage in sexual relations. At least before the later fifteenth century most couples in fact thought sex was acceptable from the time they first agreed to be married. Only the rather more puritanical values prevailing on the eve of the Reformation and beyond insisted that sexual activity before the church solemnization was morally wrong. Thus in 1520 Agnes Plumrige of Fingest (Bucks.) was ordered by her bishop to carry a lighted taper to her neighbours' houses on the feast of the Purification by way of penance for becoming pregnant by her husband before their marriage was solemnized.

In the absence of effective forms of artificial contraception, the beginning of a sexual relationship was invariably the beginning of a procreative relationship. Withdrawal (coitus interruptus) was the best-known contraceptive practice, but we do not know how far married couples may have practised this. Women may have used herbal contraceptives and abortifacients, but our knowledge is again somewhat speculative since the Church taught that all forms of contraception were sinful. The Church further taught that couples should abstain from sex on Sundays, feast days and during Lent. Only the missionary position was acceptable as any other was thought to impede conception. Though couples owed each other the marital 'debt' – that is, the one should agree to sex if the other asked – ideally sex was for the purpose of procreation, not pleasure. What impact this teaching had on sexual behaviour is unclear. The last actually conflicts with contemporary medical thought, which held that both the male and the female needed to experience pleasure in lovemaking in order to conceive.

The widespread practice of maternal breastfeeding probably reduced fertility in established marriages, but most mothers would have expected to be pregnant at least every couple of years even if not all pregnancies went to term. Margery Kempe's completed family of 14 children, though large, was perhaps not so unusual. Thomas Hevingham (d. 1500) is portrayed on his brass with five sons. His wife is likewise shown with six daughters. A (somewhat enigmatic) listing of families from the archdeaconry of Stafford c.1532 likewise suggests that large completed families were then fairly common, but not the norm. It does not, however, follow that these children survived infancy. High levels of neonatal and infant mortality would in practice have significantly reduced the numbers of living children associated with any medieval couple. Of the nine children listed for Henry and Alice Soke of Great Bloxwich in the c.1532 survey, for example, three were already dead.

Tradition dictated that the mother was confined near to the time her baby was expected, and birth took place ideally in a warm, dark room. At birth, the mother was attended by a midwife – probably an experienced local woman rather than a professional – and a number of female helpers, who might be kin or friends. Men were strictly excluded other than perhaps in the event of medical emergency. The newborn baby would be taken to be baptized within a day or two of the birth, such was the fear that the unbaptized child might die and thus be excluded from salvation.

The child was given three godparents, two of the same sex, one of the opposite. There is some reason to think that parents often looked to godparents of at least like, or preferably higher, social rank. Sir Geoffrey Luttrell, for example, stood godfather to some of his employees' children. One of the same-sex godparents would have the distinction of naming the child, often with their own name. Through baptism, the child was received into membership of the Church and into the community. It was the child's godparents and not the family that were the sponsors and supporters. The father had little formal role to play and the mother was absent altogether. Custom required that she wait a month from delivery to be churched and ritually reincorporated into the community.

3 MANOR AND BOROUGH

Although, as today, the medieval landscape comprised areas variously of open country-side, of woodland, of scattered settlement and of larger towns and cities, our knowledge of that landscape in documentary terms comes from records of government and admin-istration. Drawing on that perspective, we may distinguish three broad administrative units within which these different types of landscape were managed: the forest, the manor and the borough. Of these, the first declined in significance and extent through our period. Our primary concern, consequently, is with the other two: the manor and the borough. What we need to recognize immediately is that these administrative units were associated with a variety of landscapes and economies. It would be a mistake to assume that the forest, primarily a legal concept, was necessarily composed of dense woodland, that the manor was always essentially rural and agricultural, or that the borough was recognizably urban. This confusion of terminology in fact leaves room for debate about the nature of the rural economy and of urban identity. The following dis-cussion will give some thought to these questions.

The creation after the Conquest of large tracts of land subject to a separate and dis-tinctive administrative and legal tradition outside (*foris*) that of the common law gives us the term 'forest'. That these areas of forest are popularly thought of as woodland, the modern meaning of the word, is because they were created either in areas of existing woodland or, as in the case of parts of the New Forest, by planting trees even on land that had previously been cultivated. The purpose was to create large tracts of land suit-able for sustaining deer and boar for hunting, but also to provide a reserve of timber, primarily for royal building works, but sometimes used as gifts to religious houses and cathedrals. Although some 70 forests can be identified in the first part of the fourteenth century, most forest was concentrated in central southern England, the west and north-west Midlands, Lancashire and the North Riding of Yorkshire. Forest law, notoriously harsh, was concerned to preserve the hunting environment and deter poaching. In fact numbers of forests effectively fell out of use through encroachment and clearance, sanc-tioned or otherwise, during the course of the later Middle Ages, though the parallel growth in the popularity of private parks among the gentry may well have meant that the actual popularity of hunting was undiminished and may even have increased.

THE MANOR

Outside the forest, which belonged to the Crown, most land was divided into units of varying size called manors – hence the term 'manorialism' as an alternative to the Marxist 'feudalism' to describe the structure of society prior to the advent of capital-ism. The process by which manors were created was largely complete by the beginning of our period, but in some 'marginal' areas – for example, the Forest of Arden or the hill country of western County Durham, where settlement was going on into the fourteenth century – this process occurred later. Manors were held by various lords (including the king), whether great magnates, ecclesiastics or mere lords of the manor, the lowest level of the aristocracy. All these in turn held their land ultimately from the Crown. Like the forest, the manor is as much a concept as a physical entity. It represented the extent of the jurisdiction of the lord as exercised through the manorial court. This last is also known as the customary court because it operated not according to the whim of the lord, but according to custom, which was itself specific to each manor. At the beginning of our period, it was the peasant community, as represented by the older and more prosperous male villeins (or serfs), who were the custodians of this 'custom'. Increasingly, however, the collective memory of the peasant community was displaced by a written document or 'custumal'.

We find it easier to think of the manor not in ideological, but in physical terms. Here we immediately encounter great diversity. Some manors were small and tightly focused, but some – especially in pastoral and upland regions like the Pennine manor of Wakefield – were large, extending over numbers of settlements and parishes. Parish, village and manor need not coincide, as at Bottisham (Cambs.), where one parish was divided between five manors, or Aldwincle (Northants), where two manors adjoined, each associated with its own parish. Conventionally the manor had an administrative focus in the court, which was itself invariably held in the manor house. On the large manor of Wakefield, courts were held of necessity in several locations. The manor might also boast communal ovens for baking bread and a mill or mills for grinding grain or even fulling cloth. Both were provided as an investment by the lord, with a view to generating revenue.

In describing the manor, scholars invariably distinguish between the demesne (or domain), that part of the manor reserved to the lord as a home farm, and the remainder of the manor. The former was cultivated partly by a regular workforce, known as *famuli*, and partly by either the labour of customary (servile) tenants or hired labourers. The latter was leased out to numbers of tenants, both free and servile in differing proportions across the country (as shall be more fully discussed in Chapter 7). From the later fourteenth century, however, greater lords were increasingly tending to lease out the demesne, or even whole manors, and hence the distinction between demesne and individual peasant holdings was eroded. The growing fashion for enclosure during the last part of our period, whereby numbers of individual strips of land were consolidated and fenced or hedged about, often to create sheep pasture, further eroded these distinctions.

The right to hold a court and exercise justice over his (or her) tenants was one of the fundamental prerogatives enjoyed by a manorial lord. The regular meeting of the manorial court, invariably once every three weeks on larger manors, but rather less frequently on small manors, was thus central to the functioning of the manor and indeed of manorialism as an institution. Fortunately for the historian, from around the middle of thirteenth century the business of the court came increasingly to be the subject of written record. This was in part a product of the growing availability of Latin-trained clerks choosing for one reason or another not to pursue a career in the Church, but it may also have been driven by pressure from the royal (or common law) courts, which presented an increasingly attractive forum for free tenants to resolve disputes. By the 1270s manor court rolls – parchment membranes stitched end to end to form a long roll and written in abbreviated Latin – were widely kept and numbers of these have survived, especially for manors forming part of large institutional estates, great magnate estates and the Crown estate. The records of individual manors and of lesser lords have fared less well, though only a fraction of extant manorial material has ever been subject to scholarly analysis.

Because the records of the manor court are so voluminous and apparently present a far fuller record of the manor and its inhabitants than account rolls, rentals or custumals (records of tenants and their obligations), the only other written sources to survive in any quantity from the English medieval manor, they have come to assume a position of immense importance in the historiography. Certainly they are a crucial administrative record. They provide invaluable evidence for landholding and the transmission of land, the enforcement of such customary obligations as heriot (loosely understood as death duty) and merchet (the marriage fine), and labour and monetary obligations of tenants. Although lords seem often to have tolerated private transactions involving the lease or sale of peasant land, it is evident that the court jealously guarded the lord's interests by requiring any permanent transfer of land to be duly registered through the court and taking firm action where this requirement was flouted. More occasionally court rolls throw light on the enforcement of labour obligations or on attempts to bring back runaway villeins.

A fuller picture of the manor as an administrative unit, however, depends on deploying a rather more extensive range of records. Manor account records, which were produced locally on behalf of the manorial reeve and, like court rolls, in some quantity from the 1270s, offer a rare insight into manorial revenue and more specifically the demesne economy. The original function of the manorial account was to protect the lord's interests against fraud on the part of the reeve or other manorial officials. Such accounts record both the expenditure involved in managing the demesne – the cost of hired labour, particularly at harvest, the purchase and maintenance of agricultural equipment such as ploughs and carts, the cost of livestock purchased at market – and the income received, notably from the sale of produce and of livestock. By auditing annually, usually at Michaelmas (29 September), the reeve could be held answerable for any blatant inconsistencies. It was possible, moreover, to set target figures for production of grain or livestock, and measure these against the performance accounted for at the yearly audit. Rental income would likewise be accounted for as also expenditure on repair of tenants' properties. Such information could also be used in the case of larger estates to calculate the revenue of a manor and hence, perhaps, decisions as to whether and when to shift from the direct management of the demesne to a policy of leasing out, as became common from the end of the fourteenth century. Where demesnes and even whole manors were normally leased out, however, such accounting material becomes much more fragmentary.

Account rolls provide valuable data relating to the product of the demesne in terms of cash crops, and so on, and hence may provide a clue as to the prevailing type of agriculture. Peasant land conventionally comprised numbers of separate strips scattered between two or three large fields. Occasionally we have glimpses of the peasant economy from chance disputes entered in the court rolls – for example, peasants bringing litigation against their neighbours for the damage done by the neighbour's pigs to their peas, beans or leeks. In terms of the bigger picture, however, 'fields' were given over either to cereal production or, when fallow, to livestock. A two-field system, which allowed for land to lie fallow every other year, tended to be displaced by or during the earlier part of our period with a more intensive three-field system. There was some tendency towards such a norm in the central arable or champian belt of Midland England, but in practice a multiplicity of systems for organizing land usage can be found. The pattern was certainly much less simple, and probably less tightly regulated, in more upland and pastoral regions where distinctive 'fields' are not necessarily found. Such a pattern has, for example, been described for parts of County Durham where the customary unit was the furlong or 'flat' rather than the larger field. Not all land, however, was subdivided into individual peasant strips. Some land was held as common. Such common land was an essential supplement to individual family holdings, but probably also a lifeline for poor and landless peasants. Common land could comprise both cultivated land, often pasture, but also woodland.

A mill and a bakehouse were commonly found as features of the manor since lords paid for their construction and then derived an income either from leasing them out or more directly by charging for their use. Such facilities were integral to manorialism and lords would sometimes attempt to outlaw the use of querns (hand mills) so as to protect their revenues. It is striking, for example, that the famous scenes of peasant life in the earlier fourteenth-century Luttrell Psalter depict peasants labouring in the fields, a watermill – with prominent padlock! – and a windmill, but neither the manor house nor the parish church. Another common feature of many manors, especially before the Black Death, was a weekly market, again a source of revenue to the lord, but a necessary resource for the peasant population.

Later medieval England was characterized by a plethora of often intensely local markets, primarily functioning as an exchange for agricultural surpluses. Peasant agriculturalists were encouraged to think of producing surpluses if only to generate a cash income to meet the various demands of rent, monies paid in lieu of labour services, the cost of hired labour or royal taxation. Some of these surpluses would have been bought up by merchants supplying the needs of urban society. Poorer peasants would also have had need of the market to buy food they were unable to produce. In the decades following the Black Death numbers of the more local midweek markets seem to have fallen into gradual disuse, but a substantial network of larger markets, often focused on Saturdays, continued to flourish into the early modern era and beyond.

The manor was staffed not only by a team of regular manorial employees or *famuli*, who might be provided with tied cottages and regular allowances of grain, and who fulfilled such functions as ploughman, carter, shepherd and dairymaid, but also by various officials answerable to the lord or the manorial court, such as reeves, haywards and ale tasters. Foremost among these officials was the reeve, who supervised workers on the lord's demesne and was in effect equivalent to a modern farm manager. Historically, reeves were elected by the manorial tenants, though in practice it would seem that they were often the lord's appointees. From the later thirteenth century, responsibility for reporting transgressions against customary law – the corpus of rights and obligations specific to each manor – rested with a jury of more substantial male villeins. Disputes about customary law were likewise referred to a jury of inquest, though in practice the advent of written records of the court reduced the need for such inquests and, as we have noted, written custumals increasingly displaced recourse to collective 'memory'.

The manor, then, has both a physical identity, albeit an astonishingly diverse one, and an administrative identity. The lord was at the focus of this administrative identity. A substantial proportion of manorial residents were variously his tenants, his serfs, his employees or their dependants. All land was held of the lord and the manor court was held in his name, though the lord himself could often be a remote figure dependent on a bailiff or lessee ('farmer'). As we shall see in Chapter 7, the authority of the lord was in fact often greater in theory than in practice, and we can discern informal groups of residents at both the level of the village and the parish that enjoyed a degree of influence over local affairs. In so far as village and parish did not entirely coincide with the extent of the manor, then the significance of the manor tended to be eroded. In broader constitutional terms the point remains: the manor represents a unit of administration under the authority of the manorial lord regardless of physical extent or size of population.

THE BOROUGH AND TOWN GOVERNMENT

The borough is comparatively easy to define. It represents a community granted privileged forms of tenure, free of all servile obligations. Often boroughs enjoyed their own court. In a number of cases boroughs were created by manorial lords out of existing manorial possessions with a view to attracting migrants and generating income from burgage rents and market tolls, such as the classic example of Stratford-upon-Avon described some 40 years ago by Eleanora Carus-Wilson.[1] Such a process was already largely completed by the beginning of our period, though Bolton (Lancs.) and Lyme Regis (Dorset), for example, only became boroughs in 1253 and 1284 respectively. Other boroughs were established communities. Some were already described as boroughs in Domesday Book (1086). Others are noticed as boroughs in the subsequent two centuries or were granted borough charters by their lords. Newcastle is thus first noticed as a borough in the earlier twelfth century and Beverley was granted its first charter at much the same time.

Tenurial privileges associated with borough status are one thing. Self-government (or at least a degree of self-government) is quite another. It is no easy matter to generalize about the nature of urban government within our period. The only certainty is that histories of individual communities all differ. Even within the same community, considerable changes in the nature of town government often occurred over the three centuries considered here. The older historiography placed much emphasis both on the emergence of the gild merchant, a collectivity of persons engaged in trade and retail, which subsequently evolved into or was displaced by the 'franchise', and on the importance of borough status. Useful work has also been done to document the constitutional histories of a number of towns in terms of the appearance of different offices and councils and the granting of charters. Most attention has been paid as a consequence to a small group of towns, such as Bristol, Coventry, Norwich and York, that by the end of our period enjoyed an elaborate hierarchy of office holding and a range of chartered privileges. As so often, there is a danger of optical illusion since many towns did not develop particularly elaborate systems of government beyond the

---

1. E.M. Carus-Wilson, 'The First Half Century of the Borough of Stratford-Upon-Avon', *Economic History Review*, 2nd ser. 18 (1965), pp. 46–63.

functioning of the local court, but still came to enjoy a degree of effective autonomy from their lords without formal charter.

Valuable work has been done systematically to document evidence that at some point in its history a particular community may have been recognized as a borough by its seigneur, whether the king, a secular magnate, a bishop or a religious house. As we have seen, this shows that many boroughs – perhaps most, since the documentary evidence is often fragile – had been established by the beginning of our period. Very few indeed post-date the Black Death. What this evidence does not show, however, is how far distinctive arrangements for the transmission of property and for separate legal jurisdiction, the characteristic hallmarks of borough status, allowed the burgesses any real voice in their own government. Moreover, several textile communities that expanded during the later Middle Ages, and consequently are often considered to have become towns, show no evidence of having achieved borough status. This is true, for example, of the Suffolk cloth towns of Lavenham and Hadleigh.

Broadly speaking, smaller communities had to wait longer than their larger neighbours to gain formal structures of self-government, if at all. Even here, however, there is often evidence that de facto government came to be provided by a religious guild, as at Stratford, Boston and Lichfield, which itself may be related to an earlier guild merchant, even where no more formal structures existed. Likewise borough courts, though still providing revenue for the town's lord, often came by the end of the Middle Ages under the de facto control of the townsfolk in their capacity as jurors. Religious houses tended to be the most conservative of lords, and political control in such monastic boroughs was conceded reluctantly, even on occasion violently. The rebellions of the townsfolk of Bury St Edmunds and St Albans against their monastic lords during the Peasants' Revolt of 1381 are but a single episode in a much longer history of discord, though the case of Westminster is a valuable corrective to this picture. Here the townsfolk in their capacity as jurors gained a high degree of autonomy by the end of the Middle Ages without serious friction and without ever being recognized as a borough.

It was the Crown, ever ready to relinquish some of its prerogative authority for a price, that was often more yielding than other secular lords. Even before our period, many larger royal boroughs had acquired charters granting them the right to collect tolls and other revenues otherwise due to the Crown as lord in return for a fixed (firma) annual payment or 'fee farm'. By transferring responsibility for collecting revenues in the form of local levies, tolls and profits of the borough courts from a royal official to burgesses chosen by the leading members of the community, the Crown effectively allowed such towns a fair degree of autonomy. This model might also be followed by numbers of other lords, as for example the bishop of Norwich in his borough of Bishop's (later King's) Lynn. On the other hand, we should not see the acquisition of the fee farm as the sine qua non for self-government. At the very beginning of our period, for example, Henry III was willing to allow the governance of Stamford to a group of substantial burgesses. This continued under his heir from 1254, but when some decade or so later the borough was granted to John de Warenne, a degree of more direct seigneurial control was restored.

These most privileged towns adopted a variety of governing bodies and officers under a variety of names. Clearly there is an evolutionary process here and borough charters often only give formal sanction to practice that may have developed some years earlier. Some general observations are nevertheless possible. Most towns appointed a bailiff or bailiffs, who were technically answerable to the Crown and on whom formal responsibility for paying the fee farm rested. They might also elect a mayor at their head as the borough's chief executive officer. Under the mayor we invariably find a group of men, sometimes known as jurats or *probi homines* (worthy men), who, together with mayor, effectively constituted the ruling council. Often, as at Winchester, Lincoln and Great Yarmouth, these numbered 24, but groups of 12, as at Northampton, Ludlow and Southampton, are also common, hence the terms 'the 12' or 'the 24'. Oxford, for example, had by 1285 a group of eight jurats and four electors. In some towns, such as Canterbury and Scarborough, however, no mayoralty emerged and the bailiffs thus constituted the chief executive officers. At Gloucester, though there was a mayor briefly in the early thirteenth century, the office was only reconstituted in 1483 and two bailiffs exercised authority in the intervening years. The episcopal borough of Beverley, on the other hand, was governed from the earlier fourteenth century neither by a mayor nor by bailiffs, but by a group of 12, here known as the keepers.

Another level of government in these towns was provided by the division of the borough into a number of wards, or leets, each under its own official, sometimes known as alderman, and each operating its own court, serving in effect a policing function in addition to the borough-wide courts. The larger body of burgesses or citizens, themselves (as we see in Chapter 8) only a privileged section of the resident population as a whole, tended to participate in the political life of the community only episodically. Although their voice was nominally required to consent to decisions of the ruling group, in everyday practice this voice was exercised on their behalf by the 12 or 24. Wider participation was, however, both politically expedient and a reality on occasions of particularly important business. The wider body was likewise involved in the election of jurats, mayors and bailiffs. In practice this process tended to be somewhat circumscribed. Thus at Oxford in 1257 it was alleged that the jurats were appointing the bailiffs without reference to the wider community. Elsewhere – and here the reason was ostensibly pragmatic – small bodies of electors, drawn from the different wards across the borough, were charged with nominating office holders, leaving the wider body with no other role than to acclaim their choice.

During the post-plague era many larger towns already enjoying a degree of self-government under a mayor or bailiffs and council of 12 or 24 tended to add a further, lower tier of councillors. This probably served to widen and deepen the pool of the politically active at a time when lesser merchants and artisans were enjoying generally greater economic prosperity. Thus at Coventry a Common Council of 48 men was formed by creating a lower tier of 24 to the established body of 24 jurats. Real power resided, however, with the senior group of 12 jurats, all of whom had held office as mayor. In York, likewise, we find three tiers of government: a senior '12' made up of former mayors and sheriffs; a '24' comprising former sheriffs and chamberlains; and a council of 48, otherwise the 'commonalty', which supposedly represented the much larger body of citizens. This last group was drawn from the crafts, citizenship and craft guild membership being coterminous by this period. During the course of the fifteenth century it appears that it was specifically the searchers of the various guilds that served. It should be noted that this process of creating additional councillors or additional layers of government developed slowly.

It can be found in York as early as the 1370s, but in Colchester, a lesser urban centre, it was initiated only in 1519.

The effect of these developments, which often ran ahead of actual recognition in the shape of charters and hence are difficult to locate in time with precision, was twofold. On the one hand it regularized the participation in government of the wider body of burgesses or citizens by giving this wider body an institutionalized voice. It also provided craftsmen and others outside the ruling elite a role in government, albeit a minor one, and the possibility at least of access to higher office. On the other hand it formalized the distance between a small ruling group of men who had held high civic office, styled themselves aldermen, effectively controlled entry to the group and regularly adopted special robes and the wider body of burgesses or citizens who might hold a variety of minor offices, notably chamberlain (one of a small group of financial officers), but were not permitted to progress further.

This process was if anything accelerated by the increasing powers that began to be gained by some of the most important towns and cities by new charters purchased from the later fourteenth century. In particular we should note the several major towns that were granted county status and hence were permitted to appoint their own sheriffs. Bristol was so elevated in 1373, in part to address the administrative problems consequent upon the borough straddling two historic counties. York followed in 1396, Newcastle in 1400, Norwich in 1404, Lincoln in 1409, Hull in 1440, Chester in 1506. By right of these charters the Crown also granted the mayors and some of the most senior councillors or aldermen in these places judicial authority as Justices of the Peace, and so greatly enhanced their judicial authority and autonomy. This new judicial authority was not limited to the county boroughs. Beverley's keepers, for example, were granted powers as Justices of the Peace by letters patent of 1415. Colchester was similarly granted its own commission of the Peace by right of its 1447 charter. We need, however, to be a little careful about equating new charters with new rights; charters sometimes only confirmed what was in practice already the case.

Large and established royal boroughs tended to be privileged, at least in formal terms, in having gained a significant degree of self-government by the beginning of our period. The port town Hull had to wait until 1331, but prior to Edward I's foundation it had been fairly insignificant. Even a sizeable and long established seigneurial borough, on the other hand, might have to wait a long time before achieving any clearly recognized degree of self-government, but it is possible that a de facto degree of autonomy often existed informally. A good example is Doncaster, a town with Roman origins and all the attributes of a vital urban community, such as a leper hospital (probably founded in the twelfth century), two friaries (the Grey Friars founded before 1284 and the Carmelites founded before 1346), and a variety of markets and fairs. The town, like many others of its size, appears to have been recognized as a borough from at least the middle of the twelfth century and the burgesses were formally granted the fee farm in a charter of 1194 while the borough was temporarily in the king's hands. Two years later, however, the borough was granted to Robert de Thornham and was then held for some 300 years as a seigneurial borough by his successors, the de Mauleys. For the entirety of that period there survives but one formal document respecting the rights (or otherwise) of the burgesses. A letter patent issued in 1331 by Peter de Mauley IV formally relinquished any seigneurial claim to an annual levy on the town's victualling traders, but implicitly allowed this to be levied by the leading burgesses. Such a levy is in fact noted in the Hundred Rolls in 1278 and a like levy is recorded in 1172. The likelihood is that a group of leading burgesses – 'the good men of Doncaster' according to a document of 1247 – continuously collected this levy and used the income to help maintain the bridge and roads. This collectivity was thus akin to the guilds merchant that had negotiated chartered privileges and constituted the earliest basis of self-government in the century or more before our period.

Despite the promise of Richard I's charter and the evidence for some sort of body of leading burgesses, control over the borough court, and hence effective authority, rested with the de Mauley lords. By the later fourteenth century this authority seems actively to have been challenged. During the 1360s Lady Margaret de Mauley complained that armed gangs prevented her steward from holding court and for the remainder of the century a small group of leading burgesses, including a couple of merchants, a cloth trader and an apprentice at law, were the subject of complaint and litigation by the de Mauleys. It is likely that the confirmation by Richard II in 1381 of his namesake's charter was part of their campaign and that these leading burgesses met the cost of this. Only with the acquisition of the lordship by Richard Duke of York in 1454 do the burgesses appear to have been able to elect a mayor, but thereafter self-government came swiftly. York's son, Edward IV, granted the borough a charter of incorporation in 1467, and in 1505 Henry VII granted the lordship of the borough to the burgess community.

A somewhat different story emerges for the neighbouring, though smaller, borough of Wakefield. Again we need look beyond the slight evidence for formal, publicly recognized structures. The borough status of the small town is documented in a late twelfth-century charter granted by its de Warenne lords. Another seigneurial charter of 1326 confirmed the rights of the burgesses only to be sued within the borough court, but even though the borough descended to Richard Duke of York in 1434 and subsequently to Edward IV, the borough remained seigneurial until the reign of Henry VII and no other significant concessions were made during that period. On the other hand, as at Doncaster, we have evidence of the leading burgesses acting collectively for the benefit of the community, thus a grant of tolls for three years 'to the honest men of the town of Wakefield' in order to repair roads was made by the Crown in 1331. During the course of the fifteenth century, a period of generally growing prosperity for this textile town, the burgesses asserted their sense of identity in other ways too. The parish church was substantially rebuilt and, from the end of the century, furnished with rood screen and pews. Perhaps the most striking assertion of a still unrecognized civic identity, however, lies in the commissioning and organization of an ambitious play cycle for the feast of Corpus Christi sometime towards the end of the fifteenth century. The likelihood, therefore, is that an articulate and well-organized body of leading burgesses took an increasingly active role in the governance of the town and that this process was accelerated once the town was absorbed into the Crown estate. By the middle of the sixteenth century the burgesses were effectively managing their own court on behalf of their own community.

Although Doncaster was slow to achieve the level of self-government smaller royal boroughs had long enjoyed, it is striking that it is a group of leading burgesses drawn from the mercantile class that seem to have been most active in the struggle for power. This mirrors the bigger picture found even in those towns that already enjoyed chartered privileges granting a greater or lesser degree of self-government. There was, however, a significant shift over time. Before the Black Death there was a very marked tendency for civic offices to be monopolized by a small number of individuals drawn from a limited number of intermarrying elite families, some of whom were as much property owners as traders. This became less marked from the later fourteenth or earlier fifteenth centuries, and there was some opening up of high office to persons outside a narrowly constituted mercantile elite.

The structure of office holding can be illustrated both anecdotally and statistically. For example, Richard de Barbflete of Southampton, who held positions as bailiff in 1315–16 and alderman the year after, and was a close kinsman of Nicholas de Babflete, himself a bailiff in the 1280s, is indicative of the kind of man who held high office prior to the plague. Richard and Nicholas shared an interest in the wool trade, but also held a manor. Richard married the heiress of one John de Holebury, likewise a wool merchant and former alderman. In Oxford several generations of the de Eu family held office as mayor or bailiff in the later thirteenth and earlier fourteenth centuries. Adam de Walsoken, twice mayor of Bishop's Lynn (1335–36 and 1343–44), first served as jurat in 1325–26. Like the Barbfletes, he was a successful wool merchant who subsequently invested in urban property. He married twice, his first wife probably being the daughter of John de Merlowe, several times mayor in the last years of the thirteenth and early years of the fourteenth centuries. Such monopolization of the highest civic office is common enough in this earlier period. In York, John Selby, himself a mayor's son and father to a mayor, was mayor at least seven times in the years 1251–71. John le Specer, another mayor's son, and John Sampson were likewise both five-times mayor there during the latter part of the same century, but the most extreme case was that of Nicholas Langton and his son John who, between them, ruled York for 28 years during the first part of the fourteenth century.

The dominance over civic offices of a comparatively small number of prosperous mercantile traders and property owners in this earlier period can also be shown statistically. In Gloucester, two-thirds of the 21 wealthiest taxpayers in 1327 served as bailiff at least once, some several times over. Of 32 leading burgesses who were the subject of complaint by one Walter de Milton in about 1253, nine had served or were to serve as mayor and ten as bailiff, accounting for all but two of the mayors in the period 1245–70. Such statistics could be replicated elsewhere. What most obviously receded by the later fourteenth century was not so much the predominance of the mercantile elite, but the monopoly of a small number of elite families and the tendency of individuals to hold high office repeatedly. The new pattern is apparent at York, for example, where restrictions on the re-election of mayors were enacted in 1372 and reinforced in 1392. It is less clear at Southampton where several men held the position of mayor on plural occasions – in the case of the merchant Walter Fetplace, senior, five times between 1419 and 1444. In Oxford, bailiffs usually served two or three terms before 1300; after the Black Death most served only once and none occupied the position more than three times.

The slow, and sometimes highly contested, change in the pattern of office holding cannot simply be ascribed to the Black Death since it was in part evolutionary, but there is no doubt that the impact of plague accelerated the shift. The haemorrhaging of office-holding dynasties by the impact of plague demanded the drawing in of new blood. At the same time the monopoly on wealth enjoyed by a property-owning, mercantile elite was challenged by changing patterns of consumption. Wealthy wool merchants, some of whom were bankrupted lending capital to Edward III in the 1330s and 1340s, were displaced by mercers, drapers and goldsmiths, but also in time tanners, dyers, weavers, brewers, tailors and bakers. These last became slightly more conspicuous during the course of the fifteenth century. This is invariably said to be because economic recession reduced the pool of mercantile traders willing to hold office, but a fuller answer might be to point to the increasing bureaucratization of town government and the invariable requirement that senior office holders first serve an 'apprenticeship' of lesser offices. The demands of high office may thus have placed less emphasis on entrepreneurial experience and personal wealth, and more on a degree of conscientious competence. In broad statistical terms the mercantile class remained, however, predominant in all but the smaller boroughs.

It is evident that just as the mercantile elite remained singularly and disproportionately advantaged in respect of holding civic office, but particularly higher civic office, so certain other groups were conspicuously disadvantaged. This was not simply a reflection of the differing levels of prosperity associated with different craft groups, though generally poorer crafts are less well represented than more affluent trades. Butchery, a generally prosperous craft, seems to have been specifically discriminated against. At Wells, for example, during the entire period 1377–1500, not a single butcher held office whether as churchwarden, rent collector, constable or master. In contrast, the numerically rather smaller group of merchants accounted for over a quarter of all the city's constables and masters, but for very few street-wardens, the lowest level of office holding. The city's weavers, who constituted the largest single craft group, were represented at all levels, but disproportionately at the lowest level and for only 1 in 20 of the city's masters. Similar patterns of office holding, whereby craftsmen are well represented among the lesser office holders, but merchants and the like dominate the higher offices, have been described for later medieval Exeter and York. This, then, was the normal pattern in larger towns from the later fourteenth century.

The exclusion of the butchers from office at Wells is by no means atypical. Much the same prejudice tended to operate, for example, at York. On one level this was a logical corollary of the regulation of the trade in foodstuffs exercised by town governments – there would be a serious conflict of interest if so important a victualling trade also exercised a major voice in government by holding high office. Indeed this was the logic behind the 1318 statute debarring bakers and brewers from civic office, a bar apparently observed more in the breach than in fact. The 1318 statute of course reflects the central importance of bread and ale in the diet of the majority before the plague. In the more affluent conditions prevailing after the Black Death demand for meat grew markedly and with it the fortunes of the butcher's craft. Butchers, moreover, required quite a lot of capital in order to maintain or purchase livestock and hence tended to be wealthier than most other craft groups. The likelihood is, therefore, that mercantile oligarchies genuinely feared that if butchers were permitted access to office on the basis of wealth and numerical strength, their own power base would be threatened. There is another related cultural factor. The slaughtering of livestock was very much looked down upon and hence seen as incompatible with office holding. Butchers may also have been considered unsuitable by temperament since the excessive consumption of meat was held to stimulate lust and anger. Lastly the historic concern of civic government to regulate against the sale of bad meat, the disposal of offal and other nuisances associated with the craft, may have reinforced this sense that butchers were not to be counted among the 'better sort' into whose hands town government was entrusted.

URBAN IDENTITY AND THE FORTUNES OF TOWNS

We have an insight into the structure of the urban economy for a number of communities from the evidence of admissions to the franchise, where this records occupations, from the poll tax returns of 1379 or 1381, from some early sixteenth-century subsidies, or more anecdotally from probate sources. Such evidence tends to be limited to those households associated with their own workshop, and tells us nothing directly about the employment of the many who sold their labour or made their livelihood out of petty retailing. A fair proportion at least of such persons would have been employed in the workshops and businesses of those who are recorded, although we cannot know how equally this was distributed between different crafts. The value of this evidence thus lays not so much in the precision (or otherwise) of the information for any specific place, but rather in the possibility of comparison between towns and, over time, within towns.

Table 3.1 sets out some statistical evidence for the economic structure of several, mostly larger, towns. Certain features are worthy of comment. The presence of numbers of mercantile crafts – mercers, merchants, drapers and the like – was a characteristically urban feature, but one that varied in size according to the wider nature of the urban economy. In the port towns of Bishop's Lynn and Chester, or in York, a major regional trading centre, it was significantly larger than in many other towns. The victualling trades, however, account for a consistently larger proportion – about one-fifth – of the population identified by occupation. The leather trades, which provided for a whole range of basic needs, whether saddles, shoes, sheaves for knives, purses, gloves, bottles or buckets, were also prominent, though more important in some towns, notably Leicester and Exeter, than in others. In Exeter, for instance, much tanning went on in the surrounding hinterland, which supported a significant level of stock rearing, whereas the city specialized in finished products, another indication of the close ties between town and surrounding countryside. Textile manufacture was evidently another important source of employment, but only in some towns, as at Norwich, Wells or (not shown in table) the still smaller communities of Rotherham and Wakefield, was it the major employer. In such cases the industry clearly served a much wider market than merely the townsfolk. Metalworking, represented by a range of specialist crafts including goldsmithing and bell-founding rather than the generic 'smiths' that were ubiquitous in village society, is a normal feature of the urban economy. Sheffield, still an industrial village in 1379, was already dominated by the metal trades.

Other crafts are notable as much for their diversity as their numerical significance. The extent of this diversity is itself a crude barometer of the importance of any particular economy. The larger the community, the greater the degree of trade specialization that could be sustained. Small towns such as Halesowen and Thornbury supported some 35 different occupations during the later Middle Ages, whereas over 100 different occupations are recorded in respect of Norwich freemen during the first part of the sixteenth century. Later medieval Wells, a middling-sized community, is

TABLE 3.1. URBAN ECONOMIC STRUCTURE

Place	Victuals	Leather	Textiles	Clothing	Mercantile	Metal	Building	Wood	Miscellaneous
Canterbury (1400–39)	22.8	12.8	13.8	12.3	9.2	9.9	–	4.8	14.3
Chester (1450–99)	19.6	16.3	9.8	13.7	16.3	7.8	2.0	6.5	7.9
Coventry (1523)	15.6	9.3	17.4	17.2	10.4	9.9	6.5	4.1	9.5
Doncaster (1379)	20.6	15.9	12.2	8.4	8.8	10.1	5.1	6.4	12.5
Exeter (1300–48)	16.2	29.3	10.8	11.7	8.6	10.8	4.1	0.9	7.8
Exeter (1500–29)	19.6	14.2	11.4	19.2	16.0	8.2	2.3	–	9.2
Leicester (1465–99)	18.7	14.3	10.2	13.5	13.5	9.9	5.5	5.8	8.6
Lynn (1400–49)	11.8	7.3	13.4	6.4	38.7	4.8	1.6	5.4	10.5
Norwich (1450–99)	16.0	11.5	23.0	7.5	10.0	7.0	5.0	7.3	11.9
Northampton (1524)	16.1	7.6	13.0	23.2	6.1	7.8	7.3	3.7	15.2
Oxford (1381)	27.2	14.7	13.5	11.9	4.7	6.2	7.0	3.2	11.6
Wells (1377–99)	26.9	11.1	19.4	12.0	–	11.1	8.3	4.6	6.4
York (1307–49)	23.0	19.7	5.3	8.4	13.2	14.6	2.1	2.7	11.0

Sources: P.J.P. Goldberg, *Women, Work and Life Cycle in a Medieval Economy* (Oxford, 1992), Table 2.6, pp. 60–1; P.J.P. Goldberg, 'Urban Identity and the Poll Taxes of 1377, 1379, and 1381', *Economic History Review*, 2nd ser. 43 (1990), Table 8, p. 211.

associated with some 60 different trades. Diversity of crafts, together with the relative unimportance of agricultural employment, thus constitutes the most telling indicator of an urban economy, but it is not the only measure.

Various attempts have been made by scholars to rank towns in terms of size, wealth or some other measure of supposed importance. The underlying concern is not so much to provide definitive rankings for any specific date, but rather to plot the changing relative fortunes of towns over time. Writing about the later twelfth and earlier thirteenth centuries, Patricia Cullum has demonstrated a close correlation between borough status and the presence from a comparatively early date of a leper hospital symbolically located just outside the town, often at one of the points of entry.[2] The maintenance of such hospitals, some of which appear to have been founded by groups

2. P.H. Cullum, 'Leper Houses and Borough Status in the Thirteenth century', in P.R. Coss and S.D. Lloyd, eds, *Thirteenth Century England* III (Woodbridge, 1991), pp. 37–46.

of burgesses, served both to signal the caring, godly nature of 'community', and to demarcate the boundary between town and non-town or 'other'. Another indicator of urban identity, this time for the century or so after *c.*1230 and limited only to more important centres, is the presence or otherwise of friaries. Almost all the county towns attracted one or more orders of friars during this period, as did a number of other towns. Some, such as Clare (Suffolk), Marlborough (Wilts.) or Yarm (Yorks., NR), represent communities that later ceased to be of particular importance, but presumably still were at this period, although even at this date the picture may be skewed by aristocratic patronage. A few greater towns – Boston, Bristol, Cambridge, Bishop's Lynn, Lincoln, London, Newcastle, Northampton, Norwich, Oxford, Stamford, Winchester and York – attracted all four major orders of friars. Oxford and Cambridge were, of course, the university towns, but many of the localities in this list were cloth towns then at the height of their prosperity. We would not expect to see the likes of Lincoln, Northampton or Stamford to feature quite so prominently hereafter.

The foundation of friaries thus provides a fairly good snapshot of the relative fortunes of towns at the beginning of our period. The next source that is invariably used is the lay subsidy of 1334, which itself is tied to the material wealth of the resident populations rather than size of population. As can be seen from Table 3.2, there is a fair degree of overlap between the towns that attracted friaries in the century or so prior to the subsidy and those ranked highest according to the subsidy. Greater structural change would await the advent of plague from the middle of the fourteenth century.

Our next important measure of urban vitality is the poll tax of 1377. This is based on the size of the resident population and not on any measure of wealth. Most of the towns that feature most prominently in terms of size at this date coincide with those ranked by wealth in 1334, but there are some significant changes in rank order. In particular the Midlands towns of Coventry and Leicester were ranked markedly higher than in 1334. The Essex port of Colchester is likewise in a much higher ranking, whereas the Norfolk port of Great Yarmouth has fallen back, indicative of broader changes in the pattern of trade. It would be unwise to read particular significance into other smaller movements in relative ranking according to essentially different data, but we need not distrust the broader pattern.

The final measure available to the urban historian of this period is that derived from the Henrician subsidy of 1524–25, the only significant attempt to assess anew the actual wealth of the population since the 1334 subsidy. The 1524–25 subsidy returned to the system of individual assessment used prior to 1334, though the criteria adopted were more complex. Consequently we can compare both the amount of tax levied for individual towns and the actual number of taxpayers. This is an important distinction; some towns, such as Hadleigh, Lavenham and Totnes, which appear comparatively prominently when ranked by tax assessment, hardly feature when ranked by number of taxpayers.

Certain observations can be made from the evidence for the amount of tax levied, notably the shift of wealth towards the south-west – Reading, Salisbury, Totnes, Worcester and, most strikingly, Crediton and Exeter, are all ranked much higher than previously. We also see comparative growth in East Anglia and the south-east – Maidstone comes to prominence for the first time and Norwich, Canterbury and Ipswich are all ranked higher. Both these regional shifts mirror broader trends in the distribution of wealth, itself a clear reminder of how closely the urban economy was

TABLE 3.2. URBAN RANKING

Place	Assessed wealth	Number of friaries	Poll tax population
	1337 £s		1377
Large towns			
London	11000	6	23314
Bristol	1900	5	6345
York	1620	5	7248
Newcastle	1333	5	2647
Norwich	1100	5	3952
Boston	1100	4	2871
Gt Yarmouth	1000	3	1941
Oxford	914	6	2357
Lincoln	900	5	3569
Coventry	750+	2	4817
Lynn	770	5	3127
Salisbury	750	2	3373
Shrewsbury	700	3	1932
Winchester	700	4	2500
Canterbury	599	4	2574
Hereford	550	2	1903
Southampton	511	3	1152
Gloucester	510	3	2239
Middling towns			
Hull	300	3	1557
Leicester	294	3	2302
Grantham	293	1	n.a.
Reading	293	1	n.a.
Sudbury	281	1	n.a.
Pontefract	270	1	1085
Colchester	250	1	2955
Small towns			
Bodmin	200	1	n.a.
Barnstaple	187	–	680
Stafford	144	2	461
Carlisle	133	2	678
Dunwich	120	2	n.a.
Selby	120	–	586

n.a. = not available

Sources: A. Dyer, *Decline and Growth in English Towns* (Cambridge, 1995), pp. 56–7, 62; R.E. Glasscock, ed., *The Lay Subsidy of 1334* (Oxford, 1975); C.C. Fenwick, ed., *The Poll Taxes of 1377, 1379, and 1381*, 3 vols (Oxford, 1998).

integrated with its rural hinterland. Since these observations relate to relative, not absolute wealth, it follows that any upward movement must be balanced by corresponding downward movement. The northern and eastern towns of Beverley, Boston, Lincoln and York seem conspicuously to have lost out.

Although for a fair proportion of towns there is a broad correlation between numbers of taxpayers and total tax assessment, only some people paid tax; we should not assume any simple correlation between number of taxpayers and total population. The 1524–25 evidence for number of taxpayers is thus not directly comparable with the 1377 poll tax populations. Alan Dyer has nevertheless bravely attempted to calculate changes in population levels between 1377 and 1524–25 by assuming (differing) uniform relationships between tax populations and actual populations at these two moments.[3] This is probably reasonable for the poll tax, but is much more hazardous for the Henrician subsidy since different patterns of wealth distribution probably applied between different towns and regions. The likelihood is that the ratio of taxpayers to total population was higher in those towns and regions that were the most prosperous. It follows that Dyer's population totals for those towns experiencing recession by this date understate the true figure. For example, Dyer calculates the population of Coventry in 1524–25 at around 4700, but this ignores the evidence for extreme inequality in the distribution of wealth whereby a handful of exceptionally wealthy people are balanced by a very large number of persons exempted from paying tax in 1522. A much more robust estimate based on the local listings for 1520 and 1523 would suggest an actual population of some 7500. Dyer's estimates of population change must as a consequence be regarded as untrustworthy; they may still highlight regional patterns of comparative growth, stability and decline. This reading of the data confirms the pattern of growth in the south-west, south-east and East Anglia, but suggests that decline was more widespread than suggested above. In particular it embraced such Midlands towns as Coventry, Leicester, Nottingham and Bridgnorth. In many instances, however, our knowledge of the actual size of towns by the end of our period is impressionistic.

Although the perspective that the later Middle Ages was a period of economic retrenchment owes much to the work of Michael Postan, it was perhaps Neville Bartlett's 1959 article on the growth and 'decline' of York in the later Middle Ages that initiated a long-running debate around the concept and phenomenon of urban decline.[4] Evidence of vacant properties, as at Coventry, and of falling rental values are indeed telling indicators that the population of some towns was contracting, but we should not exaggerate this. Similarly, during the course of the fifteenth century numbers of towns petitioned for reductions in the fee farm obligations to the Crown on the grounds of poverty. Such pleas were of course couched in the most pathetic language, but their success owed more to the parlous state of the monarchy and its need to buy political support during the period of civil war known as the Wars of the Roses than to the veracity of the claims made. Winchester's claim of 1440, for example, that 987 messuages had fallen into decay over the previous half century beggars belief for it exceeds the likely total number of houses in the city. Much the same caution should be applied to York's frequently cited claim during the later Middle Ages to be second only to London in importance. Unlike its more successful rival, Bristol, York's claim appears to have been cultivated, for example, by using distinctively southern forms of

---

3. A. Dyer, *Decline and Growth in English Towns 1400–1640* (Cambridge, 1991), Appendix 5, pp. 64–6.

4. J.N. Bartlett, 'The Expansion and Decline of York in the Later Middle Ages', *Economic History Review*, 2nd ser. 12 (1959), pp. 17–33.

building construction in the city and the introduction of southern language forms into the official text of the city's Corpus Christi Play. Such a policy of 'spin' fails to disguise the fact that York's political pretensions to be an alternative capital, realized briefly under Edward I at the time of the Scottish wars, had little substance by the later fourteenth century; other regional centres enjoyed rather greater economic success through the fifteenth century.

It is all too easy to confuse evidence of population contraction with evidence of economic malaise, though the two are connected. We need also to distinguish between evidence for declining civic revenues and a wider contraction in private wealth. Numbers of towns saw revenues from tolls decline as a consequence of the growth in the numbers of traders exempted by charter from paying tolls. Similarly, revenue from the enfranchisement of burgesses or citizens waned as epidemic disease became less virulent and revenue from rents contracted with falling numbers. Political inertia prevented civic governors finding alternative sources of regular revenue, but it is clear that numbers of towns had little difficulty raising funds for specific prestigious projects such as the purchase of a new charter, or the construction of a civic guild or common hall. The governors of Beverley were contemplating raising money for a new guildhall at almost the very moment in 1435 they claimed that the borough was too poor to aid the king. York's guildhall was constructed on a grand scale in the 1450s precisely at the moment the city was supposedly facing accelerating recession. This may, however, provide a clue. A new common hall, a new charter, these were symbolic of a community's faith in itself even at a time of growing difficulty in much the same way as modern towns have embraced orbital roads or the construction of prestigious sports facilities.

A more useful perspective than to talk glibly of urban decline, as if this were a general phenomenon, is to describe an urban restructuring along the lines already indicated. Thus real decline in places like Wallingford, Winchester, York and, perhaps most spectacularly, Coventry in the 1520s, must be set against the continued growth of London and the evidence for the sustained prosperity of regional centres like Norwich and Exeter, or the growth of newer towns like Hadleigh or Taunton. Even this picture needs to be qualified. Local economies could fluctuate considerably from one decade to another. The continued growth of London may have somewhat sapped the fortunes of first Exeter and then Norwich by the last decades of our period. Coventry's decline from the mid-fifteenth century was neither linear nor continuous. Even in the 1520s, moreover, there were some spectacularly wealthy individuals in a city characterized by extreme inequality of wealth distribution.

Our focus thus far has been on larger towns and cities, but we need to put this in perspective. The Venetian author of a description of England written right at the end of the fifteenth century rightly commented, from the perspective of one of the most urbanized regions of later medieval Europe, that there were virtually no towns of any significance outside of London. An English observer would have taken a different view and modern scholars likewise conventionally refer to the likes of Norwich, Bristol and York, whose later medieval populations were in excess of 10,000, as 'large'. By comparison with Scottish towns at the same period, they were. Within a larger European context, however, only London can be counted as large. Even before the plague, when towns were swollen by considerable numbers of impoverished rural migrants, most towns were very small, containing fewer than 2000 inhabitants. There were then perhaps only some 50 towns with populations in excess of this figure. Based on the number of communities identified as boroughs, however, a further 400 or more could still be characterized to a greater or lesser degree as urban. By the end of our period we can identify well over 700 market 'towns', but again only a proportion of these could be otherwise recognized as urban.

A still more hazardous exercise is to calculate what proportion of the population lived in towns. This almost certainly changed over time and it is very likely that England after the Black Death saw a larger proportion of its population living in urban communities even though most individual towns had contracted in terms of absolute numbers. The pre-plague proportion was probably no higher than 10 per cent. This may indeed be a generous estimate. After the plague, however, the equivalent proportion most likely grew to nearer 20 per cent. This still contrasts with a (statistically more robust) figure of 34 per cent of the population of Tuscany living in communities containing an excess of 800 persons in 1427. How stable this proportion was over the latter part of our period is difficult to assess. The documented contraction of major urban communities such as Coventry and York was probably largely balanced by the growth of numbers of other communities, especially, as we have seen, in the south-east and south-west. London seems to have continued to grow from a post-plague low of perhaps 40,000 to over 100,000 by the end of our period, although much of this growth was probably concentrated in the early Tudor era and reflects the city's growing monopoly over trade both internally and overseas.

Towns grew (and contracted) according to their ability to attract migrants, primarily but not exclusively from the immediate hinterland, rather than the usual demographic parameters of fertility and mortality. The only significant exception to this rule is the very real impact of the Black Death; the effect of most subsequent epidemics was perhaps more ephemeral. We can explore patterns of migration indirectly. By the later fourteenth century hereditary second names – surnames – were increasingly common, but before that date names often reflected an individual's trade, place of origin or physical appearance. Consequently we can draw on the evidence of toponyms – second names derived from the names of places – as a useful clue to patterns of migration. By mapping such placename bynames ('surname diffusion') it is possible to explore migration fields both in terms of the distances travelled and in terms of the precise localities from which migrants tended to journey.

In general, the larger the town, the greater the distance over which migrants would be drawn. Thus well over half the migrants to the small town of Ludlow in the period 1250–1300 hailed from places within a ten-mile radius, whereas much larger urban centres such as Bristol or York pulled in migrants from over much greater distances. It is possible that the pulling power of these larger towns actually increased in the decades immediately following the plague. The precise shape of the migrational hinterlands of towns – a rather neglected consideration – was variously influenced by topography, the rural economy and the location of other urban centres. Migrants tended to be the rural dispossessed and hence came in greatest number from places experiencing hardship. On the other hand they were more influenced by ease of roads or navigable rivers than actual distance. London attracted migrants from all over the country, but before the plague particularly from the densely populated regions of East Anglia. In the decades following the Black Death, however, the city absorbed a large influx of migrants from the English Midlands. According to scholars of historical linguistics, this shift was sufficiently marked as to effect the actual sound of London English as reflected in the written language.

By the fifteenth century, as names become more stable, direct evidence for migration is generally harder to find. Occasionally the place of origin of members of the urban franchise is recorded, as at Colchester after 1384, Romney (Kent) in the period 1433–1523 and York for the years 1477–1566. This slight evidence mirrors the earlier pattern. About a third of the migrants to the small town of Romney hailed from within a 5-mile radius, whereas more than half the migrants becoming freemen in York travelled from outside a 20-mile radius. Again we can see distinct patterns of migration. Most migrants came from village society rather than other urban settlements. Few migrants to Tudor York originated south of the Humber or east of the Wolds, but significant numbers came from areas to the north-west of the city, extending through the historic county of Westmorland and as far as the Cumbrian coast, both regions associated with comparatively impoverished rural economies. It is clear, however, that many towns found it much harder to recruit migrants through the fifteenth century and it is this failure that accounts for the shrinking populations of numbers of towns, notably those outside the south-east and south-west. Colchester, for example, continued to draw many of its migrants from outside the immediate counties of Suffolk and Essex, but numbers were insufficient to prevent the overall population falling by some quarter or more between the later fourteenth and the earlier sixteenth centuries.

Migration was not necessarily a once-in-a-lifetime experience. Our concern with migration tends to focus on net flows, and obscures the probably considerable level of temporary movement in and out of towns. In particular there appears to have been a steady flow of adolescents and young adults – the most mobile groups in society – into towns. These often took up positions as servants or apprentices, who may subsequently have returned to the countryside. Alice Dalton, for example, was twice employed as a servant in York early in the fifteenth century, before marrying and settling in her native Poppleton. Significant numbers of probably poor and single persons appear only briefly in urban records – whether as lessees of cheap accommodation, holders of annual licences to trade (as at Canterbury) or in court records. The likelihood is that numbers of these were only temporarily resident. Turnover of tenants specifically for the cheapest properties of the York Vicars Choral, for example, is very high, few staying more than a year at a time and many only six months. Women are quite conspicuous among these temporary migrants. Women seem also to have formed the majority of all migrants to towns, at least at the time of the poll taxes. Women outnumbered men, for example, by some ten to nine among the adult (over-14) populations of Carlisle and Hull according to the 1377 poll tax returns. An even more skewed sex ratio was true of Coventry in the 1520s, though it appears that London's growing preference for male labour tended to have the opposite effect by about the same date. At present we cannot know with confidence whether pre-plague towns displayed the same imbalance in favour of women.

The impact of towns on the rural hinterland was hardly confined to the pull they exercised over migrant labour. Towns were very much dependent on the surrounding countryside to supply grain and meat. The main markets in towns would have been dominated by rural traders selling agricultural surplus, just as towns themselves provided goods and services for their rural hinterlands. It has been argued that the grain requirement of London in about 1300 – that is, when its population was at as high a level as it was to reach before the sixteenth century – was sufficiently great to determine agricultural production within a 20-mile radius and for 60 miles along riverways. Obviously the impact of lesser towns would have been much less marked. It would also have changed as the demand for meat grew significantly after the plague, though cattle, unlike grain, could be herded over long distances at comparatively little cost. By the early sixteenth century the demands of the London market found Welsh cattle pastured on the Romney Marshes and Midland cattle on the Isle of Sheppey.

We tend to think of towns as physically quite distinct from their rural neighbours, with densely built streets crowded inside high stone-built walls. This indeed is how contemporaries tended to represent towns in manuscripts or on maps, but in fact it was for the most part only the larger and more important urban centres, such as Exeter, Newcastle or York, that were ever fully walled. For these larger towns, walls could be genuinely defensive, an observation that is especially true of northern and western towns vulnerable to Scottish or Welsh raiding, or port towns that were likewise potentially vulnerable. On the other hand the incentive for such Midlands' towns as Nottingham to maintain their walls into the sixteenth century was slight. Walls also served to provide the necessary security to enforce a system of tolls on goods brought into the town for sale and to permit effective curfew, usually from nine o'clock at night. But walls also had prestige value. The cost of building stone walls was considerable and their regular maintenance a continuous drain on resources. To boast a circuit of walls, and thus to conform to the medieval self-image of a town, was to make a statement about wealth, to proclaim civic pride and to demarcate *urbs* from *rus* (town from country).

Many lesser towns, such as Doncaster or Wallingford (Berks.), possessed at best only ditches, ramparts and fortified gateways. The early fifteenth-century brick north bar at Beverley is a good example of this last, its function by this date being as much symbolic of the authority of the town's governors and the borough's prestige as a serious defence. Within these fortified boundaries there were often areas containing gardens, the precincts of friaries or other religious houses, or undeveloped land. This last was certainly true of Hull, where the town walls encompassed a rather larger area than was subsequently developed. Almost the entire north-western quarter of Wallingford was occupied (until its dissolution) by the priory, but there were open spaces elsewhere. During the course of the fifteenth century such open spaces often became more conspicuous as a shrinking population led to the actual abandonment of properties, both housing stock and churches.

The supposedly sharp contrast between town and country marked by defensive boundaries also proves somewhat illusory, for many towns had suburban growth spreading out beyond the town walls or ditch. Indeed, because the central walled area had often been laid out before the full extent of medieval growth had been achieved, some towns spilled out beyond their walls in all directions. Nearly half Oxford's housing in 1279 lay outside the walls and by 1300 Colchester had likewise considerably outgrown its walls. Ludlow had suburbs to the north-east and to the south, Ipswich to the south and east, and the much larger city of Coventry possessed substantial western suburbs. The housing stock here would often have tended to be of poorer quality, occupied by labourers and the poor, and visually not necessarily so very different from the equivalent poorer housing of the surrounding villages. Streets and houses were crowded together within the walled centre of Totnes (Devon), but taxation evidence suggests that even in 1416 more than half the population lived beyond the walls. A century later, nearly half Leicester's taxpayers lived outside the walled area. Such crowding of properties, particularly in central areas, created fire risks, and fire was indeed a perennial urban problem. Much of Chester within the walls, for example, was destroyed by fire in 1278, but the retention of firebreaks between properties, the progressive outlawing of thatched roofs and the use of other flammable materials probably made the problem less acute for much of our period.

Any visitor to a medieval town could not but have been struck by the contrast between wealth and poverty, which might co-exist cheek by jowl, but was often spatially zoned. Suburban areas were often comparatively poor. So too were areas built up against town walls. It was the central areas of the town, and particularly the principal thoroughfares running through those areas, that tended to be characterized by the largest and most substantial housing, occupied by the wealthier members of the community. In early sixteenth-century Coventry, most residents of the singularly wealthy and centrally located Bailey Lane ward occupied substantial three-storey houses, kept servants and paid more than 12s in annual rent. In contrast, in the largely suburban wards of Bishop and Spon, some half of all tenants paid rents of less than 6s a year and many fewer kept servants. The highest proportion of cheap rents, however, was in Jordan Well ward, which, though adjacent to Bailey Lane, constituted a poor, industrial enclave close to the city walls. Like patterns may be found in later fourteenth-century Hull and York, where the prosperous mercantile Hull and Coney Streets, fronting the rivers Hull and Ouse respectively, contrast with the poor suburb of Trippet (Hull) or the cheap cottages of Aldwark (York) tucked just inside the city's northern walls. Poor properties could also exist in close proximity to prosperous housing in side streets – like Grimsby Lane (Hull) and Grape Lane (York), a street associated with prostitution – running off main thoroughfares.

Alongside this social topography there was a related economic topography. One of the characteristic features of the medieval town was the tendency for certain trades to congregate in particular localities, even particular streets, a pattern that is reflected in such medieval street names as Butcher Row and Fish Row in Boston, or Souter Peth (shoemakers' street) and Fleshergate (flesh hewer or butcher street) in Durham. The same logic applied to the sale of sex for we find numbers of Grape or Grope (originally Gropecunt) Lanes, and London had a Popkirtle Lane. Marketplaces tended to be located fairly centrally. In York, the tanners and the dyers were concentrated on the south-western bank of the River Ouse, across the water from the commercial heart of the city. The rationale for this pattern is twofold. On the one hand civic governors wanted to contain smelly and hence potentially anti-social craft activities, ideally at some distance from the most affluent and desirable properties; on the other hand the regulation of merchandising of victuals, such an important part of what civic government was about, was much easier to manage when traders were not widely scattered.

The spatial distribution of crafts also reflects a logic in terms of access to water and the distribution of raw materials through the town. Tanning, like dying, required a good supply of water, hence its location by the river. The tanning craft itself depended on the supply of animal hides, but the slaughtered livestock from which the hides derived represented the raw materials of the butchers, located in York on the other side of the river. A little further on, in Hornpot Lane, were located the horners, whose raw material was a by-product of the butcher's craft. The cordwainers and saddlers, who were directly dependent on the tanners for their supplies, were located on the Ouse bank opposite them; it is likely that the tanned hides were taken across the water directly by boat. Broadly similar spatial arrangements have been described for Coventry. Butchers themselves tended to be fairly centrally located, but this caused problems. Civic regulations relating to street cleansing, the slaughter of livestock and the dumping of offal, as seen for example in various London ordinances of 1357, 1369 and 1371, regularly targeted butchers, who were thus seen as an obstacle to a magisterial concern with creating an orderly and dignified environment.

If smelly and unsocial crafts such as tanning or commercial sex were deliberately relegated to more marginal areas of the town, the intention was to render the central parts the most prestigious and godly. Coventry's Bailey Lane, the residence of gold-smiths and mercers, ran between the civic parish church of St Michael and the common hall of St Mary. Stonegate in York, a similarly well-to-do street, stood in the shadow of the city's cathedral. Other fashionable streets originated as market-places. This was true of Southampton's English Street and London's Cheapside. Bridges, as necessary crossing points, could also function as prestigious locations for shops and residences, as was true of London Bridge or Ouse Bridge in York. Periodically we can detect evidence of deliberate planning on the part of civic govern-ors or wealthy individuals to enhance a town's image. At Norwich, for example, the city took control of the main market in the late fourteenth century, and followed this by rebuilding the market cross and constructing a new guildhall on an adjacent site. Together with patronage of the parish church of St Peter Mancroft, these works gave a new focus to the city. The creation of the new Leadenhall market in London is an example of private patronage.

The economic and social topography of towns, which saw wealthy merchants living in large centrally located houses, and poor labourers and widows concentrated in cheap cottages located in side streets and poor suburbs, mirrors what we know of the distribution of wealth in English towns. There was a tendency for wealth to be con-centrated in a comparatively small number of hands and hence for extreme inequal-ity of wealth distribution. Periodically we find individual traders who amassed considerable personal fortunes, such as William of Doncaster in late thirteenth-century Chester, Roger Norman in earlier fourteenth-century Southampton, Nicholas Blackburn, senior, in early fifteenth-century York, William Canynges, junior, in mid-fifteenth-century Bristol, or Robert Jannys in early sixteenth-century Norwich. Taxation evidence prior to 1334 and again at the time of the Henrician subsidies allows some measure of this inequality. Thus at Colchester in 1301 some 60 per cent of taxpayers, themselves a minority of the total population, were assessed at less than £1, but only 4 per cent at £5 or more. At Bishop's Lynn a decade or so earlier only 43 taxpayers are listed. Of these just under half were assessed at less than £5, but four were assessed to have goods valued in excess of £100. The Henrician subsidies offer a rather sharper picture, but the same inequalities are manifest. At Coventry in 1522, where 1377 persons are listed, some quarter of the city's assessed wealth was owned by just 3 people and some half by a total of only 20. Conversely, over half the persons listed were exempted from the assessment as too poor to pay. Wealth was but slightly more equitably distributed at the smaller, but buoyant town of Sudbury the same year. Here nearly half the town's assessed wealth was accounted for by 9 persons (of a total of 221), but the poorest half of the population accounted for only 4 per cent of the total assessment.

This marked inequality of wealth distribution also largely mirrors the distribution of power in towns as discussed above. Merchants and other members of the 'merchant class' are disproportionately represented among those in whose hands wealth was concentrated. Thus of the four wealthiest taxpayers in late thirteenth-century Bishop's Lynn, Reginald Taverner was much involved in the port's trade in wool and herring, John Quitloc traded in timber, Hugh le Moygne in woad and wool and Philip de Bekx, who also owned his own ship and had a share in another, was active in the grain trade. Richard Marler of Coventry and Robert Jannys of Norwich, the highest-rate taxpayers in their respective cities in the 1520s, were both grocers, a term that came to be used for the wholesale merchant or trader. Elsewhere it was often wool merchants and clothiers who were most conspicuous for their wealth.

4 CHURCH AND PARISH

By the beginning of our period, the parish map of the country, comprising some 9500 parishes, was already established – indeed, in many instances, long established since many parish boundaries pre-date the Conquest. Parishes varied considerably in size for reasons dictated variously by population density, agriculture and historical accident. Parishes in the upland pastoral districts of northern and western England tended to be large, stretching from the focus of settlement in the valley and up the hills behind, representing the traditional pasturage of the villagers' livestock. An example is the large Pennine parish of Halifax, which contained three dependent chapelries. Elsewhere parishes tended to be more compact. In some of the towns associated with Danish settlement before the Conquest, such as York, Lincoln or Norwich, we find a proliferation of small parishes. Other towns that developed late – after the main period of establishing parishes – were served solely by the parish church of the core settlement. This was true, for example, of the ports of Boston (Lincs.), Bishop's (now King's) Lynn and Great Yarmouth (Norfolk).

At the focus of each parish was a church with its associated churchyard. Again by the beginning of our period all churches had acquired a dedication to one or more saints, who were considered the patronal saints of the parish and whose feast day was of special importance in the parish. Often the south doorway of the church would be marked out from other doorways as the principal entry into the church and might be further distinguished by a porch. Not far from this door in the western part of the church there would be a font for use during baptism. These are symbolic relationships since the right of burial was open only to those who had been baptized in the faith. The doorway represented the threshold between secular and sacred space. It was here that the infant was received by the priest prior to baptism and it was here (and not within the body of the church) that couples had their marriages solemnized. The main focus of the church was, of course, the high altar to the east, though many churches also had subsidiary altars, sometimes associated with chantries. Mass was celebrated on a daily basis at each of the altars. During the course of our period the high altar and eastern parts of the church (the chancel) were separated from the main body of the church (the nave) by means of a screen. This screen effectively demarcated that part of the church that was the responsibility of the clergy from the western parts that were the responsibility of the parishioners.

Such a division of responsibility had already been established by the beginning of our period. Parochial visitation by archdeacons further reinforced the needs of the lay community to maintain the fabric and might require specific individuals to answer for the parish. This, for example, is what we find in Exeter diocese in 1301. By the time of the Black Death, churchwardens – that is, individuals elected from among the parishioners – had emerged as formally representing the lay community and taking responsibility for the day-to-day upkeep of the fabric. Their activities in terms of income and expenditure are known to us from their accounts, which begin to survive from much the same time. Income derived from collections, from ales, hocking and other events, the leasing out of property or from cows, bees and the like. At Calne (Wilts.) in the first part of the sixteenth century, most income (85 per cent) derived from church ales and other fundraising activities, but at Bridport (Dorset) in the mid-fifteenth century, revenue was derived from collections (40 per cent) and property (48 per cent). Expenditure was in terms of the purchase of timber, nails and other building materials, the cost of hired labour, cleaning and mending. Churchwardens tended to be drawn from the middling and upper strata of parish society, but since a term of office of a year at a time was customary, there was much turnover of personnel. We even find the occasional example of a woman serving in this office: Margaret at Borston served at Morebath (Devon) in 1528.

The parish church was the focus of regular worship and the administration of various of the sacraments, notably baptism, confirmation, marriage and the Eucharist. The parish church alone had rights of burial – rights that were jealously guarded by parochial clergy, not least because associated mortuary payments were a not insignificant part of the parochial revenue. A dispute over burial rights between the secular college of St James at Sutton on Hull (founded in 1347 from a pre-existing chapel) and the parish church of Waghen, for example, led to years of litigation and dispute. At an early stage, Archbishop Zouche, as diocesan bishop, even ordered bodies to be exhumed from the chapel of Sutton and reburied at the mother church of Waghen. To cite another example, when in 1353 Bishop Trellek of Hereford buried Sir Laurence de Ludlow in the Carmelite friary he had recently founded in Ludlow, the local rector immediately wrote to complain at the way the rights of the parish church had been violated. Baptisms were also normally reserved to the parish church, but, unlike the churching of mothers after childbirth, these did not constitute a source of revenue. The presence of a baptismal font was thus a mark of a church's parochial status.

The precise extent of the parish was memorialized by the beating of the bounds, an annual procession at Rogationtide (the week before Ascension Day) during which small boys might be made to remember particular landmarks by being held upside down in potholes or slapped about the head. All who resided within the bounds of the parish were expected to attend parish mass on Sundays and major festivals. The boundaries also marked the extent of parochial rights to tithes, the payment of a tenth of all produce. Tithes were intended to support the parish priest and to provide alms for the poor of the parish. In some geographically extensive rural parishes, where individual settlements might be some distance from the parish church, or where new settlements grew up, chapels were sometimes established so as to facilitate attendance at regular services. At Hindon (Wilts.) the residents built a chapel at their own expense and petitioned the pope in 1405 to allow it to be licensed, claiming that the two-mile journey to their parish church at Enford was through woods infested with robbers and hazardous in winter. This was allowed.

At the beginning of our period most parish churches were comparatively modest in scale, often comprising an aisleless nave and chancel, as at Wissington (Suffolk), and perhaps a western tower. Some more important parishes – the descendants of pre-Conquest minsters – were built on a grander scale with an aisled nave, as at Castle

Hedingham (Essex), or cruciform with a central tower, as at Old Shoreham (Sussex). By the second half of the thirteenth century the piecemeal addition of aisles, bell towers – such as the magnificent detached bell tower at West Walton (Norfolk) – and porches became common, though this process intensified during the next two centuries. Porches were sometimes constructed with an upper chamber, as at Newark (Notts.) or Woolpit (Suffolk), that might serve as accommodation for a priest or come to be used as a schoolroom or library. It is in this later period, likewise, that we may locate so many of the furnishings – screens, font covers, pulpits, timber roofs, brass lecterns, candelabra, sepulchral monuments and (least conspicuous today) images.

Three important factors influenced the development of the fabric and furnishings of parish churches over the course of our period. Of these, perhaps the most important is the growing involvement of the parish community in supporting and financing what they increasingly identified as their church. A corollary of this was the actual prosperity of the parish or of individual parishioners who contributed to the fabric. The third factor is the fashion for chantry endowments, which often required space to be created for additional altars and sometimes resulted in the construction of entire new chapels, as at St Alphege's in Solihull. Multiple altars and chantry chapels are more particularly a feature of urban parish churches. The parish church of Newark (Notts.) came to contain 16 altars serving chantry and guild chapels. Like proliferation of altars and chantries can be found in Holy Trinity, Hull and St George's, Doncaster.

Building activity is often related to the prosperity of the parish; it would be foolish to conclude that all churches underwent a continuous programme of building work or accumulated by the end of the Middle Ages the range of furnishings suggested by uncritical appraisal of some wealthy East Anglian or Devon parishes. The simple two-cell Romanesque church at Wissington, with its late thirteenth-century wall paintings, stands out from its more prosperous Suffolk neighbours, but is no less representative. Patterns of building activity thus serve as a crude barometer of economic change. Taking the East Riding of Yorkshire as a case study, we find some distinct regional patterns. Thus parish churches located on the higher Wolds are often predominantly Romanesque, implying little investment beyond the first post-Conquest endowment. In the Hull valley and Holderness, the low-lying south-eastern part of the county – areas that enjoyed continued prosperity through most of our period due to the importance of pastoral agriculture – most churches were substantially rebuilt during the fourteenth and fifteenth centuries. Like patterns are found in the city of York. The most substantial parish churches – St Crux, St Martin's, Coney Street and St Michael le Belfrey – were associated with the wealthiest commercial districts. All were constructed in the Perpendicular style, that of St Michael le Belfrey only in the 1530s. In contrast, the surviving church of the poor parish of St Andrew is a very modest building. The same would have been true of the peripheral parish of St Helen on the Walls, whose church is known only from excavation.

Taking the country as a whole, we find very substantial rebuilding of churches, sometimes on a grand scale, during the course of the later fourteenth and fifteenth centuries in areas associated with wool growing and textile production. This is true, for example, of the Cotswolds and Somerset, famous for their impressive church towers as at Wells or Huish Episcopi, or the great 'wool churches' of Suffolk and North Essex, as at Lavenham, Long Melford and Saffron Walden. Similar remarks can be made of the woollen districts of Devon and, by the later fifteenth century, the West

Riding of Yorkshire. The economically less developed regions of the north, the north-west or the far south-west, by way of contrast, tend to be characterized by fairly modest churches of piecemeal build.

The York parish of All Saints, North Street, may serve as a case study. The surviving fabric provides evidence of a long and complex building history. What is apparent, however, is that the church was very substantially remodelled in the earlier years of the fifteenth century. To the west a tower surmounted by a dramatic slender spire was constructed, new aisle windows added and a substantial amount of glass inserted. At much the same time the chancel and side aisle were given a splendid new painted roof. We have here evidence of a programme extending piecemeal over a number of years involving the rector (who gave the chancel roofs), various merchant families (notably the Blackburn family, whose patronage is indicated by various donor figures and associated inscriptions contained in the glass) and, presumably, though less conspicuously, the wider parish. The programme may well have been prompted in part by a desire to compete with some of the city's better endowed parish churches located across the River Ouse from All Saints, but if so this rivalry was expressed in terms of (to coin a phrase) conspicuous piety. It is striking that the visual impact was achieved without wholesale rebuilding. This reflects the more modest means of a parish dominated not by merchants, but tanners.

One of the remarkable features of the church of All Saints, North Street, is its extant medieval glass. In addition to images of various saints (appropriate to the church's dedication), the earlier fifteenth-century windows include a portrayal of six of the seven corporal acts of mercy based directly on Christ's teaching, a depiction of the last days based on a devotional poem known as 'The Prick of Conscience', and a representation of the nine orders of angels. This last is especially interesting since each angel is accompanied by representatives of the social hierarchy, including working men, women and children. In part, these windows demonstrate a didactic purpose: parishioners were shown how they should be charitable to their poor neighbours; they were warned of the horrors of damnation; they were also given a positive picture of the place of ordinary parishioners in the scheme of salvation. We can read these windows in one of two ways: they could suggest a concern on the part of a parish elite, who had the necessary wealth to provide these windows, to instil certain moral values and behaviour in their poorer neighbours; equally, they could suggest a shared sense of community. What they clearly demonstrate, however, is the willingness of some parishioners at least to invest materially in the fabric of their parish church. It is likely that the relatively greater prosperity of those below the level of the aristocracy in the century or more after the Black Death saw particular investment in fabric and furnishings of parish churches, but this may have been especially conspicuous in an urban context.

This pattern of giving is apparent from wills, though this tells only about the more well-to-do within the parish community. Sometimes bequests were of a very personal nature. Thus, to take some later fourteenth-century examples, John de Whettlay left an alabaster image of the Trinity to Rainton church; Alice, the wife of Geoffrey de Dyghton gave her gold ring and amber paternosters (prayer beads) to the image of the Virgin on the high altar of St Saviour's church, York; and Alice, wife of Robert de Ripon, bequeathed her silver paternosters and a gilt crucifix to St Mary's, Gillygate, York. Elsewhere we find towels left to be used to catch any crumbs that might fall when the parish Eucharist was administered at Easter or clothing and bed hangings left to be converted into vestments or altar cloths. Margaret Gateshed of the parish of All Saints, North Street, York, even asked that her bed be used there as an Easter Sepulchre (a symbolic receptacle for the host during Holy Week in imitation of Christ's tomb and on which a lay figure of the dead Christ might also be placed). Many other bequests were of a more mundane nature, though they often provide valuable clues as to the chronology of church building and furnishing. Sums of money might be left to particular building works ongoing at the time the will was drawn up. Monies were also left for gilding images or towards the purchase of specific items such as windows, chalices or candelabra. Similar patterns of giving are demonstrated by churchwardens' accounts, though here lifetime rather than just post-mortem giving is evidenced.

Fundraising was indeed an important aspect of parochial life in the late medieval era. Routine maintenance alone was more expensive in an era of high wages and materials costs. Although some urban parishes enjoyed significant rental incomes, most parishes had to find alternative sources. In addition to general parochial collections, parishioners might act collectively to raise funds towards specific projects. The purchase of a new cross for St Ewen's, Bristol, in 1454–55, for example, was furthered by the collection of various gifts, including silver spoons and other pieces of silver, as well as bequests from a whole group of parishioners. Other forms of fundraising included church ales, whereby money was raised from the sale of ale brewed by women parishioners. 'Ales' at the beginning of our period had taken place in the church and had consequently been frowned upon, but later ales were not held on sacred ground. They became the most widespread and common form of fundraising and might occur on a variety of occasions, such as the patronal feast, St George's Day or at midsummer.

In rural parishes, the church house, with its vats and ovens, could be let out for brewing or baking by those who could not afford the necessary equipment. In some West Country, Midland and London parishes, Hocktide celebrations resulted in additional funds for the parish. This represented a late medieval sanitization of an earlier custom: hocking involved men ambushing and ransoming women on one day, and women doing the same to men another day. Such customs were frowned upon until a (presumably rather tamer) version was adopted in the fifteenth century as a way of raising money for the fabric of the church. Unsurprisingly Hocktide collections were especially popular with guilds of young men and maidens, as at Croscombe (Somerset).

For the parish of St Petroc in Bodmin (Cornwall) we have an unusually full set of accounts relating to the rebuilding of the church between 1469 and 1472. Such a substantial building campaign, costing some £270, is perhaps less common than a succession of smaller-scale projects, but the evidence of the building accounts may still reflect wider practice. In particular the accounts signal the important role of the various guilds in fundraising. Some 40 different collectivities are noted, representative variously of parish guilds, for example the guilds of Corpus Christi and of St Erasmus; of craft-related collectivities, such as the skinners' and glovers' guild of St Petroc or the cordwainers' guild of St Anian; of maidens, specifically the maidens of Fore Street and the maidens of Bore Street; and, as with the maidens, guilds associated with specific parts of the borough, as, for example, the guilds of St Margaret at the Bore or of All Saints in Pool Street. It is eminently possible that at least some of these collectivities came together as a consequence of the campaign to rebuild the church and so create Cornwall's largest medieval parish church. The craft-related guilds, in addition to their ordinary fundraising, instituted halfpenny or penny collections of all those associated with them. Many individual donations were received, including a goose and a lamb. Money was raised from selling salvaged building materials from the old fabric. Finally a voluntary collection made of the townsfolk collected over £50 from some 460 named persons, including some women giving in addition to their spouses, and some servants giving on their own account. This probably represented more than half the adult population and must mean that most families contributed.

Seating, in the form of benches or pews, only became common during the fifteenth century and represents another facet of the fashion for furnishing churches. Although the church of St Petroc, Bodmin, commissioned new seats and pulpit in 1491, the impression is that the provision of seating was sometimes a piecemeal process and it is unclear just what proportion of the parish was provided for at any given moment. At St Ewen's, Bristol, the churchwardens' accounts for the 1450s suggest that seats there were provided only for women for the payments are recorded from various men on behalf of their wives or, in a couple of instances, mother or daughter. Two of these women were married to the current churchwardens. The implication is that seating here demarcated a social hierarchy within the parish – only the upper echelons of the parish community were associated with pews – but also a rather conservative understanding of gender roles – men might stand, but women needed to be provided with seats. Some 60 years later payments are recorded in the London parish of St Mary at Hill for men's pews and women's pews. This would tend to support Margaret Aston's thesis that men and women were segregated in church, but not necessarily before this date.[1] It is likely a late trend that mirrors the proliferation of maidens' and young men's guilds from the later fifteenth century and the prevalence of a more conservative gender ideology.

Churches were also increasingly subdivided by the use of screens. Rood or chancel screens are well known because these sometimes survive. Best known are the many fifteenth-century screens associated with Norfolk, Suffolk and Devon, numbers of which still carry painted representations of saints as at Southwold (Suffolk) or, more rarely, as at Blundeston (Suffolk), angels bearing the instruments of the Passion. Again it has been suggested that the spatial division of male saints to the southern half of the screen and female to the northern half mirrors seating arrangements, but this need not be the case and, as at Somerleyton (Suffolk), very different iconographical concerns dictate the ordering of saints. The provision and painting of such screens lay with the parishioners, though we must presume that the parochial clergy would have helped decide the iconographic scheme adopted. Screens separating chantries sometimes also survive, but there were often various other screens, which have left few traces. The effect would be to create subdivisions within the church and to make some spaces more accessible than others in a manner strikingly reminiscent of domestic interiors.

Numbers of monastic churches, particularly Benedictine houses, also served a parish. Usually this involved the nave, or even an aisle as at Crowland Abbey (Lincs.), being used by the lay community, though sometimes the parish church might abut the monastery church. Parochial churches were absorbed into the precinct walls of the great Benedictine abbeys of Bury St Edmunds and St Mary's, York. In a number of instances the parishioners took over part or all of the monastic church at the dissolution as, for example, at Worksop (Notts.) or Binham (Norfolk), where the nave was

---

1. M. Aston, 'Segregation in Church', in W.J. Sheils and D. Wood, eds, *Women in the Church, Studies in Church History* 27 (1990), pp. 237–94.

retained, or at Romsey (Hants) where the entire abbey church was purchased. So long as church buildings were shared, tensions could arise between the two communities. We see this, for example, at Binham in the 1430s and more dramatically at Sherbourne (Dorset) a few years later. Here a dispute between parishioners and the abbey, focused on baptismal rights, culminated in the parish priest allegedly sending a blazing arrow up to the roof of the abbey church with catastrophic consequences. The cost of refurbishing the gutted abbey church fell to the parishioners.

Many parishes came to be appropriated to monastic houses – that is, the revenues from the parish in the form of tithes and fees were granted to support the monastery. The pastoral care of the parishioners was then entrusted to a vicar employed on a stipend fixed at a level that ensured that the religious house profited. In the case of parishes appropriated to Augustinian or Premonstratensian monasteries, the position of parish priest might well have been filled by one of the canons, as appears to have been the case, for example, at Worksop. Thus, although tithes were supposed to support the priest and to provide for the poor of the parish, in the case of appropriated churches, the tithes were taken by the religious house to which the living had been granted. This helps account for some of the substantial abbey tithe barns still surviving, but also for some of the resentment expressed periodically about the payment of tithes. The same was true of mortuary payments associated with the parochial rights over burial.

As already noted, numbers of larger parishes contained within them chapels, where a chaplain celebrated daily mass and ministered to the parishioners living at some distance from the parish church. Such chapels tended to be comparatively modest buildings if only because the material resources of the chapelry tended themselves to be modest. In some instances, however, chapels were founded not to serve dispersed rural communities, but new urban settlements established after the process of defining parish boundaries had ended. Thus the small town of Chipping Sodbury (Glos.) was served by a chapel founded in 1284 and dependent on the parish of Old Sodbury. The new town of Kingston upon Hull was likewise served by two churches, both of which were technically chapels dependent on neighbouring villages. The same was true where new settlements were created as a result of colonization, as in the Lincolnshire fenland. Likewise in some populous urban parishes, chapels supplemented the provision of the parish church. Thus at Bishop's Lynn, the parish church of St Margaret was supplemented by the chapels of St James and of St Nicholas, which last also gained burial rights (though still a dependent chapel) in 1361.

5 GUILD AND FRATERNITY

Guilds are an important facet of later medieval culture, particularly after the Black Death, until (and in the case of craft guilds long after) the reign of Edward VI. They were associations of people who shared a common identity or purpose. Many were focused on the parish, but others brought together groups of artisans or merchants, and some were more disparate. By their nature, they stressed the solidarity of members and regularly adopted a religious discourse of brotherhood or fraternity, rather than one of hierarchy and social difference. The guild of St Mary in the church of St Botulph, Cambridge, for example, required that every new member give a kiss of brotherhood to the other members on entry. In numbers of guilds, fraternity was symbolically enacted through the sharing of food at a guild feast. This discourse of fraternity often implicitly, and sometimes explicitly, encompassed women members too, though the 'typical' member was often imagined as the married man.

Guilds commonly provided important social and welfare functions for their members. The principal purpose in bringing people together, however, was a shared devotion to a particular saint, cult or image, and it is this devotion that lends its name to many of the guilds we know about. Thus we find numerous guilds of St Mary, St Katherine or of Corpus Christi, reflecting the dedication of altars and lights burning before images, but also currently fashionable cults. Even those known by other titles invariably reveal a particular shared devotion. The Norwich brotherhood of the barbers, for example, reveals a common devotion to St John the Baptist, patron variously of tailors and of barbers. Guilds also served the functions occupied in later centuries by friendly societies and burial clubs. So the guild of Killingholme (Lincs.) provided support for members who had lost a beast or their home, or had been robbed, through payments of a halfpenny from each brother and sister of the guild. Other guilds made provision for their memberships to attend the funerals of their deceased members (as, for example, the Hull guild of Corpus Christi), furnished wax torches, and even, as with the Lincoln guild of the Resurrection, provided for burial at guild expense.

Guilds are a rather misunderstood phenomenon and their early history is often obscure. Modern scholarship has tended to distinguish between 'religious' guilds (or confraternities) and 'craft guilds', though this distinction is not always helpful and would not always have been so obvious to contemporaries. In part, the distinction is a creation of the inquisition established by the Cambridge Parliament of 1388, itself a response to a petition calling for the suppression of all guilds, which led to the 1389 returns. This call was made by an essentially conservative, landed elite, still jittery in the aftermath of the Peasants' Revolt of 1381, who saw such collectivities of peasants and townsfolk as potentially subversive. They were also suspected of amassing significant funds that could otherwise be diverted for the defence of the realm. This last was the ostensible reason for inquiring into their function, privileges and assets.

Two sets of writs were issued to sheriffs to initiate the process of inquiry, of which one was directed specifically at the masters, wardens and searchers of crafts. This last asked that copies of any royal charters held by these crafts be presented to Chancery. In fact a number of associations of craft workers, such as the London barbers, cutlers, glovers, pouch makers and carpenters, made returns in the same way as other non-craft collectivities. The St Mary 'society' of shoemakers of Great Yarmouth (Norfolk) interestingly declared that it was not a guild, not because it was a craft association, but rather because it had neither a constitution nor an oath of membership. Nevertheless, the bulk of the returns relate to associations that had no formal craft association and whose function was exclusively or primarily devotional and charitable.

The comparative absence of 'craft' guilds from the extant 1389 returns probably has a fairly simple explanation. Craft guilds were still uncommon at that date and certainly outside such major cities as London, Lincoln or Norwich they would have been rare. The craft guilds that are found, however, look to be no different from the others making returns in 1389. They share similar devotions and purposes. This may itself be a clue to the emergence of craft guilds (or 'mysteries') as collectivities concerned also with the regulation of trade. Our problem is that before 1389 guilds generally tend not to be well documented, though we do have numbers of London craft guild ordinances from civic archives prior to that date. The 1389 returns are in fact our earliest source for many guilds, and certainly our fullest source for the majority of rural guilds. In trying to reconstruct an early history of guilds, therefore, they are necessarily a starting point.

The writs sent out to sheriffs in 1388 provided a rigorous schedule of questions to be asked of each guild. This schedule began with the guild's foundation, ranged through oaths, meetings, feasts and customs, asked after ordinances and inquired finally about the guild's assets. These questions framed the form of most returns, though it is evident that different guilds responded in different ways. Some acted together to obtain the necessary clerical assistance to draw up their replies. The returns made by two Ripon (Yorks., NR) guilds, for example, were contained on the same piece of parchment. In such instances there may be a high degree of overlap not only between the form of the returns, but the actual content. Such similarities may also be a product of local guilds imitating one another.

Returns from the adjacent counties of Cambridgeshire, Lincolnshire and Norfolk account for more than two-thirds of those extant. This must in part be an accident of survival, but also indicates some real regional differences. The question about foundation does provide some evidence for the antiquity of guilds, though we cannot always be confident of the veracity of information. Often this must have been a matter of oral tradition. Thus the Lincoln guild of fullers plausibly claimed to have been founded in 1297, and the Ludlow palmers in 1284. A few claimed much greater antiquity. The Chesterfield guild of St Mary, for example, stated that it was founded in 1218 and certainly there are internal reasons to believe this to be plausible. A majority of guilds claimed, however, to have been founded in the decades after the Black Death.

Two questions arise. The first relates to the apparent proliferation of guilds only after the advent of plague. The second pertains to the emergence of craft guilds as distinctive entities. The two are related since craft guilds seem often to have grown out of 'religious' guilds. It follows that we must start by addressing the first question. Although it is possible to trace to before the Conquest collectivities of people bound together by an oath and calling themselves a guild, there is little otherwise to relate these to the sort of structures found in the 1389 guild returns. Organizations of merchants and traders, known as the 'guild merchant', who acted collectively to manage trade and local government in emergent towns and so occupy the voids left by their lords, are also found before the Conquest and for a century or more after. Seigneurial and royal authority was increasingly asserted through the twelfth century, however, and so tended to displace these guilds merchant. It is apparent, however, that such associations sometimes survived, perhaps in modified form, into the later Middle Ages. The Chesterfield guild of St Mary, with its central concern for the maintenance of the liberties of the town, is indeed one such example. The Beverley (Yorks., ER) guild of St John of Beverley, which dated to the early twelfth century, was another. This guild, interestingly, declared itself as a craft guild.

The early existence of such organizations that were identified by their common devotion to a particular saint or, as with the Holy Cross guild at Stratford-upon-Avon, cult, probably provided a partial model for the later parish guilds, but this does not explain their popularity in the fourteenth century. Rather we have to look to the broader devotional climate of the period and the wider social context. As discussed in Chapter 16, we can see growing evidence for lay participation in the life of the parish in the wake of the Fourth Lateran Council (1215). In particular we have evidence for the promotion of the cults of the Virgin (St Mary) and of the patronal saint, to whom the parish church was dedicated, during the thirteenth century. Images of the Virgin and the patron were commonly erected either side of the high altar, but further images placed at other altars were increasingly common by the end of the century. It is likely that cults developed around these images and that parishioners sometimes marked their devotion by burning candles, referred to as 'lights', before these images. Indeed bequests to lights are a common feature in early wills. In 1269, for example, Adam de Collercote of Exeter left 2s to the light of St Mary Steps. The coming together of groups of parishioners with the collective purpose of supporting a particular cult, often that of the parish's patron, by maintaining a light before the saint's image, was only a development of this pious need. Over 80 per cent of the guilds that made extant returns in 1389 indeed recorded the support of such lights as part of their purpose. For some, such as the Holy Trinity guild of Wiggenhall (Norfolk), it was ostensibly their only purpose.

Another need specifically addressed by a majority of these parochial guilds, and likewise a corollary of greater lay participation in devotional life, was for the burial of members to be duly observed and for deceased members to be prayed for. The burial of the dead represents a near universal human need, but in medieval culture it was specifically understood as a Christian duty and a work of mercy. The traumatic experience of the Black Death, where on occasion bodies were buried en masse with minimal religious rites and few mourners, would only have added to the attractiveness of belonging to a collectivity that promised to bury its members with due ceremony and may of itself help account for the apparent proliferation from the later fourteenth century.

Prayers for the dead represent a still more culturally specific concern. The dissemination of the concept of purgatory, a middle place between heaven and hell, where souls could be purged of their sins and so in time be received in heaven, lies behind this. So long as the soul might be held in purgatory, the prayers of the living could hasten its progress to heaven. The aristocracy, and even some merchants, might be able to endow chantries and provide doles at their funerals, but the lower levels of society were more dependent on their neighbours for support, not least at the crucial liminal moment when the soul left the body. In that sense guilds have been dubbed 'poor men's chantries'.

Another related consideration is the extent to which the constructed solidarity of the guild came to displace, or at least supplement, the solidarity of the family and kinship network. It has been argued that this would have been particularly true of the period following the Black Death. High levels of population turnover, consequent on both mortality and migration, would, it is argued, have left many without the ties of family that had hitherto been taken for granted. In fact, population mobility was hardly new after the plague – as evidence for high levels of mobility in pre-plague Essex, for example, has shown – but the underlying argument still has much merit. In particular it is apparent that many of the older guilds recorded in 1389 are urban and hence associated with communities that grew as a consequence of the steady influx of rural migrants. Many of the people who settled in these towns would have done so as individuals rather than as family groups, and may consequently have lacked close family ties in their new homes. The shift from a stem to a nuclear family system out-lined in Chapter 2 would only have increased this need. Towns are also characterized by the prevalence of hired labour alongside or even displacing family labour. The same was increasingly true in a rural context even before the plague, but accelerated after the plague, especially in regions characterized by a diverse economy and the preva-lence of rural industry such as the Cotswolds, parts of the West Riding of Yorkshire and especially East Anglia.

A similar argument may apply to the social welfare function of many guilds, the sol-idarity of the guild substituting for familial support networks. The Hull guilds of St Mary, Corpus Christi and St John the Baptist, for example, all provided for impover-ished members and included provision that:

> If it happen that any of the gild becomes infirm, bowed, blind, dumb, deaf, maimed, or sick, whether with some lasting or only temporary sickness, and whether in old age or in youth, or be so borne down by any other mishap that he has not the means of living, then, for kind-ness' sake, and for the souls' sake of the founders, it is ordained that each shall have, out of the goods of the gild, at the hands of the wardens, sevenpence every week.

The use of biblical language here and elsewhere in the ordinances recorded in the 1389 returns shows, however, how religious ideas and ideals helped shape the prag-matic provision made by the guilds to their members.

Another possible influence in the formation of guilds was the mendicant orders (the friars). Certainly the impression is that these played a significant role in parts of Continental Europe and in the cities of northern Italy in particular. Some English guilds were associated with friaries. Thus the Norwich guild of St Mary, which made a return in 1389, was attached to the Dominican house and the Beverley guild of St Helen to the Franciscan. The Franciscans of Bodmin no doubt influenced the crea-tion of a 'congregation' of St Clare recorded in the later fifteenth century. As a pro-portion of all guilds, however, those closely tied to mendicant houses are few. This is very much a reflection of the strength of the parish, even in an urban context. A number of larger towns and cities, such as York, Lincoln and Norwich, were characterized by a multiplicity of parishes. The friars thus worked alongside an established parochial structure rather than filling a vacuum created by poor parochial provision in the context of rapid urban growth. On the other hand, towns with only one or two parishes often saw a proliferation of guilds during the course of the later Middle Ages. This is true, for example, of Hull, with only two churches, or Doncaster (one). Clearly in such instances the parish proved too large a unit to support a single cohesive parochial guild and a number of smaller groups formed. Bottisham (Cambs.), a medium-sized rural parish, supported seven guilds in 1389, but here the reason was that the parish was itself fragmented between five different manors. Bodmin (Cornwall), which is unusually well documented because of the chance survival of some accounts for rebuilding the parish church in 1469–72, supported some 40 guilds at that date, some of which related to particular areas of the town. (Cornwall is not represented in the 1389 returns.)

Guilds, then, were not new in 1389, but few dated back before the beginning of the fourteenth century and many, rural guilds in particular, were still young at the time of the 1388 inquisition. It is likely that some guilds were comparatively short-lived, not extending beyond the lifetime of the initial founders, and so the apparent youth of many individual guilds may disguise a greater antiquity of the phenomenon as a whole. Both the guild of St Mary and the barbers' guild of Norwich talk in terms of 'so long as 12 persons of them live', which might support this contention. On balance, however, the popularity of guilds, already growing through the first half of the century, was probably greatly enhanced by the experience and consequences of the Black Death. This was perhaps especially true of the more prosperous and economically developed eastern part of the country, notably East Anglia. The development of guilds is thus a litmus test of social change. In towns we see a particular concentration of guilds and, among them, a number that are associations of artisans and traders. It is here that we might look to the origin of craft guilds.

A number of factors influenced the emergence of craft guilds. Unlike parish guilds, whose members were drawn from within the parish, the craft fraternities making returns in 1389 were often associated with cults located in monastic churches and hence were not identified with a specific locality. Thus the Norwich carpenters' fraternity of the Holy Trinity was located in the cathedral priory of Holy Trinity, whereas the fraternity of the spurriers and saddlers there was associated with the image of St Mary in Carrow nunnery. Often there is a direct patronal relationship between the guild's cult and the trade associated with it. Thus the London guild of painters was dedicated to St Luke, who supposedly painted the Virgin. Sometimes the relationship is less obvious. The Norwich tailors' guild, located in the chapel of St Mary in the Fields, was dedicated to the Ascension, an association explained by the account of the persons dressed in white in Acts 1:10.

The earliest craft guilds are the various guilds of weavers that are known to us through their purchase of royal charters. The weavers of York, for example, acquired a charter in 1163 granting them a regional monopoly in the production of certain types of cloth in return for an annual payment, the collection of which required a degree of collective action. How far such collectivities were actually akin to later craft guilds is a moot point since their focus was on regional trade rather than the regulation of workshops. There is good evidence, however, for this newer type of craft guild by the fourteenth century. The early emergence of craft guilds in London probably owes much to the sheer scale of the city and hence the numbers of workshops associated with any particular craft, together with the tendency of some crafts to be concentrated in a particular locality or street, later reflected in the spatial location of guildhalls. Thus we find ordinances recorded in 1316 on behalf of the pepperers of Soper Lane. Other crafts followed the precedent of the weavers in purchasing royal charters to give authority to their collective control of trading standards: the London skinners and girdlers both acquired charters in 1327. However, most ordinances were made after the advent of plague and were registered with the city rather than the Crown.

Outside of London, craft guilds tended not to emerge before a generation or so after the Black Death, though even in some larger towns such as Exeter, where formal guilds are first found from the 1480s, their advent was delayed. Craft guilds as organizations, comprising masters or heads of workshops enacting ordinances for the regulation of the craft and the control of labour within workshops represent, however, a late stage in a longer evolutionary process. An earlier stage is the emergence of associations of craft masters, either as a result of having shared devotional interests, as already noted, or as a consequence of civic regulation. Civic government periodically made ordinances to regulate trade in the absence of established craft organizations. The London tailors were thus forbidden in 1310 to scour furs in the Cheap, though it was perhaps trades dealing in foodstuffs that were most vigilantly regulated. Their response was probably to self-regulate through the appointment of wardens.

The new fashion for the cult of Corpus Christi, which is found in England from the 1320s and came to be marked by processions and even street theatre, may also have stimulated the formation of craft collectivities that then might evolve into actual guilds. The Corpus Christi Play at York, for example, is first documented in the 1370s, and it is apparent that a multiplicity of craft groups, some perhaps very small, were involved its production. The desire of craftsmen here to be involved in this important devotional ritual probably encouraged the formation of craft associations. Much the same has been suggested at Exeter, where numbers of different craft groups are documented as responsible for the production of pageants in 1413. In other instances, town governments may have urged the formation of craft groups in order to stage like productions in imitation of those already established. This was perhaps the case at Chester and Durham, where guilds are not noticed before the advent of evidence for plays in the 1420s and 1450s respectively.

Another crucial factor influencing the coming together of masters sharing a common craft identity has been posited by Sarah Rees Jones as a by-product of shared concerns about the regulation of labour in the aftermath of the Black Death. A statute of 1363 intended to prevent price-fixing by groups of traders required that craftsmen were to confine themselves to a single craft policed by persons (searchers) drawn from within the craft, but answerable to the Justices of the Peace, who by that time also enforced the Statute of Labourers. In numbers of larger urban communities these justices were appointed from the town governors, an arrangement formalized by the creation of county boroughs. Unsurprisingly the appointment of searchers effectively provided craft associations with some kind of formal voice to represent craft interests and petition civic governors. This trend indeed broadly coincided with a growing tendency for crafts to be given a voice in civic government and it is this that underlies the pattern of presentation of craft ordinances to civic government and their recording in civic records.

The ordinances of craft guilds tend, as a consequence of the pattern just noted, to survive as registered copies in civic archives. This has prompted the argument that these ordinances represent not so much the concerns of the craft members as of the town governors, who, because drawn disproportionately from a mercantile elite, might have had differing and even conflicting agendas. They tend also to be the only substantive records relating to the majority of medieval craft guilds, so our under-standing of guilds and the way they functioned is perhaps coloured unduly by regu-lations that focus on quality control, working practices, the employment of labour and the like. We thus can too easily lose sight of the devotional, social and political dimensions of craft guilds.

The ordinances of the York carpenters' guild of 1482 go some way to throwing light on the problems just identified. Unlike most extant ordinances, they are not confined to the conventional business of workshop, employee and product. They are equally concerned with the social and devotional aspects of the craft as fraternity. Provision is made, for example, for members to be present at the funerals of deceased members, and support is provided for those who suffer misfortune. We need not regard these ordinances as exceptional in themselves, but rather as a clue as to how the fuller identity of the craft guild was regularly masked by the fact that civic clerks recording ordinances tended only to record those pertaining to economic matters, or indeed that the crafts themselves only presented such ordinances for ratification. This again would imply some sense of ownership on the part of craft masters over the ordi-nances enacted.

This last is strengthened by the details sometimes recorded of the way ordinances were presented to civic authorities and by the way the ordinances recorded can be shown to address the specific needs and concerns of craft masters. In London, craft ordinances are often recorded as petitions to the mayor and aldermen by 'the reputa-ble men' of the craft for approval. This could, of course, be a formula disguising a very different power dynamic, but there are reasons for thinking otherwise. Sometimes the names of the members drawing up the ordinances are recorded. The names of 128 masters follow the record of the York tailors' ordinances of 1386–87. In a few instances, as with the late fourteenth-century York dyers' ordinances, these include women, presumably widows running workshops.

The devotional aspect of craft guilds has already been noted in respect of their par-ticipation in a number of towns in Corpus Christi pageants and related drama. In Beverley, in addition to their support of pageant, the guilds maintained lights before images in one or other of the town's churches and played an important role in the com-memoration of the town's cult of St John (of Beverley). Each guild constructed its own 'castle' or wooden scaffold from which the craft masters viewed the civic procession of the saint's shrine on Rogation Monday. Guilds would look to provide for the poor at their annual feasts, occasions that combined a social function with significant religious symbolism. The London goldsmiths were supporting 12 'poor of the mystery' (craft) as early as 1332. During the fifteenth century some guilds even came to maintain their own almshouses. This was true, for example, of the York butchers and of a number of London guilds, including the skinners, the tailors and the vintners.

Craft guilds were not solely social and devotional associations. They are best known in respect of the regulation of manufacture and commerce. Broadly speaking, craft ordinances reflect the collective interests of the constituent masters as managers of workshops. We may here identify a 'guild ethos', which complements and reflects devotional concerns; some regulations would have made little sense if masters had followed a strictly capitalist and individualistic model, but made good sense in terms of masters following a slightly more altruistic and shared agenda. For example, at least before the later fifteenth century, many guilds placed strict limits on the numbers of apprentices any master could employ at a time. The rationale here was that apprentices represented the next generation of craft masters and hence the guild had to ensure that there would be workshops available to newly qualified apprentices, and that each was carefully trained and supervised. This would be difficult were several apprentices to be employed at a time. Individual masters, however, might have been tempted to take on extra apprentices as a cheap form of labour so as to undercut their competitors, something that was anathema to the guild ethos. However, when in late fourteenth-century York the founders guild allowed Giles de Bonoyne an exception to the one-apprentice rule 'because he has no wife', it was responding to the particular needs of an individual member. Such specific provision was hardly likely were ordinances handed down by the civic governors.

Guilds were also concerned to regulate working hours. They were especially vigilant to ban night working and to protect Sundays and other holy days. Ordinances regularly reiterate the tenor of the labour legislation against masters poaching workers before their term of contract had expired. The mobility of contract labour was at times a problem and potential cause of dispute. The York cordwainers ruled in 1417, for example, that employees must give their masters due notice of whether they wished to remain beyond their term or find a new master. From about the middle of the fifteenth century, however, it became common for ordinances to require that employees be properly trained in the craft. This suggests that it was no longer labour, but rather work that was becoming scarce. From the mid- to late fifteenth century some guilds specifically attempted to marginalize women working within the craft, an even surer sign that work was scarce. This is most dramatically expressed by some weavers' guilds, which attempted to exclude women altogether, as at Bristol in 1461 or Norwich in 1511, but most guilds recognized that wives at least were an integral and important part of the labour force. The Coventry cappers' ordinances of 1496, for example, demanded 'that no person of the craft teach no point of his craft to no person save to his apprentice and his wife'.

Much attention was focused on the proper training of apprentices and a concern that only those who were formally apprenticed and enrolled as such should have access to instruction in the craft. In fact, as the Coventry ordinance just noted indicates, informal training must often have been provided for other members of the workshop; the 1398 ordinances of the London leather sellers specifically exempt wives and children so as to conform with what was stated to be custom. Other servants employed within the workshop cannot but have been exposed to craft skills, but from the guild's perspective they were not being trained and so could never aspire to positions as masters.

There were two important areas where the authority of craft guilds was liable to be undermined, both of which help explain the need for guilds to look to civic government for support. One relates to possible challenges to guild authority by journeymen or waged employees, who were supposedly subject to guild discipline. The second relates to the encroachment of other traders on the 'mystery', such as by smiths on the work of marshals, who specialized in the shoeing of horses, or by upholders, who often sold second-hand clothing and furs, so trespassing on the skinners' craft. The first seems to have been especially problematic in London in the latter part of the fourteenth century. In particular, we find attempts by groups of journeymen to form their own confraternities, ostensibly for reasons of devotion, challenged by their employers' craft guilds. In 1396, for example, a guild in honour of the Virgin Mary set up by journeymen saddlers was suppressed as a front for demanding higher wages, in effect a trades union. The tailors likewise successfully complained against their journeymen living communally and organizing among themselves 'like a race at once youthful and unstable . . . without any rule or supervision by their superiors'.

The city governors backed the guild masters in their petitions against their employees because they had a vested interested in maintaining an essentially patriarchal order, shared a concern to keep wages down and, in the aftermath of the Peasants' Revolt, were distrustful of associations whose agendas might be more political than devotional. That the craft guilds needed to solicit this support, however, suggests that the authority of the guilds themselves at this date was not as great as their own ordinances would want us to think. The same is true of the problem guilds faced trying to regulate in respect of those who were outside the guild, but whose activities impinged upon the mystery. A common guild response was to petition civic government to allow them to collect dues from individuals. Where, as at York, the guilds supported Corpus Christi pageants, these dues were asked in support of the guild pageant. Thus the York cutlers ruled in 1445 that all who sold cutlery should contribute to the pageant. When in 1425 the cooks agreed no longer to sell fish, they at the same time cancelled their contribution to the fishers' pageant. Direct intervention by civic governors was, however, a possibility. Thus, a dispute between the masons and the tilers (bricklayers) of York led to the ruling that the tilers were to contribute to the masons should they have occasion to build a wall or foundations of stone.

The role of overseer that civic government played in relation to craft guilds has been seen as evidence that craft guilds were essentially puppets of the former, seen as a narrow and essentially mercantile group. There is some merit in this view, more especially perhaps from the later fifteenth century, but the picture is in fact more complex. Guilds came to play a significant role not just in the regulation of trade, but, as we have seen (Chapter 3), in civic government itself. At the same time we can see ways in which craft guilds themselves evolved from the more egalitarian model discussed above to more status-conscious and hierarchical organizations. This was probably reflected in the seating arrangements at the annual guild feast. We find it also in a growing tendency for the more senior members of a craft to adopt a coloured gown and hood by way of uniform or livery. Some of the larger London crafts in particular took this trend a stage further and came to relegate lesser members to a yeomen's fraternity, whilst the more substantial liveried masters – in contemporary parlance, the merchant members – constituted the senior fraternity. Thus the yeomen skinners belonged to their fraternity of the Assumption, rather than the senior Corpus Christi fraternity. The tailors' equivalent senior fraternity of St John the Baptist seems in fact to have been more open to members of the aristocracy and clergy, whose patronage could only be of value to the principal tailoring workshops, than to lesser or yeoman craft masters. This London model was, however, exceptional; for most guilds, even in London, there was no real distinction between fraternal and craft identity, and hierarchy was manifested within the same collectivity rather than by forming separate structures.

PART 2
The People

6 COUNTING HEADS

Over the three centuries that this book considers there were profound changes in the overall level of population, or the rate of growth or decline from period to period. Broadly speaking, population was growing at the beginning of our era. It stabilized and may even have slipped back modestly during the first half of the fourteenth century, but nevertheless population levels were historically high. This was profoundly changed by the advent of plague. The first pandemic of 1348–49, known since the nineteenth century as the Black Death, resulted in a huge loss of numbers, a trend that was continued in a number of subsequent epidemics. The population fell by well over half over the next century. There is little evidence of significant recovery before the second half of the fifteenth century, but much to suggest it was growing fast in the last 50 years of our era.

Before the advent of modern censuses at the beginning of the nineteenth century we have little direct evidence for the total number of people alive at any given moment, or how these numbers fluctuated over time. Moreover, before the advent of parish registration of baptisms, marriages and burials in 1538, we have comparatively little in the way of measures of vital statistics that would allow such patterns to be reconstructed. We do, however, have two benchmarks: the Domesday survey of 1086 and the poll tax returns of 1377. To these we may add a third derived from the registration of baptisms, marriages and burials in parish registers from 1538. We also have a number of more fragmentary or indirect indicators. There is little here, however, that can generate an accurate population total, let alone a set of totals that would permit secular fluctuations to be measured with any precision. The current 'guesstimates' for the population on the eve of the Black Death, which range between 3.75 million and a figure nearly twice that amount, tell their own story.

Such attempts to quantify the unquantifiable or to lend a veneer of statistical authority to highly speculative conclusions are ultimately misguided. The medievalist must consequently regard all population 'statistics' with suspicion. The lack of accurate statistics need not be such a problem. For example, in thinking about the question 'Was England overpopulated before the Black Death?' there is little point in knowing precisely how large the population was unless we were to know how large a population could in fact be sustained at that date. What matters is whether that population caused acute pressure on available resources or not, whether people fell prey to malnutrition and related disease, and whether even the poorest members of society were assured their daily bread. If we acknowledge the limitations of our evidence, we can focus instead on the more significant issues relating to the shape of population trends and the implications of changes over time. This chapter begins by reviewing the statistical evidence for overall population levels over time. We will then consider evidence relating to the key demographic variables of fertility, commencing with a discussion of marriage and of mortality. This discussion will inevitably raise questions as well as suggesting answers, but some sort of overview will finally be outlined.

Our first benchmark, Domesday Book, raises many problems since it is neither clear what its purpose was nor, as a consequence, who is recorded. In so far as it appears in part to be concerned with taxation and the assessment of taxable resources, the survey attempts to record, county by county, the landed, animal and human assets associated with any feudal tenant in any settlement. These human resources are recorded using a variety of terms, such as villein, bordar, cottar, sokeman and slave, that represent Norman attempts to make sense of a more complex and diverse system of social relations characteristic of Old English society. The traditional assumption is that these persons represent heads of households, rather than, say, adult males, implicitly because they constitute peasant tenants of the lord. Even if this is a correct assumption, it is not clear to what degree, if any, other householders may have gone unrecorded because not tenants of the lord. In a few instances the entries are patently incomplete or defective. How generally accurate the information was we cannot know. Towns are particularly imperfectly recorded, and London and Winchester are entirely missing.

It should be clear that any attempt to generate an accurate population estimate from the Domesday evidence is mistaken. Even if the recorded population does represent heads of households, we are hardly in a position to know the structure, let alone the mean size, of households in 1086. It is, however, probably safe to suggest that households would have to be unusually large by historical standards, or the survey to be very seriously defective in ways not hitherto suspected, for the English population at this date to have reached two million. Equally it is very unlikely that the population could have been less than one million. This is a crude estimate, but it is not a worthless one.

Where the Domesday survey is rather more useful, and probably more reliable, is in terms of providing evidence for density of settlement. Here we find that parts of Lincolnshire, much of Norfolk and Suffolk, north Essex and eastern Kent are the most densely populated regions, though there were a few other more densely settled pockets outside this eastern region, as along the Sussex coast or in north Berkshire. Unsurprisingly the least densely settled regions at this date were in the north and north-west of the country, essentially those regions north of the Trent. To no small extent these regional differences, and more local variation within them, reflect the distribution of differing types of land. Upland, marshland and other areas of poor soil were least densely populated. This pattern was modified during the course of the medieval era, but the broader features of low population north of the Trent and high population in eastern England remained.

Our second benchmark, one that actually falls squarely within our period, are the returns for the first poll tax of 1377. This was a head tax – poll means head – supposedly levied on all adults over the age of 14, except the very poor, the tinners of Cornwall and the populations of the counties of Durham and Cheshire, who were all exempt. Clergy and laity were taxed separately, but both paid. As a measure of total population the returns probably represent a less problematical source than the Domesday survey, but because they relate to a period immediately following the Black Death of 1348–49, the so-called Grey Death of 1361–62, and the third pestilence of 1368–69 they are at best a very indirect indicator of the levels the population may have achieved half a century or so earlier. They are, however, sufficient to show that the population had grown in the long period since 1086 and that the distribution of that population had also undergone a modest degree of change.

Until recently, the poll taxes have been a comparatively neglected source, though the population totals for 1377 have long been used. The reason for this neglect is a profound distrust of the quality of the evidence. Sylvia Thrupp's critique of some returns supposedly for several London parishes in 1377 (but now identified as Worcester and quite possibly in relation to a later poll tax), coupled with some much earlier observations by Charles Oman in respect of the 1381 returns for Essex, suggested to many scholars that the poll taxes seriously under-enumerated the population liable to tax, by ignoring numbers of single people, servants and women in particular. The criticisms of some of the returns for 1381 are undoubtedly justified, though they owe much to the almost unworkable specifications for the assessment of the tax in that year, whereby within each vill (settlement) more prosperous taxpayers were supposed to subsidize the less well-to-do. The assessment in 1377 was much simpler: a fixed flat rate of 4d per head was required of all persons over 14 years of age, the very poor alone being exempt. This was considerably less than the average (mean) rate for 1381 and did not involve any complicated manipulation on the part of the assessors. There is thus every reason to believe that the tax was much more comprehensively collected in 1377. The total number of taxpayers recorded in 1377 is indeed invariably in excess of the equivalent number in 1381 and in many instances considerably so. To put it another way, if the 1381 returns are bad, those for 1377 are considerably less bad.

For most places no detailed lists of names of taxpayers, referred to as nominative listings, survive. Instead we have merely indications of the sum of money collected and the number of persons taxed. We thus have no way of assessing the composition of the taxpaying population and hence also the credibility of the returns as a record of all those actually liable to tax. We do, however, have some nominative listings for several major towns and also for the small county of Rutland, for the Coquetdale ward of Northumberland and for fragmentary parts of Leicestershire, Lincolnshire, Oxfordshire and Sussex. There is a great deal that can be learned from these listings regarding the composition of households and marriage patterns, but our initial concern is with the credibility of the source.

Were it the case that women and single persons had been systematically under-enumerated, as was true of Essex in 1381, then we would expect to find a disproportionate number of males to females recorded – that is, a high sex ratio. Similarly we would expect to find a high proportion of the recorded population to have been married. With the exception of Coquetdale ward, this is not what we find. Indeed, sex ratios in respect of the urban listings are consistently low (i.e. there are actually slightly more females than males recorded). The proportions of taxpayers recorded as married are likewise low when compared to other historical populations. The implication must be that the tax was collected fairly conscientiously and that there is probably a generally good match between the numbers of recorded taxpayers and the actual population liable to tax. The listings for the Coquetdale ward may, however, suggest that some returns are defective, but in the absence of nominative listings we cannot tell which. Even for Coquetdale, however, it is possible to suggest some special circumstances that explain the apparent anomalies of that return, namely the exodus of the young and mobile from a region characterized historically by border raiding and poverty.

In order to convert the tax populations from 1377 into actual total populations it is necessary to allow for those who were too young to pay tax, those who were legitimately exempted on grounds of poverty and those who evaded the tax. Population totals for the clergy and religious, who were taxed separately, also need to be added to these figures for the lay population. Once again this is a recipe for compounding error with error. For example, any estimate of the proportion of the population below taxable age depends upon estimates of the birth rate and of infant and child mortality, neither of which can be known with any confidence in the absence of accurate census data or registers of vital statistics. Consequently any estimate of total population so derived must be regarded as a crude indicator rather than an authoritative total. Nevertheless, based on a recorded lay tax population of 1,355,201 persons, it is hardly likely that the total population for England in 1377 was less than two million, though Hatcher's estimate of 2.75–3 million appears to be on the generous side. This sort of range suggests a population still nearly twice that of 1086 even despite the catastrophe of the Black Death and two subsequent epidemics.

The value of the 1377 poll tax lies in much more than the crude estimate of total population that it can provide. For example, the thousands of individual returns together allow us to see population distribution and density in some detail. As in 1086, the land north of a line drawn between the Tees and the Exe appears to have been comparatively sparsely populated. (Though there is no poll tax information for Cheshire and County Durham, there is little reason to think that they departed from this pattern.) Norfolk, Suffolk, Kent and parts of Lincolnshire remained populous regions, but the particular concentration of people within the eastern part of the country is now much less marked. Rather, population was concentrated within a wedge-shaped triangle with its points at Scarborough, Exeter and Dover, the centre and eastern parts of this wedge being especially populous. This distribution mirrors to no small degree the distribution of wealth observed from the lay subsidy of 1334. Although it would be unwise to posit a simple correlation between taxable wealth and numbers of people, such an observation may suggest that this new population distribution was not primarily a product of the Black Death, but part of a longer-term development that pre-dated the plague.

The final benchmark (1525) is that derived from parish register evidence. This is no less problematic than the two previous sources. Registers of baptisms, marriages and burials do not readily convert into population totals. Although registration was initiated in 1538, moreover, comparatively few registers are extant from quite so early a date. We must rely, therefore, on the statistical wizardry of the technique of 'back projection' (or 'inverse projection') that relates recorded vital events to known population totals derived from nineteenth-century censuses and then estimates backwards through time population totals to match vital statistics recorded for earlier periods. This was undertaken by Jim Oepen of the Cambridge Group for the History of Population and Social Structure back to the beginning of parish registration and indeed one generation further back, hence our 1525 benchmark.[1] The results are probably imperfect, but equally they are probably about as good as we are going to get. The pertinent estimates are tabulated (Table 6.1) against those already discussed for 1086 and 1377, together with the estimates for the pre-plague population peak, the post-plague nadir and the last decades of our era.

---

1. E.A. Wrigley and R.S. Schofield, *The Population History of England, 1541–1871* (London, 1981).

TABLE 6.1. ENGLISH POPULATION ESTIMATES, 1086–1551

Date	Total
1086	1–2 million
1315	3.8–6.5 million
1377	2–3 million
1450	2–2.5 million
1525	2.3 million
1541	2.8 million
1551	3 million

Though the foregoing discussion deliberately shies away from the more precise estimates of the total population for Domesday Book or the first poll tax, the totals as set
out in the table are still revealing. In the light of the sixteenth-century totals, the lower
end of the ranges suggested for the earlier dates is perhaps usually to be preferred. For
the entire post-plague era as far as 1550, it can be seen that the population remained
between two and three million, and had indeed reached this upper figure only by the
very end of this period. Furthermore, population levels at the end of the Middle Ages
failed to regain or even significantly approach the level achieved at their pre-plague
peak. On the other hand, population must have grown considerably during the first
part of our period, though the present table is unable tell us anything about the rate
and timing of that growth. This must be our next objective.

To state the obvious, growth is a product of fertility – the propensity of people to
produce children – outstripping mortality. Several factors will influence fertility,
including contraceptive knowledge and practices relating to breastfeeding, but the key
variable is the age at which people and, more specifically, women marry. So long as
she has achieved sexual maturity, the earlier a woman marries, the more childbearing
years she has ahead of her, but also the more fertile, and hence likely to conceive, she
is. Unfortunately before the era of parish registration we have only very limited direct
evidence to work with. This evidence will be discussed shortly, but our discussion will
begin with some very speculative remarks concerning the indirect evidence for fertility, propensity to marry and marriage age.

There are two stages to our argument. The first, focusing on Domesday evidence,
attempts to relate population growth to patterns of landholding and inheritance.
Regions associated with high levels of personal freedom and partible inheritance, it will
be suggested, may historically have sustained higher rates of population growth. The
second, focusing on poll tax evidence and so pertaining more immediately to developments taking place within our period, argues that regional structural differences in
householding and the economy may have tended to reverse the earlier pattern.

A striking feature of the Domesday evidence is that the highest proportion of free
peasantry coincided with the eastern region of greater population density. Domesday
Book thus highlights important structural differences between regions that remained
a feature of English society throughout the medieval era. In some ways such cultural
differences have their roots in the pre-Conquest era and may even extend as far back
as Romano-British times. The area of West Saxon rule, which saw the development
of a powerful state and a degree of political centralization even before the Conquest,

emerges as significantly different from the eastern regions associated with the Danelaw. Eastern England was characterized by the high incidence of personal freedom and often with the practice of partible inheritance. These are also regions often associated with what has been termed a wood-pasture economy and a high proportion of dispersed settlements. In contrast, the majority of peasants in what we can identify as the champian belt of Midland England (including the county of Yorkshire) were villeins. Here forms of impartible inheritance were the norm. So too were nucleated settlements. The position in the west and south-west was more mixed.

These differences are likely to have been reflected in different population growth rates. Whereas impartible inheritance may have encouraged inheriting sons to delay matrimony until the father's death, and discouraged younger sons from marrying altogether, partible inheritance, which might result in land being held jointly by all the heirs, together with a more diversified economy, may conversely have enabled more youngsters to marry and to marry sooner. If this hypothesis is correct – and it is a problematic 'if' – then population would have tended to grow more quickly in regions, notably Kent and East Anglia, characterized by free tenure and by a higher incidence of partible inheritance, than in the champian country of Midland England.

The population distribution derived from the 1377 poll tax has many broad similarities to the pattern observed in 1086. The northern and western counties are least densely populated, but Norfolk and Suffolk remain among the most densely settled. There are, however, some interesting changes. Cornwall now appears more densely populated. More striking still is the intensity of settlement in the by now drained and fertile south-eastern division of Lincolnshire known as Holland; in 1086 it had been the two other divisions of Lindsey and Kesteven that were the more populous. The most significant shift, however, is the greater density of settlement now found in the Midland counties of Bedfordshire, Leicestershire, Northamptonshire and Rutland, a density of settlement no less marked than that found in parts of East Anglia.

Clearly whatever particular factors underlay the high level of population settlement in East Anglia at the time of the Domesday Inquest (stage one), they can do little to explain how the population of this very different Midland England region was able to catch up (stage two), presuming we do not simply have a pattern of population redistribution consequent upon migration. The small number of surviving nominative listings allow an almost unparalleled insight into households and their composition, and hence into household formation, but also into the proportions currently married and hence, tangentially, into age at marriage and levels of fertility. Because the evidence surviving from 1377 is so heavily skewed to urban populations, however, there is reason also to draw upon like evidence from the second poll tax of 1379, where some returns appear to be of good quality. Poos has even made ingenious use of the patently defective Essex returns from the third and final poll tax of 1381.

Two observations may immediately be ventured. First, households consisting of no more than one married couple – to use demographic jargon, 'simple conjugal' households – *appear* to be the norm. Indeed there is reason to think that by the later fourteenth century this was actually the case outside the champian region of Midland England. Whereas many households consisting of persons apparently living by themselves are to be found, there are very few where more than two generations live together. Evidence for more than one married couple living within the same household is hardly to be found. Households may contain any combination of parents, children and servants, but very rarely other kin or non-kin. We may conclude from these observations that new households were formed at marriage (since households contained no more than one married couple) and that married children did not normally live with their parents, either because they did not remain within the natal home even once a parent was widowed or because elderly parents did not join the households of grown-up children.

As discussed in Chapter 2, closer scrutiny of the returns for parts of Midland England suggest another pattern or, more precisely, the traces of another pattern that may have been more normal prior to the time of the poll tax. There is little evidence for the sort of complex households characteristic of parts of the Balkans or Russian serf society even within the recent past. There are, however, indications of extended or multiple households – that is, households containing unmarried siblings, married children or three generations. Such a strategy is logical where family land is normally conserved intact from one generation to the next, precisely the model that some scholars, including Zvi Razi, have suggested for this region. Razi has argued that this model, prevailing in the English Midlands at least before the plague, encouraged comparatively early marriage for both sexes. This would explain a high level of fertility and hence a high population growth rate, but it does not explain why implicitly this was not the case at a rather earlier period.

Razi's evidence for age at marriage rests on an analysis of the very extensive records of the customary court for the manor of Halesowen (War.).[2] His methodology depends upon his making a series of assumptions that he then seeks to confirm from the evidence itself. He assumes that male peasants were liable first to be recorded in the court rolls once they achieved their customary majority – 20 years at Halesowen – and that parents would endeavour to provide a son coming of age with some land without compromising the integrity of the family holding. He assumes further that sons would invariably marry at much the same time as they were provided with land, and hence that they would marry and be liable to father children from about 20 years of age. Razi goes on to demonstrate these propositions by showing that sons often first appear in the court rolls some 20-odd years after their father's appearance and that in turn their own first named son appears some 20 years after. In the case of daughters, he calculates their age at marriage by the interval between the father's first notice and the recording of merchet (the marriage fine) in the court rolls.

Razi's evidence is very plausible, but it depends on several assumptions and is weighted to the experience of the oldest surviving sons and the children of the better-off. Fathers may well have had a particular interest in seeing their heirs married within their lifetime so as to ensure the succession of family land. Such concerns may thus have resulted in male heirs marrying earlier than their brothers. The possibility remains, however, that early marriage was common in central England in the later thirteenth and fourteenth centuries.

An alternative hypothesis has been proposed by Richard Smith, but drawing upon evidence for the rather different region of eastern England. In particular he uses the somewhat fragile evidence (dating to the 1260s) of the Spalding Priory serf lists for the villages of Weston and Moulton in the Holland division of Lincolnshire, and the apparently more robust evidence of the 1377 poll tax returns for Rutland to argue for

---

2. Z. Razi, *Life, Marriage and Death in a Medieval Parish* (Cambridge, 1980).

the existence of a nuclear household system. He goes on to suggest that hand in hand with such a pattern of householding went – to use demographic jargon – a marriage regime characterized by comparatively late (i.e. in the twenties rather than the teens) marriage for both sexes. This last follows from the logic, intrinsic to the nuclear household system, that young people should set up their own households on marriage.

Significant numbers of adolescents and young adults would appear to have left home prior to marriage since this is the only way to explain variously the comparative paucity of children still living with their parents, the numbers of servants contained within, especially, urban households, and the comparatively low proportion of the population recorded as currently married, observed in 1377. Such children would no longer have been subject to their parents' authority at the point at which they got married. This itself may indicate that some young people, including young women, were able to make marriages that were not specifically arranged for them by their family. Because younger children are more compliant to the parental will than older, arranged marriages tend, moreover, to be early marriages. Conversely, it may be suggested that the young women who made their own marriages married later rather than earlier. Smith uses the proportions of males recorded as currently married from the 1377 Rutland poll tax to show just this. He refrains, however, from repeating the exercise in relation to women lest doubts as to how satisfactorily single women are enumerated leave any conclusions open to challenge.[3] If a more upbeat assessment of the 1377 returns is accepted, then there is reason to believe that a similar later marriage pattern is indeed also true of females.

Two observations follow. First, if we accept Razi's findings, we would expect a higher birth rate associated with the peasant households of Midland England at the time of the poll taxes than was true of the more commercialized economies found in the city, in parts of eastern England or the south-west. Second, we might expect a picture of rapid change as the fallout from the demographic catastrophe of the Black Death and the second pandemic of 1361–62 – the so-called Grey Death – worked through peasant society in terms of the much more ready availability of land, the willingness of peasants to move to take up land on more favourable terms, the increasingly uneconomic nature of arable farming other than on the most fertile soils, and the growing attraction of less labour-intensive pastoral farming. It may indeed be that earlier forms of householding are already largely obscured in the extant 1377 poll tax listings as a consequence both of structural change and of the impact of very high mortality.

Smith's 'hypotheses' have subsequently been lent some support by evidence relating to the ages of servants and unmarried and married witnesses within the church court of York. This evidence, which relates primarily to the later fourteenth and earlier fifteenth centuries, suggests that, in town society at least, men were marrying in their mid-twenties to women only a couple of years younger than themselves. On the other hand, the same evidence – albeit a rather smaller sample – suggests that rural couples married a little earlier and that there was a slightly larger age difference between spouses. This observation would tend to bring post-plague rural Yorkshire a little closer to pre-plague Halesowen than Smith's analysis of the Rutland poll tax returns would suggest.

---

3. R.M. Smith, 'Hypothèses sur la Nuptialité en Angleterre aux XIIIe–XIVe Siècles', *Annales: E.S.C.* 38 (1983), pp. 107–36.

Smith's hypothesis of a late marriage regime operating at least in eastern England by the later fourteenth century also conflicts with my own tentative remarks concerning high levels of population growth within this same region around the time of and after the Domesday survey. Here I would like to suggest another, earlier process of structural change that would reconcile these different perspectives. The areas that were most densely populated at the time of the Domesday survey in time inevitably afforded only comparatively small individual holdings. Such holdings could of course be held jointly in a version of the frérèche; we see a glimpse of this in the 1377 poll tax returns for the Holland (Lincs.) village of Freiston, where William Roberd and his wife apparently co-resided with his two married sons.

Another consequence of sharing insufficient landed resources would have been for those who lost out to abstain from marriage and reproduction. In the context of a culture where children could be seen variously as additional labour on family land, successors to that land and as security in old age, marriage and childrearing would have been de rigueur for peasant agriculturalists. The incentive to beget children on the part of the landless or near landless, however, was but slight. Such a hypothesis accords with the evidence derived, for example, from the poll taxes for Essex and Howdenshire (Yorks., ER) that peasant labourers were less likely to be married than husbandmen. It also fits with the observation that in the case of smallholders on the Suffolk manor of Redgrave before the plague, where partible inheritance was customary, brother often inherited from brother.

A third possibility is that the prevalence of smallholding encouraged peasants to pursue a wide diversity of economic activities in order to sustain themselves. Such economic diversity would have been possible within the wood-pasture economies that characterize many areas outside the champian belt of Midland England. Economic diversity is also the leitmotif of descriptions of the rural economies of the Lincolnshire fenlands, the Norfolk breckland, the tin-mining country of the duchy of Cornwall and the lead-mining districts of the Mendip Hills or the Derwent Valley in Derbyshire. One facet of this economic diversity is the emergence of rural industry. We find numbers of rural craftsmen – tanners, carpenters, weavers – who invariably combined craftwork with smallholding, and whose craft activity relates closely to the product of the local agrarian economy. Again we see this clearly from the poll tax evidence, as in parts of the West Riding, the Cotswolds or North Essex, but it almost certainly has longer historical roots.

The emergence of a 'complex' society in which a variety of possible livelihoods existed, all requiring different skills, provided the framework for the emergence of life-cycle service as a way of training youngsters in skills their own parents did not necessarily possess. The poll tax evidence again shows that it is craft households, conspicuously in towns, but also in the countryside, that were most likely to contain servants and again we may suppose that this pattern was not entirely new. Although we should be wary of exaggerating the numbers involved, for those youngsters who did go into service the effect may well have been to encourage a drift towards a pattern of later marriage as such youngsters became more independent of familial influence. The emergence of an active peasant land market at much the same time may also have served to undermine parental influence by making the acquisition of land less dependent on inheritance and the goodwill of parents. Again the effect would have been to depress fertility.

Long-term changes in the propensity to marriage and in the age at which young people customarily got married are not mutually exclusively explanations of movements in fertility. The important point here is that we should not turn immediately to changes in levels of mortality to explain population decline any more than population growth. Rather we need to explore both, which is the intent of the paragraphs that follow. The advent of parish register evidence from the very end of our period shows that the population was growing fast. The conventional wisdom would be to explain this in terms of a marked decline in mortality associated with endemic plague, but the continued high levels of mortality demonstrated at least by the monks of Canterbury Cathedral Priory through the fifteenth century suggests that this is an insufficient explanation. Any decline in levels of mortality must also have been accompanied by a real increase in levels of fertility consequent upon higher marriage rates and a reduction in the age at which people customarily married.

Both these last must be possibilities. Whereas the demand for live-in servants may have grown rapidly in the post-plague decades as the cost of day labour spiralled the cost of food – the main expense in maintaining servants as members of the household – tended to fall in real terms, by the later fifteenth century the pendulum was beginning to swing the other way. Fewer youngsters, consequently, would have spent time in service. As a corollary, more would have continued to reside within the parental home and hence be subject to greater parental influence in matters of courtship and marriage. As we shall see (Chapter 15) the opportunities for single women – never-married women to use demographic jargon – to support themselves independently in the labour market, or for widows of artisans and traders to continue to manage businesses previously run jointly with husbands, was being eroded from much the same time. It follows that women would have become more dependent on finding marriage partners to support themselves. This would be reflected in a higher incidence of marriage, a reduction in the age at which women customarily first married and, consequently, a higher birth rate. This in fact accords well with the picture suggested by the earliest parish register evidence.

Two further factors impinge upon fertility, but are both very indifferently documented and impossible to quantify. The practice of extended maternal breastfeeding will tend to depress the chances of a woman conceiving even if there is no cultural taboo against sexual relations while still feeding. Conversely the employment of a wetnurse will tend to improve the chances of conception. There is good evidence from aristocratic household accounts and the like that the aristocracy regularly used wetnurses, but it is much more difficult to ascertain how far down in society the practice extended. A disputed marriage case of 1366 from the neighbourhood of York clearly shows the arrangements made for a woman at the very lowest level of gentry society to secure peasant women as wetnurses immediately before the births of her two children. The same source indicates that local peasant women would normally feed their own children for at least 18 months, a finding that is also supported by recent archaeological evidence. The aristocratic practice may well have extended to the urban mercantile elite. Margery Kempe, who was the daughter of a well-to-do mercantile family and who married another Lynn merchant, had 14 children in some 20 years of marriage, a rate of reproduction that would have been unlikely had she followed peasant practice.

If clerical commentators and preachers sometimes deplored the failure of mothers to suckle their own children – and here the image of Mary feeding the Christ child was a powerful propaganda tool – so they were still more voluble in their hostility to any form of contraceptive practice. This tells us that contraceptive knowledge existed and implicitly that it was practised. Peter Biller has argued that such commentary is most conspicuous in the first part of our period before the advent of plague, and tentatively suggests that people were indeed trying to limit their fertility at this time precisely because resources were scarce.[4] This must remain only a hypothesis, though a tempting one. Coitus interruptus (withdrawal) was probably the method most likely to have been known, but it is perhaps more likely that such practices were used, if at all, to avoid conception on the part of couples who were not married rather than to control fertility within marriage.

Many of the remarks above respecting nuptiality (marriage and the propensity to marry) are necessarily speculative. We are on only slightly surer ground when we turn to mortality. Mortality crises and epidemic disease are comparatively well documented. They are likely to elicit comment from contemporary chroniclers and, by the later fourteenth century, wills are sufficiently numerous that we can use them to pick up years, and even seasons, of high mortality. Incidence of mortality can also be calculated in respect of the secular clergy from bishops' registers. The mortality of manorial tenants can likewise be discovered from court rolls so long as these are of sufficient quality and completeness. Problems arise, however, when we move from tracking epidemic disease and focus instead on endemic disease. ('Epidemic' is where large numbers of people die in a short space of time, whereas 'endemic' relates to disease present within the population and causing deaths over a long period.) Bishops' registers, manor court rolls and wills are most useful for studying the experience of adult males drawn from the middling levels of society and above, but are much less satisfactory for women and the poor, and entirely overlook children. The invisibility of children in the records is indeed perhaps the major lacuna; we know almost nothing directly of infant and child mortality, and we must not assume that it will mirror that of adults.

Chroniclers provide useful evidence for years of unusually high mortality and may well offer some explanation, though the terminology used is often vague. It is from chronicle sources that we have the most apparently immediate and graphic accounts of the suffering and actual mortality caused by the relentless rains falling between 1315 and 1317, a period known to scholars as the Agrarian Crisis. In fact, it can be shown that these are sometimes modelled on scriptural accounts of pestilence and famine, and contain a certain amount of embellishment based solely on hearsay. On the other hand, Trokelowe's account of seeing dead bodies lying in the streets of London carries more conviction. Much the same caveats are true of chronicle accounts of the pandemic of 1348–49 (the Black Death). Chronicles are nevertheless a valuable and demonstrably reliable source for the timing and geographic extent of subsequent plague epidemics.

The chronicle evidence usefully alerts us to the way in which any discussion of mortality over this period falls into two phases. Before the advent of plague the focus is on mortality associated with malnutrition and related disease. From 1348, however,

---

4. P.P.A. Biller, 'Birth-control in the West in the Thirteenth and Early Fourteenth Centuries', *Past and Present* 94 (1982), pp. 3–26.

the focus shifts to the severity and chronology of plague mortality. The wider context of these two phases will be treated at length in the third part of this book ('The Dynamics of a Pre-industrial Economy'). The present discussion will attempt to focus objectively on sources, taking each phase in turn.

Direct evidence for mortality in the first phase, beyond the essentially anecdotal evidence of the chroniclers, is limited and specific to particular localities. Razi has used evidence for the deaths of tenants from the Halesowen court rolls to map levels of mortality from 1270. Periods of high mortality occurred in the earlier 1290s, but more especially in the early and the later part of the 1310s. This last peak coincides of course with the Agrarian Crisis and represents one of the more compelling pieces of evidence that there was significant mortality at that time since these are the deaths not of the landless, but of actual tenants. For the remaining two decades prior to the plague, recorded deaths seem largely unremarkable save in the years 1343–45 where a sudden peak in deaths of female tenants, always a minority, is noticed. Razi argues, however, that despite phases of high mortality the manor continued to grow through the period and only the rate of growth declined.

Other sources are perhaps a little more difficult to interpret. Poos has presented important evidence for fluctuations in the population of resident males over the age of 12 for 4 Essex communities in the form of records of payments of tithing penny. These payments seem to have been fairly stable until around the time of the Agrarian Crisis. The number of pennies accounted for then tumbled by an average of about 15 per cent over the critical years 1315–17, although even within this one region we can observe variation between the three communities then under observation. Like data for Taunton (Somerset) show a more modest fall. What is more striking, however, is that payments continued to fall steadily up until the time of the Black Death. What we cannot know is how far this last represents actually mortality, depletion of numbers due to migration or, the most intriguing possibility, the non-inclusion of young men in life-cycle service who were exempted from tithing membership because not regarded as long-term residents within the community. Any increase in demand for servants – the argument made tentatively above – would effectively have reduced the tithing population without impinging on actual numbers.

Another source that turns out to be not quite what it seems relates to payments of heriots recorded in manor court rolls. Postan and Titow related heriot payments to fluctuations in grain prices to suggest a causal link between years of poor harvest and high levels of mortality. This will be considered at greater length in Chapter 11, but the main caveat is that the heriot payment is symbolic of the lord's title to a peasant holding. It was due whenever a holding was given up by the tenant to whom the lord had first granted the holding regardless of whether the holding passed to the heir, reverted to the lord for lack of heirs or in fact (but not within the fiction of the legal record) was sold. In this last instance heriot payments are not an indirect measure of mortality. Only where heriot was payable solely at death or the court rolls specify actual deaths can we tie higher than usual death rates to poor harvests, but even then the evidence is ambivalent and certainly much less clear on some manors than others. Price series for grain remain, however, very good indicators of harvest shortfall, so 'inelastic' is demand for this staple foodstuff. Particularly high grain prices were reached in 1258, 1272, 1289, 1297 and through the whole of the second decade of the fourteenth century. It may well be that the most vulnerable in society – the landless poor, particularly poor women, infants and the elderly – may have suffered higher incidence of mortality in these years. We have some hint of this, albeit again anecdotally, in the form of presentations in the coroner's court relating to the deaths of poor women due to exposure.

One further oblique window on mortality is provided by measuring the numbers of children still living at a parent's death, a measure known as the replacement ratio. In general terms, the lower the replacement ratio, the higher mortality is understood to be. Evidence for low replacement ratios – specifically ratios below unity implying that the older generation is being replaced by a smaller number of the younger generation – sustained over a period of time is, therefore, compelling evidence of demographic recession. Once again, however, we cannot treat mortality as the only factor operating. Replacement ratios will be influenced by expectation of life, age at marriage and, more obviously, by fertility. The later a person marries, for example, the shorter the interval between the births of their children and their own demise, and hence the greater the probability that any one of those children born will survive to the parent's death, but not necessarily reach sufficient age itself to marry and reproduce. Suffice to say, replacement ratios are only suggestive indicators of trends over time. They should not be read as hard statistical evidence.

Replacement ratio evidence relating to recorded sons of male manorial tenants again offers ambivalent evidence. At Halesowen, ratios were depressed in the four decades prior to the Black Death, but suggest actual population contraction in the decade spanning the Agrarian Crisis. At Coltishall (Norfolk), on the other hand, the replacement rate evidence suggests that population grew steadily right up to the arrival of plague. A similar pattern of apparent growth is more briefly detected for Udimore (Sussex) in 1321–23, precisely at the moment population levels appear to be falling on the Essex manors studied by Poos. Equivalent replacement rates calculated from Inquisitions Post Mortem respecting tenants-in-chief of the Crown, and hence an exclusively aristocratic population, likewise suggest continued growth until 1348. This last is perhaps less surprising as this privileged group would have been sheltered from the sort of hardships caused by acute scarcity of resources that were experienced in peasant society.

Two observations follow by way of a conclusion. First, though the direct demographic evidence pertaining to mortality is pretty slender, there is enough here to demonstrate much regional and local variety of experience, a picture no doubt complicated by the movements of people in and out of communities over time. In due course new local studies will help us flesh out this regional geography rather more clearly. The second observation is that there is every reason to believe that the Agrarian Crisis, centred on the second decade of the fourteenth century, was a major disaster with real demographic implications. It is less than clear that the implications, in terms of mortality at least, necessarily extended beyond that decade. The real problem, however, is that the groups most vulnerable – the poor and the landless – are also the least visible. The same is true again of the next, far greater demographic cataclysm, the Black Death.

MORTALITY DURING AND AFTER THE BLACK DEATH

The advent of what contemporary chroniclers referred to as *pestilencia magna* (the great pestilence), but which modern historians have called the Black Death, is well documented. In addition to the many chronicle accounts, few of which venture any statistics on mortality and none that are reliable, pestilence is frequently noted in manor court rolls. These regularly record a high turnover of peasant holdings due to the deaths of tenants. Where we have good evidence for the actual number of tenants on the eve of the plague it is possible to calculate death rates for this section of the population. This evidence is likely to be particularly robust. It is also surprisingly uniform. Although variations can be found between different manors within a larger estate or the different constituent parts of large manors, on average it would seem that nearly half of all tenants perished. This is the sort of level found variously on manors in north Essex, Cambridgeshire, the West Midlands and east Cornwall, though slightly higher rates are found in the south-west and some rather lower rates elsewhere. A rather different measure, the decline in numbers recorded paying heriot 'because he is dead' on the manors of the large Glastonbury Abbey estate, shows a death rate as high as 55 per cent.

It is difficult to ascertain with any confidence how far rates of mortality differed between different sectors of the population according to gender, age or social status. Clerical mortality, calculated from the proportions of parochial livings that changed hands due to deaths as recorded in diocesan registers, suggests that this population of moderately well-to-do adult males suffered a death rate in the region of 40–45 per cent. A similar level of mortality can be shown for a number of religious houses and the heads of such houses. The mortality of bishops, who constituted a sort of clerical aristocracy, was, however, only 18 per cent, a figure more in line with the 27 per cent aristocratic mortality calculated from Inquisitions Post Mortem, albeit there were many fewer bishops than tenants-in-chief. This may suggest that the very topmost levels of society were less severely afflicted by the pandemic of 1348–49. (Once again the mortality experience of the lowest social echelons remains obscure.)

The Black Death became known as the 'great pestilence' not least to distinguish it from subsequent pestilences or plague epidemics. The second pestilence of 1361–62 was clearly of lesser magnitude, but probably on a par with the earlier Agrarian Crisis in terms of its immediate demographic impact. Tenant mortality on the manor of Bishop's Walton (Hants) had been 65 per cent in 1348–49, but in 1361–62 it was only 13 per cent. A total of 14 per cent of the beneficed clergy of the large diocese of York also died in the second pandemic, as did 23 per cent of tenants-in-chief. More anecdotal evidence relating to the deaths of senior officials in the service of central government likewise shows that the pestilence of 1361–62 was, for this level of society at least, not so much less acute than in the first pandemic. It is tempting to speculate that these higher echelons of society, having been less severely affected than the general populous in the first pandemic, found themselves more vulnerable to the second.

This last point – that each subsequent epidemic particularly afflicted those who had not been exposed to the immediate earlier epidemics – is generally assumed and makes sense of the point stressed by the chroniclers that it was children that perished in the greatest number. This is, for example, the point made by the Anonimalle, Louth Park and Lynn Grey Friars' chroniclers of the 1361 pandemic. The Anonimalle chronicler makes similar observations of the plagues of 1369 and 1374. Interestingly, Walsingham and the continuator of Ranulph Higden's *Polychronicon* report specifically of the 1361 pandemic that men were much more vulnerable than women. It is difficult to know what weight to put on this evidence, but it accords with probate (will) evidence that women may have been less susceptible to plague.

Wills survive with increasing frequency from the later fourteenth century. The bunching of wills in particular years can be shown to tie up closely with reported epidemics. Though wills do not record either the precise date of death or the cause of death, we can attempt to tease out information about both. Wills are normally recorded in the form of registered copies. These record both the date of making and the date of subsequent probate. Death obviously occurred at some point between the two, but since in a significant number of instances the one followed the other by a matter of days, we may assume that probate need not normally be particularly delayed after death. Certainly the sense that wills were regularly made on the deathbed – even if an earlier will may have been made some years before – is confirmed. If we use this evidence for approximate date of death to allocate deaths by season, then most errors will be insignificant. Using probate evidence in this way it is possible to show – as has been done for wills registered in the diocese of York – that men's wills tended to be most numerous in the autumn, whereas women's wills bunch in the spring, which last is the normal pattern prevailing by the early modern era. Given that plague tends to be most active in the autumn, we may tentatively conclude that men were indeed more vulnerable than women to the disease. What we can be less sure of is how similar the population of female testators is to that of male testators, or indeed how representative are either of the wider population.

Another finding that has been suggested, this time from a study of East Anglian wills using a slightly different methodology to that just described, is that by the 1470s plague was on the wane as the major cause of death. This observation raises two related issues. The one pertains to the virulence of *endemic* as opposed to *epidemic* plague, the other to the level of mortality associated with diseases other than 'plague'. The chronicle accounts continue to tell us of plague epidemics far into the fifteenth century. These, however, seem increasingly to have been localized phenomena, plague experienced in one place not touching another. It would be wrong to take this as evidence that even by the end of the fourteenth century plague was waning. Rather the disease had become spread through the population by the process of epidemic and was now endemic within the community. Instead of large numbers dying in a finite space of time, people were dying all the time in ways that were neither noticeable to the chroniclers, nor worthy of notice. Endemic disease may in fact have accounted for as many deaths over, say, a ten-year period as would have been caused in one or two epidemic visitations over the same period.

If we follow the East Anglian probate evidence, endemic plague would appear to have remained a major killer through the first two-thirds of the fifteenth century. Evidence relating to the mortality of monks during the course of the fifteenth century cautions, however, that any possible waning of plague in the last third of the century is not to be read as evidence for a slackening in levels of mortality more generally. John Hatcher's analysis of the obituary evidence for the large and singularly wealthy Benedictine cathedral priory of Canterbury shows that tuberculosis and the so-called sweating sickness (perhaps influenza), major outbreaks of which are recorded in 1485, 1508, 1517 and 1528, were also significant killers. He concludes that there was no significant downward trend in mortality over the century.

His findings further suggest that within this adult population the age group 25–34 years experienced a generally higher level of mortality than older age groups.[5] If this were translated into the wider population, it could suggest that people were particularly vulnerable to the ravages of disease at precisely the time they would have been most likely to reproduce. Mortality here may thus have had a depressing effect on fertility. Like patterns have been found for the monks of Westminster. Both populations show a general marked deterioration in the life expectancy of young adults (20 years) through the second half of the fifteenth century, reaching a nadir in the very early years of the sixteenth century. Significantly this trend is sharply reversed at Westminster for the three decades prior to the dissolution (1540).

How far we can extrapolate from the experiences of the rather artificial, overfed world of the wealthy Benedictine cloister to the wider population, particularly given the fragility of our knowledge respecting the poor, women and children, is a matter for debate. The evidence is, however, a salutary warning that we cannot explain the apparent strong recovery in the population by the early sixteenth century solely in terms of a fall in mortality occasioned by a decline in the incidence or virulence of plague. Rather we must consider the possibility that – as has been shown for the early modern era – fertility is at least as big a dynamic in explaining long-term trends in population. One position is to argue that whereas mortality was unusually severe in the two decades following the Black Death, mortality, especially child mortality, remained very high at least through the fifteenth century. This is suggested anecdotally by evidence for the high ratio of child to adult burials at Sutton on Hull in 1429 and the very high rate of infant mortality recorded in German later medieval autobiographical evidence. What allowed population levels to recover, therefore, was not so much a slackening of the mortality regime as a gradual growth in fertility levels by the latter part of the same century. This can only have been a product of a higher rate of marriage and, a more powerful influence on fertility, a lower mean (average) marriage age on the part of women.

To date, the statistical evidence that is needed to demonstrate or challenge this last hypothesis simply does not exist, but there are some more circumstantial indicators to support this view. Parish register evidence has been used to suggest that marriage rates were exceptionally high (and falling) at the very end of our period, but this cannot inform us of trends prior to that date. A reading of disputed marriage cases within the church courts would suggest a generally higher degree of parental and familial involvement in the making of marriages by the later fifteenth century in London and York or, even more markedly, the earlier sixteenth century in Kent than was necessarily true of the later fourteenth and earlier fifteenth centuries. Such family involvement is compatible with a pattern of earlier marriage for women, though hardly conclusive proof. The expansion of pastoral agriculture and associated rural manufacture – textiles, tanning, woodworking – may also have encouraged earlier marriage. For the early modern era Barbara Todd has shown that widows were more likely to remarry when

5. J. Hatcher, 'Mortality in the Fifteenth Century: Some New Evidence', *Economic History Review*, 2nd ser. 39 (1986), pp. 19–38.

the opportunities open to them to support themselves were most circumscribed.[6] As we shall see in Chapter 15, this appears to have been true at least of urban widows from the later fifteenth century.

While the broad trend of population growth at the very beginning of our period, sharp and sustained decline following the advent of plague in 1348 and renewed growth by the end of our period is beyond dispute, what happened in between is less certain. Likewise we can be confident enough that the English population as a whole was about 3 million by 1550. With somewhat less conviction we can suggest that at its peak in the earlier fourteenth century it was around 5 million and at its nadir in the mid-fifteenth century it was nearer 2 million. These are the broad outlines. What the foregoing discussion has tried to show, however, is that these broad patterns are shaped by a whole variety of factors – fertility, mortality, patterns of inheritance and land util-ization, forms of employment, patterns of migration – and may consequently have been subject to degrees of regional and even local variation that are now hard to recover.

The Agrarian Crisis and its impact on population will be explored in more depth in Chapter 11. Similarly, the Black Death and its aftermath are discussed at greater length in Chapter 12. Part of our purpose here, however, has been to show that mor-tality is not the only dynamic of population change. We have tried to show that fer-tility was at least as important. This last could be held in check by landless labourers choosing not to enter into marriage and childrearing, by adolescents postponing mat-rimony until after they had completed an extended period of training, by prolonged maternal breastfeeding or by women in employment exercising greater control over decisions relating to matrimony. Alternatively it could be accelerated by greater avail-ability of land making it easier for peasants to support themselves through agriculture or by women turning to marriage sooner because they could not readily support themselves otherwise. Such considerations follow no simple pattern. In some places new land continued to be colonized well into the fourteenth century and as a conse-quence high rates of marriage may have followed. In older more densely settled regions, however, the difficult years of the early fourteenth century may have prompted a polarization in landholding and a growing underclass of landless (or near landless) labour, who of necessity opted out of marriage and family life.

The way forward probably lies in local studies that are located within and sensitive to the wider debates, and in the realization and analysis of a greater range of sources. Some records of churchings have, for example, been found. Since a mother was rou-tinely churched a month following her delivery, such records are a proxy for births. Similarly, medieval cemetery evidence offers some possibilities, but only where skele-tal remains can be located chronologically with some confidence, which, by the nature of cemeteries, is in fact rarely the case. Skeletal remains do offer a source for the inci-dence of certain types of disease that impact on the bone structure. Lacunae are still likely to remain. Infant and child mortality, which does not necessarily show even in cemetery evidence, is essentially unrecorded before parish registration, yet may have been a major factor restraining population recovery in the fifteenth century. In talking of infant and child mortality, however, we are again reminded that there can be no understanding of demography without consideration of births as well as deaths.

---

6. B. Todd, 'The Remarrying Widow: A Stereotype Reconsidered', in M. Prior, ed., *Women in English Society 1500–1800* (London, 1985).

7 HUSBANDMEN AND LABOURERS

It is a commonplace of 'school' history that within the 'feudal system' there was a simple hierarchy comprising the king at the apex, lords beneath him and peasants at the base. Peasants are thus imagined both to be subservient to their lords, but essentially undifferentiated in terms of their own level of society. One highly influential group of scholars associated with the School of History at the University of Birmingham has offered a much more sophisticated window on peasant society which nevertheless, by stressing the conflicting interests of lords and peasants, tends only to reinforce this perspective. In fact peasant society is highly diverse and if anything this diversity is accentuated over the period.

Medieval peasants are popularly imagined as living on manors comprising a village with a church, manor house, tumbledown cottages and fields divided into strips. Each would work their own strip, but would also labour for the lord of the manor. They would grow their own food, seldom venture beyond the nearest market town and rarely move away from their natal village, indeed would be prevented from doing so by their lord even if they so wished. Their agricultural practices would be backward and unchanging, their minds cluttered with folklore and superstition, their knowledge of politics or the wider world as slight as their grasp of relativity theory or rocket science.

There is much that is attractive to us at the beginning of the twenty-first century in imaging the past in these terms. It would, moreover, be too easy to dismiss this picture as entirely erroneous for myth often captures certain truths. It is not, however, a useful starting point. Our problem as historians is, as always, that we can only access the past through the sources that have come down to us. The principal sources that medievalists have used to explore peasant society are the records of the manor court. These survive in great number, but often very patchily. They tend to be fullest and most well preserved in respect of institutional lords – religious houses, bishops, the Crown – and for those areas of the country where the institution of the manor and the manor court was most well developed. Consequently we tend to know more about 'Midland England', the predominantly arable central swathe of the country, than we do of the upland and pastoral districts of the north and west. We also tend to know more about the fourteenth than the fifteenth or earlier sixteenth centuries: court rolls tend to survive from the later decades of the thirteenth century and so the temptation to engage in local studies commencing with the earliest extant rolls is marked, but because of changes in estate management consequent upon demographic recession, later court rolls tend to be briefer and have attracted much less interest.

Another 'optical illusion' created by our reliance on manor court rolls is that we know most about the sort of peasants who are most frequently recorded in the court rolls, but relatively little about those who are not. Thus our knowledge is skewed towards the experience of adult, male, villein tenants, especially more substantial tenants. Women, the young, the landless, subtenants and smallholders, even peasants of free status, are all poorly represented in the court rolls and hence the historical literature. Finally, it should be recognized that the record of the customary (manor) court necessarily relates only to those matters that fell within the jurisdiction of the court – litigation between neighbours, transactions involving land, the enforcement of customary law and obligations – but leaves obscure many areas of daily life that were of little interest to the court. The record is thus weighted towards conflict, towards the activities of the more prosperous and litigious, and to the most impersonal facet of the interface between peasant and seigneur (lord).

Any discussion of peasant society must involve the deployment of a variety of technical terms. The term 'peasant', which derives from the French for someone who dwells in the *pays*, or countryside, is not one that was much used at the time. Chroniclers, writing in hostile and pejorative terms after the Revolt of 1381, talked of *rustici* – rustics – and *villani* – villeins (or villains). This last is a term that is related to the word 'vill', denoting a settlement, and defines a person tied to the land by reason of their birth. Again it is a term that has pejorative overtones in literary discourse, but need not elsewhere. Serf, neif (like the Latin *nativus*, a term that stresses the hereditary nature of villeinage) and bondsman are all alternatives to villain; neif and bondsman are contemporary usages. Modern scholars distinguish the villein from the freeman – that is, the person who has no legal ties to the land or the lord who has jurisdiction over that land. Even this distinction between free and servile is an oversimplification; close reading of the evidence reveals subtle gradation within this broader framework. Turning again to the context of 1381, peasants themselves used the term 'commons' to describe themselves collectively.

Whether free or servile, peasants did not own the land on which they worked and lived. The land was instead held by various lords, whether great magnates, ecclesiastics or mere lords of the manor. Such lords regularly reserved part of the manor, the demesne (or domain), for their own use. This last was cultivated partly by a regular workforce, known as *famuli*, and partly either by the labour of customary (servile) tenants or by hired labourers. The remaining land was leased out to numbers of tenants, both free and servile in differing proportions across the country. In Kent, where a particular form of tenure known as *gavelkind* prevailed, the peasant population enjoyed a degree of personal freedom that distinguished them from villeins. Free tenure was common, but not universal in the old Danelaw region of Lincolnshire and East Anglia. On manors that formed part of the royal demesne or had historically belonged to the Crown, tenants enjoyed the privileged status of villein sokemen, which again was more akin to free than servile tenure. In Midland England, however, villeinage, though not universal, was the norm.

The distinction between persons of free status and serfs was one that was dear to medieval lawyers. Because we so often study peasant society through the lens of the customary court, moreover, this legal differentiation appears very significant to us also. Villeinage was hereditary through the father. Villeins, because tied to the land over which the lord exercised jurisdiction, were debarred from seeking justice outside their lord's court, the customary court. If an unfree person tried to bring an action in the royal courts, their personal status was immediately challenged. Villein sokemen, however, did have access to the royal courts because their lord was in fact the king.

Heriot, which is normally understood as a death duty, but was in fact due whenever a servile tenant gave up their holding, was paid only in respect of persons of servile status. This was symbolic of the lord's actual ownership of the land, but also of the tenant's status. This last was also true of chevage, the fine paid for the lord's consent to reside outside the manor, of merchet or the marriage fine paid in respect of villein women to obtain the lord's licence to marry and of leyrwite (or legerwite), the fine payable where a woman was presented for fornication. The lord could also levy tallage, that is a periodic taxation of his servile peasantry, not least when his oldest son was knighted or his daughter married.

These legal constraints and obligations may appear oppressive, but we have to see them in perspective. Few peasants would have had the need or the resources to enter into litigation in the royal courts; the customary court provided an adequate forum for the resolution of most disputes between peasants. The obligations of heriot, tallage and merchet were rarely a serious financial burden on unfree peasants; though they represented a useful source of revenue to manorial lords, their purpose was also repeatedly to demarcate persons of servile status. When, for example, in 1278 Reginald son of Benedict claimed he was of free status, the manor court of Elton (Hunts.) was able to disprove this by reason of the merchets paid by his sisters for their marriages. The levy of the leyrwite fine depended, as we shall see shortly, on representatives of the peasant community (the jury of presentment) bringing sexual transgressions on the part of villein women to the attention of the court. It may thus have functioned as much as an instrument of social control on the part of the peasant community as a reason to resent villeinage.

Perhaps at least as important as the implications of personal status are those of tenurial status. Villeins were supposed to hold villein land associated with specific labour obligations, whereas free peasants supposedly held free land in return for a money rent. In practice these distinctions were eroded during the latter part of our period; before the plague they mattered. The labour obligations attached to lands held in villeinage varied both according to the size of the holding and manor. They could also vary over time, not least because even at the beginning of our period lords often chose to commute part or whole of these labour services to a money payment. At Littleton (Hants) in 1265–66, for example, 5s worth of services per virgate (or yardland, a unit of land – usually some 30 acres – that varied according to the locality and the quality of the soil) had already been commuted. In addition, each virgater (holder of a single virgate) owed a miscellany of labour services on the lord's demesne, including harrowing, weeding, haymaking, planting, sheep shearing and harvesting. (Ploughing here was presumably the responsibility of one of the *famuli*.) Smallholders had lesser obligations including collecting nuts. These services could be particularly resented as they took labour away from the family holding at precisely the busiest moments in the agricultural year, notably the hay and grain harvests, though there was nothing to prevent more affluent tenants from employing labour to render these services on their behalf. It should also be noted that the lord looked to the labour not just of the (usually male) tenant, but the family as a whole since weeding and sheep shearing were specifically women's work and nut gathering might be delegated to children. From the later fourteenth century, however, labour services were little more than a memory.

It is tempting to assume that legal status and economic status were closely related, but this is not so. The extent of a bond tenant's obligations to their lord depended, as we have seen, on the size of his holding. This itself was often a product of inheritance. There was also a market in peasant land, which from the early fourteenth century especially could be quite active. The important point here is that, though the land legally belonged to the lord, in practice local custom regarding inheritance was respected and enforced through the manor court. Likewise the lord permitted land to be bought and sold so long as these transactions were duly registered through the court. (They appear not as market transactions, but as surrenders to and grants by the lord so as to acknowledge his ownership, but the effect was also to secure the purchaser's title.)

Across medieval England we find two different traditions of inheritance. In one (partible inheritance) all the male children inherited equally. Such a pattern was common among the free peasantry of East Anglia and within the distinctive traditions of Kent, but was uncommon among the unfree. Rather most villeins and many free peasants practised a form of impartible inheritance, either primogeniture (inheritance by the oldest surviving son) or ultimogeniture, otherwise known as borough English (inheritance by the youngest surviving son). In both systems daughters invariably inherited equally in the absence of male heirs, though we do find the occasional exception. Thus at Badbury (Wilts.) the eldest daughter alone inherited in the absence of male heirs.

The effect of these systems was either to subdivide holdings into units that were potentially too small to be viable or to favour one son at the expense of the others. Peasant parents would sometimes endeavour to provide some land for their non-inheriting sons just as they would provide materially for their daughters. The effect was still a very unequal distribution of land between peasant families, both free and servile. By the early fourteenth century, there were significant numbers of substantial villeins just as there were large numbers of impoverished freemen, especially in eastern England, where partible inheritance among the free was common. Peasants, however, were not always bound by custom. As we shall see, maintenance agreements made between elderly tenants and a younger generation sometimes resulted in land being transferred away from the heir, for example to a married daughter, or even outside the immediate family. Similarly, by the latter part of our period it is not uncommon to find tenants disposing of land by will, often in order to provide for their widows rather than allowing property to pass directly to the customary heir.

Peasant society displays a complex social hierarchy. At one end of the spectrum there were numbers of prosperous villein families with substantial holdings. It is the men from these families that made up the various juries of inquest (juries appointed to determine the veracity of disputed claims made within the customary court) and, from the late thirteenth century, the jury of presentment on which the customary court was so dependent. The jurors of presentment were required to bring various transgressions against customary law to the notice of the court. Although they could on occasion be punished for concealment, in practice this gave jurors some discretion and considerable power within the community. Substantial villeins were also the most prominent litigants within the courts, often engaging in business concerning land and the transfer of land or acting as pledges (sureties) for poorer neighbours. At the other end of the social hierarchy we find the landless (sometimes noted as *valletti*) and the near landless, both villein and free, who as a group are relatively invisible in the records.

This latter group might include smallholders holding land of the lord and may be referred to in manorial documents as cottars. On the manor of Tuxford (Notts.) in 1297 there were, for example, 19 cottars (who performed some labour services) and 5 further smallholders in addition to 14 bond tenants (who likewise performed labour services) and 9 rent-paying free tenants. It is possible, however, that some such persons would be concealed in manorial extents (records of the lands and properties associated with a manor drawn up by inquest). Those who held land as subtenants or even squatted on common land are much less visible, though we do find reference to undersettles. Some of these poor probably lodged with other peasants. They represented an unusually mobile group within society since, holding no land of their lord, there was nothing to tie them. Indeed before the plague lords probably had little interest in trying to hold such peasants even if they were of servile status. Only in the context of labour shortage following the plague did the lord, through the customary court, try to curb this movement.

Rather than talk about peasants as if a homogeneous group, we need instead to distinguish between peasant agriculturalists or, to use a contemporary term, husbandmen and labourers. Husbandmen held sufficient land to support a family; a peasant holding was only viable when the family as a whole contributed to its management. Labourers conversely sold their labour to others. Even this may be an oversimplification; peasant agriculturalists would sometimes sell their labour (or that of family members), especially when labour was most in demand and hence commanded the best wages. This goes some way to explaining the numbers of persons, particularly women, presented during the course of the later fourteenth century for taking 'excess' wages at harvest time. Likewise, smallholders need only be partly dependent on hiring themselves out. Indeed, it is an enigma how agricultural labourers got by, for where we have records of employment, as Larry Poos found for Porter's Hall (Essex) during the 1480s, few names occur with any regularity and certainly not through the entire year.[1] Much the same has been observed in relation to labourers contracted by Durham Priory. Lastly we should note the small numbers of craftsmen, notably smiths, carpenters and, in arable districts, millers, who were an essential part of all but the smallest villages. Such craftsmen likewise invariably supplemented their livelihood as smallholders.

The demand for hired labour tended to increase over much of our period. From the later thirteenth century to the time of the plague, lords were more and more likely to commute most labour services, other than at harvest, and employ hired labour in its place. There were two reasons for this. The first is simply that customary labour was inflexible and liable to work badly. The second is that, in a period of high population, labour was abundant, cheap and, of necessity, willing. But it was not lords alone who relied upon hirelings to work the land. Numbers of substantial peasants depended on supplementing familial labour by hired labour to work their own large holdings. This was perhaps particularly true in the aftermath of the Agrarian Crisis (1315–17), which accelerated the trend towards a polarization in landholding between substantial peasants on the one hand and the landless or near landless on the other. After the Black Death labour became scarcer and hence more in demand. There was little incentive for labourers to try and accumulate land when wages were buoyant, but every incentive for

1. L.R. Poos, *A Rural Society after the Black Death: Essex 1350–1525* (Cambridge, 1991), pp. 217–20.

those with land to augment their holdings and hence indirectly to increase their need for hired labour. Lords, especially religious houses, may have attempted briefly to turn the clock back and reimpose customary labour services, but in the longer run such a policy was effectively resisted by peasants voting with their feet.

It need hardly be observed that the labourers of the preceding two paragraphs are identical to the *valletti*, cottars and undersettles of the two previous. One intriguing possibility is that numbers of substantial tenants may have sublet part of their holdings in return for labour in much the same way as the lord historically demanded labour services of his own servile tenants. Certainly some tenants were significant landlords in their own right. In one exceptional case we know of a tenant of the manor of Meon (Hants.) who in *c.*1250 had some 25 subtenants. There would be little purpose in these all paying cash rent since their landlord would in all likelihood also be one of their employers. In the thirteenth century some more substantial villein tenants may even have resented the commutation of labour services since it was cheaper for them to provide their own hired labour to perform their labour services than it was for them to pay the lord in lieu of those labour services. In the post-plague era, some manorial lords were sufficiently anxious to secure a reliable supply of labour that they provided tied cottages for labourers who would contract themselves to serve the lord.

As our previous discussion (Chapter 2) of household and family has shown, hired labourers were invariably adults, who might be married but were in fact often single, and lived separately from their employers. They represented only one form of extra-familial labour employed by peasant agriculturalists. A small proportion of peasant households (and a larger proportion of husbandmen) employed youngsters as live-in servants. These were mostly boys and young men hired primarily for bed, board and clothing. In pastoral districts we do find women servants too. Such servants were part of the landscape before the plague, but in the century following the Black Death they were in particular demand because it was then cheaper to provide workers with food than to pay them wages.

We have come a long way from the notional peasant society comprised entirely of essentially self-sufficient family groups, or a peasant society polarized between prosperous freemen and downtrodden serfs. We need now to ask questions about the peasant economy, peasant politics, and, most problematically, peasant ideology and culture. For all these questions we are again very dependent on manorial rather than peasant sources, though by the end of our period we do find wills and even inventories (lists of possessions drawn up for probate purposes) of husbandmen. Peasants can also be found as deponents (witnesses whose testimony is recorded as a written deposition) in church court litigation. Archaeology has contributed to our understanding of the material culture of peasants and literary sources can also provide clues.

In a later fifteenth-century poem, unhelpfully dubbed by its nineteenth-century editors 'The Ballad of the Tyrannical Husband', we learn of a ploughman (the contemporary term for the skilled agricultural worker) who goes out to plough, but on his return finds that his dinner is not yet ready. He angrily accuses his wife of passing her day in idle chatter with her neighbours. She responds that from early morning to night she spends her time caring for the children, carding wool, spinning, weaving, brewing, baking, taking the geese to pasture, milking the cows, making butter and cheese, feeding the ducks and chickens and preparing flax. Without a servant to assist her, she has not a moment to spare. This satirical verse alerts us to both the multiplicity of economic activities essential to the functioning of the peasant household and the question of the gender division of labour.

The ploughman of the poem cannot, of course, spend every day at the plough. The agricultural year was characterized by a variety of tasks, which themselves varied according to the region and wider economic parameters. Where grain production was the norm, the land had to be ploughed, harrowed, sown and weeded. The grain had then to be harvested, transported to storage, threshed, winnowed and finally taken to the mill to make flour. Peas and beans had likewise to be sown, weeded and harvested. Weeding and winnowing were women's work. At harvest, husbands and wives probably normally worked as a team, alternatively reaping and binding. Some of these activities, notably ploughing and harvesting, required co-operation between neighbours for no peasant could sustain a plough team of his own and harvest necessarily drew on all available labour.

Where livestock was reared, lambing and calving would be a busy time and would again draw heavily on all available labour, likewise the hay harvest, essential for winter fodder. Mowing using a scythe was men's work. The daily task of tending, feeding and milking livestock – both cows' and sheep's milk was used – would have drawn upon all members of the peasant household, including children, to do the tending in the fields and women the milking. These daily demands made it attractive for more affluent peasants to employ servants. Where dairying was a significant part of the family enterprise, moreover, wives and women servants would have spent time making butter and cheese, and may even have marketed these, together with eggs, chickens and other poultry; the poultry market of medieval Nottingham was referred to as the Woman Market. Washing and shearing sheep also appears to have been women's work and, to judge from manuscript depictions, women sometimes worked alongside men as shepherds. Once again, the demands of a pastoral economy necessitated co-operation between peasants, not least in determining when livestock could be pastured on common land. As with harvest, and prior to enclosure, such collective enterprise was regulated at a communal level. This is sometimes recorded in the form of ordinances or village by-laws such as those for Wymeswold (Leics.) made in the early fifteenth century.

Only peasants with a sufficiency of land could readily sustain cereal production or maintain livestock. Smallholders probably preferred to produce vegetables in a manner akin to the modern allotment keeper, but more substantial peasants likewise tended to maintain 'gardens' used to grow vegetables, herbs, flax, hemp, apples and sometimes even flowers to sell in the market. Such gardens tended to be the responsibility of peasant wives. As 'The Ballad of the Tyrannical Husband' indicates, however, the peasant economy depended not just on growing produce and rearing livestock. Where sheep were raised there was much work created carding, spinning and weaving woollen yarn. Similarly, where flax was grown, it needed to be processed and the linen yarn could then be woven. As the 'Ballad' implies, these were all historically women's work, though where a commercial rural textile industry emerges, notably in East Anglia, the West Riding of Yorkshire and the Cotswolds, we find numbers of male weavers.

Brewing has been much studied because the assize of ale, a regulation designed to tie the price when sold to the market price of barley, was regularly enforced at the manorial level by means of fines. These were nominally for 'breach of the assize', but in practice served as a licence for commercial brewing. Ale was a staple product in a society that did not have ready access to a safe water supply. For the most part it appears that brewing was confined to slightly better-off peasant households since there was some capital investment in brewing equipment. Much brewing would have been for domestic consumption and, judging from records of brewing fines, only a small proportion of brewsters (female brewers) brewed ale for public consumption on a very regular basis.

Another commercial activity where women appear conspicuously is petty retailing. The village would have depended on such retailers for a variety of basic daily needs, including bread and ale. This may have been an extension of women's role in marketing goods and purchasing against household needs. According to Fitzherbert, writing in the early sixteenth century, wives were to sell not just poultry and dairy products, but grain and pigs too. On the other hand, as Helena Graham found at Alrewas (Staffs.), most such petty retailers (hucksters or tranters) were married to smallholders and landless labourers or, like Maud Molet and Lettice Souter, supported themselves.[2] We have already noted that even peasant families with moderate holdings might periodically hire out the labour of family members as another source of income.

A comparatively marked gender division of labour is apparent, but we need not accept the simplistic model of the man going out while the woman stays at home, as presented by 'The Ballad of the Tyrannical Husband'. On one level this was a necessary plot device to set up the debate about the value of women's work, but it also performs a normative ideological function: we are meant to believe that is how things are because the author's notion of valuing women depended on placing them in the biblical paradigm of the good mother and household manager. Barbara Hanawalt has offered a similar model from her analysis of the records of accidental deaths recorded in coroners' rolls. She found that men died in work-related accidents occurring in 'the fields and forests', whereas the equivalent pattern for women was in the home.[3] Because deaths are most likely to occur in relation to hazardous work activities, Hanawalt's analysis overlooks many of the tasks noted above. In fact we can discern a more complex pattern in which men indeed tend to work outdoors, but where women periodically move between the house, the area around the house and the fields or beyond – to fetch water or produce from the garden, to feed livestock, to milk cows and sheep, to take produce to market, to engage in the hay and grain harvests.

The peasant economy was, then, essentially one of make do and mend. It depended on a range of activities and the labours of all members of the household other than the very young and the very old. Indeed the prevalence of economic openings besides agriculture may have been crucial in sustaining numbers of smallholders and labourers. Proximity to a market or town often explains the greater evidence for petty retailing on some manors. The rural worsted industry, to give a specific example, helps explain the high proportion of smallholders in later medieval Norfolk. This was also, as we have seen, an economy that depended on the availability of labour beyond the

---

2. H. Graham, "'A Woman's Work . . .": Labour and Gender in the Late Medieval Countryside', in P.J.P. Goldberg, ed., *Woman is a Worthy Wight: Women in English Society* c.*1200–1500* (Stroud, 1992), pp. 134–5.

3. B.A. Hanawalt, *The Ties that Bound: Peasant Families in Medieval England* (New York, 1986), p. 145.

immediate family group, whether this was collective enterprise, as at harvest time, group solidarity between neighbours, as for example in putting together a plough team, or contractual labour. The peasant household that bought in labour on a seasonal basis or engaged live-in servants through the year looked beyond self-sufficiency. Such households aimed to produce a marketable surplus in order to generate a cash income both for the benefit of the household members, but also to provide wages for employees and to pay rent to the lord. Conversely those whose livelihood depended to a lesser or greater degree on selling their labour were dependent on their more prosperous neighbours and employers producing surpluses, whether they purchased these in the market or were provided with food as part of their remuneration.

The material circumstances of labourers varied considerably over the era. Before the plague, peasant labourers tended to be in a fairly weak bargaining position: the combination of high population levels and consequent land scarcity meant that the numbers of landless and near landless who depended on selling their labour to others was greater than the actual demand from lords and more substantial peasants. These were lean years for the poor despite a modest improvement in wages in the three decades before the plague. It is likely that the custom of providing workers hired by the day with food, primarily in the form of bread, in addition to money wages helped keep numbers of poorer families afloat. (It should be noted that married labourers probably worked as a team; certainly the food allowances noted in manor account rolls were, as Christopher Dyer has found, sufficient to feed an entire family.)[4]

The bargaining position of labourers was transformed by the experience of the Black Death and the sustained demographic decline that followed in its wake. The consequences were improvements in wages (continuing until the last decades of the fifteenth century) and in the quality and diversity of the food provided by employers. Now meat, fish and ale formed a larger proportion of the diet. Food was frequently cooked and served hot where bread and cheese had hitherto been the norm. A more benign work discipline also followed: before the plague, competition for employment was acute and workers were consequently keen to please; after the plague workers could afford a more relaxed attitude. These changes occurred in spite of the new labour legislation initiated in 1349 and 1351, but repeatedly revised and enforced thereafter. This is not to say that this legislation had no effect – it almost certainly put a modest brake on wages – nor did it go unchallenged since it was a significant factor in the Revolt of 1381.

It is hard to document the many ways in which different peasant households made their livelihood. It is not much easier to recover the material culture of the peasantry. We may start with the peasant home. Some peasant housing survives from around the beginning of the fourteenth century, much more by the fifteenth and early sixteenth centuries. As always, however, what survives is probably skewed towards the buildings of the better-off. For the earliest part of our period, and for a sense of the broader range of peasant housing, we must look to archaeological and documentary sources. It used to be thought that most peasant housing stock before what W.G. Hoskins dubbed 'the great rebuilding' of the Elizabethan and early Stuart eras was poorly constructed, using materials such as mud and rubble, and essentially ephemeral, being

---

4. C. Dyer, 'Changes in Diet in the Late Middle Ages: The Case of Harvest Workers', *Agricultural History Review* 36 (1988), pp. 21–37.

rebuilt every generation or so. The pendulum has since swung the other way. It is now thought that much peasant housing was moderately substantially built, often timber-framed and certainly designed to last more than a single generation. Much work has yet to be done both to identify regional types and to establish some kind of hierarchy in terms of ownership, but two broad types are invariably identified: the longhouse and the farmstead or courtyard farm.

The longhouse seems to have been a widespread form from the beginning of our period. It comprised, as the name implies, a long, narrow, rectangular structure, divided internally between a byre for livestock and a living area. This last might itself be subdivided. Entrance was at the midpoint between the living area and byre. A central hearth provided warmth and a place for cooking within the living area. A drainage gully cut though the earthen floor ran down from this part of the building and through the lower, byre area. In winter, the animals sheltering in the byre would help generate additional heat, but the general arrangement must have been (to modern eyes) smelly, smoky and lacking in privacy. Later developments of the same basic structure allowed for the creation of an upper chamber within the domestic area and latterly for further living space to be created with the removal of livestock to a separate structure. During the fifteenth century chimneys also became more common. These larger structures would have allowed greater privacy and would also have provided accommodation for servants.

Although the longhouse remained a common type within the more pastoral-based rural economies of upland northern and western England, other forms were widely found in southern and eastern England. Here hall structures were associated with separate farm buildings, including barns. These might all be loosely arranged around a yard (the crew yard). Whereas before the Black Death these hall structures tended to be long and low, from the later fourteenth century we see evidence of a fairly significant rebuilding to create more substantial elevations that more readily allowed for accommodation at the first-floor level. Once again, these newer structures facilitated greater privacy, greater specialization of room function and the possibility of accommodating live-in servants. This last must again alert us to the fact that this narrative describes only the homes of the more affluent peasantry, husbandmen holding at least half a virgate.

The housing of poorer elements of peasant society, notably labourers and the elderly who had retired from the family home, is less conspicuous both in terms of the archaeology and of standing buildings. Maintenance contracts registered in the customary court rolls, whereby a tenant's heir (or others) took over the principal dwelling before the death of that tenant in return for support (maintenance) in old age, sometimes provide either for the creation of a separate room within the main home – akin to the modern 'granny flat'. Other contracts stipulated that the retiring person or couple was to be housed elsewhere on the family plot. Sometimes this took the form of finding, assigning or converting an existing cottage or farm building. When Agnes Mom of Great Waltham (Essex) surrendered her house and land in 1394 for the use of John atte Noke, she retained the use of the bakehouse as her home and was assigned use of the kitchen, a garden, fuel and an annual pension of 20d. In other instances a new cottage would be specially constructed. In 1281 the widow Agnes Brid of Ridgacre on the manor of Halesowen (Worcs.) handed over to her son Thomas. He in return agreed, among other things, to build her a timber-framed home 30 feet by 14 (10m x 5m) containing three 'new' doors and two new windows. That these last are specified as new is a reflection of the frequency with which worked timber was regularly reused for building purposes.

Agnes Brid could afford to be particular about the quality of her retirement home. It is likely that the many references to cottages in manorial documents describe inexpensive and insubstantial structures that would often have accommodated labourers. Such cottages were probably small, cramped and, by comparison to the more substantial two-storey houses of the later Middle Ages, with privies overhanging cesspits and the use of smoke hoods and smoke bays to channel smoke away from living areas, squalid. Such cottages were often cheaply constructed by the lord and in the fifteenth century were leased out at an annual rent of only 6d or at most 1s. As the population as a whole contracted from the later fourteenth century, numbers of these cottages were allowed to fall into ruin and were then cannibalized for their timber. Other labourers probably rented rooms in the houses of their more substantial neighbours.

Some peasant housing does survive, at least for the latter part of our period. The same cannot be said for most of the furniture and fittings that it contained. We do, however, have numbers of inventories, particularly from the second half of the fifteenth century. Even though limited to husbandmen, these suggest two things. They demonstrate precisely the same diversity of prosperity suggested by the evidence for landholding. If labourers were also represented, this would appear yet more marked. They also suggest certain peasant priorities. Most capital was tied up in livestock, grain and farm equipment. The value of household goods tends to be more modest. Thus William Atkynson of Helperby (Yorks., NR), whose inventory is dated 1456, possessed livestock valued at £4 11s 4d, grain (both stored and growing) of similar value and farming tools (including a horse and plough) worth £1 7s 10d. Atkynson was conscious of his status as a moderately prosperous husbandman: among his household goods were a salt cellar and some pewter saucers, a sideboard and a feather bed, but these goods as a whole (including brewing utensils) were worth less than £2. We may contrast this with the inventory of Robert Forcette, a York pewterer, dated 1460. The contents of his shop, the equivalent of the peasant's livestock, grain and tools, were similarly valued at £8 11s 4d, but his household goods were worth just over £8.

More modest were the possessions of Emmota Cowper of Dunnington (Yorks., ER) appraised in 1461. Her goods as a whole were valued at just under £1, of which her cow (worth 8s) together with a rent income of 4s (listed as an outstanding debt), together with what she might earn from carding wool, grinding pepper and selling the eggs from her three chickens, provide clues as to her meagre livelihood. Her clothing was valued at a mere 1s 8d and her bedding at 2s. Curiously, her few itemized possessions included a 'citole', a stringed instrument, but whether for her own entertainment or because she sang for her supper we cannot know. Emmota Cowper may be indicative of what may be dubbed the feminization of poverty, but she was hardly at the bottom of the heap. Numbers of peasant deponents in a lengthy church court case of 1365–66 include Joan Symkynwoman of Rawcliffe (Yorks., NR), who stated that she had 'almost nothing in goods save her clothing for body and bed, and a small brass pot'. Agnes de Polles, who was married to one Ralph de Hesyngwald, claimed to possess no more than a spinning wheel and a pair of cards (for carding wool). Such women probably found the opportunity to glean (collect stray stalks of grain) after the harvest, which was reserved to poor women and widows, the casual charity of their neighbours and doles provided at funerals, necessary supplements to a precarious existence.

Just as Emmota Cowper does not represent the lowest strand of peasant society, so William Atkynson probably does not represent the topmost level. The problem is that the boundaries between the upper peasantry – the sorts of people who are designated 'franklin' in some of the fourteenth-century poll tax returns and are dubbed 'yeomen' by the early sixteenth century – and the 'parish' gentry are not clearly delineated. They are blurred even more by the tendency of lords from the later fourteenth century to lease out the demesne and even entire manors to just such persons. On the other hand, we may discern a particular 'peasant' mentality that preferred to invest in land, livestock and agricultural tools rather than in household goods. There are probably a number of factors that underlie this observation, but one may relate to the power dynamics of the peasant household. Given the conservative gender ideology characteristic of peasant society, it is likely that male householders were the principal arbiters of how any surplus income should be spent or invested; their priorities were not with the domestic – that is, the furnishing and comfort of the house as home.

How far peasants invested in leisure and cultural pursuits cannot readily be recovered, but the alehouse was undoubtedly a focus for communal activity. Deposition material for the canonization of Thomas Cantelupe provides a rare glimpse of communal dancing and singing focused on a Herefordshire village pub in the late thirteenth century. The dancing took place outside the pub but, inside, food was served alongside ale. Football seems to have been played widely by peasant males, though we should probably distinguish between the sort of informal games between small groups of men and the occasional village-wide games such as the game held in Wistow (Yorks., ER) on the eve of Lent recalled by one Margaret Pyper in a church court deposition of 1422. Archery in the form of shooting at butts was encouraged as another activity for males following the renewal of war with France in 1337, even to the extent of outlawing (presumably to little effect) other sports. It is for this reason that archery practice, but not football, is depicted in the Luttrell Psalter of *c.*1340.

Recent scholarship, notably the work of Ronald Hutton, has drawn attention to the plethora of seasonal games, plays, 'mumming', dancing and the like that were a feature of peasant life. Numbers of these represent long-standing if evolving traditions with roots in a pagan past. The period following Christmas was a time of particular revelry, as bemoaned by Mirk in his *Festial*, a compilation of model homilies or sermons. May and Whitsuntide was another time of widespread festivity. In numbers of places we have evidence of May games involving particularly the local youth, who would elect a May king and queen. The day-long activities of the youth of Wistow involved the use of a barn as their summer hall. The 'royal' couple were supported by an entourage of soldiers and office holders. Midsummer or St John the Baptist's eve likewise saw festivity, usually revolving around the burning of bonfires. Other festal activities include mumming or folk drama involving players disguised as animals. Robin Hood plays also enjoyed popularity from the fifteenth century, but particularly in the earlier years of the sixteenth century. To these and other essentially secular activities we should add others revolving around the parish and the devotional life of the community, though to no small degree the two converged; a great deal of our evidence for the activities just described comes about because they were used as fundraising activities for the parish church. Church ales, whereby ale was brewed and sold for the benefit of parish funds, were also commonplace.

8 MERCHANTS, ARTISANS AND LABOURERS

One of the characteristics of urban society was that the majority of the resident population made their livelihood not out of agriculture but from trade and manufacture. Merchants were primarily traders. They might supply craftworkers with raw materials or they might trade in the goods such craftworkers produced, but they were not usually involved in manufacture themselves. Most craft activity was focused around small workshops owned by independent craft masters. Contemporaries sometimes described these craftsmen as artificers, but the more modern usage, artisan, is preferred here. Such workshops provided employment for the immediate members of the master's family, though sometimes it was his widow that took the place of the master. Also employed within these workshops were male and female servants, including apprentices, who lived with their employer as part of the household, and men and women who were employed within the workshop on a daily basis. Because these last worked by the day or (in French) *journée*, they are often referred to as journeymen by modern scholars. Contemporaries tended to talk simply of servants, and thus not to distinguish between live-in and other employees, or of labourers. We may thus distinguish between several categories of person in urban society: merchants, artisans, apprentices, live-in servants and journeymen or labourers.

The primary distinction between the merchant and the artisan is that the merchant trades in goods produced by others, be these wool, grain, timber, lead or a whole variety of manufactured goods, whereas the artisan is the actual producer of manufactured goods. Merchants might variously engage in local trade, regional trade or even international trade, as for example in respect of salt, cloth, timber, dyestuffs or wine. It follows that among the possessions associated with the merchant we may find horses and packsaddles and, in the case of wealthier merchants engaged in long-distance trade, ships or at least shares in ships. In the first part of our period especially, periodic fairs, including the great cloth fairs of St Ives or Stamford, represented a significant location for mercantile trade. By the fourteenth century, however, merchants came to be primarily located in an urban context and were able to display merchandise as part of their stock throughout the year. Similarly, whereas before the plague the aristocracy probably constituted the principal clients of merchants, latterly their client base probably broadened.

Artisans were essentially self-employed managers of small workshops who made their livelihood by purchasing raw materials, working them and then selling the finished product. Building craftsmen – masons, tilers (bricklayers), carpenters and the like – represent a significant exception to this pattern in so far as they frequently worked on a piece-rate basis, hence the use of building craftsmen's wages to determine wage series and standards of living. Tailors invariably worked with cloth supplied by the client rather than speculatively buying up cloth themselves. We should also include numbers of providers of services within the category 'artisan', notably scriveners, who provided essential writing and legal services, hostillers or innkeepers and barbers. The workshop could also function as a shop simply by having an opening with a counter on to the main street frontage, but we also find numbers of separate shops.

As always, these categories are not entirely clear or watertight, but they are still useful. Merchants or mercers can be understood as much in terms of their cultural and political aspirations as their involvement in trade. As we saw in Chapter 3, it was invariably groups of merchants who dominated civic government, and their commercial and magisterial interests were inevitably bound up together. Since Sylvia Thrupp's 1948 study *The Merchant Class of Medieval London*, scholars have regularly talked of a 'merchant class', a group that extended well beyond those styled mercer or merchant. Heather Swanson more recently articulated the perspective that merchants and artisans had essentially different and conflicting interests and outlooks, thus placing a Marxist spin on the term 'class'.[1] It is, however, clear that the boundaries are in fact fuzzy. Some artisans did not confine their economic activities to the business of their own workshop. Some, such as dyers or bookbinders, to cite a couple of examples, might sometimes subcontract other textile and book trade craftsmen and so control the finished product in a way that is indistinguishable from merchants. There were, moreover, a galaxy of retailers – tranters, hucksters, chapmen – that might collectively be described as petty traders rather than merchants, though the case of the York chapman, John Gryssop, is much less clear-cut to judge from the very extensive stock of goods and of wool listed in his 1446 probate inventory.

The medieval workshop, then, was often made of persons of different ages, marital status and gender. The division of labour between males and females tended to be generally less marked than in the countryside, but perhaps more subject to change over the period. Central to the medieval conception of the artisanal (and to a lesser extent the mercantile) household was the working partnership between husband and wife. This is implicit from guild ordinances. Once widowed, women from this level of society were ordinarily expected to take over the running of the workshop, an expectation that necessarily follows from their participation in the workshop while still married (and periodic, temporary management of the same during their husbands' absence or illness). This pattern probably became less common in the last part of our period. It is much harder to say whether the same was also true of the pre-plague era.

Before the later fifteenth century, the main gender differences in relation to work were neither spatial – home and workshop tended to be in essentially the same location – nor even type of work in so far as the activities of the workshop involved both husband and wife. Rather they were differences of work identity: men tended to be involved solely in the business of the workshop; women were expected to manage a variety of work activities, only some of which directly overlapped with those of their husbands. The household economy was not limited to the profits of the husband's craft, but depended instead on a range of activities in which the role of the wife was also of importance.

---

1. H. Swanson, 'The Illusion of Economic Structure: Craft Guilds in Late Medieval English Towns', *Past and Present* 121 (1988), pp. 29–48.

That the partnership of husband and wife in the workshop was understood as a given is reflected as much in the silence of the records about the role of wives. We have to look very hard to see this norm. Thus we find the London girdlers, in their ordinances of 1344, requiring that 'no one of the said craft shall set any women to work other than his wedded wife or his daughter'. In 1394, in a case before the church court of York, John Wyrsdall, a York barber, testified that one Juliana del Grene 'is a wife and lives by the labour of her husband and of her own hands', but went on to explain that Juliana carded wool and 'also follows the craft of the saddler with her husband'. At much the same date and from the same city, we have already seen (Chapter 5) that the founders' guild, then revising its regulations to limit to one the number of apprentices allowed to be employed in each workshop, made an exemption for Giles de Bonoyne 'because he has no wife'. It may be that close reading of records elsewhere will provide a few like examples, but the point is not that this evidence, because rare, is atypical, but that the social practice that underlies it is so normal that it is hardly ever commented upon.

It is only from the later fifteenth century, and then specifically in relation to weaving, an industry that seems to have been particularly vulnerable to economic change, that we begin to find evidence of craft guilds regulating against the employment of women in workshops. Perhaps the best known instance of this trend is found in the ordinances of the Bristol weavers of 1461, which talk of how 'various of the king's subjects, men liable to do the king service in his wars and in defence of this his land, and sufficiently skilled in the said craft, go vagrant and unemployed'. This they ascribe to the numbers of weavers who used their wives, daughters and female servants as part of the workforce. But even here the guild conceded that members 'may employ their wives during the natural life of the said women'. By 1511, however, the Norwich worsted weavers were prepared to take a more dogmatic approach, debarring women from the craft 'for that they be not of sufficient power to work the said worsteds as they ought to be wrought [worked]'.

Similar observations may be made in respect to widows as for wives. As a general rule, widows are simply not noticed in guild ordinances until the later fifteenth century, when we begin to find regulations designed to circumscribe the ability of widows to run workshops. Thus the weavers of Shrewsbury ruled in 1448 that widows could only trade for three months after their husbands' deaths and then solely to work through remaining materials. Once again, the appearance of ordinances designed to force widows to give up workshops is a telling indication that previously widows ran workshops without comment. Probate (will) evidence shows this to have been the case in as much as men sometimes bequeath tools to their widows, and widows likewise leave tools and name apprentices. Thus, to cite two examples from mid-fifteenth-century York, John Walton left his widow 'my best woollen loom and the things that pertain to it' and Emmot Pannall left her servant (perhaps apprentice) Richard Thorpp 'every single tool of my workshop relating to the saddler's craft'. Because it was assumed that any man taking up a workshop and being admitted to his craft as a master (and into the 'franchise' as a burgess or citizen) would be married, widows normally continued to enjoy these privileges and did not have to be separately registered. Guild and franchise records are therefore silent about the widows who formed part of their membership, though interestingly numbers of widows are named as attesting the ordinances of various of York's craft guilds during the latter years of the fourteenth century.

Guild ideology, then, constructed the workshop as a shared enterprise in which husband, wife and indeed other household dependants, both children and servants, were fully and perhaps wholly engaged. Two questions arise: how far did this ideology mirror practice and why was there a shift in thinking from the later fifteenth century? We will focus here on the first since a fuller consideration of the second belongs with our discussion of the economy of that period contained in Chapter 15. To summarize briefly, however, one key factor is the failure of the economy to keep pace with the supply of labour: as competition for work grew, men strove to hang on to work by eliminating competition, whether from 'aliens' (foreigners), 'foreigns' (persons who were not members of the franchise) or women. The result is that women end up being constructed as part of 'the other'. The language deployed by the Bristol weavers in 1461 is particularly revealing in this respect, touching as it does on the then topical issue of military service – only men fight, so only men can in this respect be loyal English subjects – and fear of the outsider – in the disordered world in which women take men's jobs, skilled weavers will become vagrants.

If instead of looking at the internal dynamics of the workshop from the perspective of guild ordinances, we turn instead to a variety of other records, including wills and probate inventories, it becomes clear that, like the peasant household, the economic viability of the artisanal household depended on a variety of activities going on under the same roof. Thus the York mason Hugh Grantham also possessed a substantial brewing business at his death in 1410, but there is reason to believe that it was his wife Agnes who actually managed this, for she was actively involved in it after his death. John Somerforde, an Exeter fuller noted in the later fourteenth century, also traded in hides, animal skins and meat, while (we may surmise) his wife dealt in dairy produce and poultry. Half a century on, the inventory of John Cadeby, a Beverley mason, shows his household also to have been involved in processing wool and flax, to have engaged in commercial brewing – he had brewing equipment, nearly £12 worth of malt and measures for selling ale – and to have kept a few pigs, ducks and chickens. Again it is likely that his wife and women servants would have been much involved in all these aspects of the household economy.

These examples could be repeated many times over. A like pattern is hinted at for a rather earlier period in the extant subsidy returns for Bishop's Lynn dating to sometime around the later 1280s. Henry le Iremonger, for example, as his name suggests, traded in hardware, but he seems also to have had interests in malt and herring. Emma, the wealthy widow of William Burel, probably traded in grain, but also sold ale and kept a cow. Assessed alongside her were her servants Roland and Isabel. Of course, Emma, by her very wealth, cannot be regarded as typical. It is likely that the first part of our period was one of great hardship for many women, including widows. As has been seen, for example, at Halesowen (Worcs.), women hucksters or petty retailers are sufficiently conspicuous in borough court rolls during the later thirteenth and early fourteenth centuries for being in breach of borough customs relating to trade as to suggest the fragility of their position and their poverty.

We have seen that by the later fifteenth century some guilds were attempting to exclude women from running or participating in the craft workshop. Although this is only explicit in some guild ordinances, and notably within the textiles sector, there is from this date much less evidence of widows continuing to manage workshops. No less significantly, whereas in the later fourteenth and earlier fifteenth centuries many artisanal households employed female servants alongside male, by the late fifteenth century such households were tending only to employ male servants. Certainly this appears to have been the case at York, to judge from the pattern of bequests to servants. Mercantile households, on the other hand, seem increasingly to have preferred to employ female servants. The pattern in early sixteenth-century Coventry is not as clear, but mercantile households again looked to employ numbers of female servants. This trend did not of course exclude women from the other economic activities of the household, but its effect would have been twofold. Its primary intended purpose was to protect male employment and to make it easier for young men who had served apprenticeships to gain access to workshops, but it would also have served to create spatially gendered spheres – that is, the male area of the workshop and the female area of the house. Once again this ties in with the language used by guilds to justify their policy of exclusion. The Bristol weavers in 1461 effectively invent the ethos of the male bread-winner; similarly the Norwich worsted weavers construct, by reference to women's supposed want of strength, a gendered model of roles 'natural' to men and women.

The division of townhouses into physically distinct craft and 'domestic' areas is difficult to establish and still more difficult to locate specifically in time, but there are indicators that it happened and that it happened at this time. In terms of more modest townhouses comprising at ground-floor level a shop facing the street at the front and opening on to a room or rooms behind (with further rooms on the upper floor) we can sometimes find evidence that a more solid partition has been inserted to separate the shop from the domestic area behind. The division is encapsulated in a later fifteenth-century deposition from London: the apprentice William Taylbos was able to assure the court that Rose Langtoft, a fellow servant, had never left her employer's house on a particular afternoon. He explained that he sat in the workshop all afternoon and so would have been able to see her leave, but he was only able see Rose washing clothes on the occasion that he went from the shop into the hall. Half a century earlier, however, John Colstan was able to see simultaneously into both the hall and the 'work-house' when inside the house of John Goddeshelp, a Scarborough weaver.

Quite a lot is known about the sort of houses townsfolk occupied, though more especially the well-to-do and during the last two centuries or so of our period. What is much harder to determine is precisely what sort of people occupied what sort of building and how the internal space was actually used. The picture is complicated by the way in which properties were often subdivided and sublet. In the thirteenth century we can find examples of larger properties comprising a principal block and subsidiary accommodation associated with people who were linked with the principal property holder by ties of kinship or trade. By at least the later fourteenth century it was not unusual for parts of properties to be leased out to provide a rent income to the occupants of the main dwelling or sometimes to an absentee (institutional or other) landlord; by the late Middle Ages most people rented their homes, though sometimes on long leases. In particular we find evidence for numbers of shops that appear to have been detached from the structures in which they were located and that feature separately in rental accounts. These were perhaps purely retail outlets, unlike the shops (cum workshops) that were an integral part of the houses of artisans.

Certain broad types of structure have been described by archaeologists of standing buildings. These vary regionally, between different parts of the same town and perhaps between different types of landlord. The core element, however, was always the hall. This could be 'parallel' to the street frontage, with services and solar or chamber placed further along the same frontage, or at right angles to the street. The latter had the advantage of allowing for subsequent development to extend into the burgage plot while maximizing the number of shops fronting the street. The most prosperous mercantile families might alternatively be accommodated in structures arranged around a courtyard. In origin some of these probably represent adaptations of rural housing, but the scale and complexity of houses, especially in the more prosperous central areas of the medieval town, and the proliferation of shops both as integral and semi-independent structures, would have appeared distinctively urban.

Focusing, so far as we are able, on housing associated with artisans, it would seem that the basic hall and solar/chamber structure was increasingly subdivided from some point in the post-plague era: the solar was subdivided to make two or more chambers and the hall was sometimes divided to create an additional floor. Occasionally a whole additional floor was added to the upper part of the house. Certainly fifteenth-century probate inventories reflect an increase in the number of rooms designated as chambers. By the late fifteenth century, it is apparent that space was assigned to specific members of the household, such as servants, or for single rather than multiple purposes. What we cannot know at this stage is how far and in what ways space within individual rooms might itself be subdivided by the use of screens or hangings, but probate inventories regularly list such items and also suggest that bed curtains were increasingly popular by this period.

The possibilities of privacy, and of shifting cultural values that are bound up with this, are tangentially reflected in evidence from various other disputed marriage cases from York. As we have seen, marriages could be made as a consequence of consummating a future contract. Such contracts were both more common in urban society than rural and also vulnerable to dispute since the man (for it was invariably the man) could either admit to sex but deny the contract, or concede the contract but deny sex. It fell to the female plaintiff to prove both. Through the fourteenth century, witnesses were called by the woman to give evidence that the couple had been seen in bed together unclothed. From the early years of the fifteenth century, however, such testimony ceases even though consummated contracts continue to be alleged for some years more. The implication is that by the early fifteenth century couples were beginning to retreat behind bed hangings or into separate chambers.

It follows that not only did artisans come to live in houses that were distinguished by the multiplicity of rooms they contained, but that this very proliferation may have encouraged or facilitated growing spatial demarcation along status and gender lines, with certain persons and certain tasks limited to particular areas of the building. At the same time we may detect a growth in privacy as it became possible for the married householders to sleep separately from their servants and children, and parlours were created as more intimate living areas separate from the hall. In a York marriage case, for example, when a young man called to see the daughter of the house, her mother showed the couple into the parlour – and then spied on them through a low window.

The bourgeoisie, if we may collectively so dub the level of society that were members of the franchise, employers of labour and managers of businesses, appear to have enjoyed a generally higher standard of living than their rural counterparts. They ate better, dressed better and, as we shall shortly see, furnished their homes more substantially. This is evidenced in the preference for wheaten bread over barley bread, the high consumption of fish and meat – mostly from young animals and hence tender cuts – and the use of wine in addition to the ubiquitous ale and, from the mid-fifteenth century, increasingly beer brewed with hops. Wills and probate inventories indicate not just the value of clothing worn, but the number of items each person possessed. The modest possessions of the Londoner, William Massyngere, for example, worth only 42s 6d in 1543, nevertheless included three gowns, which together accounted for just over half this sum. This pattern of consumption is not simply a product of wealth; it represents a difference of outlook and values that distinguished the bourgeois from the peasant even though the bourgeois was often, but a generation or two back, of peasant stock. It is likely, moreover, that these were self-conscious differences. The humour of the fifteenth-century 'Ballad of the Tyrannical Husband', written about a quarrelsome peasant couple and found uniquely in a London merchant's collection, no doubt depended in part on sophisticated city dwellers finding country bumpkins an object of ridicule.

Urban artisans seem generally to have invested much more freely in material possessions than their rural cousins. This can be seen after the Black Death when probate inventories become more common, but it is in any case likely to be more a feature of society after the plague. John Collan, a York goldsmith, had at his death in 1440 moveable goods worth just under £16. The contents of his workshop account for over £9 of this. What is striking, then, is not so much the value as the range of other household possessions spread between the hall, parlour, kitchen, two storerooms, a principal chamber and a second chamber. Each of the living rooms was hung with decorative hangings. Of those in the parlour, one depicted the Trinity, the other St George and the Virgin. Similarly, a representation of Our Lady of Mercy hung in the main chamber, which clearly functioned as a bedroom. The hall hangings depicted flowers. Trestle tables, benches, stools and beds were scattered between these same rooms. The main chamber contained in addition a quantity of bedding, towels, some tablecloths, several chests and, bizarrely, a cider press. The kitchen contained various jars, basins and pans, plus a pewter vessel valued at 6s 10½d. Many of the individual items, including the hangings, were in fact valued at only a few pence and much was described as 'old'. The impression, nevertheless, is of a house that was well furnished, comfortable by the standards of the day and not without some aesthetic appeal.

The rather more modest possessions of William Coltman, a York shoemaker (d. 1486) still suggest the same pattern. His goods were valued at only about £7, only a small part of which was accounted for by the contents of the workshop. The rest was contained between a hall and a parlour, both of which had hangings. He owned much the same range of furnishings as Collan, though on a more modest scale. These included a mazer and six spoons, two salt cellars and a pewter basin (valued at a mere 6d). The best feather bed, however, replete with bolster, tester and curtains, was valued at £1, nearly as much as the entire contents of the workshop. Right at the end of our period, the 1543 inventory of Robert Fosster, a London tailor, listed goods valued at a sum only slightly higher than Coltman's, but worth less in real terms due to the effects of price inflation. The range of items is strikingly similar. Again we find painted hangings, stools, cooking utensils, vessels, chests and bedding, but his bed was worth only 3s 4d. New fashions are modestly reflected in the possession of a carpet (valued at 8d) and a cotton nightgown (5s), though this last could be part of his stock. As with the other inventories, there is also the usual evidence of supplementary economic activity in the form of spinning wheels and a heckle for working flax.

The common presence of cooking utensils in artisanal households, and the frequent provision of such utensils to women servants alerts us to the fact that mercantile and artisanal households served as the locus for the preparation and consumption of food. This is an important point since, as we shall see shortly, journeymen and labourers may often have relied in part on meals provided by employers and on food purchased in pubs or from street vendors rather than on home cooking. The shared consumption of meals has long been regarded as one of the ways in which a household is defined, but here we see it also having a social significance. The kinds of food consumed can probably be read in similar ways. Bread and ale were very much staples in any context. Meat, poultry and fish, including shellfish, seem to have been consumed on a regular basis, especially in the generally more prosperous post-plague era. When a York apprentice wanted to impress his prospective father-in-law, he brought a goose for them to dine on. In earlier fifteenth-century Norwich, the Lollard Margery Baxter, the wife of a carpenter, was detected when a visiting servant found bacon cooking on a Friday, a day of fast (when her orthodox neighbours would have eaten fish). Various fruits seem also to have been an important component of the urban diet.

Our discussion thus far has emphasized the way in which the household economy depended upon the varied contributions of all its members. The presence of items such as wool, cards (for carding), spinning wheels, heckles, malt and brewing equipment alongside the tools and stock of the workshop is clearly indicative both of this and of the part played by women. Women, as household managers, likewise played a key role in determining what food was purchased and consumed at the various mealtimes. In the century or more after the Black Death, if not before, wives in particular participated actively in the business of the workshop in addition to these other activities and hence may have been seen by their spouses very much as business partners. It follows that over that period wives may have enjoyed rather more influence over the way in which the profits of production were expended than was true, for example, of peasant women. This must remain for the moment a hypothesis, but it would help explain the observed differences in patterns of investment in household goods and furnishings between artisanal and peasant households of similar economic standing. Indeed it is possible that, as in the first period of industrialization in the later eighteenth century, the spending power of women (or at least the influence women had over how money was spent) significantly stimulated demand for a whole range of household goods and services within the urban economy.

Journeymen and labourers are not as visible in the records as we would like. Often the sources that record them, both guild and civic, are hostile. In so far as most urban adolescents would – at least after the Black Death if not before – have been servants in the live-in 'life cycle' sense, labourers represent an older age group, albeit one extending from young adulthood to old age. As in rural society, it is likely that only a proportion of these would have been married. How far others lived together in more informal, and even transitory, relationships is likewise difficult to say. Even less visible are the children born to this labouring population. No doubt they played in the streets from an early age since their homes would have been cramped, and perhaps for large parts of the day either empty or housing harassed mothers too busy balancing the demands of a breastfeeding baby and the need to earn money from spinning, sewing or whatever to be able to play. Parents were no doubt relieved when their youngsters were of sufficient age to go to work in the households of artisans and merchants, so beginning a lifetime characterized by economic dependence and, because labourers had no access to the franchise, political subordination.

A substantial body of labourers found employment as assistants in the workshops of artisans or as employees of merchants. Numbers of these may have been skilled in the craft of the workshop and, in the earlier part of our period, may even have been identified by occupational bynames (surnames). We may suspect, for example, that Richard Wright, John Sporier and Thomas Lokesmyth, noted in the 1381 Derby poll tax listing, worked respectively as a carpenter, a spurrier and a locksmith. Such skill may have been learnt informally from having first worked in the workshop of the pertinent craft while in service as a youngster. It may also have been more formally acquired through an apprenticeship. The conventional view, based on German sources, that former apprentices would spend some time as journeymen, moving between workshops in different towns to gain experience of different practices before settling down as a master in their own right, has yet to be demonstrated for later medieval England. What is apparent, however, is that by the later fifteenth century guilds were tending to permit masters to employ several apprentices at a time or, at least, failing to enforce their own controls. Ex-apprentices, consequently, were finding it increasingly difficult to find openings and so a growing proportion would have had to resign themselves to careers as employees rather than as independent masters. By the end of our period it is likely that most former apprentices became and remained journeymen, and that the status of the apprentice was consequently eroded.

The journeyman employed in an artisanal household would have lived apart and walked to work. The long working day was tied broadly to the hours of daylight. In summer this could extend from about 5 am to 7 pm, though there appears to have been a degree of variation over time, between crafts and between localities. Employees were not, of course, expected to work these long hours without a break. They were allowed three or four meal or rest breaks, that in the middle of the day being at least an hour in length. Most of their food requirements would have been provided at work. Evenings, later Saturday afternoons, Sundays, all major feast days (and the later afternoons preceding them) would normally have been free from work and would have represented the only time many labouring families could have spent together. It is likely, however, that the pub, with its opportunities to socialize, to drink, to play games or sing, to gamble and even, in the case of unattached males, to purchase sexual services, would often have been the journeyman's preferred place of relaxation. Again this sort of conduct tended to be frowned upon by moralists and civic governors alike, thus re-enforcing the social hierarchy.

There are interesting hints, at least from post-plague London, that journeymen sometimes associated collectively. Inevitably we know this from hostile sources. In the aftermath of the events of 1381, the governors of London were fearful of any kind of potentially subversive collective activity, so such perceived threats are readily recorded. In 1387, the leading members of a group of cordwainers' journeymen were imprisoned for starting a journeymen's guild in the house of the London Dominicans. A guild of journeymen saddlers, referred to as 'yeomen', meeting in the church of St Vedast was likewise suppressed in 1396. The journeymen may well have been reacting to developments within their employers' guild that saw the acquisition of a charter of incorporation and the construction of a guildhall near St Vedast's at much the same time. The most interesting record, however, relates to the journeymen tailors who in 1415 were accused of renting entire houses together. The logic is that these were unmarried male employees whose behaviour contravened the bourgeois ideals of family, hierarchy and discipline. This also makes sense of the repetition of the term 'yeoman', which derives from 'young man'. A different perspective on journeymen enjoying a collective identity is hinted at in a marriage case from York in 1394. Here we find a group of four young unmarried saddlers going on a trip together one weekend. They only returned to York at ten o'clock on the Sunday night and then they all drank together in the lodgings of one of the group before making their way back to their respective homes.

Not all members of this labouring class would have so specific a work identity or have been contracted on a regular basis to assist in a workshop and so form part of their employer's household during working hours. Numbers of people were employed on a piece-rate basis or were self-employed, mainly in service occupations or petty retailing. Women were prominent among these groups; service occupations included, for example, laundry work, nursing and prostitution, all three dominated by women and all representative of the commercial application of roles traditionally assigned to women in the home. The primary textile processes of carding and spinning wool depended on large numbers of women workers. As we have seen before, such work was also undertaken by the women members of the artisanal household, but it is evident that numbers of other women attempted to support themselves by working on a piece-rate basis.

There is every reason to think that carders and spinsters were an exploited group who had to struggle to make ends meet. Indeed, Fitzherbert, writing in 1523, observed that 'a woman cannot get her living honestly with spinning on the distaff'. Textile entrepreneurs would supply the women with raw wool to be worked in their homes and would then pay them for the spun wool by weight. In Coventry, however, the authorities had repeatedly to attempt to regulate these weights to protect the spinsters. We find ordinances in 1449, 1451, 1513, 1518 and 1530; on these last three occasions truck wages (payment in kind rather than cash) were also prohibited. The Worcester civic ordinances of 1467 likewise outlawed the payment of truck wages to spinsters and other poor textile workers and at the same time required employers to give work exclusively to those resident in the city and its suburbs.

Spinning was seen as 'natural' to women, part of their gender identity; proverbially spinning, weeping and deceit were all part of a woman's birthright. The spinster, then, was viewed not as a skilled worker but specifically as a woman. Her conditions of employment were not protected by any guild. Rather, as just noted, civic government attempted to shield her from the worst excesses of exploitation very much as a work of charity. The logic behind this is not hard to determine. The woman who supported herself by spinning necessarily lacked a husband. Because her labour was proper to her gender – after the Fall, an angel gave a spade to Adam and a distaff to Eve – it was honest. Consequently she both merited and was in need of a guardian, a role that civic governors seem willingly to have adopted. At the same time employers from the same level of society as provided the civic government can be found leaving bequests to their spinsters as if a work of charity. Alice Chellow, a York merchant's widow, left 4d in 1466 to 'each poor woman who served me in the past by spinning'.

Substantial bequests of spinning wheels to support poor women can likewise be found in early sixteenth-century Coventry.

Women spinsters represent but one part of the spectrum of piece workers, petty traders, journeymen and labourers that made up the majority of the residents of urban and small-town society. Only some members of this broader labouring population enjoyed a stable trade identity; a number would have been single and some may have stayed single throughout their working lives. Many would have engaged in a variety of activities at different times in order to get by, sometimes crossing the boundary between the licit and the illicit. Borough court records contain numerous entries relating in particular to trading offences: selling goods in non-standard quantities (regrating); buying for resale goods before they come to market (forestalling); or a miscellany of deceitful practices such as selling candles without wicks, seen repeatedly in late fourteenth-century Nottingham. Once again it is noticeable that many of these traders were female. There is plenty of evidence to suggest that poor spinsters, laundresses, seamstresses and the like might periodically sell sexual services to supplement their meagre earnings. Civic ordinances likewise regularly targeted alehouses in connection with a whole sub-economy of thieving, gambling and prostitution, an understanding famously represented by the poet William Langland in his description of the clientele of the London alehouse patronized by Gluttony.

Part of the attraction of the alehouse would have been that it offered an opportunity to escape an otherwise impoverished and drab existence. We may suspect that football or the sorts of street games such as wrestling and shooting at cock that the Goodwife advised her eponymous daughter to shun were also aspects of this labouring culture. Part of that drab existence must have been the kinds of rented accommodation available to the labouring classes. The housing occupied by piece workers, petty traders, journeymen and the like does not survive as well as that of their employers, but some impressions are possible. We can discern two kinds of provision. First, there are cheap, purpose-built cottages and rows of inexpensive houses. These might be located away from the main commercial heart of the community, down passages between more substantial houses opening on to the street, or on the margins of churchyards. These last, of which Our Lady Row in York, dated to 1316, is the earliest and best known example of a fairly common type, were invariably built specifically to generate a rent income used to support a chantry within the church itself. Our Lady Row comprised a number of two-storey houses with a ground area somewhat less than six metres by four. Second, there was the accommodation provided by the subdivision of larger houses to provide rental income. Such properties could either represent a subdivision of houses once inhabited by more prosperous townsfolk or be purpose-built. This last appears to be the case, for example, with the many Wealden houses – a type otherwise associated with more prosperous peasant households in Kent and East Sussex – in Warwickshire towns, including Coventry.

Such inexpensive accommodation was represented, at the cheapest end of the market, by single rooms let out for no more than a few shillings per half year. The 1522 Coventry muster roll, for example, shows groups of labourers renting adjacent properties with rental values of four or five shillings. Rental evidence reveals the high level of turnover of tenants at this bottom end of the market. How far this represents a movement of tenants between properties, whether to avoid paying outstanding rent or otherwise, or a broader movement of people in and out of town is difficult to ascertain. We may also notice the tendency for groups of female tenants to bunch together within a particular area or group of properties as, for example, Grimsby Lane in Hull as noted from the 1377 poll tax or in the Aldwark area of York some 20 years later. For the early modern era this phenomenon has been described as 'spinster clustering', but it is in fact likely that numbers of the women observed were widows. No doubt they found some security and also a level of solidarity in the company of women.

The paucity of provision for cooking that must have been a feature at least of rooms at the bottom end of the market begs questions. Those labourers who were in regular employment in a workshop – journeymen in the way the term is conventionally used – would, as we have seen, have been given meals by their employer and would only have had to cater for themselves on Sundays and holidays. This group no doubt included numbers of single males, who may not have expected to cater for themselves. Those who supported themselves in piece work or service trades and did not spend their working day in someone else's house or workshop would, however, have been less well provided for. Women, as spinsters, seamstresses, laundresses, dealers in second-hand clothing and such like, would have been disproportionately represented among these, though such women were perhaps better socialized to improvise cooking. It is tempting to speculate that women who lived in close proximity may also have co-operated to a degree in terms of preparing food and cooking. The other factors in the equations are the public house as a place where cooked food could be purchased – ale itself also had some nutritional value – and the many (usually female) retailers of the medieval equivalent of fast food. In particular we may notice the vendors of hot pies, presented periodically in the borough courts for selling pies that had been reheated. These vendors were very much an urban phenomenon, but they are almost certainly also a class phenomenon.

Our discussion so far has focused on the material circumstances of the different levels of urban society. In particular we have described a bourgeois identity and values that, to continue a Marxist discourse, differed markedly from those of a labouring proletariat. We have also noticed the rather different circumstances of men and women at different levels of society. Poor spinsters, seamstresses, petty retailers and the like seem to have been particularly conspicuous at the margins of society, suggesting a particular gender dimension to poverty. These differences of experience can in part be understood by adopting a rather different perspective that focuses on life cycle and life course.

It is no easy matter to outline the stages in the life courses of the later medieval bourgeois or bourgeoise achieving adulthood. Any such attempt must be hedged about with caveats. The conventional wisdom, based on little evidence, is that children were expected to begin to contribute to the household economy from about seven years of age. We can be more confident that many youngsters – at least from the time of the Black Death – went into service in or by their early teens and may well have remained there until their early twenties. Boys going into formal apprenticeships probably did so at 14 and, by normally serving for a period of 7 years, would complete their term when aged 21 or thereabouts. For the first part of our period, however, it may have been more common for children to remain within the natal household and even for boys to be apprenticed to their own fathers. The length of apprenticeships also tended to be less standardized at this date. The point at which young people left service was the point at which they might look to marry, though our knowledge of actual marriage ages is fragile. It likewise represents the point at which more well-to-do young males would first take up the urban franchise as burgesses or citizens, and simultaneously be enrolled in a craft guild.

Charles Phythian-Adams' study of the career cycle of Coventry citizens in the earlier sixteenth century found that some guildsmen achieved minor office in their craft by their early thirties.[2] By the time they were about 40, those with political ambitions may have obtained their first civic position as chamberlain, though evidence elsewhere suggests that such men may first have held office at ward level. At the same time they would first be included in the membership of the city's common council of 48. Several years later they might be appointed a leet jurat or gain higher office as sheriff. Only by their mid-fifties, and hence towards the end of their working career and ordinary lifespan, might they first serve as mayor and become a member of the inner group of 12 jurats. What is apparent here and at York is that young men from the most privileged mercantile backgrounds and families might enjoy accelerated promotion. Men from artisanal crafts rarely progressed beyond minor office. A significant proportion of adult mercantile males probably had some experience of civic administration, but only a minority of artisans.

The life course of women, for whom a career in civic government was simply not a possibility and who rarely played much role in guild politics even as widows, must be treated separately. For most, marriage would lead to repeated childbearing. Margery Kempe, the Bishop's Lynn merchant's wife, it will be remembered, bore 14 children before she obliged her husband to abstain from sex. The likelihood, then, is that many wives were bearing children over a period of some 20 years and no doubt continued to be actively involved in the rearing of those born at the end of that time for a further decade or so. If they and their husband lived into their fifties, however, it is likely that they would have been free of childcare responsibilities by the time they were widowed. At least before the later fifteenth century, such widows would have been free to continue to run the family workshop, if only for a comparatively brief interval before their own death. Women widowed younger, especially those with young children to support, may often have remarried, though we can find examples of women who enjoyed long widowhoods. One such is Marion Kent, the widow of a York mercer who held office in the guild during the later fifteenth century. The comparative rarity of such long widowhoods explains why widows are not more conspicuous as heads of workshops or as active members of their craft guilds, and hence also their political weakness in the face of growing restrictions on their running of workshops from the later years of the fifteenth century.

For those born to the ranks of the bourgeoisie, then, there was much emphasis on being trained, particularly through service and apprenticeship, in both the skills and the values needed to run a family enterprise. Male apprentices would aspire to become masters in their own right and to manage a workshop. They would expect to marry at the same time, so marriage represented a sort of social coming of age. Conversely, as the mid-fourteenth-century verse 'What the Goodwife Taught her Daughter' indicates, girls were socialized to assist their husbands and might only head the family business in his absence or on his death. (Even that last option was eroded by the very end of our period.) Girls might thus learn craft skills, but not with a view to setting up their

---

2. C. Phythian-Adams, *Desolation of a City* (Cambridge, 1979), Table 8, p. 126.

own businesses. Bourgeois parents would also provide for their children materially in ways that poorer parents simply could not match. Towns were never closed communities, however. Immigration was the main means by which towns sustained and indeed increased their numbers. Consequently there had always to be means by which outsiders could be absorbed and socialized into different groups. In the labour-scarce conditions following the plague it is likely that numbers of sons of peasant agriculturalists were taken on as apprentices, just as at other times rural artisans came to the town or city to take advantage of the larger market. Both groups could gain access to the urban franchise, by which the boundaries between householding and labouring households came to be defined, by right of apprenticeship or redemption (purchase), respectively.

Children from poorer families, whether born within the town or the surrounding countryside, lacked the advantage of hereditary wealth by which to be taken on as apprentices, to purchase tools or raw materials beyond the most basic and inexpensive, or to acquire workshops or admission to the franchise. The journeyman weaver, for example, owed his loom to his employer; the journeyman tanner could never have afforded the hides that were his raw materials, nor could he have had access to tanning pits other than his employer's. The seamstress could afford her needle and thread, but her materials were those supplied by her clients. The journeyman's son or the spinster's daughter might well be taken on as servants, but never as apprentices. They might acquire craft skills, but would never aspire to running a workshop. If they married, the costs of childrearing would have ensured that their capacity for saving, even in the comparatively prosperous years of labour scarcity, would have been limited. It is likely in fact that any surplus income was treated as a windfall to be spent quickly. The gulf between the haves and the have-nots was wide.

9 LORDS, KNIGHTS, ESQUIRES AND GENTLEMEN

The traditional medieval social model comprised three elements: those who labour; those who pray; and those who fight. Each supposedly needed the other: the authority of the lord was predicated on his ability to defend the priest and the peasant alike. The Marxist model of medieval society describes but two classes of people: those who own the land – lords; and those who work the land – the peasantry. In Marxist terminology this social arrangement is called 'feudal' since the relationship between lord and peasant was determined by law and custom rather than by a money nexus, such as is found within capitalist social relations. The effect of this latter model is to stress the conflict of interest between two monolithic groups, those who owned the means of production and those that were the means of production. It is this conflict that defines class boundaries. Within this Marxist model there is nothing remarkable about peasant resistance and even revolt or seigneurial exploitation or oppression. We have already seen that peasant society is rather more diverse than might be suggested from either model. The same can be said of the aristocracy. The boundaries between the two groups are, moreover, more fuzzy on close inspection than might otherwise be expected.

The terminology that is used to describe the landowning classes needs some explanation. Broadly speaking, most scholars use 'aristocracy' as a blanket term to describe all levels of society from lords of single manors to holders of vast landed estates. Many, however, distinguish between a 'lesser' aristocracy – knights, esquires and gentlemen – and a 'greater' aristocracy – barons, earls, dukes. Sometimes the terms nobility, nobles, peerage or peers are preferred for the latter group. The lesser aristocracy are often collectively referred to as 'the gentry'. What needs immediately to be understood is that the term 'gentry' does not solely describe 'gentlemen', which itself is in any case a usage not found before the end of the fourteenth century. 'Gentry' also encompasses those people who were dubbed knights or styled esquires and their immediate families, hence the title of this chapter. The term 'gentleman' is itself sometimes qualified in modern scholarly literature, the lowest echelon being labelled 'parish' or even 'mere' gentry, persons who normally exercised lordship solely at manorial level (and sometimes not even that).

These latter usages in a sense recognize the very real gulf that exists between such petty landowners and persons of greater rank, and warn us that the boundaries between well-to-do peasants and the lowest levels of the aristocracy are not always clear. Indeed where by the later fourteenth century peasants were renting the manorial demesne or in some cases even 'farming' (paying a fixed rent for) entire manors, and hence exercising de facto lordship through the customary courts as part of the manorial revenue, these differences would not have been immediately obvious.

Similarly, we know that numbers of gentry families, most famously the fifteenth-century Norfolk gentry family who took their name from the village of Paston, emerged from peasant stock within a couple of generations. We need, therefore, to look not just at patterns of property holding or wealth, but also at cultural values and ideology. Likewise we should not confine ourselves to the political ambitions of lesser aristocratic men, but consider gentry society more generally.

The actual numbers of individuals and households associated with the different ranks of aristocratic society obviously fluctuated over time, but some very rough estimates can be offered. At the beginning of our period there were perhaps some 200 persons who could be described as belonging to the upper ranks of the aristocracy. By 1500, a low ebb, there were only some 60 peers – that is, persons who were liable to be summoned personally to Parliament by virtue of their rank. Much more numerous were men of knightly or lesser rank. In 1300 there were some 1250 to 1500 knights and a perhaps slightly larger number of esquires. Again, these numbers had contracted somewhat by the earlier fifteenth century and still further by the earlier sixteenth century. The term 'gentlemen' does not emerge until the late fourteenth century and, because the term lacks any definition, numbers become particularly difficult to calculate. By 1524 there are thought to have been some 4000 to 5000 gentlemen and esquires. This may be a conservative estimate of the actual number who aspired to be known as gentlemen even at that date. Certainly the redistribution of Church lands following the dissolution of the monasteries heralded a long period of growth in gentry numbers.

The actual numbers and distribution by status group varied considerably not just over time, but geographically. By the end of our period, Surrey had the highest proportion of resident gentry. The western counties and Kent may also have seen larger than average numbers. Most villages, however, had neither a resident knight nor resident esquire. This can be seen from the later fourteenth-century poll tax returns, which are sometimes arranged with the person of highest social rank at the head of the return for each vill. Of 23 villages in the Tunstead hundred of Norfolk in 1379, 4 were headed by knights or their widows, 1 by an esquire and 1 by a franklin's widow. Likewise, the 30-odd villages and hamlets of the Blackburn wapentake of Lancashire in 1379 included a knight and 7 esquires at their heads. Of 19 communities (including Liverpool) in the West Derby wapentake of Lancashire, however, 3 were headed by knights, 10 by esquires and 1 by a franklin. The esquires were themselves variously assessed at 20s, 6s 8d and 40d according to their landed possessions and hence, in some instances, below the level of the franklin. The franklin is here and in numbers of other cases – the West Riding of Yorkshire is but one example – probably representative of the sort of men who would a generation or so later be styled 'gentleman'.

The boundaries between the lower echelons of the aristocracy and men of lesser rank were always permeable and seem to have been as much cultural as economic. During the course of the later Middle Ages it is apparent that the gentry were fashioning an identity for themselves. The reasons for this are various. The essentially military nature of aristocratic society had but limited utility in a stable and increasingly bureaucratic system of royal government. It had to a degree been sustained by the war with France, but military prowess and valour in battle ceased to be the qualities (if they ever were) that served to enhance the fortunes or political ambitions of the lesser aristocracy at the end of the Middle Ages. Warfare had come to depend much more on the firepower of unmounted archers or of early artillery than costly, but vulnerable mounted knights. By the fifteenth century knowledge of the law and expertise in how to manipulate the law to one's own ends were as important as knowing how to wield a sword. Indeed by this time it was becoming usual for gentry sons to spend time at the Inns of Court specifically to acquire some kind of legal grounding.

Just as military expertise, nurtured by training from childhood, came to matter less, so legal and administrative capacity became more important. By the second half of the fourteenth century the Crown was regularly turning to the upper echelons of the gentry to carry out administrative and legal responsibilities as Justices of the Peace, (briefly) Justices of Labourers or on various commissions. The esquire, Thomas Farnham of Netherhall (Leics.), is an unexceptional fifteenth-century example. He several times sat as a JP, on commissions of gaol delivery and on a commission of array in a career spanning some 20 years. The rationale from the Crown's perspective was that these men of lesser rank made effective servants because their social and political standing could only be enhanced by royal office, whereas the greater aristocracy enjoyed power in their own right. In practice, particularly during the course of the fifteenth century, the Crown's purpose was frequently subverted by the manner in which the greater aristocracy attempted to influence these appointments, but this did not alter the changing role of the gentry themselves. On the other hand, the civil wars of the later fifteenth century ensured that the military capacity of the gentry remained a facet of their identity and it is this that is regularly memorialized in sepulchral monuments and brasses; the dead knight's actual helm (helmet) was invariably hung above the tomb.

To the ranks of a hereditary lesser aristocracy, new men were always being added. Wealthy burgesses or citizens, particularly those who had held office as mayor or as burgess member of Parliament were sometimes made knights. William Walworth, the then mayor of London, and Nicholas Brembre, both knighted by the young Richard II for their support during the events of 1381, probably represent the earliest instances of a pattern that became more common from the late fifteenth century. Between 1472 and 1550 some 21 mayors of London were knighted. Sir John Gilyot of York was knighted in 1503 during his second term as mayor, having also sat in Parliament. He consolidated his new status by marrying a daughter of an established knightly family after the death of his first wife. Even without formal title, some city mayors and aldermen might identify themselves as of gentle status, perhaps particularly where they had been associated with royal service. Nicholas Blackburn senior, mayor of York in 1412, for example, is represented in full armour in a window in his parish church. The daughters of such men sometimes married into more established gentry families.

Another route into gentry society was the law. The most famous example is that of the Pastons, a Norfolk gentry family documented through the fifteenth century by their voluminous archive of correspondence. Clement Paston was a peasant agriculturalist, who used the ready availability of land after the Black Death to his advantage. He married the sister of a lawyer and subsequently invested some of his income in schooling their son William, who was born in 1378. William Paston gained a legal training and embarked on a career first as a lawyer in Norwich, but subsequently in royal service as a sergeant-at-law, becoming in time a judge in the court of Common Pleas. He used his success to invest in land, but also to make a 'good' marriage. In 1420 at the late age of 42 he married an 18-year-old heiress. When the oldest son of that marriage was 19 he then arranged his marriage to another heiress. Through a process of land acquisition and shrewd marriages, therefore, the Pastons were assimilated into gentry society. By 1466 the family was even able to use their legal skills to fabricate an armigerous pedigree going back to the Conquest.

The Pastons' arrival into the middling rank of aristocratic society is perhaps atypical, but from the earlier fifteenth century we can find numbers of men with a legal training in civic, aristocratic or royal service, who were styled and styled themselves 'gentleman'. The Cornishman, Simon Yerll, a clerk employed in the exchequer, is thus named in a grant of land dated 1419. Yerll's position reflects a broader shift whereby laymen came to displace clergy in administrative and bureaucratic posts. There was also a growth in demand for men more skilled in the law, letter writing and accountancy than in the art of war. Such men were able to invest in land over time, but the windfall created by the dissolution allowed a whole generation of new men to become landed gentry.

The comparative fluidity of the ranks of the aristocracy does not, of course, mean that change, the emergence of new names and families, the creation of new titles went unremarked or unchallenged. Richard II's unprecedented appointment in 1397 of several of his allies to the rank of duke was a cause of considerable resentment. The new creations were contemptuously referred to as *duketti* (little dukes or 'dukelets'). The rapid rise of the de la Poles, from Hull merchant family to dukes of Suffolk in two generations, was noticed unfavourably by older magnate families. The intense hostility shown by Thomas Howard, third duke of Norfolk towards Thomas Cromwell, culminating in his destruction of Cromwell in 1540, was no doubt fuelled in part by Norfolk's dislike of the Putney brewer's son who had risen to be the king's chief minister and had been created earl of Essex that same year. The sensitivity of the Pastons to their peasant origins is well known.

Aristocratic standing seems sometimes to have depended on the respect afforded individuals by their social inferiors. In line with medieval social theory, members of the aristocracy seem to have been looked to in order to provide leadership at times of crisis. In one sense we find this in the willingness of peasant men in the marches to go in the service of their lord to defend against Welsh or Scottish incursions. We see it again in the way peasant risings seem sometimes to have tried to co-opt members of the local gentry to their cause. The other side of this phenomenon is suggested by two incidents from the Peasants' Revolt of 1381. Among many properties attacked was that of John Reed of Rougham (Norfolk). Neither a justice nor a tax collector, he still seems to have roused an unusual degree of hostility, particularly among his tenants. One clue is that he owed his position as lord of the manor to his marriage to Alice de Rougham and not to his own more humble ancestry. Another victim of the Norfolk rebels was Sir Robert Salle. Unlike the comparatively small number of other victims of the rebels, he had played no obvious role in royal government or administration. His mistake, according to Froissart's account, was that he disparaged the rebels, who had wanted to co-opt him to their cause, even though 'he was not by birth a gentleman'.

Froissart's narrative of Salle's death is telling not for its authenticity, but for the fact that he was addressing an aristocratic audience. In writing of Salle he contrasts his humble birth with his 'great renown for his ability and courage'; 'he was the most handsome and strongest man in England'. Froissart's point is that nobility was not necessarily the accident of lineage, but rather an innate quality that manifests itself in terms of martial virtues and physical appearance. It is these qualities that distinguish Salle from the peasant gang who, by reminding him of his humble origins – 'you are not a gentleman, but a poor mason's son, much like ourselves' – had asked him to be their leader. Contemporary romances such as *Havelok the Dane* likewise tell of nobles abandoned as infants and brought up in poverty, ignorant of their true status, who show great courage and perform remarkable deeds of arms on coming of age. The romances, however, though they define nobility in terms of particular deeply rooted values and virtues also emphasize that nobility is a product of birth.

The concern to place emphasis on family and on lineage follows as a reaction to precisely the sort of influx of new men and new families just described. Gentry families seem to have been concerned to impress their name on the locality where they held their lands. Older established families may have enjoyed ties of patronage with religious houses, as for example different branches of the Roos family at Kirkham Priory (Yorks., ER) and at Belvoir Priory (Leics.). Some possessed their own private chapels. Lesser families, however, seem to have exploited their parish churches to this end. Thus we may find family arms prominently displayed on the fabric, in stalls, in windows and on monuments. Sometimes, as at Harewood near Leeds, a parish church became in effect a family mausoleum, a sort of parochial Westminster Abbey, though brasses rather than three-dimensional sepulchral monuments often fill the limited space available. We see this, for example, in the brasses of the Eyre family at Hathersage (Derby.) or the late fifteenth-century brasses of the Peyton family at Isleham (Cambs.). One of the most striking examples is the parish church of Cobham (Kent), elevated in 1362 to a college by John de Cobham, who effectively converted the parish church to a family chantry and memorial to the family.

The effect of this proliferation of ancestral monuments and the memorialization of family members through daily masses was, as in the Luttrell Psalter, to draw the parish community into the process of remembrance, but also to assert a historical sense of ownership. Where the family manor house was adjacent to the church, as was true of the Griffith manor house at Burton Agnes (Yorks., ER), the church indeed became akin to a private chapel. Even comparatively new families could, through a judicious degree of patronage, ensure that their arms and their monuments were conspicuously displayed in the parish church and so give the impression of permanence and possession that might be entirely fictional. Slightly different was the purpose of Sir William de Etchingham at Etchingham (Sussex) in the 1360s where the windows served to promote an old-established family's ties to members of the nobility. Comparatively few families, however, could have matched the grand glazing scheme of this knightly patron.

The proliferation of heraldry in manuscripts, in glass, on church architecture and on monuments from the beginning of the fourteenth century serves to assert lordship, but by the fifteenth century the quartering of arms, whereby the shield is divided into four sections, suggests a new trend. Heraldry moved from being primarily a means of identification in battle, for which simple, bold designs were obligatory, to a signifier of estate and pedigree. The association of heraldry with a martial culture was not, however, lost. Members of even the lesser aristocracy are represented in glass, on their sepulchral monuments or their brasses in full armour, their armorial bearings clearly displayed.

Such a masculine and martial culture was sustained through our period by the extended periods of warfare in Wales, Scotland (notably under the first two Edwards) and France, and even by civil war in England. It is probable that most young men, and particularly younger sons, of greater or middling aristocratic parentage had some experience of actual fighting even if very few were to make their career as soldiers. The example of the Gloucestershire knight, Peter le Veel, who served in 14 campaigns between 1349 and 1381, contrasts markedly with the norm of a single campaign associated with other gentry of the same county during the fourteenth century. It follows that military service marked something of a coming of age against which a boy had to be trained and subsequently equipped, specifically with armour, horse and saddle; John Woodcock, a Yorkshire gentleman, held no land at the time of his execution in 1424, but he did possess a fully equipped horse, a sword and long dagger, a silver belt and a furred gown. These needs demanded a degree of wealth, but also a particular upbringing.

Aristocratic culture is popularly associated with jousting and tournaments. These were means by which military skills and prowess could be displayed outside the context of war. They may also have become primarily concerned with display, entertainment, even propaganda. Hunting, jealously guarded as an aristocratic preserve, would have provided a much more frequent opportunity to develop skills in horsemanship. But military training was not confined to the practicalities of swordsmanship or riding a horse. It also came to encompass a whole ethos known as chivalry, by which virtues such as courtesy, generosity and piety were grafted on to a warrior culture.

Such values permeate contemporary literature, notably romances, but also some history writing. It was the specific concern of treatises by authors such as Geoffrey de Charny and Ramon Lull, whose *Book of the Order of Chivalry* was translated and printed by Caxton in 1494. Alongside these we may set such didactic writings as Jacques Legrand's *The Book of Good Manners*, a publishing phenomenon at the end of the fifteenth century, John Russell's *Book of Nurture*, or various texts on table manners such as Lydgate's *Stans Puer ad Mensam* (the boy standing at the table), so necessary, as we shall see, in a culture that placed much emphasis on communal eating. In the early sixteenth century Henry Percy, fifth earl of Northumberland, had his castles of Wressle and Leconfield (Yorks., ER), his principal residences, decorated with verse inscriptions of a didactic nature. Some of these seem specifically intended to provide moral instruction to the younger members of the earl's household, including his heir, whose private room at Leconfield contained verse proverbs that urged him to 'virtuous exercise'.

In writing about a military aristocracy much emphasis has been placed on warfare, on the associated activities of the hunt and the tournament, on their role in politics and government, and on the idea and practice of chivalry. This perspective tends to privilege the higher-status adult male in respect of certain very public activities. On the other hand, the aristocratic female, junior members of the household and activities focused on the place of residence rather than the court or the field of battle, are not seen as so pivotal to an understanding of this level of society. They are in fact central. Happily, scholars have begun to take an interest in such issues, notably Jennifer Ward and Barbara Harris on aristocratic women, and Christopher Woolgar on the (greater) aristocratic household. It is clear there is still much work to be done, not least in terms of the lives of lesser gentry.

The aristocratic household tended to be composed of numbers of people, though it was only the noble household that comprised some tens of persons, even in some cases 100 or more, particularly by the early sixteenth century. Hugh Audley, the husband of one of the Clare heiresses, had a household calculated at some 96 persons in 1320. Edward Stafford, duke of Buckingham, had some 157 persons in his household at Thornbury in 1507–8. We tend to know less about lesser households, but it is evident they could be much more modest. Thomas de Saltmersh, esquire of Saltmarsh (Yorks., ER) is listed with just seven servants, including a nurse, in the 1379 poll tax returns. Likewise Sir Richard de Goldesburgh of Goldsborough (Yorks., WR) is recorded the same year alongside his daughter and ten servants, again including a nurse. Sir Roger Townshend of East Raynham (Norfolk) employed at least 15 resident servants at the end of the fifteenth century.

The immediate family need not be large, although it is less than certain that a nuclear system prevailed. It was the presence of numbers of servants, including, in the case of greater households, retainers and office holders, that swelled the overall size. Gentlemen and even knights served in magnate households, sometimes filling the role of counsellors, but, in respect of young men and boys, including pages, effectively following a kind of aristocratic apprenticeship. The lady would invariably have one or more female attendants. In a great household she might have a number of ladies to attend her as much as companions as menials. Many of these were young women (damsels) being similarly groomed to run a large household in their own right once a little older and married, but also to make potentially valuable social connections with families of rank. This, for example, is precisely what Margaret Paston hoped in seeking such a position for her daughter Margery. For the best families the prize was service in the queen's household, but this required political connections, physical beauty and suitable disposition. Households might also employ female nurses, laundresses and the like. Most household staff, however, were male, this being especially true of higher-status households and particularly the royal household.

The physical structures – the manor houses, the fortified houses, the castles – that contained these households likewise varied considerably in scale and grandeur according to the rank of the occupant. Great lords, moreover, often had several residences on different parts of scattered estates and might move between them through the year. This was especially true during the earlier part of our period. The 1296–97 itinerary of Joan de Valence, the widowed daughter of the earl of Pembroke, shows, for example, her residing at eight different locations on her estates, though she stayed briefly at several further while travelling. At the heart, both metaphorically and physically, of these houses was the hall. The hall might serve a variety of functions beyond being simply the place where communal eating took place. In manor houses it was probably the venue of the regular sessions of the customary court. It was also where entertainment in the form of music, acrobatic performances and plays took place.

The hall lent itself to drama. Indeed the hall was specifically a dramatic space in which social relations were played out and appropriate conduct learnt. The lord sat with his immediate family and more important guests on a dais at the 'high' end of the hall, visible to all present. Others sat along the sides of the hall or, by the latter part of our period, at separate tables arranged in descending order of seniority within the main body of the hall. The late medieval greater aristocratic household seems to have been particularly status conscious: the lord's table was presented with a different range of meat, including veal, ceremoniously carved at the table, and fish, including freshwater fish, from that served at the tables of those of gentle rank; those below the rank of gentry ate differently again. The fashion for large oriel windows at the high end of the hall by the late medieval era likewise served to illuminate the high table and focus attention on the lord. At the same time there is reason to believe that lords might ordinarily eat separately and only dine in the great hall on more important occasions.

Communal eating served a number of functions beyond the purely pragmatic. It was an opportunity to display the chivalric quality of largesse – what social historians would dub 'conspicuous consumption'. It was a vehicle for reinforcing a sense of community in the service of the lord. It was a means by which the piety of the lord, another chivalric virtue, could be marked through the annual cycle of feasting and fasting, but also by the provision of food for numbers of poor. A lord's claims to political influence and the exercise of government in his locality could likewise be demonstrated through his observed good management of the household gathered in the hall. These different functions are well documented, but only for the greater aristocratic household, hence our choice of examples.

In the early fifteenth century Dame Alice de Bryene, a wealthy Suffolk widow, dined regularly with local landowners of knightly rank, local clergy and visiting friars as well as kin, estate officials and even estate workers. On New Year's Day she provided for some 300 persons made up of tenants and others. In this way Dame Alice was kept informed of regional politics, asserted her authority over her estate and manifested good lordship by rewarding her tenants and employees. During the festive season of Christmas the importance of hospitality reached new levels. That of the duke of Buckingham at Thornbury was particularly lavish: 294 persons dined there on Christmas Day 1507, considerably more than twice the usual household, but on the following Twelfth Night numbers had risen to 459. Easter was liturgically the more important festival and was likewise marked by large-scale entertainment.

From the high table the lord and his immediate family could retreat through doors located on the wall behind them into their own private apartments. These might comprise a number of rooms including a chapel. At least at the beginning of our period, the other members of the household, guests and others, who might include poor persons supported by way of charity, shifted as best they were able, even bedding down in the hall. The accommodation afforded by the great house seems to have become progressively more generous with the passage of time. At the Scrope castle at Castle Bolton in Wensleydale (Yorks., NR), built at the end of the fourteenth century, we find two smaller halls in addition to the great hall. This suggests that, here, the lord may sometimes have dined more intimately with his immediate household. It may also suggest, as we find in the remodelled facilities at the neighbouring Neville castle of Middleham, that some members of the lord's household were allowed their own familial accommodation. Sir John Fastolf's Caister Castle, built around the middle of the fifteenth century, boasted some 50 rooms, including two halls, of which 28 offered sleeping accommodation totalling 39 beds. The traditional defensive castle, with its often rather cramped accommodation and necessarily modest windows became something of an anachronism; Fastolf's choice was determined by the desire to locate himself within the upper echelons of aristocratic society despite his obscure birth, rather than defence. The great house, still castellated as at Haddon Hall or, somewhat later, South Wingfield, became the more normal aristocratic residence by the latter part of our era.

Piety has already been noticed as a chivalric virtue. Conspicuous devotion, to coin a phrase, may perhaps be identified as another aristocratic characteristic. Significantly, heading the catalogue of pieces of evidence presented by the Pastons in 1466 to prove their gentle ancestry were licences to maintain a private chaplain and evidence of patronage of religious houses. In fact the proliferation of private chapels and private chaplains seems to have taken place during the course of our period. The greater aristocracy might employ more than one chaplain and additional staff including numbers of children maintained as choristers, but the gentry household made do with much less. Friars seem also to have cultivated well-to-do households and they appear not infrequently where we have evidence for guests at high table: Sir Geoffrey Luttrell is famously depicted at his high table with two Dominicans seated nearby to his right.

In some particularly devout households – notably those headed by certain great dowager ladies of which the household of Cecily, duchess of York, at the end of the fifteenth century is best known – the rhythms of the household mirrored those of the canonical offices. Princess Cecily's routine is known through the survival of her household ordinances, which effectively serve to draw attention to her ostentatious piety (and to defuse her potential political importance following the accession of Henry VII). The creation of private oratories within or overlooking larger chapels as survives, for example, in the Scrope chapel of St Anne at Bolton Castle built at the very end of the fourteenth century, was ostensibly to afford the immediate family greater privacy. They may, however, also have served to draw attention to these high-status worshippers, glimpsed behind their screens.

Most studies of the lesser aristocratic family focus on the arrangement of marriages to the neglect of other issues. This is to no small extent a product of the kinds of sources we have available, but it also reflects a certain lack of scholarly interest. Particular weight has been placed on a (very) small number of marriages selected from the major gentry letter collections that survive for the fifteenth century. Thus the marriages (or would-be marriages) of Elizabeth and Margery Paston, Margery Brews or the infant granddaughters of Sir William Plumpton feature disproportionately in the literature without due consideration of how representative these are either specifically of fifteenth-century marriages or later medieval gentry marriages as a whole. In fact these are very difficult questions to answer at present.

It is probably fair to say that gentry marriages were in part a business arrangement. Dowry, in the form of cash (rather than land) paid by the bride's father to the groom, had necessarily to be agreed by the two families and entered into a formal written contract. In the last century of our period the dowry paid in respect of a knight's daughter was usually a little under £200. The groom's father had also to agree what settlement he would make on the couple in the form of land, cash or annuity. It follows that a marriage could not normally occur without the agreement of the respective families. Margery Paston's secret marriage to the Pastons' agent, Richard Calle, departs from this norm and is probably entirely atypical, but equally it warns that the parties contracting cannot be dismissed as mere ciphers. Gentry males were expected to take the initiative in seeking out marriage partners. Brothers sometimes exchanged information about prospective brides. In 1481, for example, Richard Cely wrote to tell the younger George Cely that a certain woman he had seen was as good-looking, sensible and in as good health 'as any I have seen this seven year'. Mothers, likewise, would look out for their daughters.

The letter collections also show that prospective couples might exchange letters, though we should be wary of reading too much into this formalized conduct. Much has been made, for example, of the valentine sent by Margery Brews to John Paston III, as if this were evidence of real affection on Margery's part. The occasion of St Valentine's Day provided Margery with the authority to write to John and dictated the language of the letter, but its ultimate purpose was to secure a marriage that was at risk of foundering because her father was unwilling to pay a larger dowry. Letters like this, written with the aid of a scribe, tell us little of the actual thoughts and emotions of the parties concerned. On the other hand, gentry women were socialized from an early age to see marriage as the chief goal in their lives, and many young women may well have been satisfied to comply with their parents' wishes. Equally, parents would not have wished to force marriages on their daughters where there was obvious hostility since such a marriage was open to challenge in the church courts and would not be conducive to the begetting of children.

One indirect measure of the degree to which marriages were arranged is the ages at which the parties married. The younger the parties, the more compliant to parental choice. Unfortunately the ages of gentry couples at marriage have not been much studied. Analogy with the greater aristocracy would suggest that heirs and heiresses were likely to be married younger than other siblings. Harris found the majority of her sample of aristocratic brides from the period 1450–1550 married in their early teens, but acknowledges that her sample is skewed in favour of heiresses. Child marriages can certainly be found, but the much cited example of the double marriage of Sir William Plumpton's 'heiress' granddaughters was a reckless and cynical act even by contemporary standards; he was subsequently to reveal that he had secretly married and fathered another heir. Perhaps a little more revealing is the marriage of Alice de Rouclif, heiress to lands in Rawcliffe near York, and John Marrays, a kinsman of the then abbot of the wealthy Benedictine abbey of St Mary's. Alice was formally contracted when still only about 11 and hence below canonical majority, but was then taken to live with Anabilla Wasteleyne, her prospective sister-in-law, prior to the formal solemnization. During that time she received various small presents from John and allegedly told Anabilla of her desire to be properly married to John. This, then, was an arranged marriage, but, so far as a girl not yet in her teens can know what a marriage means, it was one that Alice was willing to go along with. The voice of Katherine Willoughby, who was married at 14 to Charles Brandon, duke of Suffolk, her senior by 35 years, offers a unique riposte: 'I cannot tell what more unkindness . . . than to bring our children into so miserable a state not to choose by their own liking.'

The rationale behind Alice's marriage was that as an heiress she could attract a rather more prestigious or wealthy spouse than might otherwise be expected for a family with no title and only modest lands. Because still below the age of 15, however, she was a legal minor and as an orphan – her father was already dead – subject to the authority of her guardian, who was thus free to arrange her marriage. In fact her guardianship and hence her marriage was disputed between her mother and another male kinsman, and it is for this reason that we know about her. Analogy with the greater aristocracy would suggest the marriages of girls below their legal majority (15), though probably not their canonical majority (12), were quite common. However, the majority of women at this level of society probably married in or even some time after their later teens and may thus have taken a somewhat more active role in approving or rejecting suitors. A few women patently remained unmarried even by their later twenties and consequently may even have missed the chance to marry. Such women went instead into aristocratic service.

Gentry males would normally have been older than their wives at marriage and probably enjoyed rather greater initiative in choosing whom they married. Interestingly the contemporary culture demanded that men woo their prospective partners. We see this from the evidence of giving gifts – silks, gloves, rings and the like – and the sending of love letters. Similarly, within marriage it became conventional to represent couples as bound to one another by ties of affection. This is sometimes seen in the language of letters between husbands and wives. It is also seen in the way couples came to be depicted on monumental brasses and, for those who could afford it, sepulchral monuments. From the later fourteenth century it was fashionable to depict husband and wife holding hands in a gesture that speaks of intimacy and affection, but of course is symbolic of marriage (otherwise known as handfasting). The ideology was thus one of marital affection, but though some (even many) gentry or greater aristocratic couples may genuinely have grown to care for one another, even in an arranged marriage, we should be careful not to confuse ideology with actual experience.

The most telling evidence of family pressure to impose marriages on unwilling individuals comes not from the marriage of younger, previously unmarried women, but of widows. It may be that gentry families were unwilling to shoulder responsibility for the younger widow. Equally it may be that a widow with dower lands was seen as a valuable marriageable asset. The younger widow, however, unlike the young teenager, enjoyed both theoretical legal autonomy and a greater experience of the world. She would have been more likely to challenge such family pressures, hence the evidence of matrimonial litigation. One example is the forced marriage of Sir Robert Harrington's widow, Christiana, to Sir Thomas Saville, himself a widower, in 1441. Thomas Harrington, a relative by marriage, had urged the union 'on account of the honour of my name and of my friends and blood kin', but warned that if she refused he would be her enemy and would attempt to deprive her of her possessions. Christiana went through with the marriage ceremony, but doggedly refused to sleep with her new husband at his manors of Elland and Thornhill (Yorks., WR).

The remarriage of gentry widows and widowers was probably quite common, though it is unclear how often gentry widows were pressurized into marrying again. Custom allowed widows a year of mourning before a second marriage was permitted and, as Patricia Cullum has shown, numbers of widows took advantage of this year's grace to take a vow of chastity that effectively protected them against such pressures.[1] This is not to deny that such widows were also, or even primarily, motivated by reasons of personal piety, but the numbers who took their oath as their year's mourning expired is suggestive. Once again gentry practice may mirror greater aristocratic exemplars such as Cecily, duchess of York, already noted, or even Lady Margaret Beaufort, mother to Henry VII.

---

1. P.H. Cullum, 'Vowesses and female lay piety in the province of York, 1300–1530', *Northern History* 32 (1996), pp. 21–41.

10 CLERKS, CLERICS, ECCLESIASTICS AND THE RELIGIOUS

During the later Middle Ages a significant minority of the population could be described as clergy or religious of one kind or another. Strictly we need to distinguish between the religious – that is, those who belonged to a *religio* or monastic order – and the secular clergy – that is, persons in holy orders (subdeacon, deacon or priest) not otherwise a member of a religious order. The former included both male and female religious (monks and nuns, but also 'regular' canons) since it was not necessary to be in holy orders to be a member of a religious order, though by the later Middle Ages most monks were in fact also priests capable of saying the mass. The religious included both those attached to enclosed monasteries and nunneries belonging variously to the Benedictine, Cistercian, Augustinian, Premonstratensian, Cluniac and Carthusian orders (to name the most important), the military orders of the Knights Templar (suppressed in 1308) and Knights Hospitaller, and the mendicants or friars, sometimes referred to as the 'voluntary poor'. Whereas the monastic orders had their roots in a form of devotional life that involved a retreat from the world that went back to the very beginning of the medieval era, the mendicant orders – the Dominicans (Preaching or Black Friars), Franciscans (Grey Friars or Friars Minor), Augustinians (Austin Friars) and Carmelites (White Friars) were the four main orders – established themselves specifically in centres of population and were of more recent foundation. Many of their houses were founded within the first 100 years of our period.

The secular clergy formed a diverse group. There were the higher clergy that variously comprised bishops, archdeacons and secular canons, but also included the beneficed clergy and, at the bottom of this hierarchy, the unbeneficed clergy. (The picture is actually a little less clear-cut, as some livings were poorly endowed and might actually be less attractive than a well-endowed chantry position.) With the exception of the unbeneficed, most were university educated if not actual graduates. Some higher clergy were of aristocratic lineage. Richard Scrope, bishop of Lichfield and subsequently archbishop of York, was a member of the Richmondshire gentry. George Neville, a slightly later archbishop of York, was younger brother to Warwick 'the Kingmaker', though most bishops were of more plebeian origin. The Church was to a degree a meritocratic institution, and there was scope for any bright and capable boy, if funded through school and university, to build a good career for himself.

A benefice, or 'living', represented the revenue accruing to a parish from tithes and from any parochial lands given for the support of a priest. Many benefices were in lay control and a substantial number belonged to the Crown. These were used as an inexpensive way to reward royal 'clerks', the medieval equivalent of the civil servant. Because a beneficed priest was permitted to hire a deputy or 'vicar', it follows that many did not personally serve the parishes for which they held the living. This fell instead to the vicar. The same was true where benefices were 'appropriated' by religious houses (monasteries): the house would add the living to the revenue of the house as a whole and appoint a stipendiary priest as a vicar. Augustinian and Premonstratensian houses invariably appointed their own canons to this task and so further maximized income.

Unbeneficed clergy represent the bottom level of a clerical hierarchy. They have justifiably been referred to as a clerical proletariat. Often of humble social origin, they tended to be indifferently educated and lacked patronage. Even within this group we may distinguish some sort of hierarchy. Clergy appointed as vicars within parishes probably enjoyed the most security and were in some instances moderately well remunerated. The growing fashion for chantry foundations, whereby a patron would make an endowment to support a priest to say mass for his soul, provided employment for numbers of other clergy. This fashion was only cut short in 1547 with the abolition of chantries. Not all chantry foundations were 'perpetual' since to make such an endowment was very costly; many were founded to last for a period of a few years or even just a year. The implication is that prior to 1547 numbers of priests supported themselves through holding a succession of temporary chantries, as has been observed, for example, in the large parish of Scarborough.

The lay demand for masses grew considerably over the later medieval era and this in turn created a demand for clergy since only an ordained priest could celebrate mass. By the fifteenth century some wealthier guilds were beginning to support their own priests. Others may have hired the services of a priest when celebrating a guild mass. Most demand lay, however, in the post-mortem provision of masses for the benefit of souls in purgatory. Just as only a few could afford perpetual chantries, so only some could endow even temporary chantries. Testamentary evidence shows, however, that by the later fourteenth century, and probably somewhat earlier, all who could afford it – merchants, artisans, substantial peasants – left money to support masses. Often this was in the form of an obit, an annual mass on the anniversary of the death of the founder. The likelihood is that there were numbers of jobbing clergy picking up such work as they were able, but enjoying limited means and little job security.

In addition to the regular and secular clergy, together with the nuns and canonesses associated with both the monastic and mendicant orders, there are a few other groups who should be mentioned. These mostly comprised lay persons (in the sense of not being in holy orders). The Cistercians made especial use of large numbers of lay brothers (*conversi*), who were originally responsible for the working of the monastic estates and the menial and service functions of the monastic community, leaving the 'choir' monks free to focus on the collective devotion of the monastic offices and private study. From the middle of the fourteenth century, however, the order seems not to have relied on lay brothers and, in common with the other orders, preferred to use hired employees. Numbers of hospitals, such as St Bartholomew's in London or St Wulfstan's in Worcester, were founded in the larger towns during the High Middle Ages and run on monastic lines following the Augustinian rule. The material (as opposed to the spiritual) needs of the sick poor for whom the hospitals were founded were provided for by the sisters, who might themselves be assisted by lay sisters.

In addition to those who followed a communal life within a monastic or quasi-monastic community, there were the 'solitaries': hermits, anchorites and anchoresses. All represented individuals who chose to retreat from the world and lead a life of prayer. Whereas the anchorite or anchoress was physically enclosed, indeed literally walled into the anchorhold, the hermit was not so constrained. Numbers of solitaries appear to have been religious who found the communal life of the cloister insufficiently rigorous and spiritually fulfilling. Some anchorholds were even attached to monastic houses. Hermits tended to be attached to chapels, including bridge chapels, and so helped minister to the spiritual needs of the traveller. Some maintained lighthouses to aid mariners.

THE RELIGIOUS

Monasticism was very well established within our period and virtually all the houses of the major orders of monks had been founded by the early thirteenth century. The oldest, largest and wealthiest houses tended to belong to the Benedictine order and included the royal foundation of Westminster, St Mary's Abbey in York, Reading Abbey, the cathedral priories of Canterbury, Durham, Norwich and Winchester, and the great abbeys of Chester and Gloucester, made seats of bishops following their dissolution in 1540. There were also numerous lesser houses. Most were urban foundations, though in some instances the town had grown up around the monastery as at Selby (Yorks., WR) or Battle (Sussex).

A second major order, not least in terms of its impact on the landscape, was the rather more austere Cistercian order. Their houses were largely sited away from centres of population, particularly in the upland regions of Yorkshire or the Welsh marches. These lands were used extensively to raise sheep; revenue from wool was a major source of income for the English houses. Often located in sparsely populated areas comparatively plentifully supplied with stone, their physical presence, represented by such romantic ruins as at Tintern (Herefordshire), Rievaulx and Fountains (both Yorks.), is still apparent. The same could not be said of the mendicant orders, though arguably their impact on culture and learning over the period was much the greater. Only Fountains began to rival any of the great Benedictine houses in terms of wealth.

The orders of regular canons, principally the Augustinians and the Premonstratensians, who otherwise had much in common with the Cistercian order, were entirely made up of men in holy orders. Two Augustinian houses – Haltemprice (Yorks., ER) and Maxstoke (War.) – were founded in the earlier fourteenth century and a priory of Gilbertine canons was founded at Poulton (Glos.) as late as 1350. Prior to the dissolution, there were some 200 houses of Augustinian canons scattered between rural and urban locations. This is the largest number of all the orders, but most were comparatively modestly endowed. Bourne Abbey (Lincs.), for example, was endowed with the livings of some 11 appropriated churches. This pattern made the initial cost of endowment for the founder comparatively modest, hence the popularity of the order, especially with aristocracy of lesser rank. Frequently, parochial churches that had been appropriated as part of such endowments were served by canons from the appropriating monastery. It follows that the Augustinians in particular had an interest in pastoral care. John Mirk, the author of the *Festial*, a collection of homilies, and *Instructions for Parish Priests*, was a canon of Lilleshall (Shropshire), and Walter Hilton (d. 1396), a canon of Thurgarton (Notts.), wrote *The Scale of Perfection* and his *Treatise Written to a Devout Man* as guides to Christian living.

The military orders of the Knights Templar and the Knights of St John of Jerusalem (Knights Hospitaller) were products of the crusading movement of the High Middle Ages and their focus of activity lay in the Holy Land. Their importance in England is more in terms of the lands they were given and administered than their numerical presence. Only their chief houses at the London Temple and Clerkenwell, respectively, were of any size. Most of their other establishments were small preceptories served by a few religious and larger numbers of lay servants. The Templars were effectively suppressed in 1308 (and formally in 1312) on trumped-up heresy charges. Their property and preceptories were largely transferred to the Hospitallers. The London Temple came latterly to be largely leased to lawyers and was by the late fourteenth century associated with two of the inns of court.

The popularity of the religious orders in our period is not to be measured by the extreme paucity of new foundations, but rather by the level of patronage and recruitment. Estimates of the numbers of religious at any given date must be treated with circumspection. They were greatest (some 18,000) around the beginning of our period, fell back sharply in the decades following the plague (to 9000), but recovered somewhat until the early sixteenth century. At any given moment, monks and canons probably outnumbered nuns and canonesses by about three to two. The number of friars appears to have fallen most as a product of the arrival of plague. Whereas friars had outnumbered monks and canons before the Black Death, their numbers thereafter were broadly similar.

Despite the differing traditions of the orders, which were probably more marked at the beginning of our period than by the fifteenth century or the eve of the dissolution, many elements of the monastic life were essentially the same. At the heart of monastic life was the routine of church services (or offices) through the day and into the hours of darkness, namely Matins, Lauds, Prime, Tierce, Sext, Nones, Vespers and Compline. The precise timing of these offices varied through the year according to the hours of daylight. In winter, the office of Matins fell at midnight and at cockcrow in the summer; the monks or canons would descend directly from their dormitory into the church and return to sleep after. The remainder of the day, mealtimes and chapter (the daily assembly of all the brothers or sisters held in the chapter house) excepted, was to be spent in private study or manual labour. In practice most manual labour was undertaken either by lay servants or, in the case of the Cistercian order, at least before the plague, lay brothers, though numbers of religious spent time on business and administrative affairs relating to their house.

Although only the Carthusian order insisted on strict silence through most of the monastic day, the other orders discouraged conversation. Meals were to be taken in silence while a reading was given. Monks and canons were to dress simply and eat adequately, but not extravagantly, abstaining from meat other than when sick. According to their vows, they were to have no personal possessions and were bound to live chastely and in obedience to their monastic superiors. We see, however, a general relaxation in the way a number of the rules were enforced, a process formalized and regularized in Pope Benedict XII's constitutions for the Benedictine order (1336) and for the Augustinian order (1339). These matters were also the subject of particular scrutiny and potential dispute at visitation, the periodic inspection of most (but not all) religious houses by the local bishop.

Visitation evidence, which may comprise depositions by the religious themselves and, more commonly, the bishop's injunctions, designed to correct any faults observed, gives us an unusual insight into monastic life. As may be expected of an institutional existence, issues relating to diet loom disproportionately large. Canons at Northampton Abbey complained in 1442 about their food and alleged that the kitchener was allowing his kinsman, a Northampton butcher, to provide bad meat to the house. Like grumbling characterized Newnham Priory in the same year, but it was also observed that the canons often missed services because they were too busy taking mid-morning snacks. Discipline is also an issue and under the wrong leadership, some houses appear divided and unhappy. This was probably true of Newnham, where the prior seems to have lost the respect of the canons. At Peterborough Abbey in 1437 problems of discipline and poor management owed much to the incapacity of the ageing abbot.

Another issue that commonly arises is the frequency with which religious absented themselves from services in the church and even from the cloister. At Peterborough, Brother William Beupho told the bishop that the townsfolk were scandalized that only a handful of the house's 44 monks were observed at divine office. The prior explained that some absenteeism was due to excessive 'watching and drinking in the evening', but mostly to the demands of office holding. Each monastery had its own hierarchy of office holders, or obedientiaries, though numbers would mirror the size of the house. The head of house was normally the abbot (abbess) assisted by a prior (prioress). In the case of 'daughter houses', which were founded from another house, the prior (prioress) was the local head, subject to the oversight of the head of the parent house. Very large houses might have a subprior. Other obedientiaries were the bursar (responsible for a large part of the monastery's revenues), the cellarer (responsible for seeing the house was supplied with a whole range of goods), the kitchener (responsible for supervising the provision of foodstuffs), the almoner (responsible for charitable provision), the sacrist (responsible for the sacred vessels), the infirmarer (in charge of the monastic hospital) and the pittancer (responsible for paying the members of the community their annual allowances for clothing and other petty expenditure). Each had their own particular sources of revenue assigned and was responsible for keeping accounts relating to their office and to answering for these in chapter. Other offices, such as precentor and succentor, were concerned with the management of divine services, but carried no financial responsibilities.

Because the quality of leadership and personality of the head of house made so much difference to the lives of its members, the election of abbots and priors was a matter of the highest importance. It was also potentially a matter of great friction, particularly where the right to appoint did not rest with the members of the house themselves or was disputed. Monk Bretton Priory (Yorks., WR) effectively broke with the Cluniac order over this issue in 1281. In 1396 Abbot Burley of Fountains sent archers to enforce his choice of Thomas Burton to the abbacy of its daughter house of Meaux, near Hull, against the opposition of his order's English chapter. Further dispute arose with Abbot Burley's death in 1410 as Abbot Ripon of Meaux challenged the English chapter's candidate, Roger Frank, for the vacant abbacy. With royal intervention, Ripon ultimately prevailed, but Frank and his immediate supporters then roamed the countryside in secular clothes stirring up dissent. An attempt was made on the life of Abbot Ripon, the abbey itself was plundered in 1423, and trouble still raged a decade later.

During the course of the later Middle Ages, heads of houses increasingly set themselves apart from their communities. A small number of abbots – the 'mitred abbots' because entitled to wear a mitre – drawn mostly from the larger and more prestigious religious houses, such as Reading and St Albans, but also some lesser houses such as Selby, had the distinction of serving alongside the bishops in Parliament as ecclesiastical peers. Other heads of houses cultivated something of the manners of the rural aristocracy. They occupied their own private apartments and could enjoy considerable revenues by right of their office. When John de Elveley stepped down from heading the Augustinian priory of Kirkham (Yorks., ER) in 1310, he arranged his own private lodgings, an annual pension of £20, generous food allowances and his own staff of an esquire, chaplain, cook and two boys.

This last is only an extreme example of a more general pattern among the better-off male houses. The sometimes lavish provision of foodstuffs, including wine, a wide selection of fish and even meat for non-fast days enjoyed by the community as a whole mimicked aristocratic consumption. The presence of hunting dogs and a monastic predilection for hunting – noted, for example, in the visitation injunctions at Newnham Priory, reflects a similar hankering after an aristocratic identity that was at odds with the peasant and bourgeois origin of most monks and canons. An interest in hunting also betrays a concern to assert a more aggressive masculine identity, noted also in complaints about monks drinking in taverns and womanizing. It would be unwise, however, to so characterize all monks. Late medieval monasticism also cultivated a distinctive clerical identity for monks, particularly through the cultivation of Latin learning.

Benedict XII's reforms for the Benedictine order provided for each house to send at least one monk to university, and more in the case of the larger houses. During the later Middle Ages numbers of monks and canons of the three largest orders studied in the two universities. At Oxford there were monastic colleges, notably Gloucester College, founded in 1283 and common to the entire Benedictine order, the later fourteenth-century Benedictine foundations of Canterbury and Durham colleges, and the mid fifteenth-century foundations of St Bernard's College (Cistercian) and St Mary's College (Augustinian). Many greater male houses accumulated substantial libraries, in which works of theology were especially well represented. Such provision could sustain a certain level of scholarship among those monks of a scholarly inclination, and occasionally produce scholars of the calibre of Uthred of Boldon or Simon Suthery. We should note, too, the long tradition of monastic chronicle writing, notably at St Albans Abbey, but more widely as well; of the two most famous fourteenth-century chroniclers, Ranulph Higden, author of the *Polychronicon*, was a monk at the Benedictine abbey of Chester, and Henry Knighton a canon of the Augustinian abbey of Leicester.

The mendicant orders represented a new devotional movement at the end of the twelfth century, designed to fight heresy and instruct the laity in the faith. Their mission was not the monastic, eremitic ideal of retreat from the world, but rather engagement with the world. Equally they rejected the conspicuous wealth associated with the monastic orders, reflected in substantial property ownership and grand buildings. Friars targeted towns as centres of population and imitated the lives of Christ and his disciples in their teaching in the form of sermons and reliance on the lay population among whom they ministered for alms. The earliest friaries were wooden buildings, invariably located on vacant land at the margins of the town. By the beginning of our period, this early missionary zeal had waned. Increasingly, friars accepted endowments in the form of property and built their houses in stone. Their collection of alms became more systematic; friars would routinely collect within a recognized area around their house and would cultivate individuals known to be sympathetic. Their ministry extended beyond sermonizing to include hearing confession (and here they trespassed on the province of the parochial clergy) and the provision of masses for deceased patrons.

The main wave of monastic foundation was already over by 1250, patronage having largely shifted to the mendicant orders. A number of new houses were, however, established after the Black Death, though the fashion was initiated before the plague by the likes of Marie de St Pol, countess of Pembroke, and Elizabeth de Burgh, lady of Clare, wealthy East Anglian dowagers with shared devotional interests. New foundations included the Cistercian house of St Mary Graces, London, in 1350, built in association with a massive plague cemetery and as an act of repentance for the sin that had provoked this divine wrath. Other new houses belonged to less well known orders that were seen to be in tune with new devotional fashions. Particularly favoured were the Carthusians, noted for their rigorous adherence to the eremitic ideal. Although the monks worshipped communally, they spent most of their day in their individual cells, each with its own little garden, in much the same way as other recluses. They lived frugally and, unlike the other orders by this date, abstained entirely from eating meat. Early houses of the order had been established at Hinton and Witham (Somerset), and Hethorpe (Glos.). A second wave of aristocratic foundations commenced just before the advent of plague. Beauvale (Notts.) was founded in 1343 and Marie de St Pol planned a house at Horne (Surrey) about the same time. Four houses were founded between 1371 and 1396 – London (also associated with a plague cemetery), Hull, Coventry and Mount Grace (Yorks., NR) – and a final house at Sheen (Surrey) founded by Henry V in expiation for his father's judicial murder of Archbishop Scrope.

Two other royal foundations favoured new orders for women. Edward III founded a house for Dominican nuns at Dartford (Kent) in 1356, a house that built a reputation for learning and strict adherence to its rules. The Bridgettine house of nuns and canons at Syon (near London), founded in 1415 and conceived as a sister foundation to Sheen on the opposite bank of the Thames, was the only English house of this new order. The Franciscan nuns (Minoresses or Poor Clares) also received much patronage over this same period. Marie de St Pol chose to be buried at her (re)foundation at Denny. Her friend, Elizabeth de Burgh, another notable patron of religious houses, including Denny, and founder of a Cambridge college, lived for part of her later years at a house she had built at the London Minoresses and was buried there in 1360. Eleanor de Bohun (d. 1399), the widow of Edward III's youngest son, Thomas of Woodstock, also ended her days there. Sir William de la Pole had planned a Franciscan nunnery on the site in Hull on which his son Michael subsequently established the Charterhouse. Bruisyard Abbey (Suffolk), the last of the order's nunneries, was founded by Elizabeth de Burgh's granddaughter, Elizabeth and her husband, Lionel, duke of Clarence.

Unlike monks, who were often of peasant stock drawn from the estates held by the houses they joined, nuns were drawn primarily from the lower echelons of the aristocracy and from the upper levels of urban society. Though more common in the earlier part of our period, we do find a few nuns from noble families and even the royal family: Princess Bridget, daughter of Edward IV, became a nun at the royal foundation of Dartford by way of political exile. Although there were several prestigious royal and pre-Conquest foundations, such as Romsey (Hants) and Barking (Essex), in per capita terms nunneries tended to be less well endowed than male houses. They tended to be comparatively small and have made less impact, architecturally speaking, in terms of extant remains. There are exceptions, such as the church of Romsey Abbey, which was taken over by the parishioners at the dissolution, but many have disappeared almost entirely. The same is true of the documentary record. We have little in the way of account rolls or other records of the internal administration of women's houses, though there are some important survivals such as the English register (cartulary or register of deeds) of Godstow Abbey (Oxon.).

We know most about nunneries during our period from the injunctions issued by the local diocesan (bishop) at visitation. Read unproblematically, these provide a negative view of the devotional life of the later medieval nunnery. Regularly the bishop would demand more rigorous financial administration, the implication being that financial difficulties were solely the product of mismanagement. He would insist on careful vigilance of the younger nuns and strict enforcement of enclosure, again implying a certain moral laxity. Likewise he would insist that the nuns sleep in the common dormitory and eat together of the same fare in the common refectory; the abbess or prioress was to show no favouritism among her nuns.

We may read these injunctions in a number of ways. On one level they are about the power relationship between the bishop and nuns within his diocese. The right of visitation reinforced the bishop's authority and his injunctions focus on administrative rather than spiritual matters. Indeed the bishop was solely concerned with how the nuns adhered to the monastic rule, but the impression created by the void is that the nuns were without vocation and were spiritually lacking. This impression is questionable. Henry V's foundation in 1415 of the Bridgettine nunnery of Syon or Barking Abbey under the contemporaneous rule of the reform-minded Abbess Sybil de Felton suggest otherwise. The mobilization of these royal foundations as bastions against the Lollard heresy may, however, be equally misleading evidence. The sometimes not so genteel poverty of many later medieval nunneries may still have been closer to the spirit of monasticism than the relative affluence experienced by numbers of male houses.

The visitations do provide some evidence for the ways in which the nuns themselves adapted to the demands of the religious life. What emerges is the influence of the nuns' social origins. The nuns at Elstow Abbey (Beds.) were instructed in 1421–22 not to wear silk gowns, numerous rings or silver hairpins in contravention of their vow of poverty, but this may have been their modest way of asserting their social rank. At Godstow, an unusually privileged house, 'parties or drinks after compline' were proscribed. During the last century or so of monasticism nuns began forming themselves into groups. At Godstow this process became sufficiently rooted by 1434 that the bishop sanctioned these distinct 'households' so long as there were only three. The creation of private chambers and separate eating places can sometimes be found, but as late as 1514 a nun of Redlingfield (Norfolk) could complain to her bishop that the beds in the common dormitory did not even have curtains to separate them. Despite their vow of poverty, many nuns came regularly to be allowed an annual clothing allowance and, at Denny, each of the sisters was allocated the revenue from a specific part of the abbey's estate.

Nunneries came to sanction the residence of aristocratic widows, no doubt because of the patronage they could bring. The most extraordinary example of such lay association with a house of nuns was Marie de St Pol, countess of Pembroke's relationship to the Minoresses of Denny Abbey (Cambs.). She constructed her own home within the church of the former Templar house there and had a new church built to accommodate the sisters who were (unwillingly) transferred from neighbouring Waterbeach about the time of the Black Death. The countess's home was thus located literally at the very heart of the religious community. A more common situation was that at Polsloe Priory (Devon). At visitation in 1308 the bishop ordered that the secular women living in the nunnery observe the rule of silence and that no married woman be allowed to reside there for more than a month. At Godstow the bishop demanded that one Felmersham's widow and her household, together with 'other mature women', leave since their presence, their visitors and their worldly dress were a bad influence.

The concerns of bishops as visitors reflect patriarchal values as much as they reveal life in a nunnery. The assumption that nuns could not readily manage their financial affairs ignores the real problems consequent on insufficient endowments and, latterly, declining revenues from land, a problem common to all religious houses. The concern with enclosure reflects an emphasis on virginity as integral to the identity of the female religious in a way that was not true of men. This is also revealed, as Roberta Gilchrist has shown, in the design of nunneries where access to the dormitory is as difficult as access to the sacristy (room containing the sacred vessels) of a male house.[1] The concern with silence – found, for example, at Polsloe – sees talkativeness as a distinctively female vice. Finally the concern with the erosion of communal life or departures from the vow of poverty, though not specific to women's houses, is represented in terms of vanity or other sin, but may say more about the nuns' concern to assert their social rank.

Just as we can question the rather negative view of convent life suggested by visitation evidence, so we should rethink the view that nunneries were intellectually moribund. The supposed lack of Latinity of later medieval nuns has been contrasted unfavourably with evidence of Latin learning in a high medieval context. This probably has little to do with the calibre of intake or the quality of vocation of the nuns themselves. Rather it may be the product of a paradigm shift consequent upon the Gregorian Reform movement. Whereas in the High Middle Ages few monks were in holy orders, by the later Middle Ages it was normal for monks to be ordained as priests in order to provide a chantry function for lay patrons. In the High Middle Ages, therefore, the only significant distinction between monks and nuns was one of gender. Nuns followed – with more or, in the case of the Cistercian order, less encouragement – the same ideals of monasticism as their male counterparts. The use of Latin, the reading of Latin, even the creation and copying of Latin texts was very much part of that monastic culture. The impact of Gregorian Reform, however, was to create a new binary of celibate cleric and married lay person. Latin, the language of the Church, became part of that binary. Indeed in English law, benefit of clergy, the

---

1. R. Gilchrist, *Gender and Material Culture: the Archaeology of Religious Women* (London, 1994).

right of 'criminous clergy' to be tried only in ecclesiastical courts, came to be extended to all (implicitly males) who could read Latin. At the same time, monastic scriptoria (writing workshops) became less important as book production passed to secular craftsmen. The monastic reputation for learning likewise transferred to the new mendicant orders. Learning and Latinity, it could be argued, thus became less central to monasticism, but Latin remained integral to male monastic houses because most monks were also clergy. The same could not be said of women's houses where Latin must have seemed increasingly inappropriate.

If instead of focusing on Latin as the yardstick of learning we turn instead to French, the vernacular of the aristocracy until the beginning of the fifteenth century, and latterly to English, a different picture begins to emerge. Although most nunnery libraries were probably comparatively modest – Dartford Priory with over 50 books at the dissolution may not be typical – there is evidence for the ownership of vernacular scriptural and devotional literature. Thus we find a French Old Testament at Flixton Priory (Suffolk), a *Mirror of the Life of Christ* at Barking, the *Epistle of Love* at Nun Cotton (Lincs.) and Swine (Yorks., ER), *The Pilgrimage of the Soul* at Marrick Priory (Yorks., NR) and the *Revelations of St Bridget* at Thetford (Norfolk). Such a literature may not have provided a basis for the sort of academic theology associated with the Oxford Divinity School, but it may have encouraged an interest in a form of contemplative devotion over the last two centuries of the Middle Ages, and suggests a common devotional literary culture between nuns and lay aristocratic women. It is also likely that most nuns were able to read French or English, even if comprehension of Latin was more limited, and so could have had access to such a literature. The most telling evidence for learning, however, is confined to a small number of women's houses, notably the royal foundations of Barking, Dartford and Syon.

Anchorholds at the beginning of our period were usually located away from major centres of population and sometimes saw two or three recluses living in close proximity or in a shared cell. (Indeed the distinction between anchorite and hermit was then still very hazy.) By the end of the Middle Ages, most anchorholds were located in towns – frequently in churchyards – and invariably housed a solitary recluse. We see here a marked change in the understanding of the eremitic ideal, the desire to escape the temptations of the world by retreating to the desert. The anchorites of the High Middle Ages treated sparsely populated and woodland areas as desert and so their retreat was literal. By the later Middle Ages the cell itself became the desert and the retreat became an inward, mental process of spiritual contemplation. The bustling world of the town glimpsed through the outer window of the cell remained a source of temptation, but, following Christ's example, the anchorite grew spiritually through resisting this temptation. Equally significantly, the anchorite (or anchoress) became an integral aspect of the devotional life of the medieval town, offering an alternative source of spiritual counsel to that of the parochial clergy or the friars. Margery Kempe, for example, recalled the guidance given to her by the celebrated anchoress Julian of Norwich. Indeed, for women, anchoresses represented the only sanctioned source of same-gender spiritual support.

The vocation of the enclosed recluse was demanding and candidates were supposed to be interviewed carefully by their bishop (or his proxy) to determine their suitability. The successful candidate was then formally shut into the anchorhold, frequently a stone building attached to the north side of a parish church. Julian of Norwich's cell, for example, was attached to the parish church of St Julian after which she took her name. The cell would have a window or opening on the inside, permitting the anchorite or anchoress to witness mass at the high altar. A window or other opening on the outer wall would allow food to be brought to the cell, waste matter to be passed out, and the laity access to the anchorite. It was common for a servant to be attached to the anchorhold who could minister to the immediate physical needs of the recluse and, if need be, solicit alms and restrict visitors so as not to disturb the recluse when engaged in spiritual contemplation. Such servants were sometimes aspirant recluses who learned the reclusive life by serving a recluse master or mistress.

SECULAR CLERGY

The secular clergy were primarily associated with either the administration of a diocese or the cathedral church, which was the focus of the diocese, or the parish. To these two groups, we should add those clergy associated with a substantial number of often small secular colleges, some of which were also parochial. There were 17 later medieval dioceses. Of these, Canterbury and York were the seats of archbishops who administered provinces. The Province of York encompassed the sees (dioceses) of Carlisle, Durham and York (plus from 1458 the island diocese of Sodor and Man), though its claims of jurisdiction extended over the Scottish border. All the other English (and Welsh) dioceses were subject to Canterbury, which also claimed to be the senior English province. Individual dioceses varied considerably in size. Lincoln extended well into the Home Counties, whereas the dioceses of Rochester and Ely were comparatively modest. Each diocese took its name from the seat of the bishop (literally his *cathedra*, hence cathedral). In the cases of Bath and Wells and of Coventry and Lichfield, two churches shared cathedral status within the same diocese. Following the dissolution, Henry VIII established six new cathedrals from the large abbey churches at Bristol, Chester, Gloucester, Oxford (initially Osney), Peterborough and Westminster. (This last survived only to 1550.)

Bishops alone could ordain clergy and perform the sacrament of confirmation, both onerous responsibilities that, ideally, required regular travel around the diocese. Bishops also consecrated churches, churchyards, chapels, altars and, where churchyards or churches were deemed to have been 'polluted' – for example, by the shedding of blood – reconsecrated ('reconciled') them. They enclosed anchorites, authorized devout widows to make vows of chastity and licensed private chapels. The oversight of parochial clergy was another responsibility of the diocesan bishop. Bishops had overall responsibility for the appointment of clergy to parishes. They could license non-residence, appoint confessors and approve preachers, though bishops often devolved the responsibility to visit individual parishes to their archdeacons. The bishop's right of visitation of religious houses, other than those that were exempted from the bishop's jurisdiction, was usually performed in person. John Longland, bishop of Lincoln, on the eve of the dissolution, however, used deputies other than where particular problems were anticipated. Each visitation was in effect at least a full day's work. The task would once again take the bishop through the extent of his diocese as is revealed, for example, by the voluminous records of Bishop Alnwick of Lincoln's visitations in the period 1436–49. The necessity of constant touring of the diocese helps explain the sometimes generous provision of manor houses and palaces.

All too often bishops were, both by background and of necessity, administrators first and spiritual leaders and pastors only second. Some did take these latter responsibilities to heart as the examples of Archbishop Pecham of Canterbury in the later thirteenth century or Archbishop Thoresby of York in the decades after the Black Death demonstrate. It may also be that our picture is too much coloured by the evidence of bureaucratic efficiency contained in the many extant bishops' registers. Some bishops were undoubtedly genuinely if conventionally devout. Thomas Cantilupe, bishop of Hereford in the later thirteenth century, venerated the Virgin Mary, but shunned the company of women, refusing even to kiss his own sister, an incident used to help promote his canonization. In the later fifteenth century William Wayneflete, like William Wykeham before him, used some of his wealth derived from the extraordinarily prosperous see of Winchester, to found a grammar school and an Oxford college (Magdalen).

Most bishops were seculars, though a number were religious and had honed their skill as administrators within a monastic environment. The promotion of someone like Richard Redman, abbot of the comparatively obscure Premonstratensian house of Shap (Westmorland), to the Welsh diocese of St Asaph in 1471 and then to Ely in 1501 is probably atypical. Less remarkable, though equally unusual, was the advancement of Simon Langham, abbot of Westminster, to be bishop of Ely and, in 1366, archbishop of Canterbury. Two fifteenth-century bishops of Hereford, Robert Mascall and John Stanbury, were Carmelite friars. In every instance, however, appointment to episcopal office followed royal service, in the case of Langham as treasurer, in the case of the Carmelites, as king's confessor.

Bishops were assisted, particularly in their sacramental duties of ordination and confirmation, by assistant or suffragan bishops. Many carried the titles of eastern dioceses such as Chrysopolis or Serbia; some were non-resident Irish bishops. Numbers of these assistant bishops were religious, including members of the mendicant orders. The implication is that their services were no great drain on the resources of the diocese. Bishops sometimes had to be absent from their diocese, as for example when Parliament was in session or where the exercise of royal office took them away. On such occasions a vicar general deputized. Their functions were more administrative than sacramental. The same was true of periods between the appointments of bishops. Archbishop Greenfield of York's vicar general Nicholas de Dene was a senior ecclesiastic with a diplomatic career in his own right. His self-importance is projected by his magnificent early fourteenth-century window depicting the life of St Katherine, placed opposite the memorial window for his master in the cathedral nave.

The judicial authority of bishops under canon law ranged quite widely. The bishop had authority to correct a variety of forms of transgressive behaviour ranging from heresy to clerical non-residence, assaults on clergy or sexual misconduct. Thus John Inglie appeared in the bishop of Lincoln's court in 1518 to answer for not communicating at the Easter mass and for laughing 'stupidly' at the elevation of the Host. The same year the rector of Husbands Bosworth appeared to answer charges of non-residence and allowing the chancel of his church to become ruinous. Disputes about parochial rights and tithes, about the probate of wills or the validity of marriages likewise fell within the bishop's jurisdiction. Even disputes about debts or allegations of defamation sometimes came to the attention of the bishop's court. A few cases, often those involving clergy, were heard by the bishop in person in his court of audience, but even here cases could be delegated. Most cases were dealt with in the consistory court under an officer called the Official, assisted by a staff of trained canon lawyers, invariably graduates in canon law not necessarily in holy orders. Despite contemporary satirical comment about the taking of bribes, recent scholarship suggests that the court applied the norms of canon law with scrupulous care.

Bishops were also assisted by archdeacons, who headed subdivisions of the diocese known as archdeaconries. The archdeaconry mirrored the administrative function of the diocese; some archdeaconries, such as the York archdeaconry of Richmond or the Lincoln archdeaconry of Buckingham, even enjoyed a high degree of autonomy. Archdeaconries might be further subdivided into rural deaneries. Archdeacons had particular responsibility for the quality of parochial provision within their jurisdiction, ideally by conducting regular visitation of parishes. Here their concern was that adequate vessels, vestments and service books were maintained, that buildings were in good order and that the parochial clergy were conducting themselves appropriately. In their supervision of parochial clergy, they were supported by the rural deans. Both also took an apparently increasing interest in the conduct of parishioners. In particular, where notice of sexual misconduct (fornication or more rarely adultery) was given at visitation or otherwise, such transgressions were liable to come before the rural dean's or archdeacon's courts. Presentments for non-attendance at church or the use of charms to cure sick livestock occur only infrequently in comparison.

Diocesan administration was kept entirely separate from the running of the cathedral churches. English cathedrals were either monastic foundations served by monks or secular foundations served by a community of canons. Each may have been the seat of a bishop, but their government belonged to the prior or the dean and his chapter respectively. The monastic cathedrals, known as cathedral priories, were, with one exception, prosperous Benedictine houses (Bath, Canterbury, Coventry, Durham, Ely, Norwich, Rochester, Winchester and Worcester) with fairly substantial numbers of cloistered monks. Carlisle alone was Augustinian. Most became secular colleges at the dissolution while retaining their cathedral status, but Coventry was demolished. The other pre-Reformation cathedrals (Chichester, Exeter, Hereford, Lichfield, Lincoln, St Paul's, Wells and York) were all secular colleges.

In the secular cathedrals the dean had responsibility for the functioning of the cathedral church as a place of worship and ministry. Together with the cathedral chapter, moreover, the dean exercised quasi-episcopal authority over all those parishes that fell within the special jurisdiction of the dean and chapter, including the right to hold a court. The dean's duties were many: it was his responsibility to celebrate mass on the major feasts; he installed the bishop on his throne; he washed the feet of the poor on Maundy Thursday. The three other key offices within the cathedral comprised the chancellor, the treasurer and the precentor. The chancellor took responsibility for the chapter's secretariat, for the cathedral school, and for maintaining the cathedral's archives and library. The treasurer, as his title suggests, had charge of the liturgical vessels, the vestments, furnishings and other requisites of cathedral worship. The precentor, who ranked second to the dean, took responsibility for the cathedral's music and service books. Each of these offices had its own staff.

The other canons comprising the chapter might hold a variety of other lesser responsibilities relating to the functioning of the cathedral church as a centre of worship. Their numbers varied considerably between cathedrals. Salisbury had a maximum of 54 canons, Exeter a much more modest 25. In practice, only some of this group seem to have been resident at any given time. Many, including numbers of royal and, at least before the Black Death, papal officials given prebends (livings) as a form of patronage or payment, saw their appointments primarily in terms of the income these provided. At York some half to two-thirds of the cathedral's total revenue was being diverted into the hands of absentees. The duties of singing at divine service came to be delegated to vicars choral; periodic attempts to enforce communal living proved ineffective. Even the precentor might delegate his responsibilities to a succentor and most of the secretarial duties of the chancellor to a chapter clerk.

In monastic cathedrals the bishop nominally filled the place of abbot, but in practice the prior enjoyed the same almost absolute authority over the cathedral church that a dean enjoyed in the secular cathedrals. The administrative structure of the cathedral thus followed the usual monastic pattern, with various offices held by members of the monastic community known as obedientiaries. The office of precentor was analogous to that in the secular cathedrals, whereas the sacrist filled a role equivalent to that of treasurer. However, whereas in the secular cathedrals overall management was vested in four key office holders, a rather larger group of monastic obedientiaries shared this responsibility between them.

The secular cathedral as a collegiate community of canons endowed with prebends represents but one particular variety of secular college. Nearly 200 such colleges can be identified as operating at some point within our period, many to 1547–48. A small number of colleges were of ancient foundation and of some size. Beverley and Southwell (Notts.), for example, acted in effect as pro-cathedrals for the diocese of York. Most colleges, however, were smaller and a number were founded during the course of our period. Part of the attraction of founding a secular college of priests was that the cost to the founder was invariably much less than that for a monastery. The founder also had more control over such a foundation, which was bound by the founder's ordinances rather than a monastic rule. Some, such as John Giffard's 1339 foundation of Holy Trinity, Cotterstock (Northants), where the chaplains were required to study divinity, followed the monastic model of a common dormitory and refectory. Others comprised separate accommodation arranged around a quadrangle with a common refectory. In other instances, the arrangements were probably rather more informal.

Colleges could also be seen by ecclesiastics as a vehicle for imposing control and discipline over the 'clerical proletariat'. The secular cathedrals invariably had colleges to house the vicars (or vicars choral) who deputized for the canons to sing the various offices in the cathedral church, but in fact might assist more generally in the administration. Indeed, it is apparent that for some vicars choral, this was effectively a form of apprenticeship from which they might graduate to higher office. Once chantry priests became numerous, we find a similar drive towards communal living. Thus concern that the chantry priests of York Minster represented a disorderly group led to the foundation of St William's College (licensed 1455, but built 1461) to impose some discipline by requiring the priests to live communally. A similar college at Wells had been established soon after 1400. The same rationale explains the Northampton college of All Saints founded with only minimal endowment in 1460 by the vicar for a community of 16 guild chaplains. Many other colleges were essentially chantry foundations, often with royal or aristocratic patronage, supporting in modest comfort small numbers of priests, often graduates, and, in some instances, variously clerks, choristers and scholars.

Another group of clergy supported primarily by aristocratic patronage were household priests. A corollary of the evidence contained in bishops' registers of the grant of licences for members of the aristocracy to hear mass in private oratories is a likely growth over much of our period in the employment of household chaplains. The provision of private chapels in the castles and manor houses of great magnates is often apparent from extant architectural evidence, and great households might employ a staff of several clergy and numbers of choristers. The case of Henry VI's private chapel, which had a staff of 49 in the middle of the fifteenth century, is clearly atypical. What is apparent is that the fashion for private chapels and the employment of household chaplains percolated down to the lesser aristocracy from the later fourteenth century. In 1397, for example, Thomas Sheffelde, a mere esquire, was licensed to have mass said in his house at Braithwell (Yorks., WR). By the fifteenth century even some wealthy merchants were employing household chaplains. The household chaplain was evidently a mark of status, a public statement of a family's piety; he was also a potentially useful adviser, confidant, clerk, scribe, informant, tutor. We see something of this with James Gloys, the Paston family chaplain.

The majority of secular clergy were associated not with cathedrals, colleges or private households, but with parishes. Only some actually held parochial livings as incumbents enjoying an income from tithes, glebe lands, mortuary fees and the like. Most constituted the clerical proletariat, clergy employed on contracts of varying length and answerable to an employer like any other wage labourer. Many parishes were appropriated during the course of our period by religious houses as a source of revenue. Some were also appropriated to support Oxbridge colleges. In such instances the monastic or college community would employ a vicar (deputy) on a fixed stipend or even supply one of their own community to serve as priest while collecting tithes and other dues for their own benefit. In a number of other instances livings, particularly those controlled by the Crown as patron, were given by way of payment to clerical administrators, 'royal clerks' and the like, who had no intention of venturing beyond Westminster to care for souls in distant parishes. Sometimes more than one living was held in plurality (i.e. at the same time) so that the holder could at most only be present in one of his parishes. Cardinal Wolsey is usually cited as the archpluralist, but even the subsequently canonized Bishop Thomas Cantilupe of Hereford (d. 1282) held numbers of rectories in addition to an archdeaconry and two prebends. On the eve of the Reformation some quarter of all livings were held by pluralists. Well-to-do families also used their patronage to secure livings for sons who might still be comparatively young and not yet in major orders, though this was perhaps more of a problem before the plague than after. It follows that the de facto priest in charge was often the vicar rather than the rector.

We can get a snapshot of the actual composition of parochial clergy from the later fourteenth-century clerical poll tax returns. Using the 1379 returns for the archdeaconry of Bedford we find that of just over 100 parishes, some 47 (or little short of half) had been appropriated. This accords broadly with a suggestion that perhaps some two-fifths of all 9000-odd English parishes had been appropriated by the eve of the dissolution. Even where the rector answered for the tax under the pertinent parish, it does not follow that he took a significant role in the pastoral care of his parishioners.

William Constable, rector of Tempsford, for example, was only in subdeacon's orders. In a number of instances one of the chaplains is distinguished by the title 'parochial chaplain', a role that may be akin to that of the vicar of an appropriated parish. Larger and more prosperous parishes are associated with numbers of clergy and lesser clerics. Thus St Andrew's, Biggleswade, had, in addition to its university-educated rector, eight chaplains and six clerks. Similarly St Mary's, Luton, a parish appropriated to St Albans, was served by the vicar, eight chaplains and five clerks. On the other hand, St Owen's, Bromham, was apparently served only by its vicar and St Mary's, Stotfold, by a parochial chaplain and a clerk. In some instances the number of clergy could fluctuate considerably over time. In fifteenth-century Scarborough, for example, there were at any moment in addition to the vicar and three priests serving perpetual chantries, between one and eight additional priests employed to serve temporary chantries. Some larger parishes, such as Oakley, contained chapelries served by their own parochial chaplains. The clerical poll taxes as a whole suggest a population of some 25,000 secular clergy, an average of rather below three per parish.

The calibre of the parochial clergy varied considerably. A wealthy parish like Long Melford (Suffolk) enjoyed a distinguished line of incumbents during the later Middle Ages, many of whom were university graduates, some with degrees in theology. Such a parish would moreover have enjoyed additional clergy, not least in the form of chantry chaplains. This was especially true of numbers of more prosperous urban parishes. Where livings were in the gift of the Crown, however, the bright university graduates appointed were often employed in the king's chancery or exchequer, and their parishes served by less qualified vicars. The same is true of the many parishes that came to be appropriated by monastic churches to augment their endowments. All Saints', Scraptoft (Leics.), for example, was appropriated to Coventry Priory. None of its medieval vicars appear to have been graduates, though they were sometimes supplemented by a chaplain. Such vicars enjoyed comparatively modest livelihoods and might well serve until death for want of alternative means of support: John Bisshop, noted as Scraptoft's vicar in 1496, was then said to be about 80. In the case of parishes appropriated to houses of canons (and latterly sometimes even houses of monks), the incumbent was invariably provided from within the monastic community. Thus in 1397 Br. Thomas de Hoveden was appointed to the parish of Aughton (Yorks., ER) from the neighbouring Gilbertine priory of Ellerton.

The gulf between those clergy who secured parochial livings, often in the control of aristocratic patrons, and those who did not was commonly a product of birth. The sons of gentlemen, merchants, artisans and more substantial peasants who constituted the majority of entrants to the clerical profession did not enjoy equal opportunities in terms of the financial support their families could offer or the connections they commanded. Canon law debarred serfs and required that candidates for ordination had some means. This largely excluded males of lesser birth, though serfs could be manumitted and, exceptionally, a bright boy might win a supportive patron as an act of charity. The cost of formal schooling and, more particularly, of a university education nevertheless effectively restricted the pool of graduates to those from more substantial backgrounds. On the other hand, there were indeed some who went up to university or took major orders only after they had been provided with a living; patronage, not merit, determined their appointments. Some young men seem to have spent time in the households of senior ecclesiastics and this no doubt provided them with additional sources of patronage if they were lucky enough to be taken on in the first place. In a significant number of cases a clerical career was seen as an appropriate niche for the illegitimate – and so non-inheriting – sons of gentle birth (and likewise the sons of clergy). Canonical impediments on the ordination of males born out of wedlock were regularly and apparently invariably dispensed.

Although a university education, encouraged by the papal decree *Cum ex eo* of 1296, was often the surest means towards a successful clerical career, especially for those who were not especially well connected, the growth in the numbers of graduates from the later fourteenth century – coinciding with a marked increase in college foundations – led to greater competition. Certainly it became harder to obtain a parochial living solely on the basis of having a degree and it appears that numbers of graduates had first to find lesser positions before so advancing. Many clergy, however, would have had neither the opportunity nor the ambition to gain a parochial living, especially some of the more lucrative livings since their value varied very considerably; the Bedfordshire living of Biggleswade, for instance, was assessed at 80 marks (over £53) per annum in 1379, but that of Stondon at only £2. Such men would instead have occupied various positions as vicars, chaplains, chantry priests and the like, enjoying varying degrees of security and remuneration. The value of a parochial vicarage, a comparatively secure position, also varied. Again using the 1379 Bedfordshire evidence, some were worth as little as £2, many about £4 and a few substantially more. It is likely that the vicar would also have been provided with a house. Parochial chaplains and chantry priests, other than in respect of the most well-endowed chantries, probably commanded similarly indifferent remuneration. By the fifteenth century the going rate for a chantry priest appears to have been £5 per annum.

We know all too little about the education of the lesser clergy, but it does not follow that, because they were invariably not university graduates, they lacked vocation or were inadequate for their duties. It is likely that much of the training of would-be priests, other than those destined for (at least the more substantial) parochial livings or higher ecclesiastical office, derived in effect from a form of apprenticeship. Formally there was a series of four minor orders – doorkeeper or porter, reader, exorcist and acolyte. These were followed by the major orders of subdeacon, deacon and priest. In practice the first three of these minor orders seem to have little particular significance for our period, but the generic term 'clerk' is frequently found to describe persons associated with the functioning of the parish, possibly tonsured, but not necessarily in major orders. There is indeed a whole genre of ballad literature concerning 'clerks' who end up seducing village women. In some instances these may represent adolescents or young men who assisted the priest in his duties and so familiarized themselves with the various forms of service. This view is reinforced by references in wills to 'little' clerks. Adolescent boys ordained as acolytes or subdeacons might also be given the paid post of holy water clerk in order to support them through a grammar school education.

A degree of literacy and, more specifically, Latin literacy, was required of the clergy, but again, outside the context of the grammar schools that became increasingly numerous from the second half of the fourteenth century, we know less than we would like about educational provision, particularly elementary education. One place to look, discussed at greater length in Chapter 19, are the various song schools run by parochial clergy. This is suggested, for example, by the 1440 bequest of a parishioner of 2d 'to each scholar not yet a priest' in his parish of Rothwell (Yorks., WR). Numbers of male religious houses operated schools for the sons of their tenants, though in the latter instance it may be that boys showing aptitude would be groomed to enter the noviciate.

The level of learning of the lesser clergy before the plague is very difficult to ascertain. No doubt much was learnt by rote and performed from memory. Once clerical wills become common, however, we have some more insights. Later medieval wills reveal a degree of Latin literacy and a genuine commitment to the ministry. Service books, particularly the breviary or mass book, are commonly noticed, though the possession of this tool of the trade is hardly surprising. We also find a fair scattering of other para-liturgical and devotional works. The York chaplain John Chaloner left copies of the *Alphabet of Tales* and the *Deeds of the Romans*, both sermon manuals, in his will of 1458. Lesser clergy may also have benefited from the increasing provision of service and devotional books chained within the chancels of parish churches. We also know of 'common profit' books designed to circulate among those who could not afford to purchase books of their own. William Wilmyncote, another York chaplain, for example, left at his death in 1405 a group of books, including a bible, to a succession of poor priests.

The advent of inexpensive printed books by the end of the fifteenth century considerably extended the range of material accessible to clergy with only limited resources. Thus Robert Bechame, a chantry priest in the York parish of All Saints, Pavement, left four books in his will dated 1521. Two were service books and two devotional, including a copy of Ludolph of Saxony's Latin *Life of Christ*. The 1523 inventory of Thomas Barton, vicar of St Lawrence in the same city and previously a chantry priest, lists six books, including both service books, but also sermons and theology. Similarly William Broke, a London chantry priest, left a copy of Peter Lombard's *Sentences* at his death in 1515. Many other lesser clergy wills, though they provide little evidence of an interest in learning per se, are invariably conventionally devout. For many, no doubt, ordination represented the means to a job and a wage rather than a vocation, but most were probably both competent and moderately conscientious.

This view is reinforced by visitation material. Such material, by its nature, highlights perceived or alleged faults and transgressions – absent clergy, negligent clergy, incontinent and promiscuous clergy – but also provides clues as to more general patterns of pastoral care. Bishop Stapeldon's visitation of his diocese of Exeter in 1301, for example, provides plentiful illustrations of clergy said to conduct themselves 'well and honestly in spiritual matters'. The vicars of the Devon parishes of Branscombe and Sidbury are also complimented on their preaching, undermining the assumption that preaching was neglected in the pre-Reformation church. More enthusiastically the parishioners of Dawlish said that their chaplain 'teaches them excellently in spiritual things', though they complained that their vicar was not himself resident and that another chaplain within the parish kept a mistress. Significantly in most cases it was not the rector, but his vicar that provided spiritual and pastoral leadership in the parish.

The broader period is marked by efforts to improve the standard of parochial clergy and to equip them for the needs implicit in the canons of the Fourth Lateran Council of 1215. Making provision for clergy with livings to spend some time at university – getting a degree as such was not a medieval priority – was but part of a wider campaign. A whole genre of literature, known as pastoral manuals, was created and comparatively widely circulated. Only some manuals confined their focus to the conduct of confession. A number were written in England. Thomas of Chobham's *Summa Confessorum* was more or less contemporaneous with Lateran IV. Most were produced through the fourteenth century: William of Pagula's *Oculus Sacerdotis*, dating to the 1320s; a cluster of manuals compiled in the 1340s – Higden's *Speculum Curatorum*, the (anonymous) *Regimen Animarum* and William Doune's *Memoriale Presbiterorum*; John de Burgh's *Pupilla Oculi* of 1384, based on Pagula's *Oculus* ('The Priest's Eye'). These were (sometimes extensive) Latin texts. As such, they were accessible only to the more educated of the clergy, but in any case could not have been used directly by a busy priest with a whole parish to confess. They were perhaps more used by higher clergy – probate evidence would tend to support this – who had responsibility for the training of parochial clergy. Nevertheless they offer useful clues as to the sort of areas in which the clergy were encouraged to offer moral guidance. Thus questions were posed about the payment of tithes, not working on holy days and sexual conduct.

Clergy were also given guidance in how to instruct the laity from the pulpit. In particular we may note John Mirk's *Festial*, a popular and long enduring collection of short English sermons tailored to the needs of the liturgical calendar. Mirk likewise produced in English verse his *Instructions for Parish Priests*, which served to make accessible the *Oculus Sacerdotis* to a less educated clergy. How many clergy had direct access to such texts is an open question, but it is likely that their indirect influence was considerable. The corollary of a clergy better equipped to instruct the laity was, however, a better informed and hence sometimes more demanding and critical laity. The Devonshire parishioners cited above who generally spoke in such positive terms about their clergy at visitation in 1301 were perhaps undemanding and easily satisfied. Of the former parochial chaplain of Norton (in the parish of Newton Cyres) they said he

> was accustomed to read the Gospel to the parishioners . . . to sprinkle holy water, and to distribute holy bread, to sing mass each Wednesday and Friday, and to celebrate a full service for them at Christmas and Easter, and to hear their confessions in Lent and likewise baptize their children.

Two centuries later, with the advent of a literate laity, the proliferation of parish guilds, the much greater sense of ownership parishioners enjoyed in respect of their churches, and the existence of an alternative and highly critical ethos contained in Lollardy, the dynamic changed.

PART 3
The Dynamics of a
Pre-industrial Economy

11 THE YEARS OF HUNGER, 1250–1348

The period between 1250 and 1348, the advent of the Black Death, is of particular importance in shaping the relationship between the Crown and the political classes. The latter part of the reign of Henry III (1216–72) was marked by civil war – the Barons' War – and effective civil war characterized a substantial part of the reign of Edward II (1307–27). On the other hand, Edward I (1272–1307), at least until the last years of his reign, managed to contain his powerful subjects, not least by engaging them in his military campaigns in Wales and Scotland, while at the same time consolidating royal authority through his rigorous approach to the demands of kingship and his pursuit of an ambitious legislative and administrative programme. The final years of the period saw the young Edward III (1327–77) emerge from under the shadow of his mother and Roger Mortimer, her lover, to assert his authority by successful campaigning in Scotland and then by reactivating a long smouldering dispute with the French Crown over the duchy of Gascony, which last is seen retrospectively as the beginning of the so-called Hundred Years War.

The corollary of warfare being so much a feature of this era was that the Crown needed to be confident of the support of the political classes as a whole. It was also regularly dependent on grants of taxation to augment its revenue from the royal estates, from royal boroughs in the form of fee farms (fixed annual payments) or from the sale of wardships – that is, the Crown's control of the estates (and persons) of under-age heirs to lands held directly of the king. Edward I, following precedents from the previous reign, realized that his authority could be extended (and taxes more effectively collected) if he involved a wider body of people, including persons outside the ranks of the nobility (the shire knights), who might nevertheless have influence in their own localities, and merchants, who could increasingly be identified as a source of wealth, in the process of consultation, an aspect of good government. Another function of parliament was to receive and debate petitions. The record of these petitions is a useful indicator of the anxieties and ambitions of the political classes at any given moment. This sense of a representative assembly as a political barometer was also appreciated by adroit rulers. Finally, the support of such assemblies in enacting a legislative programme was also a powerful bulwark against the narrower interests of particular baronial factions. In these representative assemblies lie the origins of Parliament, a body that only subsequently came to be formally constituted or to exercise real authority in its own right; at this early date it was little more than an extension of the king's council.

We cannot divorce any overview of the main political events of the period from their economic implications. Warfare was a costly business and this cost was not sustained solely by the political elite represented in Parliament. Rather it was shared with a substantial body of slightly more well-to-do peasants and townsfolk, representing perhaps some third of all householders. Between 1290 and 1348 over £1 million was collected in direct taxation of the lay population. A further £216,500 or more was raised from clerical taxation. The peasantry as tenants would also have contributed indirectly in so far as their rents and labour helped pay their lords' tax obligations. Warfare impinged even more directly in terms of fighting on the Welsh and Scottish borders. This sucked in men to fight, but also resulted in the pillaging of crops and property. This was particularly acute in respect of the Scottish raids of Edward II's reign. The royal right to purveyance – that is, to collect foodstuffs against military need – further impacted on the rural economy. Finally it should be noted that the disastrous era of Bannockburn (1314) and the near civil war culminating in Boroughbridge (1322) coincided with the Agrarian Crisis, a period of near famine followed by a series of livestock 'murrains'. These were dark days indeed.

In 1250 Henry III had been king for 34 years, though his effective rule had commenced only in 1227 when he had declared his majority. His was a rule characterized by a clear sense of his own authority, his right to choose his own counsellors and, consequently, a growing friction with his magnates, who considered themselves his rightful advisers. That same year the Holy Roman Emperor Frederick II Hohenstaufen died. Frederick's demise sucked Henry into imperial politics and the ambitions of Pope Innocent IV to contain Hohenstaufen rule. In particular, Innocent IV aimed to reclaim the Kingdom of Sicily, which Frederick had effectively absorbed into the Empire. Failing to interest other princes, Innocent turned to Henry and in 1254 offered him the Sicilian crown on behalf of his second son Edmund, earl of Lancaster. Henry was unwise enough to accept. In return he agreed to meet the pope's considerable debts incurred fighting in the Sicilian kingdom. Henry thus promised enormous sums of money to secure a new overseas kingdom that was in fact rapidly passing into the effective control of Manfred von Hohenstaufen, Frederick's illegitimate son.

The political debacle forced Henry to yield to pressure from his magnates, culminating in the Provisions of Oxford of 1258 whereby Henry agreed to the appointment of a Council of Fifteen and to hold regular sessions of a Great Council, so giving formal voice, and supposedly influence, to a group of magnates elected by the wider body of the higher aristocracy. Further reform in respect of feudal law was attempted by the Provisions of Westminster the year following. These political concessions failed to distract Henry from the Sicilian project. He continued to appease the papacy and in return was absolved from his oath of agreement to the emasculating Provisions of Oxford. He likewise secured peace with Louis IX of France by the treaty of Paris (1259) whereby he renounced claims to Normandy, Maine, Anjou and Poitou, territory lost by King John over half a century earlier, and agreed to pay homage to Louis for continued possession of the duchy of Gascony. The full significance of this settlement, the roots of the conflict misleadingly known as the Hundred Years War, was only subsequently to emerge.

The failure of Henry to be bound by the spirit of the Constitutions, together with disquiet on the part of some magnates about the extent to which the royal prerogative was theirs to limit spilled over into civil war. Simon de Montfort, the earl of Leicester and leader of the radical faction, struck the first blow, capturing Henry and his heir at the battle of Lewes in 1264. For a brief interval, de Montfort exercised effective rule, but Prince Edward ('the Lord Edward') escaped and killed de Montfort at the battle of Evesham a year later. By the dictum of Kenilworth (1266) Henry attempted to write de Montfort out of history, though by the Statute of Marlborough (1267) he reiterated much of the earlier Provisions and reaffirmed Magna Carta. The same year, by the treaty of Montgomery, he recognized the claims of Llywelyn ap Gruffydd to rule as prince in Wales in return for his homage, by implication surrendering his own claim to lands and to vassals in the principality. Llywelyn's subsequent failure to renew this homage to Edward following Henry's death in 1272 was to provoke war.

Edward I assumed the throne on his return from crusade. As we have seen, he served his apprenticeship confronting Simon de Montfort and the baronial opposition to his father's rule at the battles of Lewes and Evesham, respectively the high and low points of de Montfort's power. His objective from the beginning of his reign was to win back royal rights eroded, as he saw it, by baronial usurpation, although as so often in seeking a restoration of the *status quo ante*, he was in fact claiming powers that had never previously been exercised by the monarch. Rigorous inquiries into breaches of regalian rights during 1274–75 (Ragman) and into the extent of the royal demesne and associated rights in 1279 were attempted, both of which built on precedents set by Henry III during the 1250s. Further inquiries demanding by what authority (*quo warranto*) magnates held their lands or exercised various rights culminated in the *de Quo Warranto* statute of 1290. These initiatives, aside from generating substantial and invaluable historical evidence, were perhaps more significant for signalling Edward's intentions than for what they actually achieved, but they do represent a seizing of the initiative and in that sense alone strengthened the king's authority.

The legislative programme that followed these inquests was no less ambitious. The first statute of Westminster (1275) attempted to address abuses of power by royal officials shown up by the Ragman inquiry by codifying a range of earlier laws. Significant codification and reform of the law relating to property holding, policing and the delivery of justice were contained in the statutes of Gloucester (1278), Winchester (1285) and Westminster II (1285). Mercantile law was also addressed in ways mutually beneficial to the Crown and the merchant community now regularly consulted in Edwardian parliaments as burgesses (representatives of boroughs). The effects were, among others, to considerably increase the volume of litigation dealt with by the royal courts, and hence both the Crown's authority and revenue.

Further significant reforms, this time of mutual advantage to the Crown and the aristocracy, were the statute of Mortmain (1279) and the statute *Quia Emptores* (1290), otherwise Westminster III. The former forbade the alienation (gift or sale) of land to the Church. This discouraged rather than halted such pious endowment on the part of the landholding classes while in practice providing the Crown with an important source of revenue in the form of licences to circumvent the statute (licences to alienate in Mortmain). The latter outlawed subinfeudation, whereby vassals (aristocratic tenants of lords) continued to claim feudal rights in respect of lands they themselves alienated (sold). *Quia Emptores* ensured that, when land was sold, the new owner owed feudal services directly and exclusively to the lord. Edward also undertook a total recoinage between 1278 and 1280, and embarked on a substantial reminting of coins between 1299 and 1301 so as to ensure a standard silver content. The corollary of this was a long tradition of stable currency that benefited the economy.

Edward I's ruthless bureaucratic drive is also reflected in his changing policy towards England's small – no more than 4000 in the 1270s – Jewish population. This was primarily an urban population, though it is possible that a few Jews lived outside the main urban centres, which encompassed many of the larger towns of the era. Historically the Jews enjoyed religious freedom and limited self-government under royal protection as, in legal fiction, the king's chattels. In practice the community was periodically the target of violent persecution as at Worcester in 1262, London in 1265 and Lincoln a year later. These attacks were often instigated by aristocrats indebted to Jewish money lenders. Although Jews engaged in a range of trades, they came to be particularly associated with money lending and hence a source of revenue to the Crown. The Jews were regularly tallaged (taxed), paying some £5000 a year at the beginning of our period and still some £1600 a year under Edward. As a popularist strategy for gaining aristocratic support, however, Edward curtailed the Jews' ability to lend money. By statute of 1275 he outlawed the levying of interest; as the revenue figures indicate, by destroying the Jewish community's most lucrative source of income, he also significantly reduced the utility of the Jews to the Crown. The community became instead a convenient scapegoat, restricted to a small group of towns and forced to attend preaching by friars aimed at their conversion. Little was done to stem anti-Jewish sentiment and, in 1290, the remaining Jewish population was expelled.

The Edwardian reform programme was important in extending the authority of the Crown through the administration of government and justice, but it was warfare that probably had the most immediate impact on English society as a whole. In terms of government, the tendency is to describe a shift from a 'law state' to a 'war state'. In terms of the economy the impact was seen in providing troops, paying taxes or, in the case of Wales, supplying masons, smiths and other building craftsmen to build castles and migrants to settle the new towns. English lordship in Wales was of long standing and had been extended by Henry III. Parts of Wales were settled on Edward in 1254, but much of west and central Wales remained effectively under Welsh rule. English rule was, however, effectively challenged by the emergence of Llywelyn ap Gruffydd. A truce was established in 1267 (Treaty of Montgomery), but in 1276 Llywelyn led a further rebellion. This provided the pretext for Edward, now king, to mount a major campaign of conquest. Despite further revolts in 1282 (leading to Llywelyn's death), 1287 and 1294, Wales was effectively annexed to the English Crown. A like aggressive imperial policy, designed to secure the kingdom as a client state, was pursued by Edward in Scotland.

The death of Alexander III of Scotland (1249–86) leaving only his infant granddaughter, Margaret of Norway, as heir created a power vacuum that Edward I was invited to fill. By the treaties of Salisbury and Birgham, Edward was to exercise guardianship over the kingdom and the person of the young queen, who was to be betrothed to Edward's own heir. Margaret's death in 1290, however, curtailed these plans and precipitated a succession dispute in which Edward I was asked to arbitrate. Edward's price for preferring the claim of John Balliol over that of Robert Bruce went beyond Balliol's homage, given at Newcastle at the end of 1292, to include rights to hear legal disputes appealed from Scotland and to demand military service from Scottish lords. Conflict over this last provoked a savage military response. Early in 1296 Berwick was sacked and its inhabitants cut down by the English soldiers. Shortly afterwards Edinburgh was taken and Balliol became Edward's prisoner. The brutality of Edward's policy, however, inevitably provoked active resistance. A rebellion by William Wallace the following year saw the English defeated at Stirling Bridge, but Edward responded with his usual aggression, defeating the Scots at Falkirk in July 1298. Scottish resistance continued and Wallace was only captured in 1305. The following year Robert Bruce, grandson of the earlier claimant, renewed the rebellion and had himself crowned king.

The legacy of Edward's Scottish policy was to be border conflict, periodic Scottish raids well into the northern counties of England, and the high cost of defending the northern counties. The border region came effectively to constitute a semi-militarized zone characterized by castles and fortified houses; political authority tended to be exercised by a small number of powerful magnate families, most notably the Percys and the Nevilles, rather than the Crown. Edward II inherited an ongoing revolt, but lacked either the will or the resources to reverse this. The English forces were defeated at Louden Hill in 1307 and English rule in Scotland was progressively eroded. The nadir was the crushing English defeat at Bannockburn in 1314. All Edward I's Scottish policy was effectively undone, though warfare continued with new campaigns in 1316 and 1319, and concerted and highly damaging border incursions by the Scots in the 1320s, until a truce was concluded in 1328 by the treaty of Edinburgh-Northampton.

Edward II's disastrous failures against the Scots served only to undermine his political authority, but his military failings were matched by his unbalanced patronage and favouritism at court. His first great protégé, the Gascon, Piers Gaveston, had focused resentment both as an outsider and as a man of comparatively lowly aristocratic pedigree, but his capture and subsequent murder (1312) by Edward's aristocratic opponents left a legacy of mutual antagonism. Thomas of Lancaster, whose ambition was matched only by his wealth, set himself up as the leader of the faction seeking to constrain his actions by enforcing the so-called Ordinances drawn up by the magnates in 1310 and issued the year following. His faction was lent strength by Bruce's repeated incursions across the border, by Edward's singular patronage of Hugh le Despencer and his son, and by their reckless and provocative conduct. By 1321 the rift was tantamount to civil war, but Lancaster's defeat at Boroughbridge in 1322 temporarily checked effective opposition while creating a political martyr. Edward was finally overthrown in 1326 in a coup led by his own queen, Isabella, together with Roger Mortimer, a politically ambitious and wealthy baron (later created the earl of March). Edward was murdered within a year, and Isabella and Mortimer ruled in the young Edward III's name until the latter's dramatic coup of 1330.

The Scottish war was renewed again after Edward III wrested power from Isabella and Mortimer, and promoted Edward Baliol as a client king against the boy king, David II, son of Robert Bruce. David was defeated at Halidon Hill in 1334, but returned in 1341 after a period of exile in France. In 1346 he led a large Scottish invasion force into England, but was routed at Neville's Cross, near Durham, and himself taken prisoner together with the relic of the Black Rood of Scotland.

David II's ambitious foray into England was at the behest of Philip of Valois (Philip VI of France) precisely at the moment that Edward III was besieging Calais. This conflict, too, had long roots. Henry III had consolidated what remained of the Angevin Empire, namely the duchy of Gascony (Aquitaine or Guyenne) by the treaty of Paris (1259), recognizing in return the suzerainty of the French Crown and doing homage to Louis IX for the duchy. These treaty conditions were strained, however, as a consequence of the centralizing policy of Philip IV (the Fair). In much the same way as Edward I was to do in Scotland, so Philip encouraged Edward's Gascon vassals to appeal disputes over the head of their suzerain to Parlement of Paris. Frictions between the conflicting interests of the French and English Crowns precipitated actual hostilities in 1294, which ran on until late in 1297, but were temporarily resolved by treaty in 1303, by which Edward married his heir to Philip's daughter Isabella.

Hostilities over Gascony were renewed again in 1324. Edward I had actively pursued a policy of planting fortified towns, known as *bastides*, in Gascony so as to secure new commercial centres to generate income and strengthen the rule of the English dukes. Edward II actively continued this policy, but the provocative action of Charles IV in planting his own *bastide* of St Sardos in the duchy provoked war once more. The set-tlement made three years later in the young Edward III's name was unfavourable to the English Crown and there is a clear sense that renewed hostilities would in time become inevitable. The English Crown could not exercise effective control in Gascony so long as the French Crown exploited its sovereign rights, but equally the French Crown could not hope effectively to extend the authority of the king over the whole realm so long as territorial princes such as the duke of Gascony resisted. The renewal of war in 1337 thus appears as a continuation of the earlier conflicts over Gascony – a third Gascon war – rather than the beginning of a Hundred Years War. Even Edward III's 1340 assertion of his claim to the French Crown by right of succession through his mother, the daugh-ter and only surviving child of the late king Philip IV, can be seen as a necessary diplo-matic ploy rather than a primary military objective. Significantly, it was a claim he was prepared to trade in for sovereign rights over Gascony by the Treaty of Brétigny (1360).

The few years before the advent of plague were thus overshadowed by warfare and the demands of warfare. Portsmouth and Southampton were both attacked in 1338. Edward launched a series of raids across the channel, in Brittany in 1341 and in Normandy in 1346. This last culminated in the victory at Crécy and the capture of Calais. At the same time, war was renewed by David II of Scotland, since 1334 in formal alliance with the French Crown, leading to his unsuccessful invasion of the northern counties in 1346. The impact, once again, must be understood in terms of the manpower diverted to warfare, the disruption of overseas trade, the material and human damage inflicted by border raids, but, most of all, the actual financial burden, sustained through direct and indirect taxation, of supporting the fighting forces. The economic costs of the Hundred Years War have indeed been long debated, most notably by Postan and McFarlane. In the early stage of the war, prior to the advent of plague, the impact on manpower must have been slight. The impact on the wool trade was prob-ably much more severe.

Under Edward I, direct taxation in the form of a levy of a proportion of the value of subjects' moveable goods (as opposed to lands) became the norm at times of acute need (i.e. war) from the time of his 'fifteenth' of 1275. A further 'thirtieth' was granted in 1283, but from 1290, right until the advent of plague, such subsidies became much more regular in the face of continued hostilities in Wales, Scotland and Gascony. Between 1290 and 1346, subsidies were levied in 25 different years (and two separate subsidies were levied in 1336). Several modest debasements of the coinage were made from 1344 in order to stretch resources a little further, and the clergy too were taxed. In total these taxes yielded well over £1 million. This primarily represents profits from agriculture and hence revenue that was not available to be reinvested in agriculture. Although the subsidies were levied only on the more prosperous members of the community, whether lords, merchants or substantial peasants, it was possible for manorial lords to offset their own costs by imposing a tallage on their servile tenants.

The consequent comparatively high burden of taxation was especially marked during the 1290s and again with the commencement of Edward III's campaigning in France during the 1340s. Under the system of subsidies operating until 1334, this burden was largely shouldered only by the more prosperous members of peasant society. Wage earners and smallholders were specifically protected from tax, though town governors were not always so scrupulous about preserving this principle. Only about a third of households normally paid tax prior to 1334 as a consequence, but this pattern changed with the imposition of a new system that year. Rather than requiring a new assessment of individual taxpayers for each new subsidy, each vill was assessed as a whole. It then fell to the (invariably more substantial) members of the vill to decide how the tax should be paid within their community. What evidence we have suggests that the result was to extend the taxpaying population by including numbers of persons who had been protected by the earlier conventions precisely at the moment that the frequency of taxation accelerated. In Kent, for example, the number of taxpayers rose from 11,000 in 1334 to 17,000 four years later.

Indirect taxation took the form of customs charges levied, from 1275, on wool and leather exports. The level of this duty varied over the period. The 'ancient' custom paid by all traders was levied at 6s 8d (33 pence) on every sack, whereas a 'new' custom from 1303 to 1311 and again after 1322 was levied only on aliens – that is, merchants who were not the king's subjects – and at half the 'ancient' rate. In addition to these regular levies, additional (much higher) charges, known as maltoltes, were imposed at time of war. These were levied in 1294–97, 1317–18, 1322–23, 1327, 1336, 1338, 1340–41 and from 1342 for the subsequent 20 years. The maltolte was at a very high level in 1294–97 and it returned to high levels under Edward III, being fixed at £2 a sack in 1342. Duty was also imposed on cloth imports from 1303 and from 1347 on exports as well.

The effect of these heavy duties latterly was profound. They had a disruptive effect on the Flemish textile industry and served to significantly reduce the demand for wool from that market. In the short term, sudden hikes in export duty, as in 1294–97, had the effect of glutting the domestic market with cheap wool, causing hardship for producers. In the longer term, on the other hand, the twin effects of duty on exported wool and on imported cloth acted as an artificial, if unintended, protection of the domestic cloth industry. It is likely that domestic cloth manufacture, which had tended to contract during the thirteenth century, was recovering strongly by the eve of the Black Death. The best evidence for this derives from the customs accounts themselves, which show declining cloth imports as well as declining wool exports, the implication being that locally produced cloth was supplanting the market for imported cloth, but ideally we need to know much more about domestic production and markets.

Commercial cloth manufacture was historically located in a number of urban centres, such as Beverley, Gloucester, Lincoln, Oxford and Stamford. The conventional view is that many of these urban centres were hard-pushed to compete with Flemish imported cloth by the beginning of our period. On the other hand plenty of evidence has been found for the proliferation of rural water-driven fulling mills as investments by manorial lords. Particular concentrations have been found in North Lancashire and Cumberland, the West Riding of Yorkshire, the Cotswolds and the West of England, and along the Thames Valley. This trend represents the foundation of new centres of cloth manufacture that were to come to greater prominence after the Black Death. How far this rural industry undermined traditional urban centres of production is a moot point.

Part of the evidence for the supposed decline of urban textile manufacture lies in the inability of numbers of weavers' guilds to pay the Crown the annual fee owed in return for their chartered privileges. There are several reasons for treating this evidence with caution. The willingness of the Crown to allow very significant arrears on these payments to accumulate with impunity – at York they had reached £790 by 1309 – would hardly have served as an incentive for the various weavers' guilds to enforce payments from their members. It may also be that the supposed privileges stemming from the charters came not to seem of much value as new rural manufacture infringed local monopolies with apparent impunity. The ability to pay the fees may have little relation to the actual number of weavers operating. At Lincoln in 1348 an inquiry into the weavers' guild found that numbers of weavers were employees of citizens, but as such were not members of or contributory to the guild. To maintain that urban cloth manufacture was unaffected by a growing rural industry would, however, fly in the face of clear evidence that some centres – notably Leicester, Northampton, Oxford and Stamford – effectively ceased to be centres of production, although merchants from these towns had instead traded in Flemish cloth.

Historical writing on the wool industry is also skewed towards what can be learned from the export trade, but in fact there is much manorial evidence relating to production, size of flock, wool yields and the like. Customs on wool are first recorded from 1279. These show that exports peaked (at some 45,000 sacks) in the first decade of the fourteenth century, but fell back substantially (to some 25,000 sacks) in the period spanning the Agrarian Crisis (1315–17) and the murrains (animal disease) that followed, to recover somewhat in the 1330s, data being lacking for the final decade before the advent of plague. Most wool was exported from London, but Boston, Hull and Southampton (in that order) were also significant wool-exporting ports, reflecting in part the importance of Yorkshire (where the Cistercians in particular ran extensive flocks of sheep), Lincolnshire and central southern England as wool-producing districts, although some exported wool came from rather further afield.

It is likely that the decline in exports in the earlier decades of the fourteenth century reflect a real fall in actual production consequent upon the loss of livestock due to murrain, but the 1270s had also witnessed high sheep mortality associated with scab. The numbers of sheep on the extensive estates of the bishop of Winchester were particularly depressed in the late 1270s and 1280s, but, this trough aside, the figures tend to show a slow decline in numbers up to the time of the Black Death, after which stocks were rapidly expanded. This must partly be explained by the expansion of grain production, which commanded high prices, at the expense of pasture. In this respect the Winchester figures do probably throw some light on the national picture.

A significant volume – perhaps two-thirds – of wool produced was associated with peasant producers, though the historical literature tends to focus on the one hand on large monastic and aristocratic growers and, on the other, on substantial wool merchants, many of whom were Italians. English merchants, however, came to displace Italians and other 'aliens' by the eve of the plague since they paid less export duty. Native merchants also regularly acted as middlemen between local producers, especially smaller producers, and larger-scale traders. Larger producers might deal directly with overseas merchants. For example, Meaux Abbey near Hull sold 120 sacks of wool in the 1280s, a period, as we have noted, of serious sheep disease, to merchants from Lucca, but by selling in advance of the actual clip, Meaux and other producers ran into serious debt. Some of the larger Italian companies were subsequently ruined lending to Edward III to finance his Gascon war. Half a century later, most wool exported from Hull, including we may presume that from Meaux flocks, was being traded by native merchants of whom the best known is Michael de la Pole, who himself became heavily involved in royal finances in the 1340s. De la Pole also travelled extensively within the region to buy up wool from the numerous small producers, so some of the profits of the industry ultimately found their way into the pockets of the rural peasantry.

The century prior to the Black Death has often been seen as a period of growth. Towns proliferate and expand. New markets are established. New lands are colonized and brought under cultivation. Old land is used more intensively. The population grows. The demand for luxury goods increases. Lords and merchants alike enjoy considerable wealth, which they are not ashamed to flaunt. Parish churches and cathedrals are augmented or rebuilt in opulent style, their windows fitted with figurative glass, their walls painted and their interiors filled with images. The cathedral at Exeter, for example, was substantially rebuilt over this period and the Octagon and Lady Chapel at Ely are masterpieces of the first part of the fourteenth century. The rich and powerful erect elaborate tombs for themselves – the Percy tomb in Beverley Minster is a particularly splendid product of the very eve of the Black Death – and endow chantries to speed their souls through purgatory. The commencement of the Hundred Years War sees remarkable military success and a conscious revival of chivalric values. The lilac- and orange-clad peasants of the Luttrell Psalter labour uncomplainingly for their lord in a rural utopia.

This perspective may be qualified in a number of ways and from a number of perspectives. Those who would endorse the broad outline above would suggest that it characterized the period before c.1320 more than the three decades following. Others would point to a more complex and regionally diverse pattern: lands were being abandoned in some areas at precisely the same time as new land was being colonized elsewhere. Historians working within a Marxist framework would suggest that, rather than representing the apogee of feudal society, this period represented the beginning of a 'crisis of feudalism'; revenue generated from the labour of peasants was squandered on lavish buildings and luxurious lifestyles rather than reinvested in the land. The present chapter heading reflects the perspective not of those at the top of the social ladder, but rather the majority towards the bottom. The wealth that was amassed by the feudal aristocracy and which served *inter alia* both to sustain significant cultural patronage and to finance war represented but one facet of a broader polarization in the distribution of wealth. Just as the rich tended to get richer over this period, so the poor tended to get poorer. Only in the imagination (or wishful thinking) of the manuscript's patron did the Luttrell peasants wear lilac and orange and go about their task ever uncomplaining.

One debate that was initiated in the 1950s by Professor Munia (otherwise Michael) Postan concerns the question of whether continued population growth over some three centuries led, by the last decades of the thirteenth century, to overpopulation and indeed to a catastrophic crisis – a 'Malthusian crisis' – of population in the early decades of the fourteenth century. The term Malthusian crisis derives from the writings of the Reverend Thomas Malthus, who wrote on population in the early years of the nineteenth century and whose ideas helped shape the New Poor Law. He wrote that population will tend to grow at a faster rate than the ability of agriculture to increase production. Consequently a point of crisis – a 'positive check' – will occur in the form of starvation and deaths from malnutrition, or in the form of warfare as peoples compete for scarce resources, unless a 'preventive check' intervenes to hold populations back. Malthus understood this preventive check in terms of young people either refraining from marriage or delaying marriage, and hence reproduction, until they had amassed a sufficiency of resources. Postan argued that a positive check was indeed reached with the Agrarian Crisis of 1315–17, and he attempted to demonstrate how increasingly frequent harvest shortfalls were matched by sharp rises in mortality, culminating in the catastrophic harvests of the crisis years.

The crisis of 1315–17 represented but the final phase in Postan's larger model, which is now termed the Postan thesis. Postan argued that population growth led, on the one hand, to the increasing utilization of unsuitable ('marginal') land for cultivation and, on the other, to the over-intensive use of lands already under cultivation. Thus we see a gradual shift from two-field systems (whereby half the land was left fallow each year) to three-field systems (whereby only one-third of the land was fallow at any time), and the continued expansion of the amount of land under the plough. Arable crops – wheat, barley, oats – are always a more efficient way of using the land to feed a growing population, but Postan's argument is that arable production expanded at the expense of pastoral – primarily sheep and cattle. The result was that the amount of fertilizer in the form of animal manure available to sustain grain production declined at precisely the same time that grain production intensified. Whereas newly colonized lands and lands brought under the plough for the first time, according to the Postan thesis, would have been exhausted within a few years, lands that had traditionally sustained arable production would have seen a slow, but inexorable decline in yields. Together with his collaborator, Jan Titow, he attempted to demonstrate this thesis by intensive study of the manorial records of the large southern English estate of the bishop of Winchester, though it is generally agreed that their work on Winchester yields provided less than convincing proof that fertility declined in quite the clear and consistent way they had hypothesized.

Although the Postan thesis is now some half a century old, it has remained very influential, either because scholars continue to be influenced by it or because they explicitly position themselves against it. Some general caveats should be spelled out before we go any further. When looking at the rural economy, scholars are increasingly sensitive to regional diversity. The nature of the rural economy owed much to local geography and climate. In the comparative absence of inexpensive bulk transport, agricultural surpluses could not readily be transported great distances and, consequently, the possibility of regional specialization was constrained, though by no means absent. It follows that any overview that depends on findings from one single region is necessarily flawed. To study the rural economy, moreover, we are very dependent on the survival of manorial account rolls. Our knowledge is consequently largely limited to the experience of the seigneurial demesne, particularly in respect of the more heavily manorialized regions of the country and for the greater estates, particularly episcopal and monastic estates, since their archives are more likely to survive. All too little is known of the peasant economy, especially in less heavily manorialized regions.

The problem is not solely a question of record survival. The relatively complete run of court rolls of the extensive Yorkshire manor of Wakefield, for example, has been relatively little used to date, though the paucity of accounts for the same manor would make analysis of the agrarian economy problematic. On the other hand, scholarship on peasant society to date tends to be associated with specific institutions such as the School of History at the University of Birmingham (the Birmingham School) and the Pontifical Institute of Medieval Studies, Toronto. The former is associated with primarily West Midlands manorial studies following a Marxist perspective, whereas the latter is more dependent on Public Record Office sources and is characterized by a distinctive methodology for classifying peasants by office holding. It follows that much work still needs to be done, particularly to redress these regional and institutional biases, though approaches derived from historical geography and deploying a wider variety of sources are beginning to address this need.

There is much about the broader outline of the Postan thesis, which, despite the caveats just noted, remains attractive. As we have already seen, the period between 1250 and *c*.1315 saw a continuation of an earlier pattern of population growth. If we look around, we can still find areas associated with the colonization of previously under-utilized land, as for example at Bilsdale (Yorks., NR) or in West Devon and Cornwall. Within the main arable regions of Midland England, three-field systems were more common by the early fourteenth century than had been true a century prior to that. Substantial numbers of royal licences to hold rural markets or fairs continued to be granted even after 1300, which again could suggest a growing level of production. The level of rents (for free tenants), entry fines and (in respect of servile tenants) customary amercements (such as merchet and heriot) all tended to rise, again reflecting increasing competition for land within the peasant community, though an adherence to 'custom' significantly blunted the effects on villein rents of what today would be dubbed 'market forces'. In particular it has been noted that merchet payments in respect of villein widows, who controlled dower holdings, remarrying in the early years of the fourteenth century rose to unprecedented levels, a sure indicator of how lords were able to exploit the acute underlying demand for land, and, as at Cottenham (Cambs.), men married such widows in preference to younger, never-married women.

By the later thirteenth century grain prices were beginning to fluctuate markedly and by the time of the Agrarian Crisis this pattern was greatly accentuated, clear evidence of the frequency and severity of harvest failure – demand for grain is comparatively 'inelastic' and prices will rise markedly against any scarcity. At Tickhill (Yorks., WR), for example, the price of wheat rose to 22s a quarter in 1315–16, more than five times the normal level, and way beyond the means of many consumers. Contemporary chroniclers frequently noted prices even in excess of that. In a landmark article, Postan and Titow show that years characterized by high grain prices correlate with those years associated with larger numbers of recorded heriot payments, and notably heriots paid in cash.[1] The heriot was a fine paid to the lord whenever the tenant gave up (often involuntarily as a consequence of their demise) a customary holding; it represented a fraction of the value of the holding and was symbolic of the lord's ultimate title to that holding. For more substantial peasants, whose holdings might support livestock, the heriot was normally levied in the form of the best beast, but a simple money payment was normal in respect of smallholders. The high volume of money heriot payments in years of harvest shortfall are thus interpreted as reflecting high malnutrition-related mortality among smallholders, precisely those most vulnerable to harvest failure.

Tempting though it is to accept this as evidence that the population had indeed outstripped resources by the early years of the fourteenth century and that a Malthusian positive check was operating, there remains another possibility. Peasant smallholders, whose ability to feed themselves depended on their producing good harvests year in, year out, would always be vulnerable to harvest shortfall. Such shortfalls would need to be made up by purchase precisely at the moment when the market price was inflated. Initially such peasants would be able to draw upon any savings they may have accumulated or rely upon credit from their better-off neighbours, but these are strategies appropriate for isolated years, not for runs of poor harvest. Once both savings and credit had been exhausted, the options available to the smallholder would become both narrow and bleak. By selling smallholdings to more substantial peasant neighbours, peasants were able to find some capital, but would thereafter need to sell their labour to make their livelihood. There was indeed a ready market for such small-holdings in so far as more substantial peasant agriculturalists, who were able to grow surpluses even when yields were depressed, saw these not as plots too small to be viable, but as opportunities to enhance production. Indeed there is reason to think that substantial peasant producers were able to earn more from reduced surpluses when prices were most inflated, than from larger surpluses in years of more modest prices. The rapid increase in the number of recorded money heriot payments represents, therefore, not high mortality, but a frenetic land market, and a consequent and lasting polarization in landholding in peasant society between, on the one hand, more substantial peasants, and landless and near landless labourers on the other. The Agrarian Crisis thus accelerated social change within peasant society, even if it did not represent quite the Malthusian crisis that Postan postulated. Indeed, if we are to look for evidence of crisis mortality, it is not to those with land, however modest, that we should look, but to the landless.

The chronicler Trokelowe described seeing bodies lying in the streets of London and we have a harrowing account of deaths of 55 poor men and women crushed to death while waiting for a distribution of alms at the Dominican friary in London in 1322. Even as early as the 1270s we can find examples from the coroners' rolls for Bedfordshire of deaths due to the exposure and hunger of indigent women, always the most vulnerable group. The likelihood is that conditions were particularly severe in the larger towns and cities since their populations would be swollen by dispossessed

---

1. M.M. Postan and J. Titow, 'Heriots and Prices on Winchester Manors', *Economic History Review*, 2nd ser. 11 (1959), pp. 392–411.

rural migrants, precisely those most at risk of dying on the street because homeless. During the height of the Agrarian Crisis we find royal licences issued for the supply of grain to various towns, but the likelihood is that food was both scarce and expensive. During 1316 the London civic authorities were several times obliged to prosecute bakers for selling bread that was variously underweight or made from rotten or adulterated grain. At the same time, thefts of foodstuff were rife, even though, if caught, perpetrators were liable to be hung. This is anecdotal evidence, but it points to a picture of acute hardship for those at the bottom of society and to a heightened level of mortality associated with malnutrition and even simple starvation. We should be careful, however, not to exaggerate that level.

The disastrous harvests of 1315–17 were accompanied in many places by high levels of livestock mortality, particularly of sheep, as disease spread on saturated grazing lands. Bolton Priory (Yorks., WR) saw its flock of some 3000 sheep reduced to a mere 913 over these years, though mortality elsewhere was often more modest. A second wave of livestock disease was to follow in the years 1319–21. This time it was cattle and oxen that were most affected by the impact of what contemporaries dubbed 'murrain'. Again we need to put these disasters into perspective. High levels of livestock mortality were not confined to this period, moreover sheep scab, which raged during the last quarter of the thirteenth century, may have had a more profound impact on the size of flocks and on wool production. The indications are that the effects of livestock mortality during the Agrarian Crisis were acute, but numbers of sheep and cattle recovered fairly rapidly and the longer-term impact was probably slight.

The Agrarian Crisis hardly spelled an end to an era of poor harvests and high grain prices. There were, for example, poor harvests in 1321 and large parts of the north were overrun by Scottish raiders in the decade following Bannockburn (1314). Raiding, in which livestock was seized and crops burned, stretched across the entire breadth of northern England and far south of the border. In the west, for example, the vicinity of Furness Abbey, already raided in 1316, was subject to further burning and plundering by Robert Bruce in 1322. Fountains Abbey, in the heart of Yorkshire, likewise suffered badly, and Durham, in the east, was subject to widespread burning. In Northumberland enormous destruction was wrought, and income from landed possessions there temporarily evaporated. Conditions were only exacerbated by effective civil war in 1321–22, caused by Thomas of Lancaster's opposition to Edward II, until Lancaster's defeat at Boroughbridge. The fighting also resulted in the deaths of numbers of peasants caught up in the fighting, and caused others to flee. To add to these woes, the murrains of sheep that we find at the time of the Agrarian Crisis were compounded by cattle murrain in the years 1319–21. It is hard not to agree with Sandra Raban that 'the years between 1315 and 1322 must have been among the grimmest on record'.[2]

Social trends in the years immediately prior to the Black Death of 1348–49 are not easy to summarize since it is possible to juxtapose examples of communities that seem to have been little affected by the earlier crisis with those that suffered badly. Wage rates show some evidence of falling back in this period, though this is in part a return to levels prevailing before the crisis, but grain prices also tended to rise for the last decade before the plague. This suggests that for the lower echelons of society conditions did

---

2. S. Raban, *England under Edward I and Edward II, 1259–1327* (Oxford, 2000), p. 19.

improve somewhat. Lords, conversely, may have found that the income from their possessions, which had hitherto tended to grow, was now checked or even reduced.

The very conditions that tended to make it tough for those (the majority) towards the bottom of a very unequally distributed heap tended also to benefit those higher up. The Agrarian Crisis in particular served to accelerate what was probably a longer-term trend, whereby smallholders tended to be squeezed out and more substantial peasant agriculturalists consolidated their landed holdings. So long as grain prices were high, peasants producing a surplus were in a strong position, even to the extent, as we have seen, of buying out smallholders. Large landowners, whether secular lords or institutional landlords, were particularly advantaged. The sale of surpluses from cultivation of the demesne and low labour costs ensured a healthy revenue. At the same time, competition within the peasant population sustained rents and entry fines at a high level. Lords, bishops, abbeys and the like thus enjoyed substantial incomes that allowed for expenditure on building, plate, clothing and food. This is not to imply that lords failed to invest in the land, and certainly not to endorse the notion that medieval agriculture suffered from backward technology or poor yields. The use of vetches and legumes, for example, is now well documented, and grain yields found for parts of Norfolk were considerably in excess of those recorded for the Winchester estates.

The aristocratic demand for skilled masons and goldsmiths, or for fine cloth, silks, imported wines, spices and the like, provided employment for a whole range of workers and craftsmen as well as for the merchants who were able to satisfy these aristocratic tastes. Philip Lovecok, merchant and ten times mayor of Exeter in the earlier part of the fourteenth century, for example, imported among other items significant quantities of wine, but also saffron, almonds and salt cellars, all of which suggests an aristocratic clientele. Merchants, mercers, drapers, goldsmiths, grocers, vintners and the like represented the economic driving force (and often the governing elite) of larger English towns, but they in turn helped provide employment for numbers of craftsmen and petty traders, and this helps explain the continued attraction of towns both for the rural dispossessed and the ambitious rural craftsmen or traders hoping to further their careers.

The aristocracy were not the only component of rural society to be materially advantaged by the very conditions of scarce resources that made life for the majority so tough. Significant numbers of more substantial peasant agriculturalists, both villein and free, regularly produced surpluses for the market. This helps explain the proliferation and vitality of numbers of local markets, whose primary purpose was the exchange of these agricultural surpluses. Such surpluses were essentially both to feed those peasants who were not self-sufficient and to supply the needs of a swelling urban population. By marketing these surpluses, peasant agriculturalists gained access to cash. On the one hand, this allowed them to pay rent to their lord or to hire additional labour to work their holdings, or even to engage in the land market and consolidate their possessions by systematically buying up small parcels of land when they became available. It also permitted a degree of investment in moveables such as farming tools, livestock and the like. William de Cranmer of Walsham le Willows (Suffolk), for example, was running a flock of 72 sheep in the earlier fourteenth century. On the other hand, it represented cash that the Crown could tap into by way of taxation.

12 THE BLACK DEATH AND ITS AFTERMATH, 1348–1381

The main themes of this chapter are the profound social and economic consequences associated with very high mortality at the time of the 'great pestilence', as contemporaries termed it, and the subsequent decades of renewed epidemic. We need, however, to distinguish between short-term and longer-term, and between direct and indirect consequences. In terms of the process of government (as opposed to government policy) and the contemporary politics of war, however, the impact of the demographic catastrophe does not seem to have caused more than a pause. The period between the Black Death of 1348–49 and the Peasants' Revolt of 1381 saw a continuation of the war in France and, until 1360, of Edward III's record of military success.

After a period of effective truce associated with protracted negotiations during which Edward III used his position of strength, augmented by alliance with Charles, king of Navarre, and by rebellion in Normandy, to demand full sovereignty of his French possessions, full-scale war broke out with a mounted expedition, or chevauchée, led by Prince Edward (the Black Prince) in the autumn of 1355. This chevauchée set out from Bordeaux in Gascony, and in September 1356 encountered and defeated the much larger army of John II of France at Poitiers. King John's capture in battle added to Edward III's negotiating position, while parts of the realm of France degenerated into lawlessness and near anarchy as a consequence of the power vacuum so created. In 1358 there were major revolts both in Paris and among the peasantry (the Jacquerie) of parts of northern France, particularly against an aristocracy that had failed in its duty to protect those who worked the land.

In the negotiations that followed, Edward III reiterated his demand for land in full sovereignty. Although the captive John II was prepared to concede to Edward III's demands, the ruling council in France was not at first prepared to yield sovereignty. A new, albeit unsuccessful, expedition in 1359 concentrated minds and resulted in the Treaty of Brétigny the following year. By this treaty Edward agreed to lay aside his claim to the French crown in return for full sovereignty over Gascony together with a substantial ransom for John II. The main terms of this treaty were never ratified, but a truce prevailed until 1369, and with it the problems associated with the return of soldiers used to the relative lawlessness of a livelihood associated with fighting and looting. In 1367, however, Edward III permitted the Black Prince to intervene in a war of succession in Castile on behalf of Peter the Cruel against Henry of Trastamara, who had secured the active assistance of Charles V, John II's successor. Prince Edward defeated Trastamara and his French allies at Nájera in 1367, but failed in the longer term either to oust Trastamara or to break his alliance with France.

The Black Prince's intervention in the Castilian dispute was in effect an extension of the Hundred Years War by proxy, but it indirectly led to a collapse of the truce of

Brétigny. Because Peter the Cruel failed to honour the cost of his campaigning in Castile, and was himself killed by Trastamara in 1369, Prince Edward attempted to recoup this expense instead by raising taxes in Gascony. This was resisted, notably by the lord of Albret and Jean d'Armagnac, who appealed first to Edward III and then to Charles V. By answering the appeal, Charles V knowingly abrogated any sense of surrendering sovereignty over the duchy (now claimed as a principality by Edward III). The renewal of war that followed was inevitable, but after several years of truce, the French were now in better shape to regain the initiative, especially as illness effectively incapacitated the Black Prince.

Between 1369 and 1377, the declining years of Edward III who came to be entirely under the influence of his mistress Alice Perrers, Charles V progressively regained much of Gascony. A new chevauchée led by John of Gaunt in 1373 achieved little. A year before, a Castilian fleet had routed an English fleet at La Rochelle leaving the south coast vulnerable to French attack. The lack of effective kingship, the continued haemorrhaging of funds and the abysmal reversal of years of military success prompted a political crisis, first with the Good Parliament of 1376 and again with the Peasant's Revolt of 1381, the subject of the next chapter. A temporary truce between 1375 and 1377 ended at much the same moment as the boy king Richard II succeeded his elderly and senile father, leaving John of Gaunt as effective ruler. His policy focused on consolidating the English hold on the channel ports of Brittany and Normandy so as to deter French raids on England. This proved a further drain on resources and failed in its stated objective.

To sustain the cost of fighting, the Crown had repeatedly to turn to taxation, which did not entirely go away even during the years of truce created by Brétigny. Direct taxation from 1334 had taken the form of assessments imposed on communities as a whole, on the understanding that payment would devolve to the better-off within those communities. Increasingly, however, the aristocracy and local elites appear to have tried to pass part of the tax burden down the social hierarchy. The renewal of the war after 1369, in particular, caused a renewed surge in the Crown's demands for revenue and stimulated a degree of creativity and experimentation in the way taxes were raised. In 1371 a parish subsidy was levied, though its yield proved very disappointing because the government had seriously overestimated the number of parishes in the realm. The poll (literally 'head') tax of 1377, however, formally extended the principle that all, save the very poorest, should contribute to the tax burden. Poll taxes were repeated, each time on a different basis, in 1379 and (for the last time) in 1380–81.

In addition to direct taxation, the earlier policy of subsidies on wool exports was continued. In 1353 a system of staple ports was established in order to give the Crown greater control over the trade and hence customs revenue deriving from it. Under this new arrangement, wool could only be sold for export at selected ports and only overseas traders were allowed to export. This system was itself displaced by the establishment of a staple first at Bruges and then in 1363 at Calais, which once again allowed English merchants to participate. The creation of the Calais staple was primarily determined by the Crown's desire to find an effective way of financing this strategically important possession. Control was given over to the Company of the Staple, a council of 26 wool merchants. The policy succeeded in helping defray the cost of maintaining Calais, but did nothing to stem the downward trend in wool exports. On the other hand, any decline in wool exports within this period was probably more than compensated for by growth in the domestic cloth trade and in cloth exports. The war and the costs of war thus dominated this period, though it was the advent of plague that probably had the greatest social impact.

The political agenda, though dominated by war, also contained a range of important legislative initiatives, notably the labour legislation of 1349 (Ordinance of Labourers) and 1351 (Statute of Labourers), the Statute of Treason (1352), the (abortive) sumptuary law of 1363, and the Statutes of Provisors (1351) and Praemunire (1353) designed to extend royal at the expense of papal authority over clerical appointments, and discourage appeals by churchmen to the papal curia. To these may be added a whole raft of other statutes, many of which related to trade and numbers of which represent responses to parliamentary petitions. Not all legislation was enforced or enforceable, but we do seem to witness a paradigm shift here. The frequent sessions of Parliament, dictated by the need for political consent to taxation to fund the war, also provided a forum for the concerns and objectives of the wider political nation to be voiced and to shape legislation. Equally, parliamentary legislation was taken in new and creative directions, whether as a means for strengthening royal authority or for shaping social conduct.

The pandemic that raged through Europe from the end of 1347 and for the subsequent three years made a profound impact on those chroniclers and other contemporary writers who survived to tell the tale. It is from these sources that we can trace the course of the disease in England from its arrival in the south-west in the summer of 1348 to its departure into Scotland about a year later. It is from these same chronicles that we learn, none too precisely, of the terrible toll of deaths, and of the profound and traumatic impact of the disease on society. If the chroniclers provide a hazy picture of actual mortality and a luridly coloured picture of the plague's effects, they articulate with remarkable clarity the essential truth, as they saw it: plague was divine in origin and was punishment for sin. Bishop Edington of Winchester concluded:

> . . . it is much to be feared that man's sensuality which, propagated by the tendency of the old sin of Adam, from youth inclines to all evil, has now fallen into deeper malice and justly provoked the Divine wrath by a multitude of sins to this chastisement.

If we are to read the chronicles aright, it is this fundamental premise that we must take on board. It colours so much of what was written at the time, but it seems not to have warned numbers of modern scholars. Only when we read against the profoundly moralizing tone of the contemporary accounts can we begin to make sense of what the chroniclers claim to have seen.

The Black Death precipitated great social change. Few of these changes were a direct product of the plague itself, for its effects were often more indirect and subtle. Some apparent changes represent a consolidation or acceleration of trends that predate the plague. Other changes were short-lived, the product of sudden disruption rather than of a more profound reordering. The most immediate impact was, of course, the very sharp fall in population. The Black Death, as historians from the nineteenth century have termed it, represents the beginning of a major cycle of plague that remained active far into the seventeenth century. Because the disease struck afresh at a population that had had no exposure to it for several centuries, as with the diseases brought from the Old World to the indigenous peoples of the New World, its effects were swift and cataclysmic. The plague spread with relentless progress. Within a year or so it had probably reduced the population of England by nearly a half. Manor court rolls and bishops' registers alike suggest this level of mortality independently of one another; the older consensus that about a third of the population died now looks fragile.

Where a good series of manor court rolls survives, spanning the period of the Black Death itself, it may be possible to know the numbers of tenancies on the eve of the plague and to observe how many of these changed hands as a consequence of deaths. The laconic entries in the court rolls narrate the same harrowing story. On the manor of Wakefield a few months after the plague we read that:

> Henry son of Thomas Bate gives the lord 12d for licence to heriot [death duty] on 9 acres of land and meadow in Thornes in Alverthorpe after the death of Thomas his father, whose heir he is, to hold to himself and his heirs according to the custom of the manor. John son of Thomas Wilcok for the same on a cottage and 2 acres in Alverthorpe after the death of Thomas his father, whose heir he is, to hold likewise. William son of William Bate gives the lord 2d for the same . . .

So the litany goes on. While the proportion of holdings vacated due to death varied from one place to another, an overall proportion of about 45 per cent is widely reported. This is, for example, what Razi found on the manor of Halesowen in the West Midlands, though Page found 56 per cent on the three Crowland (Lincs.) manors.[1] Tithing evidence, relating to males over 12, for several Essex communities also generates a mortality rate of 45 per cent. These figures represent mortality primarily among manorial tenants – the tithing evidence is the exception – and among an adult and predominately male population. They tell us nothing about child mortality or sex-specific mortality, nor do they tell us much about those who held no land or were merely subtenants.

Similar caveats apply to our second major source, the registers of bishops that contain evidence for the tenure of parochial livings and thus the deaths of clergy during the pandemic. Since the number of parishes at the time of the plague is known, the calculation of mortality rates for a number of dioceses is a comparatively straightforward task. Again, considerable variation is found: 60 per cent of the parish clergy of the city of Lincoln died, but only 19 per cent in the deanery of Aston in the same diocese. The overall proportions, however, are strikingly uniform and compatible with the manor court roll statistics; nearly half the beneficed clergy in the dioceses of Bath and Wells, Ely, Exeter, Norwich and Winchester appear to have died. Once again, these figures tell us only about an adult population, but in this case an exclusively male and comparatively well-to-do population. It may be that young people born subsequent to the last epidemic were more vulnerable to later plagues. It may also be that men were a little more susceptible to plague than women. In the absence of more substantial evidence, however, we must accept the chroniclers' perspective that the Black Death respected neither age, nor status, nor gender. The 'great pestilence' seems, then, to have carried off somewhere between two-fifths and a half of the population. The overcrowding, the land-hunger, the underemployment and the

---

1. F.M. Page, *The Estates of Crowland Abbey* (Cambridge, 1934), pp. 120–5.

famines that had characterized the previous century did not entirely go away, but they were much abated.

The haemorrhaging of the population begun by the Black Death did not end there. The later years of the fourteenth century saw repeated epidemics. The second plague of 1361–62 is sometimes known as the Grey Death, but other major epidemics followed in 1369, 1375 and 1391. Further epidemics are documented through the fifteenth century, but these became increasingly localized. Indeed once spread through the population by epidemic, the disease became endemic; people were liable to die at any time rather than en masse at the time of epidemic. From the late fourteenth century, registers of wills complement chronicle evidence. These allow us to observe not just years of high mortality associated with a bunching of wills and perhaps noticed by local chroniclers as times of pestilence, but also the year-on-year pattern of mortality otherwise unremarked by chroniclers. Given that plague seems to have been particularly virulent in the late summer and early autumn it is possible to surmise the presence of endemic plague from high incidences of mortality within that season. (This must be a surmise because plague is not the only disease associated with such a seasonal pattern.) A higher than average incidence of mortality in the autumn season is noticed through the first two-thirds of the fifteenth century, but studies of wills from East Anglia and Yorkshire suggest that endemic plague was less virulent thereafter. It may also be that women were less likely to die of endemic plague than were men.

These last are tentative observations based on difficult sources. Plague (*Yersinia pestis*) was not the only potentially fatal infectious disease known to have existed at this period. Influenza, known as 'the sweat' is known to have been a major cause of death in the 1550s, but may well have been a factor in high recorded levels of mortality in the first decade of the same century if not before. Recent studies have suggested that tuberculosis may also have been a major killer during the fifteenth century and, again, perhaps earlier. The spread of tuberculosis probably displaced leprosy, which had been prevalent in earlier centuries. Continued years of poor harvest and scarcity, noted by chroniclers and reflected in high grain prices, led to deaths from diseases such as typhus or dysentery among poor folk and children weakened by malnutrition. Recent archaeological analysis of children's bones from Wharram Percy (Yorks., ER) points to poor nutrition and living conditions for children once weaned. Such deaths will not generally show up in probate (will) evidence since the underage, smallholders and labourers neither made nor had registered wills.

Plague, both epidemic and endemic, was a major killer, probably *the* major killer, well into the fifteenth century. It operated alongside other diseases that at particular moments accounted for large numbers of deaths and that serve to make it difficult to reconstruct plague's precise effect on different groups in society. Several chroniclers identified the epidemic of 1361–62 as particularly afflicting the young and, in at least a couple of instances, males more than females. Unfortunately, in several instances this testimony is patently borrowed from one chronicle to another. Nor is there any clear evidence to identify this epidemic with bubonic plague. To go further and draw speculative deductions from modern plague studies or to read conclusions as to who would be most at risk from speculations as to the behaviour of rats and fleas in a medieval environment is foolhardy in the extreme.

There are further reasons for sounding a note of caution. The conventional historical accounts of the Black Death talk confidently of the disease as bubonic plague caused by the bacillus *Yersinia pestis*, carried by fleas, and endemic in certain regions of the world and in certain rodent populations. The advent and spread of plague is explained in terms of the movement of infected rats, specifically black rats, along trade routes, but, once introduced, spreading that infection to indigenous rats and from rats to the humans whose homes are shared by rats. Analogies are drawn with the experience of the disease in a more recent, and hence better documented past, and the contemporary evidence is thus accommodated within a predetermined model. Though historians, who are neither epidemiologists nor biologists, have long been satisfied with this methodologically flawed approach, it is striking that loud dissent is periodically voiced by professional epidemiologists and biologists, who are not, of course, historians and hence have commanded little respect within the historical community.

The particular concerns raised by biologists relate to the speed with which the disease spread, the extent of its occurrence and the high level of mortality. The capacity of the disease to spread quickly even over rural areas and outside of the bigger towns has surprised. Recently it has been questioned how far the black rat would have been found outside an urban, and particularly a port, context. It has been argued that plague epidemics struck medieval Iceland even though the hostile climate meant that neither rats nor fleas flourished there. Some scholars have therefore preferred to suggest more contagious diseases, even drawing analogies with the Ebola virus, and to abandon any link with *Yersinia pestis*. On the other hand, one recent piece of French research claims to have found evidence for *Yersinia pestis* DNA in the teeth of supposed victims of the Black Death. The jury is still out and will be, no doubt, for a long time to come. What we do know is that very large numbers of people died in 1348–49 and that large numbers continued to die for a long time after. Population levels tumbled at the time of the Black Death and probably continued to fall at least until the middle of the fifteenth century. And that is all we need to know for the moment.

The sudden and dramatic fall in population had several immediate effects. First, it created local labour shortages. A number of chroniclers reported that harvests rotted for lack of hands or that livestock roamed untended. Henry Knighton also reported a marked fall in the price of livestock. At the same time certain peasant holdings became vacant for lack of heirs. Sometimes lords were able to find new tenants, but in the short term at least some lands went unlet and uncultivated. Urban landlords faced the same short-term problem, perhaps particularly in respect of cheaper properties. Other effects followed swiftly. In order to secure labour, employers were forced to offer higher wages. Employers who failed to allow their employees the new wages found that labour went elsewhere. Employers, whether lords of manors, artisans with workshops, or more substantial peasant agriculturalists, were pitted in open competition with one another. Moreover, because the relationship between employer and wage labourer was purely contractual and owed nothing to legal status or manorial custom, lords found that they could exercise no prior claims over available labour.

Plague mortality thus brought about many disjunctions in terms of patterns of landholding and employment, but in ways that appeared consistently to advantage the lower echelons of society and to disadvantage the traditional elites. Lords found themselves confronted by wage labourers who refused to work on the same terms and conditions as had prevailed before the plague and who were no longer bound by the disciplines of a saturated labour market and low wages. Some hired workers took advantage of higher wages to invest in leisure and, having earned as much in a single morning as they previously earned in a whole day, chose not to return to work from their midday break, but spent the time in the alehouse. At the same time, lords faced real difficulties finding tenants for all their holdings, particularly in respect of customary holdings to which substantial labour services were still attached, and so found themselves under pressure to reduce rents and to forgo customary obligations at precisely the moment they had most incentive to increase them to compensate for labour shortages.

These changes were difficult for contemporaries to assimilate. From the perspective of the social elite, as reflected in written sources, they could only be understood in moralistic terms. The Black Death, as Bishop Edington, quoted above, had observed, was punishment for sin. Looking around at the world on the morrow of the plague, the bishop saw evidence of that sin wherever he looked. The order of society as imagined by the landed classes of which the bishop was a part – an order that was held to be natural and hence divinely sanctioned – had been challenged by labourers refusing work on the old terms, and by peasants who were prepared to argue and bargain with their lords rather than accept without question the conditions that had bound their fathers and grandfathers before them. Such a challenge was thus a challenge to divine authority and as such a manifestation of the very sin for which the plague had been sent as chastisement. Similarly the propensity of some labourers to invest in leisure was a sign of sloth, just as their demand for better terms of service was a product of greed. The refusal of peasants to acquiesce without murmur to their lords was interpreted as arrogance and rebellion.

This moralistic perspective that understood the social and economic consequences of plague in terms of sin is most clearly to be seen in the preamble to the Statute of Labourers (1351). In response to the sudden inflationary pressures on wages an ordinance had been issued in 1349. This Ordinance of Labourers represented an emergency response by the king's council made while there was no Parliament due to the plague. It attempted by decree to peg wages at levels prevailing prior to the plague, but wage levels, driven as they were by the economics of supply and demand, failed to return to pre-plague levels simply at the king's command. New legislation in the form of the Statute of Labourers was therefore enacted. According to the preamble, the statute was directed against 'the malice of servants who were idle and unwilling to serve after the pestilence without taking outrageous wages'. It went on to deplore the non-compliance with the earlier ordinance:

> But now our lord king has been informed . . . that such servants completely disregard the said ordinance in the interests of their own ease and greed and that they withhold their service to great men and others unless they have liveries and wages twice or three times as great as those they used to take . . .

Market economics are thus translated by the statute's framers into the same language of sin as that deployed by the bishop and the clerical chronicler. Likewise the legislative response was couched in the language of order, of custom, and of maintaining or restoring the status quo.

The remedy of the statute was to peg wages, to set wages for such labour-intensive seasonal tasks as reaping, mowing and hay making, to curb the mobility – and hence the bargaining power – of agricultural labourers, and to oblige such labourers to swear to abide by the terms of the statute under pain of imprisonment in the stocks. Such a policy was not entirely without precedent. Attempts to control landless labour at a village level during the harvest season are sometimes found in by-laws dating to the period before the plague, but there is little to suggest that there was any significant seigneurial input into these. London ordinances designed to regulate the wages of building workers are also found before the plague.

Such precedents do not detract from the radical nature of the new legislation. The landed classes who backed the legislation had once benefited from cheap labour and had not previously seen need to act. It represented a new level of government intrusion into the lives of ordinary peasants and townsfolk by requiring officers of the crown in the form of justices of labourers (later justices of the peace) to regulate terms of employment in every village and hamlet in the realm. As such it was deliberately couched in the most conservative language. Wages were to be set at the level 'accustomed' in the twentieth year of the reign of Edward III and four years previously, as if wage levels were determined by custom and not supply and demand. Terms of employment, other than for building craftsmen and seasonal workers, were to be 'by the entire year, or by the other usual terms, and not by the day'. Wages above those set by the statute were described as 'excess'.

That contemporaries thought society had changed – and in the case of clerical and governmental elites understood this change in moral terms and the language of sin – is perhaps as important as the observation that society had in some ways changed. The immediate short-term consequences of the Black Death had longer-term implications. The sudden upward movement in money wages was not sustained continuously. Indeed wages fell back somewhat from their initial peak and only started to move upwards again following the second plague. The sudden upward movement in the cost of labour was, however, sufficient to make labour-intensive arable farming uneconomic in some regions. Whereas the high population of the immediate pre-plague era had sustained both high grain prices and provided an abundance of cheap labour, both factors were now reversed (although continued poor harvests tended to dampen the effect of falling demand for a further couple of decades). On lands only marginally viable before 1348, the plague served to tip the balance. This seems to have been especially true of numbers of holdings in the English Midlands, but chalky soils such as the Wolds of Yorkshire and Lincolnshire also saw a comparatively rapid contraction of arable husbandry in favour of mixed husbandry or even less labour-intensive pastoral farming. The effect was that numbers of labourers, and indeed probably peasant agriculturalists too, found themselves in search of alternative forms of livelihood even at a time of more general labour shortage. Some of this labour migrated to the towns. London, in particular, seems to have received a flood of migrants in the decade after the plague.

The movement of labour in search of work itself provoked hostile moralizing since it was hard for lords and governors to grasp that individuals could be genuinely in search of work at a time of more general labour shortage. The Ordinance of Labourers, for example, specifically proscribed the giving of alms to those who were able to work. A London ordinance of 1359 deplored the influx of migrant labour into the city since it supposedly deprived of alms those genuinely unable to work through incapacity. The reality was that the influx of labour into the capital, drawn by the lure of work and prosperity, was at that moment faster than the economy could absorb. The London poet William Langland articulated similar sentiments some two decades later, but as with the Commons' petition against vagrants of 1376, this was probably a response to the particular conditions of the later 1370s. There is little here to suggest any long-term hardening of attitudes to the needs of the poor or that there emerged a systematic policy of discrimination between sturdy beggars and deserving poor. This language and these concerns are not found again for at least a century after the Commons' petition.

The process of the transformation of the agrarian economy that caused this dislocation was accelerated once grain prices started to fall consistently by the mid-1370s. Until that date a combination of poor harvest and declining levels of production held prices stable. Now even producers who had managed to accommodate higher wage costs became vulnerable. Only in those regions best suited to arable did large-scale grain cultivation continue. At the same time the demand for the products of pastoral and stock-raising economies in the form of wool, hides and meat grew. In a number of areas, therefore, lords and peasants with sufficiently large holdings found it made economic sense to shift away from arable farming. Once again we may suppose that numbers of smallholders and landless peasants lost out and, as the evidence just cited suggests, were obliged to search for work elsewhere. The Norfolk manors of Coltishall and Martham, for example, shed residents in great number at precisely this period. The young and unmarried constituted the most mobile groups. This is suggested by the paucity of unmarried taxpayers recorded in the poll taxes in respect of villages in decline, but is reinforced by evidence for the migration history of individuals who appear as witnesses (deponents) within the church courts.

People moved as much because they saw a brighter future elsewhere as because there was no work available locally. Surviving poll tax returns for Coquetdale in Northumberland in 1377, a poor region historically vulnerable to Scottish raiding, indicate, for example, a movement of young people, but especially young women, away from their natal villages. A like exodus is suggested from 1379 poll tax evidence for the marshland settlements of the lower Ouse in Yorkshire. The ready availability of land in more propitious locations and the steady demand for labour in towns helps explain these observations. One of the striking features of the 1377 poll evidence is indeed that women tended to outnumber men in urban settlements, whereas the reverse was true for villages – clear evidence for a net movement of women from rural to urban settlements. Conversely we can find some village communities, such as Normanton (Rutland) and Golder (Oxon.), later to be abandoned, which display an extraordinarily marked preponderance of males.

The two decades following the Black Death thus saw considerable disruption and change in agriculture. But just as some peasants may temporarily have lost out in terms of employment and so been obliged to seek new openings elsewhere, many others were advantaged, at least economically. The greater availability of land encouraged peasants who already held land to further extend their landed resources as a way of increasing the surplus they could produce for the market. For numbers of peasant agriculturalists this was an effective way of accommodating increased wage costs, and indeed the short-term response of peasant producers in the face of higher labour costs must have been to attempt to maximize production even though total demand had fallen. Peasant labourers, as we have seen, benefited from better terms and conditions in the form of higher wages and better meals. In a much cited passage from *Piers Plowman* the poet complains that labourers after the plague demanded cooked meat or fish served hot, whereas before they had made do with bread and cheese. This literary gibe at labourers aping the manners of their social superiors is borne out by the evidence from manorial account rolls, which record both outlay on foodstuffs for hired labour and the employment for the first time of cooks as part of the manorial staff.

The hunger for labour that had replaced the hunger for land created additional opportunities for women and the young. Women had always been an integral part of the labour force within peasant society, but most of their energies were absorbed into the familial economy whether as mothers and domestic managers, as brewers or bakers, as spinsters and carders, as managers of gardens, poultry or dairy stock, or as general agricultural labour. At the busiest seasons of the year, the hay and grain harvests, women would have been especially conspicuous in the fields. Single women were employed as dairymaids on the permanent staff of manors and some women were probably employed as casual labour, but they were always in a disadvantaged position in the saturated labour markets that prevailed before 1348. The advent of plague suddenly enhanced the value of women's labour in the waged labour market and there is good reason to think that a proportion of women took advantage this. Numbers of women are, for example, found among the names of harvest workers indicted under the Statute of Labourers for going 'outside the vill in autumn' and receiving 'excess' wages. We can find examples of urban servant women who arranged with their employers to absent themselves during harvest so as to take advantage of the high wages available. Married women likewise absented themselves from regular familial responsibilities to benefit from high seasonal wages: Isabel Clerk of Stillingfleet (Yorks., ER), a married woman, was presented in 1363 for working in neighbouring Moreby for 6d a day through the autumn (harvest). The same no doubt was true of adolescent daughters living at home. In this way familial incomes would have been augmented. Other women may have found it easier to get by as general agricultural labour than had previously been the case.

Young people likewise hardly constituted a previously idle section of the population, but as with wives they had hitherto largely been absorbed into the familial labour force and hence were inconspicuous in the contemporary record. Some, however, found employment as servants, living as dependants within the houses of their employers. Such servants, likewise dependants, are no more visible in the manor court rolls, so it is difficult to know just how common they were before the plague. There is reason to believe, however, that they became much more in demand following the plague. Employers were keen to recapture some stability in the supply of labour and servants, customarily employed by the year, scored over day labour. Equally, servants commanded remuneration in kind rather than cash and so were particularly attractive at a time of wage inflation, but when the cost or value of food to the employer was either stable or falling. Servants were likewise valued within the context of the comparatively less seasonalized labour needs of pastoral and stock-rearing economies since they were available to provide for livestock at unsocial hours and also throughout the year. Poll tax evidence shows that a significant number of youngsters, and within arable economies young men especially, were employed as servants for periods of time in the decades following the Black Death. Female servants were much more conspicuous in pastoral regions.

Numbers of peasant families, perhaps even most peasant families, found they were better off as a consequence of the plague. Peasant agriculturalists often managed more land as a consequence of taking up holdings left vacant or buying out smallholders, but for these they owed less to their lords in return. A few peasants accumulated considerable holdings and probably explain the designation 'franklin', found, for example, at the head of various villages listed in the West Riding (Yorks.) poll tax returns for 1379. Even where higher labour costs and falling grain prices came to force peasant producers to abandon intensive arable agriculture, it was often possible to make a viable livelihood from mixed or pastoral husbandry, and the employment of live-in servants might help offset higher labour costs. For peasant smallholders and labourers, the augmented value of their own labour and that of their wives and children, made for greater security. Rents fell as an immediate consequence of the plague. From the mid-1370s the cost of food also started to fall. Married labourers may have found it easier to support families as older children left home to become servants or contributed directly to the familial economy through their own earnings.

The enhanced economic well-being of numbers of peasants, whether as individuals or members of family units, translated into new patterns of consumption. As suggested earlier, for some living through the Black Death, more money may have resulted in the purchase of more leisure as of choice rather than necessity. Certainly moral commentators were quick to condemn those who spent their time in the alehouse, but for those who had previously spent all just on staying alive from one day to the next, greater spending power was an opportunity to purchase a range of basic commodities previously beyond their reach. Here, then, was a significant new market for cheap cloth, for metal cooking utensils, for basic items of furniture, for leather shoes, and for a diet that was not solely composed of bread and pulses. The enhanced spending power of more substantial peasants probably also resulted in an increased call for housing and building work.

This pattern of consumption, some of which represents new demand and hence a real expansion in the market even at a time of profound demographic recession, itself stimulated demand for a variety of raw materials and of associated producers and crafts. Thus the demand for inexpensive cloth, generically referred to as russet, stimulated demand for wool and hence sheep farming, but also for spinsters, carders, weavers, shearmen and fullers, as well as traders responsible for distributing and marketing both the raw wool and the finished cloth, and for craft workers who made cards, spinning wheels, looms, shears and fulling mills. We find rural textile manufacture flourishing in a number of localities, notably the Cotswolds and the south-west, parts of East Anglia, the West and East Ridings of Yorkshire, and Derbyshire. Likewise the demand for furniture and housing stimulated demand for timber and for carpenters, and that for leather shoes and for meat enhanced the market for livestock and work for butchers, tanners and shoemakers. Such examples could be repeated elsewhere, nor were these patterns of consumption and demand confined to peasant society. Plague seems also to have been a stimulus to the urban economy. It was also a stimulus to urbanization.

All too often scholars have used the size of towns as a sort of economic virility symbol, but the urban populations of the pre-plague era were in fact swollen by numbers of poor rural migrants who added little to the economic vitality of the towns to which they drifted. Plague was to transform this picture by reducing numbers within the towns, and hence eliminating labour surpluses, and, in the longer run, by reducing the flow of dispossessed immigrants from the rural hinterland. In the short term, however, many towns outside the capital seem to have managed to absorb numbers of rural migrants consequent upon the transformation of the agrarian economy, such was their need for labour. The young, including young women, may have been particularly conspicuous among this flow of migrant labour. This is reflected in the disproportionate number of women to men found within the poll tax populations recorded in 1377. At Hull, for example, only 92.7 men (over 14 years of age) are noted for every 100 women. At Carlisle, close to the troubled border with Scotland, the equivalent proportion was only 89.7. The same source shows that up to a third of all urban households contained servants, and we may presume that many of these were themselves rural migrants. Only briefly in London did the influx of labour cause obvious friction.

The reason that towns could absorb migrant labour was because the contraction in the population did not cause an equivalent collapse in demand for goods and services. Rather the demand for manufactured goods held up, or at the lower end of the market increased, and with it demand for both skilled craft workers and workshop labour. The only sector that lost out was the luxury end of the market since falling landed revenues combined with increased labour costs to reduce the purchasing power of both secular lords and religious institutions. Although there has been a disproportionate emphasis on the international trade in wool and cloth, the importance of a domestic market for other manufactured goods is not to be judged by the comparative paucity of evidence. In fact in many towns as many people were employed in the leather, clothing or metal trades as were engaged in textile manufacture. This is suggested by evidence relating to the occupations of persons admitted to full membership of the urban community as burgesses or citizens and by the occupational patterns recorded in the later poll tax returns (see Table 3.1). Indeed the logic of the urban community was that numbers of different trades and crafts existed in close proximity to one another. On the one hand, different crafts were to a degree reliant on one another. For example, saddlers depended on tanners to supply tanned leather, who in turn depended on butchers to supply the raw hides, but also on other craft workers and traders to supply wood for the core of the saddle and metal for rivets and other fittings. On the other hand, the concentration of a variety of goods and services in one location enhanced the attractiveness of the town as a market centre.

Numbers of existing urban centres, such as Colchester, Exeter or York, would appear to have prospered in the decades immediately following the Black Death, but it is apparent from the evidence of the poll taxes that various 'industrial' villages, some of them nascent towns, were also flourishing only 30 years on. This is apparent from the returns for the Cotswolds or for northern Essex in 1381, or for parts of the West Riding of Yorkshire in 1379. Thus the village of Felsted (Essex) contained numbers of carpenters, tailors and smiths, in addition to textile workers and traders, out of all proportion to their resident population. Proximity to London, but also perhaps to the Low Countries, no doubt explains a significant part of the market here. A similar picture emerges for the Cotswolds. In the West Riding we find places such as Sheffield, Tickhill and Wakefield, particularly associated with metal, leather and textile trades respectively, already essentially urban in function, though politically still seigneurial boroughs with minimal self-government. Another nascent textile town, Rotherham, does not even appear in Beresford and Finberg's handlist of English medieval boroughs.

It would be unwise to assume this pattern of urban development was essentially a novel product of the plague. The poll taxes effectively represent the first opportunity to analyse comparatively and in any detail the occupational structure of English communities, but it is likely that the picture they present is not entirely new. The growth of a rural textile industry, for example, has been traced back to well before the Black Death, and scarcity of land may have prompted numbers of peasants to supplement or find alternative livelihoods through craft production. However, changing patterns of wealth distribution and of consumption following the plague may have served to stimulate these developments. It may also be that increased levels of demand permitted a greater degree of craft specialization, and provided the conditions for the development and proliferation of craft guilds from this period.

13 THE PEASANTS' REVOLT, 1381

Late in 1380 Parliament granted a third poll (head) tax following hard on those granted in 1377 and 1379. The new tax was, for reasons that will be explained anon, more complex and intentionally heavier than the two previous. In the following spring commissions were appointed to assess and collect the new subsidy (tax), but it soon became apparent that the numbers of persons accounted for as paying the tax often fell a long way below the levels achieved in the two earlier taxes. The government responded by sending out new commissions to various localities to investigate the shortfall and to attempt to remedy this. When just such a commission appeared at Brentwood in Essex on 30 May, angry villagers from a large number of local communities attacked it. What started as a local riot spread with remarkable speed during the early days of June 1381, rapidly involving large numbers of rebels in Essex, Kent and London. Groups of Essex and Kentish rebels converged on the capital, which was entered on 13 June. By this date serious unrest was beginning to be played out in St Albans (Herts.), Cambridge (Cambs.) and Bury St Edmunds (Suffolk). Such unrest spread through East Anglia as rebel bands moved from village to village. The apparent success of the rebels in London, however, prompted their departure from the city. Disorder elsewhere was quickly checked by a combination of armed and judicial violence. A renewed Essex rebellion on 28 June, designed to frustrate this judicial oppression, was unceremoniously cut down at Billericay.

Though the massacre of (according to the St Albans chronicler, Thomas Walsingham) some 500 rebels just 4 weeks after the initial challenge to authority effectively signalled the ignominious conclusion to the revolt, what happened in that brief space of time demands fuller consideration. In particular, events in London need to be related. London itself was politically highly charged as mercantile and artisanal factions played out a long-running dispute about the government of the city, a dispute that continued to be played out after the revolt itself. Into this volatile community came rebels bands from Kent and from Essex. Their entry into the city was facilitated by Londoners, who saw their arrival as a means to furthering their own factional ends. By entering the capital, the rebels had access to the Crown. Indeed Richard II's court had transferred for reasons of security from the largely unprotected vill of Westminster to the apparent safety of the Tower. Two days later, on 14 June, however, the Tower was breached and the rebels seized Simon Sudbury, archbishop of Canterbury and chancellor (also identified as John of Gaunt's man), Robert Hales, the treasurer, and William of Appleton, a friar and physician who was likewise identified with John of Gaunt. Sometime later, one John Legge, who was supposed to have been the inspiration for the commissions of inquiry into non-payment of the third poll tax, was also captured. All were executed and their heads paraded as if traitors. Much destruction of property and burning went on at the same time.

How far the Essex and Kentish rebels retained separate identities and objectives is difficult to establish from the rather confused chronicle accounts, but it is apparent that Wat Tyler, the Kentish leader, is identified by the chroniclers as also the principal leader of all the rebels. It is unclear, however, despite his association in some sources with Maidstone, whether he was himself from Kent or, as other sources suggest, actually from Essex. His name suggests that he was an artisan rather than a peasant agriculturalist. Tyler's name overshadows the other known leaders, Jack Straw (or Rackstraw) and the priest, John Ball. A similar profile is encountered with regard to rebel leaders elsewhere. John Wrawe, the leader in Suffolk, was another priest and Geoffrey Litster, a key figure stirring up rebellion in Norfolk, was presumably a dyer.

The rebels confronted their boy king on two occasions, first at Mile End on 14 June and again the next day at Smithfield. The probability is that the Mile End meeting was dominated by the Essex rebels, whereas the Smithfield meeting was mostly composed of the Kentish rebels. At Mile End Richard II was supposedly petitioned to abolish villeinage and he conceded their demand and ordered that a charter or letters patent to that effect be issued. The strategy seems to have been to try and disperse the rebels as quickly as possible by making concessions that could be revoked because given under duress; it appears to have had some success. Another large group of rebels, however, confronted the king at Smithfield and here Wat Tyler seems to have acted as leader and spokesman, though Jack Straw is said to have been present too. (There is indeed some confusion in the chroniclers' minds as to who was who.) According to the *Anonimalle* chronicler, Tyler presented a much more coherent and radical programme of demands. The demand for the abolition of villeinage was reiterated, but it was no longer the primary, let alone sole, objective. Tyler required the replacement of all law by 'the law of Winchester', the abolition of outlawry, the abolition of all forms of lordship, the disendowment of the Church (in the narrow sense of the religious and clergy), the virtual dismantling of the episcopal hierarchy, the redistribution of clerical wealth and property among the common people and, finally, the abolition of serfdom so as to create social equality.

Tyler's utopian vision, with its enigmatic reference to the law of Winchester, was again readily acceded to by Richard, but in a violent altercation with the mayor of London and a royal valet, Tyler was stabbed and then cut down, though not immediately killed. The *Anonimalle* chronicler has it that he was taken to the neighbouring hospital of St Bartholomew only to be taken from his bed and executed on the orders of the mayor. It would appear that, faced with the apparent concession of their demands, but demoralized by the death of their leader and now confronted for the first time by armed men rallying to the support of the king, the remaining rebels began to depart.

The dispersal of the rebels in London was the signal for swift and at times bloody repression on the part of the government. The charters abolishing serfdom were revoked since they had been granted under duress. Royal commissions backed by sometimes substantial military escorts were sent out to dispense summary justice against suspected rebels. Essex, the heartland of the revolt, offered the most resistance and suffered accordingly. An attempt on 28 June by Essex rebels to resist such an armed commission led to their being ruthlessly cut down. Dozens of peasants were killed. Around the same time 31 rebels were convicted and executed at Chelmsford for their involvement in the revolt. In Norfolk, Henry Despenser, bishop of Norwich, led his own force against the rebels and killed a number in the ensuing skirmishing. In early July soldiers were also sent to Scarborough to bring an end to disturbances in the town. Only by November was the purge considered sufficiently complete that general pardons could be issued at the request of Parliament, although certain individuals were excluded as being too important to ignore. Those pardoned included not just the peasant rebels, but lords who had killed rebels without due legal process.

The events of the summer of 1381 had a profound impact on contemporaries and helped shape royal policy towards the lower orders of society for some time thereafter. The revolt has also been seen by numbers of scholars as a moment of great importance in a longer history of labour relations and even class struggle. The sympathies of earlier writers, such as Charles Oman and Edgar Powell, writing around the turn of the last century, tended to rest with the ruling order. Neither work matches the standards of archival scholarship set by their contemporary André Réville, but his posthumous *Soulèvement des Travailleurs* (Rising of the Workers) represents but a fragment of his project. Interest in the revolt was revived after the Second World War, but prior to the Hungarian Rising of 1956, notably by scholars sympathetic to a Marxist ideology, and again with the 600th anniversary of the revolt in 1981. Rodney Hilton has perhaps been the key figure here. His work locates 1381 in a long history of conflict between lords and peasants. The title of the 1985 collection of his essays – *Class Conflict and the Crisis of Feudalism* – takes this Marxist analysis further.

Despite the continuing lively interest in the events of 1381, stimulated most recently by the work of Paul Strohm and Stephen Justice, who bring insights from literary critical approaches to the reading of well-known historical texts, despite the accumulation of local studies, and despite the fuller reading of a range of key primary sources, major problems of interpretation persist and some real enigmas remain. Our principal sources are either downright hostile to those who participated in the revolt – this is universally true of the chronicle accounts – or were compiled by the ruling order and so present a top-down view. It is almost impossible to recover the voices of the rebels and so understand their motivations in their own terms. It is indeed quite difficult even to know who the rebels were. The substantial body of judicial material relating to the aftermath of the revolt, coupled with local manorial records, do allow some insights, but even this evidence may be selective and tend to privilege those considered to have taken leadership roles.

In thinking about the Peasant's Revolt, three particular issues need to be addressed. These relate to the timing of the revolt, the broadly regional nature of the revolt, and the objectives of the rebels. Though it is tempting to assume that the revolt represented a widespread and spontaneous uprising by an oppressed and impoverished servile peasantry against their aristocratic masters, this is hardly borne out by the evidence. The revolt was largely confined to the eastern and south-eastern counties of England, the counties of Kent and Essex representing particular foci, though Norfolk, Suffolk, Cambridgeshire, Hertfordshire, Middlesex and Surrey were also implicated. The rebels themselves were socially diverse: rich and poor peasants, agriculturalists and artisans, free and servile, townsmen and country dwellers. The decades immediately following the Black Death may sometimes have been difficult, but by the later 1370s we can say with confidence that food prices were falling, rents were competitive, land was readily available, and the wages of hired labourers were tending to rise.

Certainly it is possible to point to exceptions to the rather tight geographic parameters just outlined. In particular there were major disturbances in the city of York and the neighbouring boroughs of Beverley and Scarborough. Hitherto these northern urban conflicts have been seen as essentially local in origin and coincidental in timing, but recent scholarship has emphasized the commonality of issues concerning who should govern and how. A modest level of discord is also glimpsed in urban contexts in the west of England: Bridgewater (Somerset) experienced some unrest focused on the hospital of St John, and there were also disturbances in Gloucester and Bristol. Other instances of rebel activity have been described in Derbyshire, on the Wirral (Cheshire), where villeins of Chester Abbey were involved, and at Halesowen, where tenants of the local abbey likewise challenged their lord. These incidents must be considered as part of the wider history of the revolt, but they hardly undermine the case that this was primarily a regional and not a national uprising.

Since Réville's pioneering work there has been little systematic attempt to document the revolt outside London, but local studies have demonstrated that we are dealing with a series of simultaneous and interconnected revolts rather than a single phenomenon, let alone a grand conspiracy with a common objective. The chroniclers consistently distinguish between 'the men of Kent' and 'the men of Essex', and certainly there are significant differences between the social structures of these two counties. There were also separate urban revolts in Bury St Edmunds, St Albans, Cambridge, Canterbury and London that should not be conflated with the rural rebellion going on around them. Many rebels chose not to join the march on the capital and directed their activity elsewhere. The Suffolk rebels seem to have targeted key local players in the royal administration, attacking, for example, the property of Sir John Cavendish, the chief justice, and of Richard Lyons, who in 1376 had been implicated with Alice Perrers, Edward III's mistress, for corruption. Cavendish was in due course captured and executed. The Norfolk rebels seem to have fallen into distinct local groups, one of which entered Norwich, the regional 'capital', under Geoffrey Litster's leadership, whereas some others briefly assembled together near Swaffham. Properties belonging variously to John of Gaunt and to some justices and poll tax administrators were attacked, but some manorial officials were also targeted. To begin to address the motives for such violence we must first determine the rebels' identity.

The chroniclers universally talk in disparaging terms of the rebels as *rustici* and *villani* – rustics and villeins – but these terms only really tell us about the social prejudices of the chroniclers themselves. Evidence from indictments and escheators' rolls, which record the material worth of those indicted, immediately informs us that the rebels were not primarily the rural dispossessed, but peasant agriculturalists and artisans of at least modest means. Of a sample of 180 known rebels observed by Rodney Hilton, nearly two-thirds had goods and livestock valued (probably rather conservatively) at £1 or more, and 15 were valued at £5 or more.[1] Although the majority of these men worked the land and hence might by any definition be termed peasants, a significant minority like John de Sutton, a carpenter, John Bettes, a tanner, and Hugh Bucher, to cite three Norfolk examples, were probably artisans. Of a like sample of 36 rebels from Essex, Hertfordshire and Suffolk, whose

1. R.H. Hilton, *Bond Men Made Free* (London, 1973), pp. 182–3.

landed holdings can be identified, two-thirds held 7 acres or more and 15 held in excess of 14 acres.

Most rebels appear, then, neither to have been particularly rich nor particularly poor, but numbers of them were drawn from the very top of village society, such as Geoffrey Cobbe of Wimpole (Cambs.), William Gildeborne of Fobbing (Essex) and the franklin, Richard Baud of Moulsham (Essex). The Suffolk rebel Thomas Sampson, who held some 200 acres and very substantial quantities of livestock, is no doubt exceptional, but cannot lightly be ignored. The greater part were peasant agriculturalists, though smallholders and landless labourers are probably under-represented in these sources. A significant minority, however, combined agriculture with craftwork and there were a large number of rebels who can justifiably be described as artisans. Of those engaged in agriculture only some held land in bond tenure. Hilton's sample, derived as it is from the evidence of property seized by the Crown, necessarily relates to free tenants. The Essex, Hertfordshire and Suffolk sample is not so biased, and this suggests that the majority in fact held by servile tenure, though again a significant minority held by either free tenure or a combination of servile and free tenure. Those Kentish rebels who held land, however, did so exclusively by free tenure.

Several points emerge. The rebels ranged across the social spectrum below the level of the aristocracy. In a few exceptional cases, such as the Norfolk knight, Roger Bacon, even the gentry participated. Substantial peasants were in a minority, but are in fact unusually well represented in relation to actual numbers. These men are important not just in economic terms, but also in social and political terms. They were often important employers of labour in their own right. They were active in the land market. Invariably they held manorial or judicial office, but this last characteristic actually extends much deeper into peasant society. Three-quarters of one sample of rebels held offices such as reeve, juror, ale taster or constable. In other words, the rebels included a significant proportion of the village elite and a still more significant proportion of those active in the administration of the manor and the vill.

The rebels also turn out to include numbers of artisans, who likewise were regularly employers of labour. Servile peasants are clearly prominent among the rebels, but servility is certainly not their characteristic feature. In Kent, owing to the distinctive and long established local customs of land tenure, it cannot have been an issue at all, but the region as a whole was one where freeholding is widely encountered. In that sense the presence of both free and servile rebels is unsurprising, but there is a case for arguing that bond tenants are disproportionately represented. Manorial evidence also suggests that these were not hot-headed youths, but rather men of middling years, implied by the high proportion of office holders, and men from established families. But they were almost exclusively men. Women are hardly noted in the records of indictments or other evidence pertaining to the revolt, though Margaret Wright of Lakenheath (Suffolk) was implicated in the murder of John Cavendish, the Chief Justice.

The picture thus far presented serves at least to challenge certain perceptions of what the revolt was about. It was patently not a revolt of the landless and impoverished seeking a radical redistribution of wealth. Nor could it have been solely a revolt of a servile peasantry against their legal status, though the resentment of servile peasants at the constraints imposed by their status may well have been felt most acutely specifically where villeinage was not necessarily the norm (as it was in parts of

Midland England). Any account of the revolt must, moreover, confront the degree to which the rebels – or at least the rebel leadership – were involved in local and manorial administration or were employers rather than employees. The urban rebels aside, these were surely men too much involved in the administration of the manor, too active in the business of the customary courts, too involved in the land market seriously to wish the radical overthrow of the whole manorial enterprise. If the Statute of Labourers and its enforcement were grievances, then they were grievances shared by small employers rather than just labourers seeking better wages. If the poll tax and its administration were grievances, then it is not the poorer levels of peasant society who had hitherto escaped personal taxation that most obviously protested.

The revolt was characterized by violence, but probably far more violence was done by the Crown and those acting in the king's name by way of suppressing the revolt than by the rebels themselves. Indeed, the rebels seem to have behaved with comparative restraint. Their targets were often property rather than people, symbolic rather than personal. (Even where court rolls were burnt, we may note a singular lack of violence towards the person of lay lords not implicated in government.) The identity of these targets and victims provides further clues as to the rebels' motivations. The picture is complicated by the fact that many personal grievances and disputes were no doubt pursued under cover of the larger revolt. This has been documented in respect of London and goes a long way to explain events in Bridgwater or the concerted attack on the property of John Reed of Rougham (Norfolk). It is also likely that some violence and destruction represents an outpouring of comparatively inarticulate resentments and as such we should be wary of extracting too precise meanings. Some violence was, however, very specifically targeted.

The deliberate destruction of John of Gaunt's Savoy Palace on 13 June is a case in point. The *Anonimalle* chronicler describes the systematic burning of cloths, beds and bed hangings. Henry Knighton laments the destruction of large quantities of jewellery and plate. Thomas Walsingham, characteristically the most given to hyperbole, describes how silk hangings were torn down and trampled underfoot, and how rings and other jewels were ground to dust in mortars. Clearly the chroniclers were struck by the orgy of destruction that went on at the Savoy and were surprised by the lack of looting. Walsingham, to press the point, indeed tells how one man caught looting was thrown into the flames by his fellows. What outraged the chroniclers was the attack on the trappings of aristocratic authority – the trampled hangings, the trashed plate, the burnt charters – and indeed the attack on the most intimate space of John of Gaunt, the Savoy's owner: the destruction of the bed and bed hangings is singled out as particularly shocking. The chroniclers, sympathetic as they are to the ruling order, are a very good source for the effect the rebels presumably intended, but we may read this in two ways.

One reading would be to see the attack on the Savoy as part of a more general attack on the aristocracy, and the inequalities and injustice of hereditary privilege. The systematic trashing and burning of all the trappings of privilege can thus be read as a profound political and cultural statement. From a peasant perspective land, livestock and the implements of agriculture was where capital might best be invested. Expenditure on possessions that had no productive value could thus be seen as both unjustified and immoral. By destroying these, the rebels could be seen as asserting a moral authority that was rooted ultimately in scripture. The duty of man, following his expulsion from the Garden of Eden, was to labour. Indeed Adam became a delver, a tiller of the soil. We are reminded of this by the rhetorical proverb supposedly used by John Ball and popular with the rebels: 'When Adam delved and Eve span, who was then the gentleman?'

Another reading of this same incident would place much more emphasis on the specific identification of the Savoy Palace not with the aristocracy generally, but with John of Gaunt, duke of Lancaster, the young king's uncle and the key figure within the government of the realm. Much the same can be said of the attack on Gaunt's college of Corpus Christi in Cambridge just two days later. According to Henry Knighton, a canon of Leicester and so likely to be well informed, about the same time a group of rebels moved from London and threatened to destroy Gaunt's manor there. Protected by his absence in the Scottish marches, Gaunt could only be attacked vicariously. To the rebels he was associated with the mismanagement of the war with France, the ostensible reason for the levying of the poll tax whose collection had first sparked the revolt at Brentwood. What was seen as his pursuit of his personal ambitions at the expense of the common good, coupled with his haughty manner, had already alienated Londoners. In the heady atmosphere of June 1381 the rebels' frustration that they could not destroy the man was vented on his property; it is this that may explain the particular attack on his chamber and bed in the Savoy.

Both readings are possible and indeed both may have applied since the motivation of some rebels may have differed from that of others, but the sense that this was a personal rather than a general attack is strengthened by the knowledge that the rebels' other victims more obviously represented royal government than the seigneurial order per se. Property was likewise targeted as a proxy for these victims. Robert Hales, the treasurer, was also prior (head) of the Order of St John of Jerusalem (otherwise the Hospitallers) in England. The evening before he was captured and executed, the mother house of the order at Clerkenwell in London was burned and three days earlier his manor at Cressing Temple (Essex) was attacked. Another manor at Highbury, London, was destroyed the very day he died.

We may trace this surprisingly disciplined attack on representatives and institutions of royal government back to the very opening drama of the revolt and the attack on John de Bampton, John Gildesburgh and others enforcing the poll tax at Brentwood. On 2 June a rebel gathering assembled at Bocking 'swore to be of one mind, to destroy various of the king's lieges and his common laws and also all lordships', agreeing further, 'to have no other law in England but those that they themselves made'. Some days later (10 June) a large group of Essex rebels again gathered near Bocking and then moved on three specific targets: Cressing Temple (as we have seen); Sir John Sewale, the sheriff and his house at Great Coggeshall; and John Ewell, the royal escheator, who lived at Feering. Ewell was killed. From these two last the rebels seized documents that they then went on to burn in the county town of Chelmsford. Steven Justice has related this bonfire to those normally held a little later, on Midsummer Eve, and has convincingly suggested that it was designed to emphasize the solidarity of the community.[2] But it was a solidarity directed not so much against lordship – lords of manors in general escaped remarkably unscathed – as against royal government. The Chelmsford bonfire symbolically destroyed not manorial records, but the

---

2. S. Justice, *Writing and Rebellion: England in 1381* (Berkeley, 1994), p. 151.

administrative archives of the senior representatives of royal government in Essex. In particular, the sheriff was responsible for the implementation of the poll tax within the county and, in January 1381, the sheriff and escheator together were charged with providing information about the tax population, which subsequently led to a fresh commission to enforce the tax. The attack on Cressing Temple was implicitly an attack on the treasurer (and hence the administration of the poll tax). Similarly, properties belonging to the poll tax commissioner John Gildesburgh were attacked and his records destroyed.

It is evident that the rebels had clearly identified targets and (implicitly) disciplined local leadership. This accords well with our previous discussion of the social origins of the rebels, and particularly the observation that many participated in manorial or local administration. These were men who were aware of the law and took an informed interest in how their own communities were governed. It was their kind who actively used the customary courts to their own advantage – to register land transactions or to engage in private litigation – or co-operated with their neighbours to draw up and enforce by-laws relating to common grazing, who periodically sat on inquest juries and coroner's juries, who employed labour both through the year and seasonally, and who determined among themselves how the communal tax assessment (under the system of tenths and fifteenths dating back to 1334) should be divided. In identifying causes of discord and friction, they looked not so much within their community, but to the ways in which royal government (identified as something without) impinged upon and disrupted the social fabric.

The intrusion of royal justice in the form of commissions of the peace, the interference of the Statute of Labourers in the ability of employers and labourers to enter freely into what hitherto had constituted private contracts, and the imposition of a head tax administered by externally appointed officials were all reasons for resentment. The sorts of men who became active in the revolt sensed with some justification that they could rule themselves rather better without this external intrusion. This perspective is voiced in the aforementioned Bocking resolution 'to have no other law in England but those that they themselves made', and was probably echoed again in the Smithfield petition to have no laws other than the laws of Winchester. But resentment at the disruptive ways in which royal justice and governance impinged upon the imagined ideal of autonomous self-governing communities was compounded by a sense that those who claimed authority by right of birth or royal office had, through abuse, neglect or incompetence, lost all claim to that authority. This was particularly acutely felt by the Kentish rebels. Despairing of the will or ability of the Crown or the local aristocracy to protect the coastline from French attack, they arranged their own defences at the time of the revolt. That a heavy burden of tax was now falling disproportionately on the lower orders of society, supposedly to fund the French war, added insult to injury.

It is appropriate here to consider at greater length two particularly contentious issues, namely the enforcement of the labour laws and administration of the third poll tax. The Statute of Labourers was, as we have seen in the previous chapter, rooted in the moral outrage and alarm of the landowning classes that wage labour had suddenly became so much more expensive. Ostensibly it attempted to hold wages at immediate pre-plague levels by outlawing 'excess' wages, curbing the movement of labourers and tying labour (other than seasonal labour) to long-term contracts. The enforcement of the Statute resulted in very large numbers of presentments and fines. In Essex some 7556 persons were fined for taking excessive wages in 1352 alone, but there is little indication that such fines succeeded significantly in holding wages down, let alone taking them back to pre-plague levels. Since this was ostensibly the purpose of the act, we may ask why it continued to be so long revised and enforced.

The enforcement of the statute was not, however, uniform across the country. Some areas were targeted more frequently than others according to the perceived acuteness of the problem. As the extant returns of the 1381 poll tax clearly attest, parts of Essex were characterized by an unusual intensity of competition for labour. Lords required labour to work the demesne, but numbers of peasant agriculturalists also had need of hired labour. What distinguished Essex from many other counties, however, is the degree of demand and hence competition for labour from rural artisans. Numbers of Essex vills were effectively busy little industrial villages. The village of Bocking itself contained two franklins, three families of weavers, four of tailors, four of shoemakers, six of fullers, five of drapers and seven of carpenters, in addition to various other crafts (including an apothecary). Some of these artisans no doubt also held land and supplemented their livelihood through husbandry, but this concentration of manufacturers and traders cannot be explained by local demand in a community of some 500 souls. Using occupational data from the 1381 poll tax returns for three Essex hundreds (Chelmsford, Dunmow and Hinckford), Larry Poos has found that over half the families identified were headed by labourers, a quarter by peasant agriculturalists and just under a quarter by artisans and traders.[3]

With lords, substantial peasants and a plethora of artisans all competing for labour, the pressure on wages was acute. There can be no surprise, consequently, that Essex was targeted by the Crown for the enforcement of the Statute of Labourers. Most presentments were indeed of labourers for receiving 'excess' wages – the mobility of labour and the terms of contract seem not have been such major issues of contention in Essex, possibly because the demand for labour was so widespread. Superficially, therefore, we would expect labourers as a group to feel aggrieved and employers, whether peasant, artisanal or seigneurial, to be supportive of the workings of the law. This appears unlikely. Although it is probable that the lowest echelons of peasant society were drawn into the revolt, those who are most conspicuous occupy middling and even upper levels, and include numbers of artisans alongside peasant agriculturalists. These persons are more likely to be employers of labour than employees.

Another possibility arises. Rather than see the enforcement of the statute to be primarily concerned with wage restraint, we should see it as a means of manipulating the labour market to the benefit of one group of employers – seigneurs – at the expense of other smaller employers. One possibility is that labourers working for lords were less likely to be indicted than those employed by lesser employers, in effect giving lords a significant advantage when competing for labour. There is some evidence that lords attempted to fabricate the actual wages paid to their employees as recorded in rolls of account. Certainly the impression that the law was partial and enforced by the gentry in their capacity of justices with the interests of their own kind was widespread. That real discontents were provoked is even reflected in the judicial evidence from the

3. L.R. Poos, *A Rural Society after the Black Death: Essex 1350–1525* (Cambridge, 1991), Table 1.3, p. 24.

enforcement itself. Here we find irate small employers desperate for labour freeing workers who had refused to abide by the terms of the statute from village stocks. When, to take a well-documented example from the chronicle of the Yorkshire abbey of Meaux, the Cellarers, a prosperous villein family, attempted to bring an action under the statute against the abbot for seizing their hired labour, the case was dismissed immediately since serfs were denied access to royal justice.

The enforcement to the Statute of Labourers cannot but be understood as an important part of the context for the revolt, but it was the poll tax that initially provoked the rising. It would be easy to dismiss hostility to the third poll tax simply as opposition to paying taxes, particularly as the third tax followed hard on the heels of the first (1377) and second (1379). Certainly the principle that all save the very poorest in society, and not merely the better-off, should contribute to the tax burden was still novel and no doubt resented. This, however, begs the question why there was not more opposition to the first or second poll taxes. One factor lies in the very real differences between the taxes. The 1377 tax was a flat rate assessment of 4d (less than 2 pence) per adult over 14. That the poorest taxpayer paid the same as the peerage was inherently unfair, but there was no scope for argument as to who owed what. The 1379 tax was more sophisticated. It was levied on persons over 16, the same population who had been taxed two years before. (This may have allowed for the reuse of some of the documentation compiled in 1377, but this is not entirely clear.) The minimum rate was again 4d, but married couples were assessed as if one person. Persons classified as artificers (artisans), merchants, franklins, mayors and such like were assessed at higher rates, with various ranks of the aristocracy heading the scale of charges. Thus earls were assessed at £4 and the dukes of Lancaster (John of Gaunt) and Brittany at 10 marks (£6.67).

The 1379 tax schedule represented a rather more equitable distribution of the tax burden than that of 1377, but the exchequer had hoped it would also have brought in more revenue. With this in mind, the third poll tax was deliberately modelled to bring in three times the income of the first simply by trebling the sum to be collected per person; rather than 4d per head, a mean of 12d (5 pence) was to be levied. Those framing the tax, however, thought it politic to retain something of the 1379 principle that the better off should pay more, so the tax was not levied on a flat-rate basis. Rather, within each vill, some taxpayers were expected to subsidize others such that no one paid more than 20s (£1), but some only paid 4d. Unfortunately the schedule failed to provide clear guidance as to how this bureaucratically complex requirement was to be achieved. In fact each set of assessors seems to have found its own idiosyncratic strategy.

The result was to create widespread anomalies. Whereas some assessors, as for example in Hampshire, seem to have tried hard to achieve a real degree of redistribution of the tax burden within each vill, others made only token effort. In Essex the degree of redistribution was comparatively slight. The effect was that in some areas a labourer might be assessed at the minimum rate of 4d, in others an equivalent labourer might be assessed (as was invariably the case in Essex) at the mean rate of 12d. This in itself introduced a degree of inconsistency and unfairness largely absent from the earlier returns, but the position was compounded on the one hand by the fact that a poorer taxpayer was more likely to be subsidized in a prosperous community (because more taxpayers could be charged above the mean rate) than in a poorer community. On the other hand, where large numbers of poorer taxpayers were encountered, the assessors could either risk antagonizing more prosperous taxpayers by shifting more of the burden on to them, alienating poorer taxpayers by assessing them at three times the 1377 rate, or blithely turning a blind eye to at least some of these taxpayers. It would appear that this last was a common and widespread response.

It need hardly be a surprising response. The assessors and collectors of the third poll tax would have seen their brief to be to collect as much tax as possible as quickly as possible, not obsessively to count heads. In what must already have been the volatile climate of the spring of 1381, those charged with administering the poll tax probably valued expediency above bureaucratic rigour. At York, the assessors consciously used earlier lay subsidy returns (based not on heads, but wealth) as their model and so excluded large numbers of potential taxpayers resident in poorer parishes. In Essex, as at a large number of other localities, the numbers of persons assessed fell conspicuously below the numbers of heads taxed in 1377. Only some two-thirds of the 1377 tax population total at Bocking was taxed again in 1381. To take another example at random, the proportion was yet lower at Thaxted.

Close analysis of the extant returns show up certain clear patterns. Young people, particularly single people, are most likely to be missed. Women are much more liable to be omitted than men. These are the very groups most likely to be unable readily to afford to pay the tax at the mean rate, unless it were paid on their behalf by an employer as was probably regularly the case with live-in servants. It is the contention here that such omissions represent a deliberate policy on the part of the tax officials rather than evidence of widespread evasion. The officers of the Exchequer, alarmed that revenue received fell below expectation, took a different view. Their suspicions had already been aroused by anomalies found between information about taxpayers separately compiled by sheriffs and escheators, and that provided by the actual assessors and collectors. The marked shortfall between the numbers accounted for in the returns delivered to the exchequer and the estimated populations derived from the 1377 tax returns prompted the appointment of new commissions to investigate these defects and enforce payment.

The first tranche of commissions were appointed on 16 March to the counties of Norfolk, Suffolk, Cambridgeshire, Huntingdonshire, Hertfordshire and Essex – that is, to most of the counties caught up in the revolt less Kent; also included were Gloucestershire, Northamptonshire and Somerset. Kent (along with Nottinghamshire, Derbyshire, Devon, Cornwall and the West Riding of Yorkshire) was included, however, in a second tranche of commissions on 3 May, and Canterbury was specifically targeted on 20 May. The correlation between the new commissions and the location of the revolt in 1381 is striking. (In addition to the main regional revolt, we should note also disturbances in Northampton, Bridgewater (Somerset) and Derby.) The actual progress of the new commissions was slow. We have new assessments, for example, from Gloucestershire, and that for Canterbury was also completed, but as we have already seen, its work was still very much in progress in Essex when the commissioners were attacked at Brentwood on 30 May.

The implication of what has just been outlined is that during the first few months of 1381, the county of Essex witnessed visitations by Crown-appointed assessors and collectors of the poll tax, separate visitations of officers working for the sheriff and escheator, also compiling very detailed information on taxpayers, and finally a new set of commissioners. Henry Knighton's account may not be reliable, but it probably captures something of the mood of the time and the rumours that circulated:

> One of these commissioners came to a certain village to investigate the said tax and called together the men and women; he then, horrible to relate, shamelessly lifted the young girls to test whether they had enjoyed intercourse with men. In this way he compelled the family and parents of these girls to pay the tax for them . . . These and similar actions by the said inquisitors much provoked the people.

The *Anonimalle* chronicler's account is probably more authoritative, but is most revealing in a factual error he lets slip. He describes how Bampton came to Brentwood:

> He had summoned before him the townships of a neighbouring hundred and wished to levy from them a new subsidy, commanding the people of those townships to make a diligent inquiry, give their reply and pay their money. Among these townships was Fobbing, where all the people replied that they would pay nothing at all because they had an acquittance from himself for the said subsidy.

The *Anonimalle* chronicler accidentally voices what the gathering at Brentwood no doubt felt: the tax had been assessed and paid, yet here was another royal official demanding 'a new subsidy'.

It now becomes much easier to comprehend the outrage provoked by the enforcement of the third poll tax. Unlike the previous system of subsidies (going back to 1334), the initiative for determining who paid and how much rested not with the local community, but with officials appointed by the Crown. It extended the requirement to pay tax to persons who had, historically, been exempt. The 1381 tax was, however, also inequitable in so far as persons of the same standing could be assessed at differing rates (or not at all) according to the whim of the assessors and the particular community in which they lived. Lastly, even after the tax had been assessed, new agents of the Crown came to demand further payments. The fury thus provoked was not the scared response of the young women and men who had not been included in the first assessment, but the righteous anger of a community sensing chronic maladministration and profound injustice.

14 DIVERSITY AND ADAPTATION, 1382–1450

The century after the Black Death has in the past been, and still is to some extent, viewed in a rather unflattering light. It has been seen as, and indeed was, a period of epidemic and endemic disease, of high mortality and of demographic recession. People were supposedly obsessed by death and the fear of dying. The image of death loomed repeatedly in art, on monuments, in the creative imagination more generally. The quality of cultural production supposedly declined. The economy supposedly reeled as a consequence of the Black Death and failed to recover significantly thereafter. This view is now being revised. The martial achievements of Edward III in France were whittled away within a generation. Likewise the brilliant success of Henry V in a renewed and essentially different campaign that so nearly brought France under Lancastrian rule was all lost by 1453. Finally, the authority of the Crown and the effectiveness of royal government is seen to have repeatedly been undermined by the 'tyranny' of Richard II, the usurpation of Henry IV, and lastly the long minority of Henry VI followed by the patent inadequacy of his personal rule.

Our concern here is not so much to offer a brief political overview as if this is somehow a more important aspect of the past than the broader discussion of the economy and society that will follow, but to signal how these are in fact intermeshed. We have already seen the close relationship between government policy, the fiscal demands of the war with France and popular revolt in the chapter on the Peasants' Revolt. Another regional rising, that of Jack Cade, concludes this period. The campaign of conquest and territorial aggrandizement pursued from 1417 by Henry V, however, had repercussions beyond simply taxation. The demand for manpower at a time when the population had probably pretty much reached its lowest ebb had a rather more marked impact on labour supply than would have been the case, even with larger armies, before the Black Death. It tended to drain money out of the economy and led to a marked shortage of coin within the realm. This can only have depressed market transactions. Though war generated demands for particular types of manufacture, it tended to be disruptive of overseas trade. In a small number of cases it created war profiteers, but in time it saw the return of large numbers of former soldiers, who constituted a lawless and disruptive element in society.

The early years of Richard II's reign saw an active pursuit of the war with France, primarily in order to secure the Channel ports of Brittany and Normandy, but at great expense. The attempt to offset these costs by a series of poll taxes culminated, as we have seen, in the Peasants' Revolt of 1381 and the poll tax was thereafter dropped. There persisted, however, the perception that taxation should only be used at times of extraordinary need and that normally the Crown should manage out of its ordinary sources of revenue. Consequently, parliament (with justification) identified the causes of the revolt with heavy-handed enforcement of excessive taxation and, as with the 1376 Good Parliament, blamed waste and corruption at court. This perspective was also part of the wider moral climate after the Black Death that was suspicious of anything that smacked of vanity, greed or idleness.

To provide the young king with a good example, the commons insisted that a committee be established to oversee the king's household. Arising out of this, Richard Fitzalan, earl of Arundel, and Michael de la Pole were required 'to advise and govern' the young Richard. The boy king seems to have got on well with de la Pole, but inevitably generally preferred the company of his own generation. In particular he liked Robert de Vere, earl of Oxford, who was some four years his senior. In 1385 de Vere was given the novel title of marquess and two years later Richard created him duke of Ireland. De la Pole, the son of a Hull merchant, was appointed chancellor in 1383 (after Richard had fallen out with his very capable and distinguished predecessor) and then earl of Suffolk in 1385. By this unconstrained patronage of his friends and promotion of what were considered new men, Richard alienated much of the established aristocracy. Aristocratic grievance was compounded by de la Pole's new policy of rapprochement with Jean de Montfort, duke of Brittany, leading to a period of truce. This was seen as a sign of weakness, a product of Richard's failure to listen to those who by virtue of their rank ought to advise.

When the truce ended in May 1385, de Montfort seized the initiative first by supporting the Scots in an attack on England and, more significantly, by threatening his own invasion the following year. Though the Scottish invasion was repulsed and the French invasion never materialized, the urgent need for funds on both occasions provided parliament with the opportunity to level criticism at the king's allegedly profligate patronage. The Parliament of October 1386 forced Richard to dismiss Suffolk and imposed a commission, composed mostly of aristocratic bishops, to investigate once more the running of the royal household. Richard responded by leaving London and attempted to rally support outside the capital. At the same time the new commission took the war once more to the French mainland, capturing French shipping and lifting the siege of Brest. When Richard returned to the capital, he found the political standing of his opponents had been greatly strengthened. In November 1387 they seized the initiative.

Thomas of Woodstock, duke of Gloucester (and the king's uncle), Richard Fitzalan, earl of Arundel, who was alienated by Richard's peace policy, and Thomas Beauchamp, earl of Warwick, together charged ('appealed', hence the term 'Appellant') five of Richard's closest allies, including de Vere and Suffolk, with treason. Suffolk escaped to France. De Vere attempted to rally armed resistance, but was defeated at Radcot Bridge in December and fled to exile overseas. Parliament – the Merciless Parliament – meeting in February 1388 found the five guilty of treason. Archbishop Neville of York, as a churchman, was spared death, but the two remaining allies were executed as was a further group of four chamber knights considered to be a malign influence on Richard. For the time being the duke of Gloucester and the earl of Arundel directed government policy.

The ascendancy of the Appellants was short-lived. Their attempt to co-ordinate a major new campaign in France failed and in August of the same year the Scots revenged their defeat three years before. Cumberland and Northumberland were raided and the English were defeated in a particularly bloody encounter at Otterburn. The commons meeting at the Cambridge Parliament in September were duly critical of their policy and Richard was thus enabled to seize the initiative and take full control of government for the first time in May 1389. This same Parliament substantially revised the labour legislation of 1351 and launched an inquest into the nature and assets of guilds.

Richard's priority was to make peace with France, though his position was informed by his concern to avoid having to call upon parliamentary taxation and hence further parliamentary constraints on his authority. Such a policy provided a degree of political stability, but failed to command the absolute support of the aristocracy. In particular, after so much sacrifice, there was hostility to the proposal that the English Crown should give up its claim to land in full sovereignty as the price of a lasting settlement. There was also hostility, not least in Gascony, to an attempt to transfer the duchy to John of Gaunt. These difficult issues were fudged by the conclusion of a 28-year truce in March 1396, cemented by a diplomatic marriage alliance between Richard, whose beloved first wife, Anne of Bohemia, had died childless in 1394, and Isabelle, the six-year-old daughter of Charles VI.

The final two years of Richard's rule are identified as his 'tyranny'. Opposition to the terms of the truce served as a rallying point for Richard's opponents, notably Gloucester, Arundel and Warwick. Richard replied by having his opponents arrested, and 'appealed' for treason in a parliament cowed by the threat of force. Arundel was executed; Warwick saved his neck through a humiliating confession and was exiled; Gloucester died in suspicious circumstances after arrest in Calais. Richard followed this retaliatory bloodletting by ennobling various of his supporters; five were made dukes. This crude assertion of Richard's prerogative rights further alienated the established aristocracy, who felt their own titles diminished. Renewed opposition was suppressed, however, by fear that the purges would go deeper. Richard blackmailed parliament into granting him customs revenue for life so as to be as free as possible of the need for parliaments. Richard's most trusted allies were given office in the northern marches over the heads of those who had historically held such positions. Lastly, Richard used a dispute between the former Appellant, Thomas Mowbray, duke of Gloucester, and John of Gaunt's heir, Henry Bolingbroke, duke of Hereford, as an excuse to exile both parties.

John of Gaunt died only months after his son's exile. Richard chose to take administration of his estates as duke of Lancaster rather than, as had earlier been agreed, to allow the exiled heir to administer them by proxy. While Richard was engaged in Ireland, Bolingbroke returned from exile with a small force and quickly rallied support from the Lancaster estates and beyond, though his signalled intention was merely to claim his rightful inheritance. Resistance crumbled quickly as Bolingbroke moved south from Yorkshire and by the time Richard returned from Ireland he had little option but to surrender and, in short order, abdicate. At the same time a formal quasi-legal process of deposition on the grounds of Richard's supposed violation of his own coronation oath and the rule of law was concluded.

Henry Bolingbroke came to the throne as a consequence of deposition and the assertion of a questionable claim to succession. He attempted a difficult balancing act of rewarding his own supporters, especially duchy of Lancaster men, while refraining from persecuting Richard's former allies, but he could not prevent disenchanted and ambitious factions exploiting the wider context of political instability. A revolt in 1400 by several of Richard's closest supporters was successfully crushed, but Owain Glyn

Dwr's revolt in Wales grew increasingly serious. Sir Edmund Mortimer, the senior representative of the Mortimer family and the claim of his nephew, the earl of March, to the throne, was defeated at Bryn Glas in 1402 and then went over to Glyn Dwr. A Scottish raid into Northumberland in 1402 was soundly defeated at Homildon Hill by Sir Henry Percy (Hotspur), son of the first earl of Northumberland, but in 1403 the Percy family likewise made common cause with Glyn Dwr. It may be that Northumberland, a key supporter of Henry IV's cause in 1399, and his son felt that they had received insufficient recognition or support for their services. Hotspur was defeated and killed at Shrewsbury, but Northumberland, briefly reconciled with Henry, instigated further rebellion in 1405. Although the wider conspiracy collapsed and Northumberland fled into exile, the hapless Richard Scrope, archbishop of York, who had been sucked into the plot, pledging to fight corruption and excessive taxation, was summarily executed for treason. Henry thus simultaneously created a martyr, with a significant local cult in York, and seriously undermined his personal authority. It coloured the remainder of Henry's reign and no doubt explains his choice of burial by the shrine of an earlier martyred archbishop, Thomas à Becket.

Scrope's execution was followed by (and perhaps precipitated) prolonged, eventually fatal, illness on Henry's part. At first government was exercised by Archbishop Arundel, but at the beginning of 1410 the prince of Wales, the future Henry V, seized the initiative. He was immediately embroiled in concerns relating to France. Charles VI had suffered periodically from a mental illness since 1393, though his condition deteriorated significantly from 1405. It rendered him incapable of rule and so created a power vacuum out of which two principal factions emerged. In 1407 John the Fearless, the new duke of Burgundy, engineered the assassination of his main rival, Louis, duke of Orleans, provoking full-scale civil war by 1411. Prince Henry saw this as an opportunity to further the interests of the English Crown and revive the agenda of Brétigny. Although a small English army assisted John the Fearless to capture Paris, little was in the event gained. Pressure on Henry IV to abdicate in favour of his able and ambitious son only provoked him to reassert his authority: he restored Archbishop Arundel to the chancellorship and switched his support away from the Burgundians to the Armagnacs. In August 1412 a new and much larger army was sent to France only to be bought off after three months by the treaty of Buzançais. A few months later, Henry was dead.

Henry V came to the throne with considerable military experience fighting the Welsh and with an agenda to exploit the civil war in France. He had also to stamp his mark as king and assert his authority: his father's claim to the throne had always been open to challenge and the first part of his reign was marked by rebellion; Henry himself was still only in his twenties and was not yet the heroic figure his own propaganda painted him following Agincourt. The fragility of his early rule is indicated first by the revolt of Sir Thomas Oldcastle in 1414. More dangerous still, Richard, earl of Cambridge, plotted to assassinate him at Southampton on the eve of his French expedition. This first foray into France in 1415 was a way of rallying the aristocracy behind a shared cause, but it should have ended in disaster when a much larger French force confronted the depleted English army heading back to the coast. The victory at Agincourt was immediately presented as divine vindication for the English cause and paved the way for grants of parliamentary subsidies sufficient to allow a much more ambitious campaign to follow.

The Normandy campaign that commenced in 1417 is invariably seen as another phase, albeit a new and very significant one, in the so-called Hundred Years War. It was not a phase; it was effectively an entirely new war. From the late thirteenth century, the primary objective of the English Crown in France had been to guarantee as full and as unfettered control of Gascony as was possible. The treaty of Brétigny (1360) had come close to delivering this, but ultimately the French Crown was neither willing nor able to surrender sovereignty over territory that was integral to the realm. English claims to Normandy, on the other hand, had effectively been lost at the battle of Bouvines (1204), and had been formally renounced at the treaty of Paris (1259). A campaign designed not simply to attack and hence pressurize the French king, but actually to conquer lands in Normandy was thus an entirely new departure. It set the agenda for campaigning in France until the end of our period and well beyond the conventional 'end date' of the Hundred Years War.

Henry's military successes reversed a long era of disappointments, but they were only possible in the context of his alliance with the Burgundian duke. While Henry was conquering Normandy, John the Fearless was capturing Paris. Any threat that the Burgundians would turn against the English and ally with the Armagnacs died with the assassination of Duke John in 1419. The Anglo-Burgundian alliance achieved its (almost literally) crowning success with the treaty of Troyes of May 1420. With Paris and the now incapable Charles VI under Anglo-Burgundian control, the treaty disinherited the dauphin, alleging 'frightful and astounding crimes and misdeeds', recognized Henry V and his heirs as successors to Charles VI, and appointed Henry as regent. The treaty, and the peace it supposedly established, was concluded by Henry's marriage to Charles's daughter Catherine, and the symbolic union of the Plantagenet and Valois lines. Henry's early death ensured that it was the infant child of that marriage who succeeded the joint thrones of England and France on Charles's own demise in October 1422.

Henry V's reputation rests partly on his proven military and administrative capabilities, partly on his early death. The writ of Troyes ran only so far as Anglo-Burgundian rule was effective. The dauphin and his claim to rule as heir to his father did not go away as the defeat at Baugé (1421) in Henry's own lifetime demonstrates. The more territory the English held, the greater the cost and difficulty of defending it, especially as advances in gunpowder made city walls vulnerable to siege. Parliamentary subsidies could readily be expected when the course of war was going well, but the willingness of the country to sustain the costs of holding territory that ought to be generating its own revenue was finite. Lastly, the utility of the English to the Burgundians was not limitless. Once the Burgundians withdrew effective support, the eventual failure of English rule in France was inevitable. Philip the Good's recognition of Charles VII as ruler of France by the treaty of Arras (1435) preceded the final collapse of English rule by but a few years.

Henry VI's minority created the usual power vacuum at the centre. In 1431 there was another, albeit short-lived, Lollard-inspired rebellion. Though the war in France was managed with considerable ability by the king's uncle, John, duke of Bedford, the position of Humphrey, duke of Gloucester, as regent was immediately challenged. There was rivalry between Bedford and Gloucester, his younger brother. Gloucester's marriage to Jacqueline of Bavaria, heiress to Hainault, Holland and Zeeland, deepened the rift by threatening to destabilize the alliance with Burgundy. His adventure into Hainault in 1425, however, ended ignominiously and he abandoned Jacqueline in Mons. (When in 1428 the pope annulled his marriage, he proceeded to marry his mistress, Eleanor Cobham.) Gloucester's most immediate challenge came, however, from Henry Beaufort, bishop of Winchester, a great uncle of the king and a cardinal from 1427. Beaufort enjoyed influence at court and with Bedford, not least because his personal wealth was so readily used to provide loans, but his policy of containing Gloucester's powers served at best to frustrate firm leadership and at worst was highly destabilizing. Bedford's death in 1435 coincided with Arras and the final collapse of the Burgundian alliance. It also left Gloucester as Henry VI's heir. This should have strengthened the duke's hand against his arch-rival, Cardinal Beaufort, but the cardinal was protected by the king, now a teenager and increasingly assertive of his own authority.

In 1437, though still only 15, Henry declared his majority. Much has been written about Henry and his (in)capacity to rule. The age demanded a martial figure in the mould of his father and uncles. To the sometimes outspoken disgust of his subjects, however, Henry eschewed these aggressively masculine qualities, adopting instead a pious and peace-loving persona. His twin foundations of Eton and King's College, Cambridge, which follow a model more obviously associated with bishops or even great ladies, seem to have occupied him more than the fate of his French possessions. The rift between Gloucester and Beaufort went unhealed and indeed culminated in a sordid plot to undermine Gloucester's credibility by implicating his wife in charges of witchcraft in 1441. Henry's favourite, however, was by then no longer the now elderly Cardinal Beaufort, but his protégé, William de la Pole, earl of Suffolk. He encouraged the peace policy in France designed to secure possession of Gascony and Normandy, but in fact singularly failed to prevent the haemorrhaging of territories. An expedition in 1443 under John Beaufort, newly created duke of Somerset, was a costly failure, and a temporary truce negotiated the following year did little to advance the situation, though it provided a breathing space for the negotiations leading to Henry's marriage to Margaret of Anjou early in 1445. The following year Henry gave up – apparently of his own initiative – Maine in return for an extended truce.

Henry's unwise concession of strategically crucial territory was resisted on the ground notably at Le Mans. Charles VII besieged the city, which capitulated in 1448. The truce itself lasted only a matter of months longer. When the English failed to take action against one of their mercenary captains who had sacked the Breton town of Fougères, Charles VII used this as sufficient excuse to retaliate. Suffolk was identified as the scapegoat; he was impeached and sent into exile, but was murdered even as his boat departed Dover (1450). As his body was brought back through Kent, widespread popular disturbance broke out (Cade's Rebellion), spreading in time over much of southern England.

The almost complete collapse of English rule in Normandy that followed the loss of Le Mans was far swifter than anyone could have anticipated; only Calais was to remain untaken. The rout in Normandy, moreover, opened the way for a campaign in Gascony. By 1453 the legacy of Edward III, of Henry V and of John, duke of Bedford, was entirely gone, though many decades were to elapse before English rulers renounced the ambition of holding territory across the Channel.

The epidemics of the later fourteenth and earlier fifteenth centuries were not on the scale of the pandemics of 1348–49 or 1361–62, but epidemic and endemic disease continued to depress population levels through the course of this period. Nor was plague alone to blame. Tuberculosis seems to have been a significant killer to judge by the experience of the monks of Canterbury Cathedral Priory. Even within a broader context of comparative plenty, the poor remained vulnerable to harvest shortfall and to famine- and malnutrition-related diseases. There was, for example, a significant regional crisis in northern England in 1438 associated with unusually heavy rainfall. The adverse mortality regime that prevailed over this period was, however, perhaps most acute for the very young, the group that is most invisible in the records. A recent examination by Klaus Arnold of German family chronicles that record the births and deaths of children – a necessarily anecdotal source weighted towards the upper echelons of urban society – suggests that some two-thirds of children failed to survive beyond childhood, most dying within the first couple of years. Records of burials at the village of Sutton near Hull in the pestilence year of 1429 reinforce this anecdotal perspective. Some families clearly lost several children within a short time. John Hogeson of Sutton lost his sons Robert, William and John, together with his daughter Alice, all aged below 12 years. At nearby Stoneferry, Peter Owgrym lost two sons and three daughters.

Demographic recession exacerbated the labour shortage that had prompted the labour legislation of 1349 and 1351 – legislation that was continuously amended and enforced through this period. The renewal of the war in France under Henry V, which probably coincided with the nadir of this population slide, served only to increase this shortage, particularly in respect of male labour. Wages paid to labourers tended to rise over these decades, peaking by about the end of this period. Most studied, because most frequently documented, are the wages paid to building craftsmen. Thus Westminster building labourers were earning an average of 3.3d (1.4 pence) a day in the first decade of this period, but 4.9d (2 pence) by the last. The manorial labourer on the Winchester estates saw a slightly more modest rate of increase, but the trend was similar. The same was true of rural Essex, but ideally we need to know rather more about wages in other regions, including the north, before we assume that this pattern was essentially uniform across the country as a whole.

Money wages probably became a more significant component of the remuneration paid both to employees hired by the day and to those hired by the task during this period, but it should be remembered that the provision of meals remained an important consideration and one employers may sometimes have used to circumvent the labour laws. We know that the quality of food provided improved – meat and ale being more freely offered – but the quantity may have increased too. Food, of course, tended to be more plentiful in this period precisely because the population had fallen, but so was land and housing. In other words, just as wages paid to day labourers were tending to rise, the cost of living was tending to fall. The consequence was that the actual spending power of wage labour tended to increase over these decades. This is regularly described as an improvement in the 'standard of living'.

In describing this phenomenon, we need to be a little cautious. Most people did not work for money wages, or at least only supplemented their livelihood through waged employment. Peasant agriculturists and artisans were at least as likely to be employers of labour as wage earners themselves. (Building craftsmen are entirely atypical in working for a wage rather than for profit.) Much work would have been seasonal; though wages may generally have been good, there would still have been lean times of the year, especially during the winter months. Labourers who relied on work not just for the money, but also for regular meals, may actually have struggled during slack times, or times of illness or incapacity. Nevertheless the broader observation that wage workers were increasingly well off in material terms still applies and is of no small significance.

The most important attempt to map the movement of wages against prices is that undertaken some half century ago by Phelps Brown and Hopkins, hence the 'Phelps Brown and Hopkins Index'. This is important because still much used by scholars. They compared the wages paid to Oxford building workers against the prices of a range of consumables, using evidence from Oxford college accounts and the like. As with modern government measures of 'standards of living', they attempted to create a standard 'basket of consumables' to reflect the likely spending patterns of their wage earners. For this period, the basket was modelled on expenditure recorded in the household accounts of two chantry priests at Bridport (Dorset), but their model did not include payments for rent (and curiously does not include butter or cheese at this period). This, then, is necessarily a crude and flawed measure since it reflects the daily wages of but one specific group, wholesale rather than retail prices, and the spending patterns of men without families. These proper concerns do not, however, undermine the bigger picture. The Phelps Brown and Hopkins Index reached its highest point in these years, a level not repeated or exceeded for the next five centuries.

Having more money to spend, labourers were able to purchase more and enjoy a greater range of goods and services. In particular the demand for ale, meat, clothing, basic furnishings, bedding and metal kitchen utensils increased. Garments, though made from inexpensive cloth, were now often lined, and dyed fabrics were more generally used. Even ceramic tableware was more likely to be of better quality and often glazed. It follows that not only was there enhanced demand for manufactured items, but that even the lower end of the market required a higher standard of and – perversely in the context of a contracting labour force – even more labour-intensive workmanship. Peasants may have come to rely more on what they could purchase from village craft workers or at regular markets and fairs than on what they could make for themselves. The corollary is that the demand for artisans and traders to service this market was buoyant, as indeed is reflected in the comparative buoyancy of the urban economy, the spread of rural crafts, at least in some regions, and the competition between artisans for labour.

Peasant agriculturalists seem also largely to have prospered in this period. By and large we find smaller numbers of manorial tenants, but the average size of holdings increased. Rents tended to fall as lords struggled to secure tenants. The graphic account at Feering (Essex) of a half virgate taken back into the demesne in 1403 'for want of a lessee' having previously been leased at 14s and latterly at 8s is perhaps atypical, but explains why lords were now obliged to yield to market forces. Elsewhere in Essex land leased at 6–9d per acre at the beginning of this period was leased at 6–7d per acre by the end of this same period. Nationally entry fines too tended to falter. On the estates of Glastonbury Abbey these declined steadily from the time of the plague, finally becoming purely nominal payments by the mid-fifteenth century. Rents generally fell, though we can find some variety in the movement including examples, as in Cornwall, of rising rental values, invariably because mineral-working opportunities or the like enhanced demand. Heriot and merchet payments by servile tenants also tended to become less burdensome. Fewer merchets were collected and it became increasingly common for lords to take cash payments rather than livestock as heriots. In this benign climate, there arose a whole stratum of substantial husbandmen and yeomen. In 1443 Thomas Jerveys of Thundersley (Essex), to give but one typical example, possessed three horses, two cows, seven piglets and 71 acres under crops.

By the beginning of this period more conservative monastic lords had already been obliged to relax customary obligations in order to secure tenants. Even on the Bury St Edmunds Abbey manor of Quiddenham (Norfolk), hired labour was employed in 1389 to supplement customary labour and harvest boon works, though the latter still accounted for two-thirds of the total. On the manors of the Westminster Abbey estate labour services were uncommon by the end of the fourteenth century thanks to a process of commutation. In effect customary tenants were becoming rent-paying tenants, a process that continued in the early years of the fifteenth century. Many lords preferred to pull back from the direct exploitation of their estates and manors, and leased out parts of their demesnes piecemeal or even as a whole. For the duration of the lease the control of the demesne and sometimes of the whole manor effectively passed to peasants, often former reeves or rent collectors, but occasionally outsiders.

From the perspective of lords, especially those managing large estates, the direct management of manors was no longer seen to be cost-effective. The changed balance between the supply and demand for land meant that would-be tenants voted with their feet if dissatisfied by the terms asked of them. Even established tenants, includ-ing tenants in villeinage, could, and did, flee by night. Around 1402 Meaux Abbey (near Hull) managed to recapture a villein who had escaped the abbey's grange at Wharram and had settled, married and raised a family in Bilsdale; his capture says more about the tenacity of a conservative and litigious monastic landlord than the lot of servile peasants generally. By and large villeinage died during this period not through manumission (the process of making villeins legally free), but because peasant resistance rendered it an ineffective way of securing labour. By passing day-to-day responsibility for managing seigneurial lands to local men through the farming out of demesnes and manors, lords assured themselves of a fixed income, but shielded them-selves from the problems of labour management and the vagaries of the harvest. For peasant farmers (leaseholders) of demesnes or of manors, however, the process pre-sented real opportunities for self-advancement. In general, this was an era favourable to the peasant agriculturalist.

As we noted previously, the sudden upward surge in the cost of labour in the imme-diate aftermath of the Black Death, followed a couple of decades or so later by a marked downturn in the market price of grain, caused significant dislocation, partic-ularly in the champian country of Midland England. This period probably witnessed greater stability. The downward movement in the price of grain was much less marked and probably compensated for by the continued downturn in rents. On the other hand, the enhanced demand for meat, for dairy products, for wool (to make cloth) and for leather (for shoes, belts, saddles, sheaves, book bindings and such like) made pastoral farming and stock rearing much more attractive and viable propositions. Many peasant agriculturalists built up small flocks of sheep or other livestock, which could be sustained by the availability of common pasture – a supply sometimes aug-mented by turning vacant holdings into pasture.

Certain regions in particular prospered with the expansion of rural textile produc-tion and the growth of other rural industries, though this is not to imply that these industries were new in this period. Textile manufacture was advantaged by proximity to supplies of wool, but was neither dependent on this, nor apparently confined to pastoral regions. What mattered more was the availability of a significant free labour force often made up, at least in the first instance, of smallholders. Rural cloth production flourished in the Cotswolds, from whence hailed the fictional Wife of Bath, of whom the *Canterbury Tales* says 'Of clooth-makyng she hadde swich an haunt [she was so skilled], / She passed hem of ypres and of gaunt [Ghent]'. It also prospered in the worsted district of north-east Norfolk, a region characterized by mixed agriculture and a high level of smallholding, the serge manufacturing districts of Devon and south-west Somerset, and the textiles districts of south Suffolk and northern Essex. Cloth manufacture likewise flourished in the West Riding of Yorkshire, although metalworking was also found in the southern part of the same county.

The expansion of rural industry was not confined to the regions just noted, nor was it continuous through the period. Our knowledge of both these matters is impressionistic. In part this is a product of the paucity of documentation relating to domestic trade, but in part it represents a lack of scholarly interest. The extant poll tax returns for 1379 and 1380–81 can provide valuable evidence for non-agricultural trades in the English countryside at the very beginning of this period. Thus the importance of wool production in Sussex is reflected in the numbers of wool traders noted, as at Lewes. In addition to the locations already discussed, textile production is noticed in Westmorland – numbers of women weavers are recorded at Bampton and Rossgill – in Surrey, as at Shalford, and in Dorset. Tanning, associated with stock rearing, is found alongside textile manufacture as at Beaminster (Dorset). In the same county we see some villages engaging in specialist trades – salt panning at Arne and fishing at Wareham. Formby in Lancashire also depended heavily on fishing. Rugeley (Staffs.) even at this date is characterized by significant numbers of cutlers.

The poll tax evidence, flawed though it is both in terms of the patchy survival and the very varied quality of the extant returns, also provides some sense of the broader geography of rural industry at the time of the Peasants' Revolt. Berkshire, Hampshire (including the Isle of Wight), Leicestershire and Northamptonshire, all part of the champian belt of Midland England, appear to be singularly lacking in evidence for rural industry and provide a striking contrast with the returns for the much more economically diverse eastern and south-eastern counties of Norfolk, Suffolk and Essex. Unfortunately no returns survive for rural Kent, though there is evidence for a variety of rural trades, including textiles, iron working and salt panning. It follows that although Midland England witnessed ongoing and marked structural changes in the agrarian economy, from an economic perspective in about 1380 it was still comparatively backward.

There are numbers of indicators to suggest that the last decades of the fourteenth century, and even the earlier years of the fifteenth, were characterized by a buoyant and dynamic economy. By the 1430s, however, the economy seems to have faltered and there are some indicators of real recession by mid-century. Several factors influenced this pattern. In particular we can identify the influence variously of monetary considerations – an issue still only comparatively recently recognized – of demography and of the climate. We should not, however, lose sight of the political context. War in France was disruptive to trade and a drain on manpower. It was also very costly to sustain, leading to high levels of taxation, little of which was invested back into the English economy, and a net outflow of bullion to the detriment of the domestic economy and trade.

The high taxation of the very beginning of this period had swiftly subsided with the long period of comparative peace initiated by Richard II. A new era of heavy taxes followed the sustained renewal of the war in France from 1417. There is little doubt that such taxation resulted in a haemorrhaging of money from England. Though certain specific sectors of the economy benefited from supplying troops, on balance the cost of war was a drain on the wider economy. The effects on the money supply of taxation were, however, compounded by the wider European 'bullion famine', a scarcity of silver and hence of silver coin caused by the drying up of silver mines in Bohemia, and subsequently in southern Serbia and Bosnia. Higher-denomination coins came to be minted in gold, but this could not address the needs of most small-scale transactions. The first famine centred on the early years of the fifteenth century, while the second was felt from the last decade of this period, though was at its most acute in the 1460s. The temptation was to reduce the silver content of coins in order to alleviate the underlying shortage of the precious metal, but such a policy of debasement, as pursued in 1412 when the silver content was reduced by a sixth, had in practice an inflationary effect. In general terms, however, a shortage of coins within an economy that had become so dependent on money transactions had a debilitating effect on trade and commerce.

Monetary factors are not a sufficient explanation. The continued fall in the population probably also had a depressing effect on the economy. Our argument thus far has been that significant sectors of the population – labourers, peasant agriculturalists, artisans – all tended to benefit from the wider economic changes of the later fourteenth century and early years of the fifteenth. The enhanced spending power of these groups compensated for the decline in numbers. Indeed household expenditure was augmented, as we shall see, by the increased earning capacity of wives and this may have had a significant effect, as in the later eighteenth century, on patterns of expenditure on clothing, household furnishings, cooking utensils and other household commodities. Continued demographic recession, however, would have come to outweigh any increase in per capita expenditure, but the return to a policy of high taxation under Henry V would in any case have eroded that spending power.

Continued demographic recession may have had yet another negative effect. By the earlier years of the fifteenth century most of the more substantial redistributions of population associated with the restructuring of the agrarian economy to meet the needs of a much reduced population had taken place. Buoyant wage levels, however, suggest that there was no surplus labour. It may be, therefore, that some sectors of the economy were adversely affected by a lack of available labour. This may have been particularly true of some urban economies, dependent always on a steady influx from the surrounding countryside, as the flow of migrants dried up. We can see this, for example, from the evidence of admissions to the franchise at York and from the decline in rental values there and elsewhere. This labour shortage would have been exacerbated by the drain in manpower to meet the needs of the renewed fighting in France. Michael Postan has argued that the numbers employed in the Agincourt campaign 'might approach ten or even fifteen per cent of the total male population aged between eighteen and forty-five'.[1] Postan's point is polemical, but it is hard to

---

1. M.M. Postan, 'The Costs of the Hundred Years War', *Past and Present* 27 (1964), pp. 34–53.

see how a labour-starved economy could have accommodated this loss of labour without some ill effect.

Climatic considerations may have had a specific impact on the economy, at least of northern England. In Chester in 1437 poor grain harvests pushed up the price of wheat and forced the poor to turn to bread made from peas, vetches and roots of ferns. Heavy rainfall in 1438 and the two subsequent years caused serious harvest shortfalls and associated disease 'throughout the realm and principally in York and the North Country', as the *Brut* chronicle put it. There is much evidence of floods and flooding in Yorkshire and the north-east, even of bridges that had subsequently to be rebuilt. Lasting damage was thus done to the regional agrarian economy, reflected in falling rental values, but actual mortality associated with disease must also have had an impact on an economy already starved of labour. Probate evidence from the diocese of York shows the highest recorded peak in deaths for the entire fifteenth century occurred in 1438, though a lesser peak is also noticed only two years before. Given that the sort of people who made wills would have been spared the worst ravages of malnutrition-related disease, it is likely that the actual level of mortality was on a scale more akin to the major plague epidemics of the previous century.

One sector of the labour force that may have been advantaged during at least the first part of this period, and perhaps particularly when the scarcity of male labour was most acute, are women workers. We have already explored in Chapter 12 how the wider labour shortage served to increase the range of economic niches available to women. It is likely that this process was consolidated in this period. Two indicators of this in relation to the economy of one regional centre, York, may be cited. First, the number of women admitted to the franchise as citizens was greater in the period 1414–43 than at any other period since the registers commenced in 1272: nearly half of all admissions of women in the period from the Black Death to 1500 were concentrated in that 30-year period. Although the number of women admitted (52) represents but a small fraction of all new citizens and is of itself hardly significant, it is still a suggestive indicator of wider trends. Second, the proportions of women leaving registered wills who appear never to have married, and of widows known to have remarried, reached their peak and their trough respectively at almost precisely the same moment. To read these statistics crudely, more women were able to support themselves outside marriage, whether as never-married women or as widows.

The evidence from York can be supported by anecdotal evidence elsewhere. Canterbury operated a system of licensing persons, who could not afford or did not want to become citizens, to trade by the year. The proportion of women within this group of 'intrants' was highest in the first part of the century and notably the third decade of the century. At Norwich, where the civic government took control of the main market in the late fourteenth century, we can trace patterns of stallholding through the fifteenth century and beyond. Once again, we find the largest number of female stallholders in the earlier decades of the century. Such evidence could no doubt be repeated elsewhere, but it is conspicuous that our examples relate exclusively to urban society.

It is much harder to find like evidence from a rural context. In part this is a product of the sources available, the lack of published scholarship in this area (at least for this period). It may also be that the more conservative nature of rural society meant that there were not the same opportunities for women to engage in paid employment as was true of towns. Indeed the likelihood is that numbers of rural women migrated to towns in this period precisely because the more dynamic culture and economy of the town attracted them. Unfortunately we have no evidence for urban sex ratios after the poll taxes of the later fourteenth century. Mavis Mate, writing from the perspective of rural Sussex, is generally sceptical of the view that women were significantly advantaged by the labour shortages of the period, but she concedes that women are more conspicuous as hired labour on the demesne as at Chalvington in the late 1430s and 1440s as a consequence of high mortality.[2]

Women's labour may nevertheless have been more in demand in the context of an agrarian economy that now placed greater emphasis on pastoralism, dairying and wool production. This was perhaps particularly true within the context of the peasant household economy (as opposed to paid employment) and hence is virtually invisible within the historical record. Wives, daughters and female servants would have taken responsibility for dairying – milking livestock (both cattle and sheep), making butter and cheese – but may have also played a role in caring for livestock. Washing and shearing sheep seems to have been women's work, as we have already noted. They would also have assisted in the hay harvest. Most would have supplemented the household economy in other ways, notably by spinning, keeping poultry and brewing. It is only the last that really impinges upon the documentary record and thus takes on a probably spurious significance in the secondary literature. A woman servant from Writtle (Essex), who had been contracted to serve her mistress for a year and a quarter at unspecified tasks, claimed in 1405 also to be owed money for additional work spinning and reaping. How far this contribution of women to the peasant economy was translated into an enhanced role in terms of making decisions about how the household budget was spent must remain a matter of speculation.

This period would also have seen an enhanced demand for the labour of servants (in the life-cycle sense) for the reasons outlined in Chapter 12. The paucity of evidence makes comparison with the picture derived from the poll taxes, which suggests that only a small proportion of rural households employed servants, very difficult. The economic case for using servants was strong: grain prices and hence the cost of food remained low, but the cost of waged labour continued to rise. The less heavily seasonalized labour requirements of mixed or pastoral agrarian economies, moreover, readily justified contracting labour by the year. We have just noted that female servants were particularly valued in relation to dairying and we may similarly surmise that the ratio of male to female servants may have shifted somewhat in favour of women. Even in 1379 in the pastoral district of Howdenshire (Yorks., ER) or the mixed, but commercialized, economies of Strafforth (Yorks., WR) or South Erpingham (Norfolk) we find fairly equal sex ratios.

One group that perhaps fared rather less well in the new economic climate was the aristocracy, particularly greater lords who possessed estates comprising numbers of manors. As we have noted, income from rents, from entry fines or from manor courts all tended to stagnate or decline. The Beaumont manor of Whitwick (Leics.), to cite a particularly dramatic example from Midland England, yielded over £52 in 1396. By 1413 it provided only just over £43 and by 1464 this had slumped to little more than

---

2. M. Mate, *Daughters, Wives and Widows after the Black Death: Women in Sussex, 1350–1535* (Woodbridge, 1998), pp. 56–7.

£24. Consequently lords were tempted to lease out their manors. At first manors were leased piecemeal and perhaps only for a few years at a time, those at greatest distance from the lord's principal residence(s) being the first to be so disposed, but longer leases tended in time to follow. In order to bolster incomes, therefore, new sources of profit were sought after. With some investment, woodland and mineral resources were exploited and rivers were used for fisheries and to create water mills. Perhaps the most significant source of revenue, however, was that derived from pastoralism, both stock rearing and sheep farming. By the 1420s, for example, the knightly Vernon family had over 1000 sheep and well over 200 cattle pastured in Derbyshire. Significant profits from wool, however, tended to come rather later in the century. Indeed, wool prices tended to fall through the first part of the fifteenth century and there is even some evidence of a temporary retreat from wool production on some lands by the 1440s. Perhaps for a military aristocracy it was the renewal of war and the campaigning in Normandy and beyond that offered the greatest attraction in terms of reward, but, as we have seen, that was fast unravelling by 1450.

Two other key events in 1450 need to be noted: the attack on the Bay Fleet by English privateers, and Jack Cade's rebellion. The first had perhaps the greater long-term impact. Some 110 Dutch, Flemish and Hanseatic ships returning from the annual expedition to bring salt from the Bay of Bourgneuf were captured and forced into port on the Isle of Wight, though all bar the Hanseatic ships were soon released. The unprovoked assault on Hanseatic shipping severed already poor relations between England and the Hanseatic cities of northern 'Germany'. English trade in northern Europe and the Baltic region was seriously damaged as a consequence, leading to a general falling off of overseas trade, especially that operating out of ports along the eastern side of the country.

Cade's rebellion flared up in the wake of the murder of the duke of Suffolk, the focus of much anti-government sentiment. Rumours raged that Kent was to be transformed into a forest by way of a terrible revenge, but Kentish men were already highly critical of the government's abuse of judicial authority and mismanagement of the war that left their county vulnerable to attack. Substantial peasants, already an articulate and politicized group in 1381, were active among the rebel bands; government officials were again carefully targeted. The rebellion quickly spread far beyond Kent. A significant body of rebels marched on London with the intention of petitioning the king. Here events took a particularly violent turn; the treasurer, James Fiennes, Lord Saye and Sele, a minister too closely associated with Suffolk and a man with Kentish connections, was but one of a number of casualties. As in 1381, the rebels were eventually persuaded to disband in the face of promised concessions and pardons, but unrest was not so quickly dispelled. As in 1381, popular rebellion may have been prompted by specific local grievances, but was ultimately symptomatic of a deeper malaise in government.

15 STAGNATION AND INFLATION, 1450–1550

The latter years of the fifteenth century and the early years of the sixteenth have often occupied a sort of historical limbo. On the one hand, medievalists would tend to label this period 'late medieval', even 'the end of the Middle Ages', whereas early modernists would see this as the very beginning of the 'early modern' era. It follows that medievalists are disposed to write about this period (if at all) in terms of distinctive medieval cultural practices, institutions, ways of thinking, beliefs, and so on, coming to an end, whereas early modernists are predisposed to look for what is new, or signifies a shift in values. It is no accident that the historiography has generated such concepts as a 'new monarchy' or a 'Tudor revolution in government'. Some recent scholarship, however, has attempted to reconsider this periodization and the assumptions implicit in it. Judith Bennett, for example, in an article polemically entitled 'Across the Great Divide', has suggested that this era was characterized as much by continuity – in family forms, marriage practices or the gender division of labour – as discontinuity.[1] It is this latter logic that determines our consideration here of the entire period 1450–1550.

The century from 1450 effectively falls into two parts, one characterized by civil unrest and economic recession partly predicated on a scarcity of coin (the bullion famine), the other by relative stability, though inflation, religious change and inept political leadership were latterly to militate against this. The period saw the effective end of the war in France, but not the ambition of English kings to rule in France and the costs that ambition necessitated. It also saw a prolonged period of civil war and the progressive establishment of a new ruling dynasty sufficiently robust as to allow, by the very end of our period, a wholesale attack on the beliefs and practices of traditional Catholicism and rule by a boy king. The power of regional magnates, so marked at the beginning of this period, was correspondingly undermined by the latter part. Population levels, at their nadir in 1450, stabilized and slowly started to recover by the late fifteenth century. By the earlier sixteenth century they were growing fast. Conversely, the spending power of those whose livelihood depended partly or wholly on selling their labour tended to decline over this period and latterly was falling sharply. Serious social problems associated with unemployment and vagrancy, with enclosure and high taxation, and with religious change came increasingly to exercise government. These problems were manifested periodically in popular revolt.

The collapse of English Normandy in the face of a concerted French assault commencing in 1449 was swift and decisive. The final loss of Gascony between 1451 and

---

1. J.M. Bennett, 'Medieval Women, Modern Women: Across the Great Divide', in D. Aers, ed., *Culture and History, 1350–1600* (London, 1992), pp. 147–75.

1453 was a little more protracted, but no less traumatic. Only Calais and the Channel Islands remained of the English possessions that had been paid for so dearly in terms of lives, careers and taxation. With no war to rally the political nation or a military aristocracy, the task of the monarch could not be easy, but Henry singularly lacked the qualities demanded of a medieval king. He was also confronted with a powerful and ambitious rival in the form of Richard, duke of York, who, prior to the birth of Prince Edward, was his heir. Richard had served successively as governor of France and governor of Ireland. On his return in 1450 he attempted to discredit Edmund Beaufort, duke of Somerset, his successor in France, a rival claimant to the succession, and a favourite at court, portraying him as the architect of the loss of Normandy.

In 1452 York unsuccessfully staged a show of force, failing to displace Somerset. With Henry's first bout of mental illness in 1454, however, York ruled briefly as protector. Somerset was briefly imprisoned. Henry's recovery (and Somerset's release) persuaded York to take up arms. He encountered Henry and Somerset at St Albans and in the ensuing battle captured the king. Somerset and Henry Percy, earl of Northumberland, a friend of Henry V and staunch supporter of the Lancastrian line, were both killed. From this position of strength York renewed his protectorate, only to have it snatched away within a few months by Henry. With no clear central authority, deep fissures between various leading magnates and their affinities were now regularly expressed in the form of feuding. By 1459 feuding gave way to full-scale war as York again resorted to force.

After the temporary debacle of Ludford Bridge, York took refuge in Calais. In June 1460 his Neville allies, Richard, earl of Salisbury, and his son Richard, earl of Warwick, returned to England and prevailed at Northampton. Once more Henry was held captive. York's allies now tried to persuade Parliament of York's proper title to the throne as heir to the March inheritance, sidelined by Henry IV's accession in 1399. Whatever Henry's defects, Parliament was not prepared to renounce the Lancastrian line and offered the compromise position of naming York as Henry's heir. Meanwhile the party hostile to York and his Neville allies rallied its forces. This party comprised Queen Margaret, who wished to protect her child's claim to the succession, and the new Percy Earl of Northumberland, whose family rivalry with the Nevilles was deeply rooted and who wished to avenge his father's death at St Albans. On the last day of 1460 this alliance trounced York's forces at Wakefield. York was slain on the field of battle, his son Edmund murdered soon after, and Salisbury captured and immediately executed.

The year 1461 probably represents the height of the anarchy created by civil war, an anarchy that was manifested in many acts of violence and lawlessness of which peasant tenants and townsfolk were probably the principal victims. The person of Henry VI commanded little support, but there were many who had no desire to renounce the legitimacy of the dynasty. Queen Margaret was distrusted as a (politically ambitious) woman, a French princess and a supposedly malign influence on her husband. York was dead, but Edward, his heir, inherited his father's ambitions and a desire to avenge his death. He gained his first victory at Mortimer's Cross, but only a couple of weeks later Warwick was surprised and defeated by Queen Margaret's army at the second battle of St Albans. He escaped to join Edward who had himself proclaimed king in a capital hostile to Queen Margaret. Edward then advanced northwards and encountered the Lancastrian royal family and a large army at Towton

(Yorks., WR) on Palm Sunday. Heavy snow blew into their opponents' faces and caused their arrows to fall short. Edward eventually prevailed, but at a terrible price in terms of casualties on both sides. Henry VI, Queen Margaret and the young prince fled the battlefield. The reign of Edward IV had begun.

Edward set about not just enforcing his own rule, but restoring kingship. His inheritance was a troubled one. His claim to the throne was always open to challenge. Powerful factions remained and continued to challenge Edward by force of arms. By attempting to conciliate the Lancastrian 'opposition', he risked alienating his own supporters; sometimes he proved too trusting of the loyalty of men who previously had fought for Henry VI. His most powerful ally, Warwick ('the Kingmaker') was too mindful of the debt the young king owed him. By his secret marriage (1464) to Elizabeth Woodville (or Wydeville), the daughter of Lord Rivers and Jacquetta of Luxembourg, and a knight's widow, Edward immediately rattled Warwick, who had plans for diplomatic alliances. He also caused difficulties for (what remained of) the established aristocracy by his conspicuously generous patronage of his bride's extensive family: her father and her brother Anthony were to hold high office, her younger brother John married Katherine Neville, dowager duchess of Norfolk, a widow much his senior in both age and wealth. Her various sisters made spectacularly 'good' marriages. Elizabeth's son by her first husband married Anne Holland, heiress to the duchess of Exeter, even though already betrothed to Warwick's nephew, George Neville.

Like Edward III and Henry V before him, Edward looked to bolster his otherwise vulnerable authority by rallying support against the French Crown, in particular through alliance with Burgundy. This policy was initially pursued with due circumspection; overtures were also made to Louis XI of France, Warwick's preferred strategy. It was the Burgundian alliance, however, that prevailed. Legislation forbidding Burgundian imports was annulled. A marriage alliance between Edward's sister, Margaret of York, and Duke Charles, who had succeeded his father in June 1467, was secured only with the promise of a substantial dowry. The marriage was solemnized in July 1468. At much the same time Edward entered into treaty with Brittany.

Edward had hoped that his elaborate diplomacy would give him leverage over the French Crown. He was bitterly disappointed. Louis launched a pre-emptive attack on Brittany while Charles of Burgundy was preoccupied celebrating his marriage. He subsequently entered into a truce with the Burgundians whereby they promised not to aid the English in any adventures into France. At the same time Louis offered succour to the exiled Henry VI and his entourage. Warwick, no longer satisfied with material rewards and frustrated by being effectively sidelined politically, turned against the man he had originally helped to the throne. Renewed civil war was the inevitable consequence.

Events moved quickly. A Neville-inspired rebellion was raised in the north under the leadership of the self-styled Robin of Redesdale. Warwick, having bought the alliance of Edward's brother George, duke of Clarence, through marriage to his eldest daughter, Isabel, raised rebellion in Kent. Edward's forces were defeated at Edgecote Moor on 26 July 1469. Edward was captured soon after. Warwick had for the moment stage-managed a coup, but he enjoyed neither the patronage whereby he might consolidate his own power base nor the authority to prevent a state of virtual anarchy that his coup had unleashed. Those hostile to the Woodville influence did not necessarily welcome rule by Warwick or the king's captivity. Released, Edward quickly resumed his authority, but at the cost of retaining Warwick. Further rebellion inevitably followed, instigated by Warwick and Clarence. Their ambitions were initially frustrated by defeat at Empingham ('Lose-Cote Field'). Soon after they fled to France into the willing arms of Louis XI and the exiled Lancastrian faction.

The subsequent invasion in support of the deposed Henry VI found Edward off-guard trying to put down another northern rebellion. He was weakened by defections as Warwick rallied a large force outside Coventry, and fled to Burgundian Bruges rather than risk battle. Edward was now in a position to undermine restored Lancastrian rule, exploiting tensions within the uneasy coalition of Warwick, Clarence and the Lancastrian party, and threatening invasion. French support for the restoration of Henry VI had, moreover, to be repaid by ending the alliance with Duke Charles of Burgundy, prompting Burgundian support for Edward. Working on Clarence's disenchantment with his diminished role in a new Lancastrian government, Edward prepared to seize back the crown. He was able to gain some mercantile financial support since good relations with Burgundy were also good for trade, but his invasion fleet was still modest and his chances of success on arrival at Ravernspur at the mouth of the Humber in March 1471 must have seemed slight. As he moved south towards London, however, support grew. London admitted him without resistance; Henry VI and his chancellor, George Neville, archbishop of York (and Warwick's brother) were consigned to the Tower. Henry was not to emerge alive. Three days later (14 April) Edward confronted Warwick at the battle of Barnet. In the course of bloody fighting conducted in swirling fog his forces prevailed. Warwick was cut down trying to flee. In early May at Tewkesbury he crushed an attempted invasion by Margaret of Anjou. Henry's heir, Prince Edward, died in the fighting. More Lancastrian supporters were tried and executed shortly after. Edward was again restored to the throne, unencumbered by the likes of Warwick.

The remainder of Edward IV's reign until his death in 1483 was devoted to consolidating Yorkist rule. He also returned to his earlier policy of renewing the war in France; after a brief foray, he was bought off by the treaty of Picquigny (1475). A de facto peace prevailed thereafter. The Lancastrian threat had been lifted with the murder of Henry VI and the death of his heir. Ironically, Edward's greatest danger came from his ambitious younger brothers, Richard, duke of Gloucester, who had served him well during the heady days of 1469–71, and George, duke of Clarence, made infamous in Shakespeare's phrase 'false, fleeting, perjur'd'. His treasonable actions came to a head in 1477 following the death of his wife Isabel. He fell out with his older brother when the king vetoed a proposed match to Mary of Burgundy, heiress to the duchy of Burgundy. He was tried for treason and quietly disposed of in the Tower early in 1478.

If Edward gained a reputation as an authoritarian monarch who would tolerate no challenge, this probably did him no harm, whatever Tudor propagandists might say. Edward's reforms of the royal household during the 1470s, improvements in exchequer administration and an ongoing campaign to recover prerogative rights represent a serious-minded attempt to restore royal finances. These efforts left the Crown solvent, a marked contrast to the latter years of Lancastrian rule. Edward also achieved some success in restoring judicial authority, primarily through the use of high-powered commissions of oyer and terminer made up of magnates and others close to the king, and sometimes reinforced by Edward's own presence. The anarchy that had characterized the latter part of Henry VI's rule was stemmed and the foundations for economic recovery laid. These were no mean achievements. The subsequent failure of the Yorkist dynasty was not so much a product of underlying political or economic weaknesses, but rather of his untimely death.

Edward's demise in 1483 at the age of just 40 left his heir, Edward V, a child barely in his teens. Though the prince was being thoroughly trained for kingship under the tutelage of Bishop Alcock of Ely, Edward had made no provision for a minority. His uncle, Earl Rivers, as his governor, saw his chance to assume effective rule in concert with other members of the Woodville 'mafia'. This was challenged by the late king's brother, Richard, duke of Gloucester. Richard had a strong power base in the north and had demonstrated ability as a military commander campaigning in Scotland. As the new king's paternal uncle, he had a powerful claim to act as regent. His decision to take the initiative by force, to have himself crowned king while disclaiming the legitimacy of Edward IV's children, subsequently disposing of the young king and his brother, was a naked act of realpolitik made possible by the unpopularity of Woodville governance and expedient by the fact that the life of the young king was the only factor uniting those who stood in the path of Gloucester's ambitions. Gloucester may even have calculated that a Woodville protectorate would have had no more compunction about eliminating him.

While the merits or otherwise of Richard III's reign have long been a matter of, at times, impassioned debate – and some no doubt will take offence at what I have written – there can be little denying that his reign was brief and troubled. His former ally Henry Stafford, earl of Buckingham, within months unexpectedly turned against him to lead an abortive rebellion in support of Henry Tudor, a claimant to the throne by right of his mother, a descendant of John of Gaunt by his third wife and erstwhile mistress, Katherine Swynford. Buckingham paid with his life, but the continued threat from the Woodville faction and from Lancastrian opposition now grouping around Henry Tudor dictated that Richard rely entirely on his trusted northern supporters. Such narrow patronage weakened Richard and did nothing to placate his opponents. Trouble was bound to follow, though Richard's defeat and death at Bosworth Field less than two years after Buckingham's rebellion owes much to the treachery of Lord Stanley.

Henry VII's victory at Bosworth gave him the crown by right of conquest. His claim by descent was tenuous. Though there were other claimants, there was, however, no obvious Yorkist or Lancastrian contender, a fact reflected in the sudden popularity of pretenders as the focus for revolt. By marrying Elizabeth of York, the oldest surviving child of Edward IV, within months of his victory, Henry aimed to give some legitimacy to his rule, to neutralize Yorkist opposition, and to forge the myth – symbolized in the fusing of the Yorkist and Lancastrian badges of the white and red roses to create the Tudor rose – that the new dynasty represented a healing of old wounds and a union of the rival houses. (The myth was strengthened by naming his first child Arthur after the mythical king of Britain.) Propaganda alone would not suffice and the first part of Henry's reign was taken up with suppressing revolts, first by Lambert Simnel, masquerading as the young earl of Warwick (defeated at Stoke near Newark, 1487) and subsequently by Perkin Warbeck, perhaps the more serious threat because backed by Margaret of Burgundy, France, Scotland and the Empire. In 1497 he led an unsuccessful revolt from Cornwall and, together with the real

Warwick, was executed two years later. By the end of the century, therefore, Henry's rule was comparatively secure.

Early in the reign, Henry flirted with the strategy of renewing the war in France, but in practice allowed himself to be bought off by the treaty of Etaples following the siege of Boulogne in 1492. More significantly he forged an alliance with Ferdinand and Isabella, whose marriage had united the Crowns of Aragon and Castile. This led to a marriage alliance whereby Henry's oldest son, Prince Arthur, was contracted to Ferdinand and Isabella's youngest daughter, Catherine of Aragon. The marriage itself was only solemnized in November 1501, when the couple were in their mid-teens. Arthur died within months of the marriage, but the alliance was maintained by negotiating a new betrothal between Catherine and Henry's second son, the future Henry VIII. The solemnization of this marriage did not take place within the reign since Henry became less convinced in time of the value of a Spanish alliance. A marriage alliance with James IV of Scotland, who wed Princess Margaret in 1503, ensured the stability of the northern border for the next decade.

Henry VII's political patronage was both more circumspect – even parsimonious – and more even-handed than had been the case under Edward IV. He had no large following of ambitious kinsmen and was much more sparing of granting peerages. Political ambitions were held in check. Henry Percy, the powerful fourth earl of Northumberland, was conveniently killed trying to suppress a tax riot. Other nobles were muzzled by judicial means, particularly by obliging potential troublemakers to enter into financially extortionate bonds against their good behaviour. The classic, if extreme, example is the £70,000 fine imposed on Lord Abergavenny towards the end of his reign for unlawful retaining – the maintenance of large retinues – subsequently commuted to a crippling £500 a year. This boosted the royal coffers while emasculating magnate power. It also created a legacy of resentment.

Henry VII's financial administration was able to build upon Edward IV's legacy of reform. Income from Crown lands, from duties paid on a variety of imports and exports – notably wool, cloth and wine – and from the profits of justice provided the bulk of what was needed to run the country; there was a mutually advantageous relationship between growing stability, economic recovery and royal revenue. Henry VII, however, also demanded parliamentary approval for taxation on a fairly regular basis through the first part of his reign even though this could not be justified by military need. Latterly – chastened no doubt by the experience of revolt in Cornwall in 1497 – he made increasing use, as we have just seen, of bonds or recognizances, but also of forced loans, and hence supplemented income by targeting those with the greatest wealth. By the end of his reign, Henry had amassed a not unimpressive collection of plate and jewellery; he left his son a sound fiscal inheritance and a budget surplus.

Although he had not yet achieved his 18th birthday when his father died, Henry was of sufficient age to succeed in his own person and unchallenged. The young king swiftly moved to solemnize the long delayed marriage to Catherine of Aragon since this was both a way of proclaiming his adult status and, like his father before him, securing the dynastic succession by begetting an heir. Sir Richard Empson and Edmund Dudley, men who had made good in royal service as the executives of Henry VII's reviled fiscal policy, were swiftly sacrificed, a populist gesture that betrays the young king's ruthless streak. Another populist move was the renewal, yet again, of the war with France. The first campaign into Gascony in 1512 was disastrous. A second campaign at the other end of the realm the year following, and led by the king in person, saw victory at Guinegate (the 'Battle of the Spurs') and the capture of Tournai. In Henry's absence James IV of Scotland invaded over the border only to be cut down with several thousands of his soldiers at Flodden Field, outmanoeuvred by the canon and archers commanded by the earl of Surrey. Surrey was rewarded with the return of the duchy of Norfolk to which he had long been heir. With James V still an infant, the Scottish threat was effectively neutralized for a generation.

The first years of his reign did much to project the young king's prestige, but at a price. War was expensive, and expenditure on armaments and the creation of a navy rapidly depleted the modest surplus garnered by his father. From within a few years of his accession, moreover, Henry was devolving much of the business of government on Thomas Wolsey, created archbishop of York in 1514, chancellor and cardinal the following year, and legate *a latere*, giving him effective rule over the English Church, in 1518. Wolsey and Henry gained prestige in the year of Wolsey's legatine appointment by sponsoring a treaty of peace (the treaty of London) between the major European monarchs and the papacy. Two years later Wolsey helped organize the extravagant and theatrical meeting of Henry and Francis I of France at the 'Field of the Cloth of Gold', but it was once again a Burgundian and anti-French alliance, and hence an alliance with the new Emperor Charles V, that Henry was to incline to and with it renewed (and fairly disastrous) campaigns in France in 1522 and 1523. The defeat and capture of Francis by Charles V's army at Pavia in 1525, however, prompted Henry to devise yet more ambitious plans for an invasion of France and, with it, a mad scramble to raise funds, notably the ill-fated Amicable Grant of that year. The demands of war were beginning to have a real impact on the economy in terms of the burden of taxation and marked price inflation.

Insufficiency of funds and lack of assistance from Charles V, who needed Henry much less than Henry needed him, ensured that the reconquest of France proved abortive. It was displaced instead by rapprochement and a switching of alliances as Henry joined Francis's Holy League of Cognac, a grand alliance, which included the pope, against Charles V. The shift reflects a new imperative: the search for personal glory and aggrandizement, or the need for a new king to make his mark now took second place to dynastic issues. Henry's queen, Catherine of Aragon, had given Henry only one surviving child, the Princess Mary. No more children were likely to be born of the marriage and the precedent for queens ruling in their own right was both slender and inauspicious. Henry had fathered a son, Henry FitzRoy, by Elizabeth Blount, one of Queen Catherine's young ladies-in-waiting. In 1525 he created him duke of Richmond and may even have considered him as a possible heir. His infatuation with Anne Boleyn clarified another option in his mind: the annulment of his marriage to Catherine, a new marriage and hence a second chance to father a legitimate male heir. Such a strategy required papal agreement, hence the diplomatic manoeuvring to be seen as an ally of the papacy.

The equation was not so simple. The alliance against Charles V had provoked imperial troops to sack Rome in 1527 and, for a time, to hold Pope Clement VII captive. It followed that Clement was more immediately responsive to Charles's wishes than those of Henry. Charles, moreover, had every reason to oppose any annulment. Henry had proved at best an unsatisfactory ally prior to Cognac. He was now effectively his enemy. Catherine of Aragon was, moreover, Charles's aunt; any annulment would be contrary to his family and dynastic interests. Clement VII prevaricated in the face of the difficult theological issues raised by the petition for annulment, namely that Henry should never have been permitted to marry his deceased brother's widow. Cardinal Wolsey, for all his legatine and other ecclesiastical titles could not bypass the pope. From this point his services quickly became expendable. In 1529 he was stripped of all his royal offices and was only spared execution by his sudden death the following year. A new minister was in the ascendancy.

Thomas Cromwell had made his reputation as a key aide – secretary in contemporary parlance – to Wolsey. Within a couple of years of Wolsey's fall from grace he had replaced him as Henry's chief minister. Whereas the churchman Wolsey always looked to his own self-aggrandizement and pursued (sometimes opportunistic) policies designed to address Henry's desire for prestige on the international stage, Cromwell, a civil lawyer by training, had a clearer vision, clearer objectives, and a rather greater interest in domestic than international policy.

The process whereby the realization that the pope would not deliver an annulment was translated into an actual breach with Rome has, of course, generated a very considerable literature. To term this breach 'the Reformation' as if this were a finite moment in history or that profound changes in belief and devotional practice automatically followed would be mistaken. More radical change was in fact postponed until the reign of Edward VI. This in turn was abruptly reversed with the advent of Mary. The process was resumed in the reign of Elizabeth and hence outside the period of this study. Some of the more destructive iconoclasm, moreover, whereby so many of the trappings of late medieval devotion were removed from parish churches even awaited the civil war era. The Henrician Reformation, therefore, must be seen for what it was: not so much a reformation as a nationalization of the English Church, a political programme designed to augment the authority and revenues of the Crown. (Discussion of the popularity or otherwise of these changes belongs to Chapter 17.)

Emphasis has been placed on the supposedly 'revolutionary' way in which Cromwell used Parliament as an instrument for bringing about change. Certainly part of the history of the Henrician Reformation can be written in terms of a succession of acts, the one building upon another. Henry, for his part, was flattered to be given quasi-papal and imperial authority over his realm as a king who was also supreme head of the Church of England following the Act of Supremacy of 1534. The year previous Archbishop Cranmer had provided Henry with his annulment and so paved the way for Henry's affair with Anne Boleyn to be legitimated through her coronation in June 1533. Less than three months later the new queen gave birth to the Princess Elizabeth. The promise of a male heir was postponed.

The turbulent and at times bloody history of Henry VIII's plural marriages has inevitably attracted much interest. Henry's serial infatuations with young ladies of the court – not of itself so unusual for a monarch – combined with his increasingly desperate, but politically expedient desire for a male heir. Where other monarchs had a series of affairs and illegitimate offspring, Henry had a series of marriages. That to Anne Boleyn lasted less than three years from her coronation. Her failure swiftly to produce a living male heir – she had two miscarriages after Elizabeth's birth – allowed Henry's attentions to stray to Jane Seymour, one of Anne's ladies-in-waiting. Seeing the way the wind was blowing, Thomas Cromwell helped set in motion an investigation into the queen's conduct and produced from this spurious charges of adultery, incest and plotting against the king's life. With indecent speed the queen and her brother were tried, condemned and executed. With like indecent alacrity Henry betrothed Jane Seymour and married her within two weeks of Anne's death. Jane herself provided Henry with the promised male heir, the future Edward VI, in October 1537, but died shortly after from complications at the birth.

Henry did not immediately cast his eyes over the now depleted numbers of eligible ladies of the court; with no queen, there were no ladies-in-waiting. Cromwell used this opportunity to persuade Henry of the merits of a conventional political marriage, in this instance with one of the German Lutheran principalities that could help act as a bulwark against any possible Catholic alliance of the Emperor Charles V and Francis I of France. A marriage to Anne, the sister of the duke of Cleves was thus arranged and solemnized in January 1540, but Henry found his mail-order bride left him unaroused and the marriage went unconsummated. What had at first appeared a strategically adroit alliance came to look embarrassing as Charles V appeared to pose a military threat. At the same time Henry became infatuated with Catherine Howard, one of Anne's ladies-in-waiting and a niece of the duke of Norfolk. An annulment was engineered and with customary alacrity Henry married Catherine.

In a little more than a year rumours of Queen Catherine's supposedly promiscuous behaviour both before and after her marriage became public, promoted no doubt by those hostile to the Howard family influence at the court. The truth or otherwise of the allegations, to which Catherine ultimately confessed, is neither here nor there. The court worked to a double standard and the infidelities of a king could not be tolerated or even suspected of a queen. She was charged with adultery, which constituted an act of treason for a queen, and by February 1542 had paid with her head. With her fell most of the powerful Howard family. Only Thomas Howard, the duke of Norfolk, saved himself by ignominiously confessing his family's supposed misdeeds.

The matrimonial roller coaster at the heart of the Henrician court was not without significance. It did much to determine which faction or factions enjoyed, or otherwise, the king's favour at any particular moment. The failure of the Cleves marriage alliance sounded the death knell for Cromwell. His demise was contrived by Thomas Howard, whose political fortunes burgeoned with Henry's love for his niece. Norfolk's influence heralded a return to more conservative, Catholic religious policy. Queen Catherine's brief unhappy marriage, however, spelled the extent of Howard fortunes. Some of Cromwell's former associates, including Archbishop Cranmer, played a key role in destroying the new queen. No new single figure emerged to replace Wolsey or Cromwell, but rather a much enhanced role for the king's council in framing government policy. This did not, however, bring an end to factionalism at court.

Henry's own influence on policy in his last years focused particularly on the international stage. He embarked on new campaigns against France and France's northern allies, the Scots. The latter were roundly defeated at Solway Moss in November 1542. The unpopular Scottish King James V died soon after, leaving the infant Mary Stuart as titular ruler and the regency disputed between Cardinal Beaton, who saw the French alliance as the best option, and the earl of Arran. Arran at first prevailed and made terms with Henry. His ascendancy, however, was short-lived because such a strategy was politically unacceptable and Cardinal Beaton's pro-French stance triumphed. Henry's French campaign of 1544 was thus conducted without the Scottish threat being contained. In the event a planned Scottish invasion in the autumn of

1545 failed to materialize and an English force under Edward Seymour, earl of Hertford, successfully counter-attacked. A couple of months earlier the French raided Portsmouth and the Isle of Wight during which the *Mary Rose* was lost with a crew of 500. As so often before, this pointless escapade was concluded by the Peace of Andres (1546). Henry secured temporary possession of Boulogne and precious little else. The cost was enormous – £600,000 for the capture of Boulogne alone – and the price was high taxation, the liquidation of various of the Crown's assets, debasement and, for a brief period, something approaching hyperinflation.

Henry's last queen, Catherine Parr, had clear sympathies for the reformed religion and this had no small influence on the way Prince Edward and his half-sister Elizabeth were educated prior to Henry's own demise in January 1547. Catherine was not the vivacious young lady-in-waiting that had hitherto caught Henry's eye. She was instead a twice-widowed mother in her early thirties. It is possible that the now ailing king was looking for a sober and devout mother for his three children and indeed a mother figure for himself, who would nurse his ulcerated (perhaps syphilitic) leg and tend him in his last years. At court a new faction around Hertford, John Dudley, Viscount Lisle and two close kinsmen of the queen, William Parr, earl of Essex, and Sir William Herbert emerged. In the closing months of Henry's reign this faction was able to assert considerable influence, entirely displacing Norfolk and shaping the politics of the succession. Hertford emerged as Lord Protector to the infant Edward VI and awarded himself the duchy of Somerset. Others of the faction awarded themselves like honours. Queen Catherine remained closely associated with the new ruling order by marrying the new Protector Somerset's brother, Thomas Seymour, but died following childbirth in September 1548.

Any substantive discussion of the upheavals consequent upon the brief reign of reform-minded Edward VI followed by the succession, according to Henry VIII's will, of first the staunchly Catholic Mary and later her Protestant half-sister Elizabeth is necessarily beyond the scope of this book. Protector Somerset attempted to make his mark by building on his military success of 1545 and subduing Scotland. The campaign of the autumn of 1547 had indifferent success, but did provoke the French to come to the aid of their old ally the following summer. The subsequent campaigning proved extremely costly, particularly because so much reliance was placed on hired mercenaries. This further drained already depleted royal coffers and prompted renewed debasement of the currency, stimulating further inflation, and yet more sales of Crown lands, mortgaging future revenues and dissipating the windfall from the dissolution of the monasteries. In this context of economic crisis, the government faced a series of serious regional revolts during the course of 1549, which were suppressed only at the cost of much bloodshed. The French meanwhile took the infant Mary Queen of Scots into their own protection and betrothed her to the dauphin. At the end of 1549 Somerset's disastrous rule was abruptly terminated, toppled from power by John Dudley, who had been created earl of Warwick early in 1547.

There is always a problem of defining what one is talking about when so abstract a concept as 'the economy' is deployed. The last century of our study began with population levels at their lowest ebb for several centuries, but the latter part of the same period was characterized by high birth rates and demographic recovery. It began with high 'real' wages for those in paid employment, but culminated in high inflation and consequently significantly reduced spending power for wage labour. The mid-fifteenth century may have seen the economic fortunes of the aristocracy at a comparatively low ebb as rental values and returns from agricultural surpluses were depressed, but by the mid-sixteenth century the fortunes of the aristocracy seem to have been in the ascendancy. Wherever we can point to a locality or region that seems to have experienced economic hardship, we can point to another enjoying apparent growth, though London alone appears to have experienced growth throughout the period. We can identify the sometimes acute financial difficulties experienced both by royal and by civic government, but these difficulties hardly constitute a barometer of the wider economy.

There is much to suggest that the mid-fifteenth century was a time of economic uncertainty, even recession. Demographic recession, war and the scarcity of silver stifled economic development. The bullion famine probably reached its final, but most acute, phase during the 1450s. At the same time a shrunken population depressed demand for agricultural produce, and hence prices and earnings. Wool was affected as much as grain. Exports of cloth slumped from a level of some 50,000 per annum during the 1440s to levels between 30,000 and 40,000 per annum for the next quarter century; raw wool exports did little to compensate for this downturn. This trend was exacerbated by poor trading relations with both the Hansards and the Burgundians. This had a very direct impact on the economies of those towns and ports – Hull, Lincoln, Nottingham and York are among the best-known examples suggestive of a broader regional trend – that had become heavily dependent on this international trade, but this picture was probably exacerbated by the growth of London and the corresponding vitality of the south-east.

As the centre of government, a major centre of consumption and a significant international port, London had always attracted migrants and exerted a powerful economic influence over a wide region. From the later fifteenth century, however, its importance begins to change exponentially. London traders came to exercise a dominant role. Even in 1450 some half of all cloth exports were channelled through London, but a century later the equivalent percentage was nearer 90. Londoners built up trading networks that reached deep into the provinces, even north of the Trent. Thomas Kitson, to cite one example, bought cloth throughout Somerset and the Cotswolds in the period 1529–40. Londoner merchants may also have fared better during the bullion famine through the greater availability of cash and credit in the capital. London thus was able to act as a magnet for labour at precisely the moment some regional centres, such (most dramatically) as Coventry were failing. Westminster shows evidence of growth from the 1470s. Southwark, another suburb, was said to be growing from the 1460s, but mushrooming from about 1500. The central parts of the City may have been a little slower to grow, but London's population was clearly on a significant upward trajectory by the end of our period.

The fortunes of London are comparatively easy to map. The big unknown, however, is how well the wider domestic economy functioned. There are, as we have seen, plenty of signs that the 1450s and 1460s were a lean period. The nominal value of the bishop of Durham's estate was over £2900 per annum, but during the 1460s actual income tended to fall below this by about £1000. Tenants were often hard to find and rents were sometimes not fully paid for years at a time. Aristocratic and institutional spending on lead, tin, pewter, fur and wine all fell noticeably. Rural centres of textile production by and large appear not to have withered in this era, though Norfolk worsteds certainly did suffer. The small size of the population ought to have ensured that those in waged employment enjoyed a high level of individual spending power. In fact, wages paid to agricultural labourers – as opposed to the much better-documented building craftsmen – may also have fallen, further depressing spending power and levels of consumption. In general, as we shall see, waged work, especially for women, probably became harder to find. On the other hand, peasant agricultural-ists by and large found land both comparatively plentiful and inexpensive. Despite this, larger accumulations of peasant land seem not at this time generally to have passed from one generation to the next. With the ending of the bullion famine and the revival of the cloth export trade, however, this picture begins to shift again.

A resurgence in the demand for wool to support a growing trade in cloth both for domestic and overseas markets was stimulated by the treaty of Picquigny (with France) and peace with the Hansards and with Burgundy. Cloth exports grew stead-ily from the later 1470s. Exports of raw wool over the same period, on the other hand, were comparatively modest and showed no sign of growth, so the bulk of English wool to be exported was sent in the form of cloth. Thus the good-quality and inex-pensive wool that had once sustained the Flemish textile industry was now absorbed in domestic production. English broadcloths found markets right across Europe either directly or indirectly having been exported to the Netherlands as semi-finished cloths and then finished in Dutch workshops. This renewed hunger for wool produced a drive to create grasslands for sheep pasture. In parts of Midland England this led var-iously to enclosure, depopulation and actual desertion. A telling example is that of the village of Fawsley (Northants), cleared of its tenants by its lord, Richard Knightley, a lawyer who made his mark in royal service and who invested his wealth in land and in sheep. The parish church alone survived to become in effect the family chapel and mausoleum. The market for wool also generated considerable wealth in some regions. This is reflected, for example, in the great Suffolk 'wool' churches as at Lavenham or Stoke by Nayland, though such wealth tended to be distributed very unevenly.

The greater political stability under Edward IV and subsequently Henry VII, the more ready, if rather uneven, availability of silver – there is some evidence that coin continued to remain scarce in the north for some time – and the revival of export markets, now increasingly focused on the Netherlands, probably marks the 1470s and 1480s as a period of modest prosperity. Coal production grew in the north-east, and the production of lead and iron seems to have fared well. Such major provincial centres as Bristol, Exeter, Norwich and Salisbury likewise all appear to have enjoyed renewed prosperity, though significantly the same could not be said of those of the North Midlands region. The north-western port of Chester, which had seen lean times mid-century, saw modest recovery at this time, partly based on trade with the Iberian peninsula. The rural textile districts of the West Riding of Yorkshire, the south-west and East Anglia, which catered at least as much for domestic as export markets, also enjoyed growth at this time. In fact we know all too little about domes-tic consumption, but cloth exports grew considerably over this period – that is, from some 37,000 cloths to some 117,000 by the early 1540s. (There are no complete records for the last few years of this period.)

Pastoralism, quarrying and lead mining also created lively industrialized communities in the Derwent Valley of Derbyshire and the Mendip Hills of Somerset, as did tin mining in parts of Cornwall. Lead output has been calculated to have grown from only 80 tons in 1464 to 715 in 1531. (The market was immediately thereafter temporarily flooded with lead stripped from dissolved religious houses.) Tin production seems to have enjoyed more modest growth, but output still doubled over the period. Production of tin and lead helped sustain the burgeoning demand for pewter, an alloy of these two metals. Mining and iron working is found in the Forest of Dean. Iron was also being produced around Walsall, in what was later to become the Black Country, in the Sussex Weald, the focus here being casting cannon, and latterly in the Mendips. Coal production was primarily concentrated in County Durham and here again there is evidence of a growth in demand and exports from the last part of the fifteenth century. The local availability of alabaster supported a major local industry centred on Nottingham. Alabaster carvings found a wide export market, but they also provided altarpieces for numerous English parish churches and, as is attested in wills, devotional images for domestic use.

The great prosperity generated in particular by the wool and cloth industries during the later fifteenth and earlier sixteenth centuries is apparent in a number of ways. It is well illustrated by the investment in buildings and notably parish churches, whether, as we have already remarked, the great 'wool churches' of Suffolk – Long Melford was entirely remodelled c.1460–95 – the majestic towers of Somerset, the magnificent wooden furnishings of Devon churches or, less well known, the substantial rebuilding of churches in the textile district of the West Riding of Yorkshire as at Wakefield or Halifax. We may note also Great Chalfield manor house built by the Wiltshire clothier Thomas Tropwell in the later fifteenth century. It is reflected also in the emergence of a number of smaller settlements as apparently prosperous communities. The examples of Hadleigh (Essex), Lavenham (Suffolk), Castle Combe (Wilts.) and Wakefield are but the best known among a multiplicity of industrial villages under seigneurial authority. Wakefield was indeed unusual in aspiring to become a self-governing borough, a fact reflected in the sponsorship of a Corpus Christi cycle by the end of the fifteenth century.

The appearance of the likes of Lavenham, Hadleigh and Long Melford (Suffolk) comparatively high up the rankings of 'towns' according to their assessment for the subsidy of 1524–25 is in fact misleading. Often their position was determined by the taxable wealth of one or two exceptionally wealthy individuals such as Thomas Paycocke of Coggeshall (Essex), the Spring family of Lavenham, Thomas Tropwell the builder of Great Chalfield manor (Wilts.), Ralph Hawley of Castle Combe, James Terumber of Trowbridge (Somerset), John Winchcombe of Newbury (Berks.) or (more modestly) John Wymer of Scottow (Norfolk). Thomas Spring of Lavenham was worth £3200 at his death in 1523. These men represent a new generation of clothiers who exercised a high level of control over all stages of manufacture. Perhaps no less significant were the large numbers of men and women who made more modest livelihoods as smallholders-cum-weavers, sometimes by the sixteenth century as outworkers not owning their own looms, and the numerous women who carded and span the yarn that fed the looms in the first place.

The latter part of the fifteenth century or the early years of the sixteenth may have seen a degree of economic stability, but there were underlying inflationary factors beginning to emerge by the time of Henry VIII's accession. These were themselves greatly augmented by the new government's fiscal policies. One factor was rapid population growth. Increased demand for foodstuffs did push prices up, but price inflation was only partly a corollary of population growth. Whereas the middle years of the fifteenth century saw economic dislocation consequent on bullion famine causing a marked shortage of silver coin, the sixteenth century saw a growing surplus of silver resulting in price inflation. The bullion famine ended as a consequence of new supplies of silver becoming available from Schwaz in the Tyrol and Schneeberg in Saxony from the 1460s, and Annaberg in Saxony and Joachimsthal in Bohemia from the 1490s. Growing levels of overseas trade resulted in a net inflow of silver into the English economy. The freer availability of silver coin also encouraged those who had earlier hoarded scarce silver – in the form of plate or coin – to put this back into circulation. Another factor was government policy in respect of the suppression of religious houses, taxation and debasement of the coinage.

Henry's ambitious foreign policy proved an enormous drain on the exchequer and the goodwill of his taxpaying subjects. In particular, the attempt to raise taxes without reference to parliamentary sanction by means of the supposedly voluntary Amicable Grant of 1525, a levy of a sixth on the goods of the laity (and twice that rate on the clergy), risked widespread rebellion. Actual rioting broke out in the textile district of south-west Suffolk, notably at Lavenham, Long Melford and Waldingfield where there were real (and justified) fears that high taxation would kill jobs. (Lavenham may also have been facing actual hardship as a consequence of 'the rich clothier' Thomas Spring's death in 1523 and the consequent ending of the Spring interest in textile manufacture.) Faced with such hostility, Wolsey was obliged to abandon the Amicable Grant and, effectively, Henry VIII's ambitions in France.

The search for revenue was not confined to taxation. The dissolution of the monasteries could clearly be understood as an attack on one of the more important institutions of medieval Catholicism and indeed on pilgrimage (since a number of religious houses supported shrines) and purgatory (since most religious houses performed chantry functions). Henry's endorsement of this policy was, however, driven not by doctrinal radicalism but by the simple fact that so much wealth and property could be realized. Although some of the income achieved in this way was immediately mortgaged in paying pensions to the ex-religious, only heads of houses received substantial payments. Shrines were stripped of their jewels and precious metals and, together with church plate, this was melted down to augment the royal coffers. Rather than adding to the royal estate – and hence increasing long-term revenue – much confiscated land was quickly sold on. This had the political consequence of creating a whole class of persons who had a vested interest in not reversing the process, but also the fiscal consequence of further flooding the Treasury and stoking underlying inflationary pressures.

Actual debasements of the coinage occurred about ten times between 1542 and 1551. These were used as quick-fix ways of raising revenue, but their inflationary effect was profound. Each debasement reduced the silver content of the coin by some third or more. The pound sterling that had contained 6.4 troy ounces of silver before the debasement was reduced to under an ounce. The result was to greatly increase the volume of coin in circulation and hence to drive inflation to unprecedented levels. The Phelps Brown and Hopkins Index, a price index centred on the period 1451–75 (= 100), well illustrates this (Table 15.1). Grain prices unsurprisingly followed much the same trend, but rents and, as we shall see, money wages lagged behind.

Prices rose, but wages did not keep pace. The failure of money wages to grow as fast as prices is not difficult to explain. Rapid population growth tended to increase the supply of labour faster than any growth in the demand for labour. Whereas in the

TABLE 15.1. EXTRACT FROM THE PHELPS BROWN AND HOPKINS INDEX

Decade	Index value[2]
1490–99	101
1500–09	104
1510–19	111
1520–29	148
1530–39	155
1540–49	192
1550–59	289

later fourteenth and earlier fifteenth centuries the waged labourer could negotiate with his or her employer from a position of strength, the employer was now in the stronger position. Attempts to peg wages by statute as seen in 1445 and 1495 effectively became redundant after 1514, which last merely reiterated the 1495 scale. The changing balance between labour supply and labour demand had two significant consequences. First, the real value of money wages, and consequently the spending power of labourers, started to slide. By the end of our period the hypothetical Oxford building craftsman studied by Phelps Brown and Hopkins had only some two-thirds of the spending power he had enjoyed 50 years earlier. Focusing on the regional economy of rural north-east Norfolk, Jane Whittle has calculated that the skilled agricultural labourer would have to work for 270 days in the period 1540–59 to earn the price of an acre of land, whereas in 1500–09 it would have taken him only 60 days. For the less skilled labourer the equivalent number of days are 327 and 95.[3] It may be that urban workers, who seem to have commanded slightly higher wages, were marginally better off, but on the other hand they may not have been so generously remunerated in terms of meals.

The second consequence of a surplus of labour were growing levels of underemployment and unemployment. This translated, as we shall see, into the growing contemporary concern with vagrancy and the sturdy beggar, a perspective last seen in London in the decades immediately after the plague. Female workers were perhaps especially vulnerable, although this is only really visible in an urban context. It is from the middle of the fifteenth century that we start to find evidence of craft guilds restricting women's access to certain kinds of employment. The three earliest and most striking examples relate to the weaving trade and date to the depressed period at the height of the bullion famine. Thus in 1448 the Shrewsbury weavers stringently restricted the rights of widows to continue trading and in 1453 the weavers of Coventry declared that for a master to permit 'his wife or his daughter or any woman

2. E.H. Phelps Brown and S.V. Hopkins, 'Seven Centuries of the Prices of Consumables, Compared with Builders' Wage-Rates', *Economica*, new ser. 23 (1956), pp. 296–314. The value at a given period is expressed as a percentage of the base period. Prices in the mid-sixteenth century rose from twice to three times the level achieved a half century or more previously.

3. J. Whittle, *The Development of Agrarian Capitalism: Land and Labour in Norfolk 1440–1580* (Oxford, 2000), Table 5.3, p. 244

servant to weave in the broad loom . . . is against all good order and honesty'. More forthright language was used by the Bristol weavers in 1461 when they claimed that 'men liable to do the king service in his wars and in defence of this his land, and sufficiently skilled in the said craft, go vagrant and unemployed' as a consequence of the employment of women in the workshop.

It may be unwise to place too much weight on evidence at a specific moment for an industry that was unusually sensitive to fluctuations in overseas trade, but we continue to find examples of ordinances directed against women weavers, as at Hull in 1490 or Norwich in 1511, in this last instance alleging that women were not strong enough to operate the looms adequately. Another indicator is probate evidence for a decline in the number of widows continuing to manage workshops. This appears to be the case at York by the later fifteenth century judging from references to servants in wills. Here female servants, previously employed alongside male in a wide variety of craft and mercantile households, came increasingly to be associated with mercantile employers. Craft workshops, it would appear, were becoming exclusively male preserves in much the same way as was true of numbers of contemporary German cities.

Other indicators of the increasingly marginal position of women in the labour market are more oblique and symptomatic of a broader shift in attitudes on the part of civic and village elites worried by disorder. One solution was the adoption of a more conservative ideology of gender. The most dramatic illustration of this shift is the 1492 Coventry ordinance stipulating that

> no singlewoman, being in good health and strong of body to work, under the age of fifty years, take or keep from henceforth houses or rooms to themselves, nor that they take any room with any other person, but that they go into service.

One way of reading this is that Coventry's ruling group could not conceive of any respectable employment whereby women could support themselves – other ordinances made at the same time concern prostitution – but the larger context is a fear of the ungoverned woman. Like concern with prostitution is reflected in ordinances issued elsewhere as at Nottingham in 1463, Leicester in 1467 or York in 1482. From much the same period we find related concern for the regulation of alehouses and a whole subculture of illicit activity. Not only were the sexual mores of the women who sold ale considered suspect, but such women were invariably implicated in gaming, receiving of stolen goods and generally corrupting young males.

An erosion of women's profile in the labour market accompanied by an assertion of a more conservative gender ideology, which saw men as the primary breadwinners and women as homemakers, mothers and helpmeets, was in fact part of a wider northern European phenomenon. The specific English chronology is as yet uncertain and different regions probably showed slightly different patterns according to their particular economic circumstances. The process in York, a community whose economy was partly dependent on trade with northern Europe, may have been comparatively precocious. It has been argued, albeit on slight evidence, that both London and the small south-western city of Wells were rather slower to discriminate against women's employment. The economy of London seems to have held up at the expense of some regional centres. Likewise at Wells, which lacked any formal craft guild structure, cloth manufacture appears to have prospered in the 1460s and 1470s. On the other hand, Judith

Bennett, in a deliberately provocative study that compares evidence from the Southwark poll tax returns for 1381 with London deposition evidence from the later seventeenth and early eighteenth centuries, even questions that there was any significant shift.[4] Bennett's conclusions are in fact deeply flawed, partly because her choice of the poor suburb of Southwark is no proxy for London, partly because her analysis is confined to single women, most of whom, like single men, were in service, but lastly because her analysis actually obscures what happened in the years between, the later fifteenth and the earlier sixteenth centuries, with which we are here concerned.

It is still harder to make any useful observations about changes in women's profile within the rural economy. The evidence, such as it is, tends to be limited to manorial and churchwardens' accounts, hence to waged work. The evidence is thus patchy and has not been much studied, at least with this question in mind. Jane Whittle, in her extensive study of waged labour in north-east Norfolk in the period 1440–1580 found only one instance of a woman labourer recorded together with her remuneration, but it would be foolish to conclude that women were as invisible in real life as in the documents. More satisfactory are the Porter's Hall accounts from Stebbing (Essex) for the year 1483–84. These show that about a third of the paid work accounted for was performed by women, at least some of whom were married, but that women were noticeably less well remunerated than men and that quite a rigid gender division of labour operated. A significant proportion of the work done by women is accounted for by sowing, exclusively the preserve of women and paid at a measly 1d (0.4 pence) per day. Even where women were employed alongside men at harvest time, women were paid 3d as against the men's 4d per day, although this precisely corresponds to the pattern at Chalvington (Sussex) in the 1430s. Women were actually fairly well represented amongst this 'casual' labour – 21 different women were employed as against 31 different men – but only one woman as against 12 men formed part of the regular staff hired by the year.

It is difficult to put this anecdotal evidence into context, but it is tempting to conclude that the wage differential operating and the markedly low wages paid to the women sowers are indicative of some sort of deterioration compared to a century previous where the evidence that women were paid less for the same work is more ambiguous. On the other hand, wage evidence from rural north-east Norfolk suggests that wages there rose in both money and real terms between the 1480s and the 1510s, and only started to decline sharply (in real terms) after the 1530s. This is indicative of a temporary scarcity of labour in an economy buoyed by the expansion of worsted production that may have been advantageous to women's employment, but it also warns that we should not generalize from the experience of specific local economies.

Significant changes in the structure and composition of the labour force represent one important change in the period. Another phenomenon – and superficially a more immediate indicator of recession – that has been much remarked is that of village desertion. The deserted medieval village – sometimes referred to by the acronym DMV – has stimulated a degree of scholarly interest on the part of historians, historical geographers and archaeologists. On the one hand, they offer archaeological evidence for peasant housing or for burials within long-abandoned and ruined churches.

---

4. J.M. Bennett, 'Medieval Women, Modern Women: Across the Great Divide', in D. Aers, ed., *Culture and History, 1350–1600* (London, 1992), pp. 147–75.

On the other, they present an interesting historical problematic relating to the chronology of and reasons for desertion. It is this last that must be our concern here. Desertion, of course, represents the end point in a longer historical process. What is perhaps more interesting is when and why this process began. As such, the discussion that follows is in some ways as pertinent to the preceding chapters as this present one, though numbers of desertions in this period were the result of deliberate clearance by landowners rather than merely the end point in a long evolutionary process.

There is a distinct geography associated with village desertion. There are particular concentrations in Midland England, especially in the counties of Buckinghamshire, Leicestershire, Northamptonshire, Oxfordshire, Rutland and Warwickshire, in Norfolk, in parts of Lincolnshire, Yorkshire and Durham, and in Northumberland. The last probably has as much to do with the troubled history of border raiding and the drift of people to less troubled settlements as the uneconomic nature of open-field arable farming after the Black Death. We see a glimpse of this in the otherwise anomalous 1377 poll tax returns for the Coquetdale ward of Northumberland; the paucity of unmarried persons, particularly unmarried females, is suggestive of a movement of the most mobile groups in that rural society even only a generation after the Black Death. The chronology of desertion in Lincolnshire and Yorkshire suggests many villages there had already been abandoned in the decades following the Black Death. The desertions in Midland England, however, can largely be attributed to agrarian change and though a significant minority of desertions may be dated to the century after the Black Death, the majority occurred at some point after the middle of the fifteenth century. Often it was historically smaller communities that went.

Two particular and related phenomena have often been noted as important factors in the process of desertion in this Midland region. One is the creation of large-scale pasture to support sheep. The other is the enclosure of former open fields and common land. We have already observed how parts of Midland England had suffered real economic dislocation in the aftermath of the Black Death as rising wage costs and subsequent erosion of grain prices made arable husbandry uneconomic for numbers of peasant producers. Already in the few decades following the advent of plague there were high levels of emigration from the countryside both into London and into other provincial towns, but a growth in the demand for cloth by the later fifteenth century now made it much more attractive to create grasslands for pasture where formerly smallholders had their cottages and open fields. As early as 1489 parliamentary legislation tried to restrain landowners from forcibly evicting their tenants and so adding to the newly emergent problem of vagrancy, claiming 'great inconveniences daily doth increase by desolation and pulling down and wilful waste of houses'.

Further legislation was enacted in 1515 and, soon after, Cardinal Wolsey initiated a sustained campaign against enclosures by means of a national enquiry during 1517–18, resulting in a large number of actual prosecutions. By 1523 Wolsey sacrificed this tough policy as the quid pro quo to persuade parliament, and hence the landowning classes, to grant a new subsidy, but new legislation curbing the size of individual sheep flocks and once more attacking enclosure was enacted in 1533 and 1536 respectively. This legislation once more resulted in ligation during the course of the 1540s. However, enclosure was not just about creating fences and hedges around previously unfenced land. It was also about landowners asserting property rights over land that had hitherto been considered common and hence the boundaries created were legal rather than necessarily physical. The issue by the last two decades of the period, moreover, was more to do with competition for land in the face of a now rapidly growing population than the creation of pasture at the expense of arable. It was consequently in this latter period that the disputes about enclosure most frequently boiled over into actual violence, although sometimes this was as much orchestrated by rival landowners as spontaneous popular protest. A fresh round of inquests into enclosure initiated by Protector Somerset in 1548–49 succeeded only in provoking yet more rioting and over a wide area. This reflects the spread of the enclosure phenomenon well beyond the Midland region as the continued growth in demand for wool, and hence strength of wool prices, rendered pasture a more profitable source of revenue for landowners than rental income from poor smallholders. Riots were provoked not just in the Midlands, but also in the south-east and the west of England.

What the Wolsey inquest of 1517–18 suggests is that land was sometimes forcibly cleared, though we should be careful not to confuse allegations for facts. Thus in 1489 it was reported that at Wretchwick (Oxon.) the prior of Bicester's 'messuages were laid waste and thrown down, and lands formerly used for arable he turned over to pasture for animals'. On the other hand, the prior appears to have had (and so destroyed) five houses there, suggesting that the community was already largely depopulated when the final clearance came. A similar story may be told elsewhere. At Barford (Northants), in 1515, 'almost the whole village' – that is, 6 houses – were destroyed and 86 acres of land enclosed for pasture, but the village had comprised fewer than 10 houses even some 100 years before. At Edgecote (Northants) the clearance of 9 houses and enclosure of 120 acres of arable land to use as pasture in 1502 reduced the population, but did not finally destroy the village. It may be, then, that contemporary concern at depopulation was at least as significant as the phenomenon itself, which as we have seen had rather longer historical roots. On the other hand, enclosure, depopulation and village clearance is symptomatic of the broader shift in power relations between lords and tenants, with the balance swinging very much in favour of the former.

This last is reflected in the emergence of numbers of 'new men', who were able to use royal service as an entrée to landed society. Numbers benefited from the flood released as a consequence of the dissolution, in some instances building their homes within the walls of the destroyed monastery as at Lacock Abbey (Wilts.). This new generation eschewed castle walls and fortifications in favour of houses built of brick with numerous windows and, latterly, fashionable terracotta mouldings. We see this, for example, in Horsham Hall (Essex), with its impressively large windows, built by Henry VII's under-treasurer, Sir John Cutte, in the early years of the sixteenth century and, more dramatically, at East Barsham, the Norfolk home of Sir Henry Fermor built a generation later. Neither of these could begin to rival the great palace begun by Wolsey at Hampton Court or indeed Henry VIII's extravagantly costly Nonsuch Palace built between 1538 and the eve of his death in 1547.

PART 4
The Dynamics of Later Medieval Culture

PART

16 DEVOTION BEFORE THE BREAK WITH ROME

Well into the last century there persisted a tradition that the Reformation was essentially progressive and later medieval Catholicism essentially sterile. As recently as 1984, Peter Heath concluded a case study of late medieval religion with the observation, echoing T.S. Eliot's 'The Wasteland', that 'when . . . Protestantism came to Hull, it came . . . as rain to a dry land'. The same year, however, Jack Scarisbrick published his revisionist study of the English Reformation and Norman Tanner his study of the Church in late medieval Norwich. Together with John Bossy's brilliant, but more wide-ranging, *Christianity in the West 1400–1700*, these represented a new Catholic perspective on later medieval devotional practice designed both to offer a more sympathetic reading and to understand late medieval Catholicism in its own terms rather than through the distorting lens of the Reformation. Tanner's book indeed deliberately ends in 1532.

To facilitate this revived interest in later medieval religion, historians have turned to two particular sources, namely wills and, more recently, churchwardens' accounts. Wills tend not to survive especially well before the end of the fourteenth century, churchwardens' accounts much before the middle of the fifteenth. Two problems arise. First, we end up appearing to know a lot about particular aspects of devotional life during the century or so prior to the break with Rome, but not before. Second, we know only about very specific aspects of devotional life representative only of certain sections of the population. Despite the lead presented by Tanner's study of Norwich, moreover, sufficient attention has not always been paid to the possibility of distinctive regional patterns or to real differences between town and country. We also risk seeing devotional practice over the course of the later Middle Ages as essentially unchanging simply because it is difficult to discern change using these kinds of sources. Finally, we are in danger of seeing an exclusively upbeat picture of popular religious enthusiasm.

The way forward must be to engage with a much fuller range of sources, including the evidence of material culture (buildings, furnishings, monuments, etc.), of devotional writings and sermons, of religious guilds, saint cults and religious drama, of visitation returns and the records of the church courts. Equally, we must acknowledge that the devotional behaviour of significant groups within the population, particularly the non-elite, must remain largely obscure. We must also acknowledge that so much of what we know relates to patterns of behaviour. To get at the beliefs that lie behind this behaviour is well nigh impossible. Heresy trials, for example, sometimes give us insights into the beliefs of Lollards, followers of the only significant heretical movement within our period prior to the earlier sixteenth century, but not into the views of their supposedly orthodox neighbours.

The Fourth Lateran Council (Lateran IV) held by Pope Innocent III in 1215 attempted, among other things, to demarcate clearly between clergy and laity, to halt the proliferation of new religious orders and to consolidate the Church's teaching on the sacraments of baptism, marriage, penance and the Eucharist. The council also marked a shift in thinking about the whole scheme of salvation from one that imagined the laity to be largely beyond redemption to one that was much more inclusive. Through the sacraments of baptism and penance, all might be cleansed from sin. As canon 1 of Lateran IV put it, 'not only virgins and those practising chastity, but also those joined in marriage, through true faith and works pleasing to God, can merit eternal salvation'.

The prevailing perception in the early Middle Ages had been that salvation was possible only for a few singularly devout persons, notably monks who retreated from the snares of the world to lead a life of prayer and service. Lateran IV projected a more upbeat view. But this was also furthered by the growth and dissemination of the concept of purgatory, a doctrine not formally spelt out until the council of Florence in the earlier fifteenth century. Instead of assuming that all those sinners unworthy of immediate salvation were summarily condemned to eternal damnation, purgatory offered the prospect of a middle place between heaven and hell. To this middle place might go the souls of men and women who, though tainted with sin, might be spared the unending torments of hell. Purgatory was thus the place where these souls could literally be purged of sin and so rendered ready for (eventual) salvation. The time spent in purgatory, imagined in terms of many hundreds of years, depended on the extent of the sin to be purged, but also on the assistance that could be offered the soul even after death in the form of prayers and masses.

This doctrine was the basis for chantries, whereby provision was made to endow one or more priests to say mass for the benefit of the patron's soul (and those of all believers) in perpetuity or, in the case of less expensive endowments, for a finite period, usually a year or several years. Our immediate concern, however, is that it represented a profound shift of emphasis in terms of the perception of the Divinity, the role of the Church and the role of the laity. Rather than imagine the Divinity very much in terms of the stern judge of the Old Testament, it became possible to identify instead with the God who was born to a mortal mother, and who suffered and died to redeem the sins of humankind. The repeated re-enactment of the Passion through the celebration of the mass reinforced this identification with the God made flesh, but was furthered also by the cult of Christ's mother, Mary, and subsequently the cult of the Holy Family.

The development of the doctrine of purgatory necessitated a transformation in the way the Church thought about those who were not called to the enclosed world of monasticism or to a life of renunciation and service. This broadly coincides with another related development, the separation of clergy and laity into two distinct orders of society. This clearly underlies several canons of Lateran IV, notably the provisions that clergy should be celibate (canon 14) and refrain from secular pursuits (canon 16). The corollary of this was the sense that each order had its own role and responsibilities and through the conscientious fulfilment of these separate callings salvation became possible. Just as the clergy were to abstain from sex, so the laity were expected to marry and produce children, hence the elevation of marriage to a sacrament. In a post-lapsarian (after the Fall) society, it was the lot of man to labour – 'In the sweat of thy face shalt thou eat bread' (Genesis 3:19) – whereas, in St Paul's words, women might be saved in childbearing. There was room, therefore, within the scheme of salvation, for the peasant tilling the fields, for the mason beautifying the house of God, the knight protecting the weak and fighting the infidel or the woman raising a family.

Just as this shift in clerical thinking led, as we shall shortly see, to a concern to instruct the laity in what constituted the true faith and works pleasing to God, so we see growing participation of the laity in the religious life of the parish. This followed as a corollary of the obligation to attend regular worship and (canon 21) to partake of the Eucharist once a year at Easter, the annual celebration of Christ's Passion and Resurrection that the mass symbolically and miraculously re-enacted. At other times, notably Sundays and other major feast days, parishioners were expected to attend mass, but were not normally invited to share the consecrated host (bread or wafer) with the officiating priest. (The consecrated wine was reserved exclusively to the clergy.) In order to prepare parishioners for the Easter Eucharist, however, the paro-chial clergy were required to hold confession and the flock to make confession and so, through penance, be absolved of their sins. This requirement, which was reiterated and disseminated through subsequent provincial and diocesan councils, notably Archbishop Peckham's constitutions of 1281, created two interdependent needs. First, the clergy had to be trained in how to conduct confession and more generally how to give instruction to the laity on how to lead a Christian life. Second, the laity needed to know what behaviour was sinful and what acceptable. As discussed in Chapter 10, this was achieved by providing the parochial clergy with appropriate training, with pastoral manual and preaching aids, by the annual process of parochial confession and by a regular programme of teaching and preaching.

The process of confession was comparatively brief, so we should not exaggerate the amount of teaching so imparted, nor was it conducted with the degree of privacy pro-vided in post-medieval times by the construction of confessionals. In an urban context the friars made confession something of a speciality, to the annoyance of parochial clergy. Preaching as an activity is perhaps better recorded. At parochial visitation in 1301 the parishioners of Sidbury (Devon) reported, perhaps unusually, that 'in all matters Walter the vicar conducts himself excellently, preaching well and laudably exercising his priestly office'. Most preaching was done by the friars. They constructed large preaching spaces in their churches, but also travelled and preached outdoors. Occasionally parochial clergy might have invited friars to preach in the parish church. At the same parochial visitation to Colyton (Devon), for example, the bishop was told that previous vicars had invited in friars 'to instruct them for the salvation of their souls', though the then incumbent 'cares not for them', a reflection of the antagonism and rivalry that could exist between the secular clergy and the mendicants.

The laity received instruction not just through the process of confession or hearing sermons preached within the parish church. The parochial clergy were encouraged to see their parishioners were instructed in the rudiments of the faith. This tended to be reduced to a programme of learning by rote the Ave (Hail Mary), Paternoster (Lord's Prayer) and Creed, the Ten Commandments, the Seven Works of Mercy and the Seven Deadly Sins. Such a programme of catechismal instruction was, for example, central to the Lambeth Constitutions of 1281 or those issued by Archbishop Thoresby of York in 1357. From the fourteenth century, the message might be reinforced by wall paintings or glass within the parish church. Wall paintings of the Seven Works of

Mercy survive at Kimpton (Beds.) and Trotton (Sussex), and an early fifteenth-century window of the same subject at All Saints, North Street, York. Likewise depictions of the Seven Deadly Sins painted in the 1340s remain at Cranborne (Dorset) and Wootton Wawen (War.). Such visual aids could be drawn upon equally by the priest in sermons or explained by parents to inquisitive children.

The rather variable instruction of parochial clergy was supplemented, particularly in the towns, by the preaching of the friars, many of whom were university educated. Their sermons characteristically were pitched at different groups in society and offered contemporary reference designed to give their teaching immediate impact. Increasingly, however, instruction was disseminated by the laity themselves. In particular, from at least the later fourteenth century drama was used variously to tell the lives of the saints, to recreate the Bible story, or, in the cases of drama cycles documented at York and Beverley, to expound the Creed or the Lord's Prayer. The texts used were the product of clerical composition, but the productions appear to have been undertaken by lay religious or craft guilds.

The major Corpus Christi drama cycles placed particular emphasis on the story of Christ's Passion and the institution of the mass. The emphasis on confession in canon 21 of the Fourth Lateran Council cannot be divorced from the Eucharist for which confession was a preparation. By insisting on annual communion at Easter, the feast of Christ's resurrection after the crucifixion, as the most important obligation of the lay parishioner, the council was reinforcing the newly developed doctrine of transubstantiation. This held that the bread and wine of the Eucharist became in substance (but not outward appearance) the body and blood of the crucified Christ. By locating annual communion as the culmination to the drama of Holy Week, the privations of Lent, and the spiritual preparation of confession, contrition and penance, and by emphasizing that parishioners were partaking of the very body of Christ, Lateran IV effectively lay the foundations for the Eucharistic devotion that became so central to late medieval devotion.

In some churches the whole drama of the Passion was symbolically re-enacted by placing the blessed host in a special receptacle on Maundy Thursday and then joyously removing it on Easter Day. These receptacles might be temporary structures or, as at Arnold (Notts.), elaborately carved stone structures. At Hawton (Notts.) and Heckington (Lincs.) the receptacles represent Christ's tomb with the sleeping soldiers. Sometimes the Passion drama was even re-enacted using an articulated image of Christ. The drama was extended through the year by the provision of the rood, the representation in wood of the crucified Christ, his mother Mary and St John (the Evangelist), mounted on a beam in front of the chancel arch. Parishioners would thus be reminded as they attended mass on Sundays or other important festivals of the relationship between Christ's sacrifice and the miraculous events going on in the mass.

During the course of the later Middle Ages it became normal to divide the ritual space of the chancel – the eastern part of the church where the priest celebrated parish mass in front of the high altar – with a screen so as to heighten the drama and make more mysterious the events of the mass. Numbers of such screens survive today in Norfolk and Devon, as at Kentisbere (Devon) or Ludham (Norfolk). The priest signalled the central moment of the miraculous transformation of bread to body by holding the host (blessed wafer) above his head. This 'elevation of the host' was the climax of the mass and was heralded by the sounding of a bell. The bell alerted the parishioners to this event, which would otherwise be obscured by the screen. Indeed parishioners were required not to focus on the Latin mass itself until the moment of the elevation, but rather contemplate the rood, other devotional images or recite prayers. For example, *The Lay Folk's Mass Book*, a guide to hearing mass, written first in French and translated in the later fourteenth century into English, advocates repeated repetition of the Paternoster (Lord's Prayer) at various points during the mass. From the second half of the fourteenth century some more well-to-do laity used primers or Books of Hours as a devotional aid during mass. These would contain a variety of prayers, but in some more lavish versions, devotional pictures and illuminations of saints.

Saints and their cults played a central role in later medieval religious practice. Again this was promoted by the Church, for example, through the requirement that images of the Virgin and the patronal saint (to whom the parish church was dedicated) be set up beside the high altar, through promotion of relics and shrines, and through encouragement of associated pilgrimage. On the other hand, the very existence of pilgrimage represents a popular desire to be close to the saint, and the belief that by this proximity and the devotion shown by undertaking the pilgrimage miraculous intervention on the part of the saint might follow. On the other hand, the church that housed the relic or shrine would take an interest in recording miracles attributed to the saint by devotees so as further to promote the cult or, in the case of new cults, to prepare evidence for canonizing the saint required under Pope Gregory IX's reform of 1234. Pilgrims were also encouraged to offer wax votive offerings to symbolize the miracle or cure supposedly worked by the saint. These would be displayed, trophy-like, around the shrine.

Many of the major pilgrimages, such as St Thomas à Becket at Canterbury, St Edward the Confessor at Westminster or St Cuthbert at Durham, had already been established by the beginning of our period, but some new pilgrimages developed and some established ones increased in popularity. The period saw a small number of native saints canonized. We may note the bishop, Richard of Chichester (canonized 1262), Archbishop Edmund Rich (also canonized 1262), Thomas Cantilupe, bishop of Hereford (canonized 1320) and the Augustinian prior, John of Bridlington (canonized 1401). There were also popular cults around Archbishop Richard Scrope of York, executed in 1405 for his part in a revolt against Henry IV, and Henry VI. Though neither was formally canonized, their tombs at York and Windsor respectively were the focus of pilgrimages. Conspicuously, we do not find many cults, let alone actual canonizations, around laity or women, such as would be true, for example, of the Low Countries or northern Italy, though we do find the adoption of the new saint cult of St Sitha (Zita of Lucca), seen first as the patroness of servants and later of housekeepers, and a renewed cult of St Anne, the mother of the Virgin Mary, and a model of married respectability and devotion.

Over the course of our period, there was a partial shift away from some of the more obscure thaumaturgic (healing) cults towards shrines and images associated with Christ or the Virgin. Thus we find interest in pilgrimages to the Holy Blood at Hailes Abbey (Glos.), a relic acquired in 1270 and quickly established as the focus of a significant cult, and the rood at Bromholm Priory (Norfolk), a cross supposedly made from a relic of that on which Christ was crucified and brought there in 1223. By 1401, when the prior was granted permission to engage priests to hear their confessions, pilgrims were said to be coming in great number and over a wide area. Both these cults are reflections of the Eucharistic devotion that characterizes later medieval Catholicism.

We likewise find pilgrimages to such Marian shrines as Our Lady of Doncaster, an image housed in the Carmelite friary there, which was itself only founded in 1350. A chance deposition from a York marriage case, for example, shows how a group including a woman servant, a tailor and a wife went on pilgrimage there from York one Sunday in 1449. Even as late as 1524 when William Nicholson gave thanks at the friary to the Virgin for saving him and his family from drowning when crossing the River Don, some 300 people were at the service. The following year Our Lady of Doncaster was believed to have miraculously revived a drowned woman. Better known, and of greater antiquity, was the Marian shrine at Walsingham (Norfolk). This attracted a steady stream of royal pilgrims and patronage, but a far greater number of ordinary folk right up until the dissolution of the priory. Even in 1534 income from offerings totalled £260.

Evidence for the revenue from shrines represents an indirect guide to the popularity of pilgrimage over the period as a whole. Ben Nilson's analysis of giving to cathedral shrines suggests that the popularity of pilgrimage may actually have grown in the decades after the Black Death and that, although income in the fifteenth century was at a lower level, there is little to suggest any significant decline before the sixteenth century.[1] The apparent popularity of pilgrimage in the later fourteenth century, the very moment of Chaucer's fictional pilgrims, no doubt reflects the greater spending power and less pressured lives of the many. Numbers of pilgrims even ventured overseas, primarily to the shrine of St James at Compostela in northern Spain, though some went to Rome. Margery Kempe also included the major new Eucharistic shrine of the Holy Blood of Wilsnack (Germany). Lesser shrines also attracted devotees: at a time of pestilence in 1430 a small group of men allegedly went on pilgrimage from Lincoln to the obscure shrine of St Theobald near Kirby Stephen (Westmorland); in 1366 a party of villagers from Scampston went on pilgrimage to Scarborough (presumably to the hospital of St Thomas) on the feast day of St Thomas of Canterbury.

Such inexpensive local pilgrimage probably remained comparatively popular with the lower echelons of society right up until the eve of the Reformation. Nilson suggests that the decline in the revenue of even the greater cathedral shrines, such as those of St Thomas at Canterbury, St Etheldreda at Ely or St Hugh at Lincoln, during the last century or so before the Reformation may represent a change in fashion in favour of Christocentric and Marian shrines, and so disguise the continued popularity of pilgrimage. What scholars have perhaps overlooked is the continuing attraction of local monastic and parochial cults focused variously on images and relics. Though some focused on new saint cults, as those of St Sitha at Eagle (Lincs.) and Clementhorpe (near York), many were connected with images such as those of the Virgin at Boxley, Caversham, Doncaster, Ipswich, Sudbury or Woolpit. At Bishop's Lynn a new chapel was constructed at the end of the fifteenth century to house Our Lady on the Mount. No less telling is the group of villagers from Burn near Selby (Yorks., WR) observed in 1466 going in their festival clothes on pilgrimage to a local image of the Virgin on one of her feast days. They prayed before the image of the Virgin, then processed to Selby to hear mass in the abbey. Finally, they spent the remainder of the day until

---

1. B. Nilson, *Cathedral Shrines of Medieval England* (Woodbridge, 1998).

sunset eating, drinking and enjoying themselves. This last is a good insight into devotional practice and the popularity of pilgrimage within a culture which did not make the same distinction between the divine and the mundane we assume in our own age.

Among the more well-to-do, pilgrimage, at least to the lesser shrines, declined in popularity. No York testator, for example, left provision for pilgrimages to be made vicariously for the benefit of their soul between 1432 and 1502, though quite a number of such bequests were made prior to 1432, including five for pilgrimages to Canterbury and a like number to Compostela. The post-mortem provision for pilgrimages by the wealthy mercer, William Vescy, in 1407 serves to locate him both as a citizen of York – he provided for pilgrimages to Beverley, Bridlington, Scarborough, Thorpe Bassett and Whitby – and a man in tune with the pious conventions of his age, mixing traditional English saint cults with Marian and Christocentric devotions. In addition to the local pilgrimages just noted, he provided for a man to go on pilgrimage to Compostela and another to visit shrines at Lincoln, Walsingham, Bromholm, Bury St Edmunds, Canterbury, St Paul's (London) and Hailes before returning to York.

Pilgrimage represents but one facet of the cult of saints. Saints were helpers and protectors. They lent identity to individuals, to families, to collectivities such as guilds, and to whole communities. As people who had lived human lives in this world they were more approachable than the Divinity, but as saints, with their own special place in heaven, they were able to intercede for their devotees. People probably used saints on a number of different levels. The most popular level was the saint as helper. Particular saints were invariably invoked to aid in particular needs; St Margaret, who miraculously escaped from the belly of a dragon, was invoked by women in childbirth. Diseases could be alleviated or cured by prayer to the pertinent saint. SS Blaise and Etheldreda were both held to be good for diseases of the throat, St Erasmus, who was martyred by having his guts pulled out by a windlass, for diseases of the stomach. The sight of St Christopher, regularly painted on the north wall of churches opposite the main entrance, protected against sudden death. St Barbara guarded against fire and lightning.

At another level saints were protectors and intercessors. People felt particular devotion to their name saint or the saint on whose festival they were born. A York clerk, John Dautre, asked to be buried before the image of St John the Baptist,

> who before [all] other saints I have held from my youth in the most passionate devotion so that same most blessed John might intercede with his holy prayers for me, a wretched John, before his merciful Cousin [i.e. Christ].

Collectivities might also feel that devotion to a particular saint would help in this life or the next. We have already seen the way in which religious guilds devoted to a particular saint flourished in the later Middle Ages. Members of a parish would tend to have particular regard for their patronal saint. This is sometimes reflected in wills. William Sokburn and John Carre of the York parishes of St Denys (Denis) and of St Sampson respectively included these otherwise uncommon, non-English saints in their will dedications, an indication of very particular devotion.

Different trade groups identified with their own patrons. The London wax chandler, Richard Whyteman, provided in his will of 1428 for candles to burn before the image of St John the Baptist in his parish church, reflecting the collective devotion of the craft. St John the Baptist was also associated with tailors since he had made his own clothes from the skins of animals. Thus the York tailor Edmund Hescham included the saint in the dedication of his will. Other saint cults reflect status and regional (and even national) identity. The cult of St Anne, the mother of the Virgin, for example, flourished from the later fourteenth century, reflecting a focus on the Holy Family growing out of an interest in the humanity of Christ. It may also have been given an impetus by Anne of Bohemia, queen of Richard II. What is striking, however, is that at first this was an aristocratic cult. During the course of the fifteenth century, however, it became a mercantile cult, Anne being identified as a wealthy, but devout and charitable householder. In one particular instance we can observe how the Richmond (Yorks., NR) merchant, Nicholas Blackburn senior, brought her cult to York in the early years of the fifteenth century having no doubt learnt it from the Richmondshire aristocracy who provided him with custom. But this was also a Blackburn family cult shared by his wife, son and daughter-in-law.

Numbers of saint cults had strong regional followings and served to signify local or regional affiliation. This is true, for example, of the cult of St Cuthbert in the north-east or of St Hugh in the diocese of Lincoln. St Erkenwald, whose shrine was at St Paul's, was closely identified with London, and St Swithun, for like reason, Winchester. By the mid-fourteenth century, notably with the impetus of the Hundred Years War, St George was actively promoted as the patron of England. Ordinary soldiers were required to wear his red cross. The founding of the Order of the Garter under the saint's patronage and the creation of the associated royal chapel of St George effectively constructed a high status and specifically English cult. By the later fifteenth century his cult was more widespread and he appears, for example, on the walls of Pickering church (Yorks., NR), at Astbury (Cheshire) and at Broughton (Bucks.).

Different saints were clearly more fashionable at some periods than at others. We find, for example, attempts from the later fourteenth century to revive interest in various Anglo-Saxon and other earlier native saints, a trend exemplified by Richard II's devotion to Edward the Confessor, but interest also in St Edmund and St Winifred. Salisbury cathedral succeeded in securing the canonization of its first Norman bishop, Osmund, in 1456 and actively promoted his new shrine. As already noted, the really important saint cults of the later Middle Ages in England tended to revolve around saints closely associated with Christ – St Anne, noted earlier, SS John the Evangelist and the Baptist, St Christopher, but above all the Virgin – or cults around Christ himself – the Holy Name, the Five Wounds and, most importantly, Corpus Christi.

The feast of Corpus Christi (the Body of Christ) was formally instituted in 1311 to promote Eucharistic devotion and appears to have spread rapidly. Processions of the Eucharistic host on the feast day became widely popular, especially in towns. Numbers of religious guilds adopted this dedication. Around the feast and the procession elaborate dramatizations of scripture also evolved from the later fourteenth century, notably at Beverley, Chester, Coventry and York, which actively involved members of the various craft guilds. This drama largely survived the Henrician Reformation. The cult of the Five Wounds (representing the wounds to the crucified Christ's hands, feet and side) also reflected Eucharistic devotion and is found by the fifteenth century. It was later adopted as a banner by the Yorkshire rebels against the dissolution of the monasteries. Eucharastic devotion thus flourished until the very eve of the Reformation.

Devotional interest in the Virgin Mary, popularly seen as a merciful intercessor with her divine Son, was very marked by the end of the Middle Ages and is reflected in a proliferation of Marian cults. Devotion to the body of Christ was married to this continuing devotion to the Virgin in the cult of Our Lady of Pity, characterized by a fifteenth-century fashion for images showing Mary cradling the dead Christ in her arms (otherwise the Pieta) as at Battlefield (Shropshire), or in a window at Long Melford (Suffolk), a mirror of the now much better-known image of the Virgin and Child. A related contemporary devotion was that of the Five Joys. Much has been made of the way Marian cults provided a role model for women, but what is in fact apparent is the popularity of her cults with men as much as with women.

The cult of St Anne can be read in a number of ways. Her regular iconography (standard form of depiction) shows her instructing her daughter, the Virgin Mary, with a book open at the words of the Psalm 'O Lord, open thou my lips; and my mouth shall show forth thy praise' (Psalm 51:15). St Anne can be understood to be teaching her daughter to pray or to read, though since early instruction in reading often used psalters and books of hours, these are related activities. This provided a positive model for women generally to offer religious instruction to their children and, at certain levels of society, to provide elementary instruction in reading. Her cult also signals a positive view of marriage in a religious culture that seemed otherwise to put so much stress on virginity. During the course of the fifteenth century she was sometimes represented as the matriarchal focus of the Holy Kindred or Family, an extended group that comprised several of Christ's disciples in addition to Mary, Joseph and Jesus. Examples are the rood screen at Ranworth (Norfolk) and a window of *c.*1470 in Holy Trinity, Goodramgate, York. By this date St Anne was used to reflect ideals of domesticity and motherhood as much as to convey a message about Christ's humanity.

This extensive discussion of saint cults is justified both in terms of their obvious importance for medieval devotees and for the ways in which they belie the notion that late medieval Catholicism was essentially static (and implicitly sterile). Parents continued to invoke particular saints to aid their sick or injured children. Adults continued to invoke saints when they were themselves sick or endangered. Saints were also invoked to give victory in battle. On the other hand, changing fashions in saint cults reflect more profound changes in devotional practice and belief. They reflect both the changing models of exemplary Christian conduct offered by the Church and the models actually embraced by the laity. If we take the pattern of canonization of English saints within our period as a guide, the model provided by the English Church was deeply conservative and authoritarian; by the later fourteenth century this may reflect a clerical response to the threat of Lollardy. The adoption of devotions such as those of St Anne and St Sitha, however, suggests a more upbeat picture. Such cults helped valorize the devotional identities of variously the laity, of women, of the bourgeoisie, of the married or of those in service.

The laity appropriated and adapted saint cults to their own particular needs. Katherine Lewis has demonstrated how the popularity of St Katherine in later medieval England was a product of the many facets of her cult.[2] As patron of philosophers, she could be a model of learning, an appropriate protector of a Cambridge college, or a suitable object of veneration for a senior ecclesiastic. She could function as an inspirational

---

2. K.J. Lewis, *The Cult of St Katherine of Alexandria in Late Medieval England* (Woodbridge, 2000).

model for young women, but she could also be prayed to by young peasant women seeking marriage partners. The cult of St Sitha, the English 'translation' of the thirteenth-century Italian (Lucca) servant saint, seems likewise to have had an aristocratic following, which probably understood St Sitha as a model of chastity and charity, but also a more popular following. This last seems variously to have identified St Sitha as a protector of women as household managers or younger women as servants. She was also held to be helpful in finding lost keys or other valuables.

Saints provided particular models or exemplars of pious behaviour, but it was Christ's own teaching, codified as the Seven Works of Mercy, that represented a key facet of later medieval teaching. The Seven Works derive from a parable of the Last Judgement.[3] Christ tells how the sheep, who are to be saved, are to be separated from the goats, doomed to everlasting punishment. To the sheep Christ says:

> For I was hungry, and you gave me food: I was thirsty and you gave me drink: I was a stranger and you took me in: Naked and you clothed me: I was sick, and you visited me: I was in prison and you came to me.

(This provided the basis of six of the seven works; the seventh work of burying the dead was added on the authority of the apocryphal Book of Tobit.) When asked on what occasion Christ had been fed, clothed or sheltered, he replied that by providing for 'the least of these my brothers', they had provided for him. Christ was thus understood to have identified himself with the poor. The poor thus became, not Christ-like, but symbolic of Christ. To give to the poor, therefore, was not about alleviating poverty or hardship, but following Christ's teaching and, by benefiting Christ, earning spiritual reward. This message was reiterated in some saints' lives. St Martin, for example, gave half his military cloak to a poor naked beggar, but, as is shown in a window at St Martin's, Coney Street, York, in a dream that night Christ appeared to him and told him that he had been that naked beggar.

The Seven Works clearly influence, and even shape, the pattern of pious bequests found in wills. Testators left food or clothing to the poor and money to prisoners. John Girdeler of Harefield (d. 1402) left a penny dole to 100 poor men and women of his parish and 4d to 120 bedridden men and women in Westminster (where he was to be buried) and Harefield. The penny dole is a common feature of aristocratic and mercantile wills and assumes numbers of poor being present at the funeral specifically to beg alms, but also, by their presence, to speed the deceased's soul through purgatory. The bedridden needed special provision precisely because they were unable to beg. Thomas Broke of Thorncombe (Devon) (d. 1417) wanted to provide food for 300 at his funeral. He also clothed 13 poor men, symbolic of Christ and the 12 apostles, in russet cloth. The London vintner John Toker (d. 1428) left money to the poor of his parish, to the bedridden of various London hospitals and to the prisoners of the city's many jails.

Evidence from York wills shows that sometimes testators put much thought into this kind of post-mortem giving. Richard Croull (d. 1460) left to poor persons variously five shirts symbolic of the Five Wounds, ten pairs of shoes in remembrance of the Ten Commandments and seven pairs of russet hose in remembrance of the Seven Works. In addition to provision of shoes to the poor, a pension of a penny a week to

---

3. Matthew 25:31–46.

five poor widows and a dole of 1000 farthing loaves, the wealthy merchant Thomas Bracebrigg (d. 1437) gave a large quantity of coal and remembered to cover the cost of delivering it to poor households. Agnes de Sutton asked that her jewels be sold to buy shoes for the poor and Cecily Giry (d. 1390) asked that three feather beds be provided in her guest chamber to provide hospitality for the poor. Richard Carlell (d. 1453), a butcher, likewise provided for five poor men and women to be dined in his house every Sunday. The thoughtfulness of these and similar bequests may imply that they sometimes represent an extension of the sort of charitable giving testators were making while still living. Women in particular seem to have asked that the poor be given fuel, and this no doubt follows from their own responsibilities as household managers. Unusually we can glimpse one York widow, Agnes Grantham, exercising such charity to her poor neighbours from a case before the church court.

The popularity of the Seven Works of Mercy as a paradigm for Christian living goes some way to explaining the fashion for almshouses (otherwise maisons-dieu or God's houses) principally between the mid-fourteenth and earlier sixteenth centuries. Unlike the hospitals run on monastic lines that had been most popular with aristocratic and episcopal founders in the century or so before our period, these tended to be smaller and more informal establishments. They received those in need, provided food and clothing, cared for the sick poor and ultimately took responsibility for burying those in their care. They were particularly common in an urban setting – some nine are recorded in Exeter and even a small town like Scarborough had four functioning in the later fifteenth century – though a number were located in the countryside. In 1397, for example, a well-to-do Tottenham peasant couple arranged to build an almshouse on a vacant holding to be maintained by their heirs. A fair number of rural almshouses, however, were aristocratic foundations, unlike the largely bourgeois and guild almshouses of the towns.

Aristocratic foundations tended to be more formally endowed, and hence better recorded, than most others, many of which are found from chance bequests in wills and hence may be seriously under-recorded. Sir Ralph Neville's hospital at Well (Yorks., NR) is stated in his foundation charter of 1342 to have been 'for the remission of my sins'. It was endowed with his house at Well, several other properties and the advowson of the church there. God's house at Donnington (Berks.), founded by Sir Richard Abberbury in 1393, was for the usual 13 poor men. The inmates were required to attend daily mass in the adjacent chapel of the Crutched Friars' chapelry founded nearly two decades previously by Sir Richard.

The best known of these aristocratic almshouses is William and Alice de la Pole's foundation of God's house at Ewelme (Oxon.), for which a royal licence was granted in 1437. Here the poor men were to begin the day by saying three Paternosters, three Aves and three Creeds for the king and the founders while kneeling before their beds. They were to wear a special hood and tabard bearing a red cross and to attend matins, mass and other services at two, three (evensong) and six o'clock daily, each with its own specified round of prayers. At some point during the day, but this time in the church, they were again to pray for the king and their founders, saying the Lady Psalter three times. After mass they were to pray around the tomb of Alice de la Pole's parents, Thomas and Maud Chaucer. At all times the poor men were required to live sober and honest lives, seldom going outside the almshouse and never begging. The ordinances that set out these rules run to several pages.

It has been argued that the significance of the fashion for almshouses after the Black Death is not that they represented any growth in charitable provision or in the social composition of benefactors, but rather that they provided for the upper echelons of society to exercise tighter social control (of the kind seen at Ewelme) over their inferiors. Miri Rubin has argued that because the old quasi-monastic hospitals were becoming supposedly moribund during the course of the later Middle Ages, the actual level of provision declined.[4] Her argument rests on the premise that because the upper levels of society tended to see a contraction of their wealth following the plague, whereas the lower orders tended to do well, a new degree of antagonism between rich and poor grew up. As a consequence, she argues, the well-to-do became much more discriminating in their charitable giving, distinguishing the 'deserving' and 'undeserving' poor. For example, the London jeweller, John Pyncheon, left in his will of 1392 money to poor men 'that have been men before of good conversation'.

Whilst Rubin is evidently correct to observe cases like that just cited, these do not of themselves demonstrate her broader thesis. Pyncheon is not entirely typical, and it is difficult to find this sort of language outside London (or Westminster) and the decades immediately following the Black Death. The language of discrimination is, however, found again by the earlier years of the sixteenth century in the context of recession and a growth in unemployment. Similarly the sort of social control reflected at Ewelme is rarely found outside aristocratic circles before the sixteenth century. Some urban almshouses required prayers of the poor. Gregg's almshouse in Hull, for example, asked for prayers at 6 am and 6 pm, but few attempted to regulate their lives so completely. Lastly, whilst it is true that numbers of earlier hospitals run on monastic lines and endowed with landed estates faced financial difficulty and so tended to prune the scale of their provision through the fifteenth century, any contraction was compensated for by the proliferation of new hospitals. (It is also the case that numbers of leper houses seem to have died out even before the advent of plague, but this seems to be in line with the actual incidence of the disease.) In the context of a declining population, actual provision was, if anything, probably more, not less, generous after the plague.

The foregoing discussion has painted an essentially upbeat picture of popular devotion in the era between Lateran IV and the Reformation. This needs to be qualified in a number of ways. First, we need to distinguish between the experience of the kinds of people who are most visible in the documentary evidence and those whose beliefs and practices are largely undocumented. We should note also that during the first 40 years of our period there was a small, but practising Jewish community. Second, we need to consider evidence for dissent, notably the heretical movement known as Lollardy. We ought properly to consider also evidence for the survival of pre-Christian traditions and practices, though in practice many of these were essentially Christianized and would thus not have been thought of as challenging the teaching of the Church.

Wills, churchwardens' accounts, records of religious guilds, extant and documented Church art, religious processions, pilgrimage, evidence for devotional literature – these all speak of a high level of lay participation in the religious life of the community. On closer inspection, however, they tell us about selected groups of people at specific moments in time. Wills in particular tell us only about the aristocracy much

4. M. Rubin, *Charity and Community in Medieval Cambridge* (Cambridge, 1987).

before the middle of the fourteenth century. By the later fourteenth century mercantile wills become common. During the fifteenth century we encounter first artisanal wills and later substantial peasant wills. Wills become still more common by the earlier sixteenth century. The apparent burgeoning of lay devotion in the later Middle Ages is thus in part an optical illusion created by the sources. In particular we should be cautious of concluding that late medieval Catholicism represented a direct response to the horrors of the Black Death. Similarly, we should notice that the majority of the lay population is unrepresented by this source.

Churchwardens' accounts, which tend to survive from an even later date than wills, allow a clearer glimpse into the level of participation of ordinary parishioners in parochial life, notably in terms of fundraising. Here a more upbeat assessment is perhaps possible, but the small number of persons who appear particularly active must be set against the many who simply do not feature in the records. The point may be repeated many times over. Guilds, by levying an entry fee and regular membership charges, consciously excluded the poor. On the other hand, men periodically presented for fornication or adultery, and the persons presented for working on a Sunday or other holy days, for failing to attend church or for stealing from the parish church hint at a larger subculture of people who were relatively untouched by the 'popular' piety of the later Middle Ages.

We should also be alert to the possibility that many essentially pagan or superstitious practices masqueraded under Christian trappings or were otherwise tolerated as posing no challenge to the faith. Ronald Hutton has made particular use of churchwardens' accounts to reconstruct some sense of the multiplicity of seasonal customs that were widely practised. Some, such as the celebration of Yule at Christmas or the burning of fires at midsummer clearly reflect pagan origins. Other clues are the occasional presentation of peasants before the church and other courts for using charms and spells variously to cure sick livestock, to serve as love charms, or to find lost objects. Some curious and essentially non-Christian beliefs and practices are also sometimes revealed as a by-product of investigations into Lollardy. There remains the possibility of a significant level of folk belief, residual pagan practice and even unbelief that has hitherto gone untapped.

LOLLARDY

Lollardy is a difficult term. We should distinguish the early Wycliffites, who followed the philosophically sophisticated ideas of the Oxford scholar, from Lollards, but whereas Wyclif himself can be associated with a number of specific teachings, most radically in respect of the mass, Lollards subscribed to no common set of beliefs. There is a sense, moreover, in which Lollardy is a clerical construct, for it was the Church that determined that Lollardy was heretical and, in so doing, attempted to identify 'Lollards' with specific heretical beliefs. In fact Lollardy was probably more a way of thinking than a creed. It was more like puritanism, with which it had much in common, than, say, Calvinism. In talking about Lollardy, therefore, it is not necessarily helpful to be bound by the same criteria as the medieval Church, even though we are so dependent on Church records when writing histories of Lollardy. Indeed in the discussion that follows the implication is made that it was possible to have Lollard sympathies and still be a devout catholic.

John Wyclif had enjoyed patronage at the court for part of the 1370s, notably from John of Gaunt, for his criticism of the very considerable landed and material wealth that had been amassed by the Church and its clergy. This patronage ended abruptly in 1381, however, once Wyclif challenged as philosophically untenable the doctrine of transubstantiation, the belief that in the mass the actual substance, but not the appearance, of the bread and wine became the body and blood of Christ. His own teaching did not challenge the Real Presence, the belief that Christ was present in the Eucharist, or the efficacy of the mass, but it was a direct challenge to the authority of the Church and its teachings. Because of his academic standing, Wyclif's heresy was tolerated in his lifetime to the extent that he was merely exiled from Oxford to his parish at Lutterworth where he died in 1384. Only at the Council of Constance (1415) was Wyclif formally condemned as a heretic; in the very different climate of 1428 his bones were disinterred.

While still in Oxford, Wyclif had inspired a number of followers within the university community, such as John Purvey. Their evangelical zeal encouraged them to preach publicly. Much of this early preaching was in the hinterland of the university, but word spread quickly and within five years of Wyclif's death there were people following his ideas in, for example, Leicester and the diocese of Salisbury. By the earlier fifteenth century the legacy of this first phase of evangelism can be detected through the south-west, the Midlands towns of Leicester and Coventry, along the Thames Valley, in the capital and into Kent, Essex and East Anglia, a geographic pattern that broadly coincides with the region that seems to have enjoyed the most dynamic economy in the post-plague decades. This is a not insignificant correlation in the light of what we know of the social composition of 'Lollards'. Though this is not the full extent of Lollard influence, there is every indication that it took firm hold in various pockets over several generations within this broad region.

The early spread of Lollardy was the product both of evangelical zeal and the inability of local bishops to do more than continually drive itinerant preachers across diocesan boundaries. There was a degree of sympathy in high places, which provided the climate in which the radical Lollard 'Twelve Conclusions' (1395) could be presented to Parliament. Only with the statute de Heretico Comburendo (1401), a product of Henry IV's policy of buying the Church's support after the deposition of Richard II, was the Church armed with an effective weapon. The statute provided for anyone convicted in the church courts of heresy for a second time, having first renounced heresy, to be handed over to the secular authorities to be burned. At the same time it signalled support from the Crown and its agents, though as yet no common cause among the political classes. In 1409 Archbishop Arundel's Constitutions were issued to prevent the circulation of heretical texts. Perhaps more significant, however, was the rebellion led by Sir John Oldcastle in 1414 designed to topple the new king (Henry V). Though easily suppressed, the Lollard sympathies of Oldcastle and his followers served to equate Lollardy with treason. Thereafter Lollardy became an underground movement no longer able to attract aristocratic support or project a political voice. Lollardy thereafter was sustained by the activities of a small number of itinerant teachers, the circulation of Lollard-inspired texts written in English and the cultivation of Lollard ideas from one generation to the next by particular families.

The ideas that crop up in association with the early (that is pre-Oldcastle) Lollards tend to focus around criticism of the Church's wealth, an associated disdain for funerary pomp, an interest in provision for the poor and the advocacy of the right of all to preach and teach. The first three overlapped with a broader devotional strand current in the later years of the fourteenth and early fifteenth centuries. It is neither possible nor necessarily helpful to draw clear distinctions between orthodoxy and dissent at this date. In particular, numbers of well-to-do people made disparaging remarks in their wills about their mortal remains or requested unostentatious funerals, preferred to endow almshouses than the religious orders or demanded high moral standards of the clergy they employed to say mass for the benefit of their souls. We also find such orthodox English texts as *Poor Caitiff* and *Dives and Pauper* circulating in both Catholic and Lollard circles since they addressed common devotional needs. A more radical position, however, which followed Wyclif's attack on transubstantiation, was to argue that all could administer the sacraments and that the Church had no monopoly on determining who was or was not a priest. In the case of Walter Brut, this was pushed to the logical extreme of claiming priestly powers for women. This was perhaps as much polemical as indicative of a radical reassessment of gender roles. Later Lollards tended to be characterized more exclusively in terms of what they rejected, notably images, pilgrimage and the mass, though Lollard suspicion of these was itself hardly new. Margery Baxter's words reported at her trial in Norwich in 1429 that the sacrament of the mass 'was falsely and deceitfully ordained by priests of the Church to bring simple people to idolatry, as that sacrament is but material bread' represents a common enough Lollard position, but one that is a long way removed from Wyclif's own teaching.

As Shannon McSheffrey has argued, Lollards came to attack precisely those things that were so much part of late medieval orthodox lay devotion.[5] Two points follow. First, Lollardy was never an especially popular movement, though we are in no position to offer estimates, especially given caveats as to what constituted Lollardy. It looms disproportionately in the historical record partly because churchmen saw it as such a threat. Second, despite a historiography that has characterized the medieval Church as unsympathetic to the needs of women, and hence that heresy had a particular appeal for women, the rather puritanical and conservative ideology characteristic of Lollardy cannot be read as liberating. Again as McSheffrey has demonstrated, women do not seem to have been particularly attracted to the sect. They were more often involved as family members and were not especially active. The enthusiasts like Margery Baxter and Hawise Moon in Norwich or Alice Rowley of Coventry nearly a century later are noteworthy, but hardly representative.

Our knowledge of Lollards, of who they were and what they believed, is largely derived from the evidence of heresy trials. These are more common from the later fifteenth century. They are hardly an impartial and objective source, since witnesses giving testimony against suspected heretics would very much be concerned to project themselves as beyond reproach in their own devotional practices and beliefs. This disguises what must be a common pattern of toleration and at times tacit sympathy, for it is otherwise difficult to see how groups of Lollards could survive through several generations. Equally, the concern of the clerical authorities not to be tainted by heresy, seen very much in terms of contagion, meant that the courts were more interested in getting suspects to renounce a range of heretical positions than to establish

---

5. S. McSheffrey, *Gender and Heresy* (Philadelphia, 1995).

the actual beliefs and ideology of any individual. This tends to make 'Lollard' beliefs appear more coherent than was necessarily the case.

What the trial evidence does allow, when placed alongside other sources, is some sense of the kinds of people who were most conspicuously active as Lollards. The aristocratic sympathy found at an early date, including a small group K.B. McFarlane dubbed 'the Lollard knights', does not extend into the period of heresy trials and was probably largely curtailed by Oldcastle's revolt. What we do find are numbers of artisans, both rural and urban, labourers, some substantial peasants and some evidence, as at Coventry in the last decade of the fifteenth century or London in the earlier sixteenth century, for mercantile sympathy. The Norwich heresy trials of 1428–31 reflect a generally lower social profile than is perhaps true of some of the later trials. Some of those tried were related to one another and there are a fair few married couples presented. To no small degree, therefore, we are looking at men and women who made their own livings as artisans, traders or agriculturalists, and who might be as likely to employ labour as to work for others. This sense of their own self-worth is integral to the Lollard identity.

Another conspicuous feature of the trial evidence is the level of literacy, particularly among male suspects. Some fifth of the males noted in heresy trials appear to have been able to read texts in English, but in the absence of clearer evidence for literacy rates more generally, we cannot know how significant this is. Literacy was an issue in the Church's fight against Lollardy because the sect produced a number of pamphlets and other writings, and was associated with the earliest complete translations of the Bible into English. These last were essentially the work of Wyclif's immediate disciples, notably Nicholas Hereford in the 1380s and John Purvey a decade later. Wyclif saw the Bible as the sole authority for the faith, implicitly rejecting the authority of the Church to augment scriptural teaching. The intention thus was to make the scriptures more widely accessible. French translations of the Bible had circulated in aristocratic circles and the Gospels had been rendered into English, but there had been no complete English translation because English was only beginning to emerge as a respectable literary language in the late fourteenth century. The effect of the Lollard translation, however, was immediately to associate scripture in the vernacular (and hence devotional writings in the vernacular more generally) with heretical sympathies, hence the provisions of Arundel's constitutions of 1409. In fact, some 250 so-called Lollard Bibles are wholly or partly extant, suggesting that its use extended well beyond a Lollard context. It is often other tracts such as *The Wicket* that actually seem to have circulated between Lollard activists.

Direct reading of scripture may not have been especially widespread among Lollards, but the sharing of other texts through reading groups was. Lollards seem to have had a particular veneration for the written word even if they were not themselves literate. This is precisely the sort of respect for the written word associated with the newly literate in a largely pre-literate culture. The supposedly Lollard fashion for reading groups and circulation of vernacular texts may not, however, be so very different from orthodox devout practice to judge by the number of orthodox vernacular devotional texts in circulation. The difference lies in the Lollard confidence that, because divine authority is vested in scripture (and by extension the written word), they had no need of clerical direction, whereas devout Catholics actively looked to the clergy for spiritual guidance, even to the extent of cultivating particular confessors.

The proliferation of trial evidence from the later fifteenth century suggests that Lollardy was flourishing, even growing significantly in numbers from this period. It could also simply represent increased vigilance on the part of clerical authorities. There is no way of resolving this, but in so far as later Lollardy represents a puritanical reaction against current orthodox devotional trends – the popularity of saint cults and associated images, pilgrimage and perhaps particularly masses for the dead – then there is a real possibility that the sect was in fact growing. Once again, however, we should be open to the possibility that Lollardy represented but an extreme manifestation of a wider devotional current. Certainly it is by this date commonplace for wealthy testators to demand that only 'honest' priests be hired to say masses for their souls. Likewise it would seem that the upper echelons of society at least were becoming less interested in the generality of saint cults and associated pilgrimages, focusing instead on Christocentric cults. The rather conservative gender ideology rooted in the Letters of St Paul, which informed Lollard thinking, was also in tune with the wider climate of the period as reflected, for example, in craft guild and civic ordinances. In London and elsewhere in those regions previously associated with Lollardy there are clear indications that Lollardy persisted into the sixteenth century and so provided a sympathetic audience for the reception of Lutheran and other Reformed teaching from Continental Europe. The join between later Lollardy and early Protestantism is, if not seamless, then at least almost invisible to the modern scholar.

17 DEVOTION UNDER THE HENRICIAN REFORMATION

The primary context for the events of the 1530s lay with the threat posed to the continuity of the Tudor dynasty by the failure of Henry VIII and his queen, Catherine of Aragon, to produce a male heir. His only legitimate child was a daughter, Mary, though he had an illegitimate son, the duke of Richmond, born in 1519, who was to die while still a child. The shadow of the dynastic conflict of the Wars of the Roses and of revolt against Henry's own father, the founder of the dynasty, could not lightly be overlooked. There was no recent precedent for succession by a queen, nor was the recent experience of queenly rule encouraging. By the mid-1520s Queen Catherine was in her early forties. The prospect of producing a legitimate son that would survive was by this date virtually nil. The idea of an annulment to the marriage consequently appealed. Henry had married the widow of his older brother Arthur, who had died aged 15 only a few months after his marriage. Henry's own marriage to Catherine had consequently depended on the grant of a papal dispensation. Hopes for a dissolution of the marriage lay with the doubts that could be cast over the legitimacy of this earlier dispensation. Henry began seriously to pursue such an annulment during the course of 1527.

Matters were precipitated by Henry's passionate entanglement with Anne Boleyn, the daughter of an aristocratic Norfolk family employed as a member of Queen Catherine's household. He had earlier had an affair with her elder sister, Mary, but his expectation of his petition's eventual success, combined with Anne's own ambitions to be more than another mistress, gave the relationship an entirely new momentum. The negotiations over the annulment, however, proved highly protracted. The central obstacle was not theological but political: Pope Clement VII was effectively in the power of Queen Catherine's nephew, the Emperor Charles V. Cardinal Wolsey's failure to deliver on this, despite holding legatine powers, ultimately cost him his position and, but for his sudden death at Leicester at the end of 1529, his execution on charges of high treason.

Wolsey was displaced as the king's chief adviser by Thomas Cromwell, whose earlier career had been in Wolsey's employ. A layman and a common lawyer by training, Cromwell had developed sympathies for reformed ideology. Certainly he had no compunction about stirring up anticlerical sentiment in a parliament dominated by common lawyers hostile to the claims of canon law, and harnessing this to push through legislation designed to force the pope's hand. In the parliamentary session of 1531, the charge of *praemunire* – that is, accepting the authority of an external jurisdiction in the form of Wolsey's legatine powers – was pursued against the clergy. This was a thinly veiled challenge to papal authority. The £100,000 levied from the Church for a pardon likewise represented a popularist move to tap into the wealth of the Church as an institution. In 1532 Parliament provisionally removed the pope's right to tax the English clergy, a measure that was confirmed two years later by the Act in Restraint of Annates. At much the same time and under extreme royal pressure, Convocation, the legislative body of the English Church, was effectively brought under royal authority by recognizing the need for the royal assent to any legislation it might make. The 1533 Act for the Restraint of Appeals effectively paved the way for Henry's petition for 'divorce' to be heard instead by the new archbishop of Canterbury, Thomas Cranmer. The same act asserted that 'this realm of England is an empire . . . governed by one supreme head and king', claims that were given substance by the Act of Supremacy the following autumn.

The latter stages of this process were progressed with a particular urgency. Once the direction of the king's policy had become apparent, Anne Boleyn had yielded to Henry's desires. By January 1533 she was carrying his child. The couple were married in secret even before Cranmer had been able formally to declare the annulment of Henry's marriage to Catherine of Aragon in May of 1533. On 1 June Anne was crowned as Henry's queen and in September gave birth to a girl, the Princess Elizabeth. Queen Catherine herself was exiled from court, recognized only as the Princess Dowager with reference to her first marriage to Prince Arthur. She died at the very beginning of 1536.

The urgency of the royal divorce combined with the realities of contemporary European power politics to precipitate a break with Rome and the assumption of quasi-papal powers by the king. Whatever the motives and religious sympathies of various players in this drama – Thomas Cromwell, Thomas Cranmer or even Anne Boleyn herself – the reasons for this breach were essentially dynastic and political, not doctrinal or religious. The Act of Supremacy represents not an attack on Catholicism as such, but a consolidation of royal authority, in effect, a nationalization of the Church in England and the creation of the Church of England as another arm of government.

Perhaps the best-known action associated with Henry's headship of the Church is the dissolution of all religious houses, including those of the mendicant orders (friars) and the larger hospitals. The 1536 act was in fact ostensibly intended only to suppress the lesser houses, whose endowments were supposedly too small adequately to sustain the religious life. The process was instead allowed to run on well beyond the initial remit. Individual wealthier houses were at first persuaded to surrender, but from 1538 a campaign of suppression steamrollered until the last house was dissolved in 1540. On the one hand, Cromwell and his agents had an interest in suppressing these supposed bastions of superstition. On the other, the lure of the immense landed and material wealth generated was irresistible to a monarch with very costly foreign policy ambitions. In total, well over £1 million was generated during the reign, mostly in the form of land and the revenues from land, but some £80,000 from the sale of jewellery and plate alone.

The first stages of the dissolution prompted a series of overlapping regional revolts in Lincolnshire and northern England, collectively known as the Pilgrimage of Grace. The attack on religious houses was not, however, the only focus of discontent. The greater fear seems rather the attack on parish churches and their assets that was rumoured to be about to follow. These risings presented potentially a very serious threat to Henry's authority, but though it attracted considerable popular support and significant gentry backing, the magnates either backed Henry or at least opted not to back the rebels. The Lincolnshire Rising was put down by mid-October 1536, the main northern rising lasted only a couple of months longer, and further risings early the following year were of brief duration. Subsequent to the Pilgrimage, opposition to Henry's religious policies from conservatives and radicals alike continued, but was never again so concerted or threatening.

In the same year as the Pilgrimage, the Ten Articles, approved at Henry's behest by the English Church's ruling body of Convocation, represented a statement of doctrine within the Church. Ostensibly this was a very conservative statement but for two ambiguous features: only the sacraments of baptism, penance and the Eucharist were noticed; the article concerning the Eucharist was doctrinally ambivalent. The reform-minded could perhaps read some comfort into this, but in fact the Articles are symptomatic of Henry's conservatism. The First Injunctions of the same year, authored by Thomas Cromwell, urged clergy to teach against pilgrimages. Much more radical – and in line with what the pilgrims had anticipated – were the Second Injunctions of 1538. These forbade the popular and widespread custom of burning candles before images of saints or in commemoration of the dead, and ordered the removal of all images that were cult objects. They also required that a vernacular Bible be available within every parish church. These new injunctions seem to have been accommodated, but not necessarily very rigorously, in much of the country unaffected by the revolts of 1536–37. Elsewhere there was resistance, though no new images were erected subsequently and the deeply rooted practice of burning lights before images seems largely to have ended. No Salisbury wills in the period after 1539 made provision for lights, whereas in the period 1530–38 half of all such wills made provision.

Aside from the implicit attack on saint cults, and the more explicit condemnation of pilgrimage, the other significant reform dating to the period of Cromwell's ascendancy was the injunction to make the Bible accessible in parishes. This was backed by a concerted effort to make approved editions of the Bible in English widely available. To this end Cromwell supported various translations and printings, culminating in the production in large numbers of Coverdale's so-called Great Bible of 1539 and a cheaper edition the year following. The effect was to make possible the intentions of the 1538 Injunctions, but also to offer an authorized translation free from the more radical Protestant traits of some of the rival translations, notably William Tyndale's. This was to be Cromwell's last significant achievement. By the time the Great Bible was being distributed the political tide had turned; Thomas Cromwell was, in rapid succession, deprived of first his office and then his head.

The Act of Six Articles (1539), driven by the duke of Norfolk and the like-minded Stephen Gardiner, bishop of Winchester, reasserted the conservative Catholic orthodoxy of transubstantiation, clerical celibacy and the like. Opposition to the act, marked in London, was firmly suppressed. The same week as Cromwell's demise, an example was made of three prominent Protestants who were burnt as heretics. This conservative position was further strengthened by the issuing of *The King's Book* (1543), with its explicit affirmation of prayers for the dead, and hence the Catholic doctrine of purgatory. Although Cranmer was able to have published his *English Litany* (1544), displacing the Latin *Sarum Use* and the basis of the later *Book of Common Prayer*, the mass remained in Latin; religious practice at the time of Henry's death looked only subtly different from that which had prevailed when he came to the throne.

The last three years of our period saw a precipitous, but not always coherent, swing back to a more radical and indeed Protestant agenda under the young Edward VI and the Protector Somerset. This agenda was to last only as long as the sickly king's life. The 1538 Injunctions were reissued, but this time vigorously enforced, resulting in the widespread removal and destruction of images. (Some were patently hidden or buried by conservative parishioners against the day when a more sympathetic regime might prevail.) The conservative Act of Six Articles was repealed and while a new Act against Revilers defended transubstantiation, it demanded communion in both kinds. Another radical measure, however, was the act dissolving chantries. This encompassed religious guilds, chapels and colleges so far as they served to commemorate the dead, even in some cases schools and almshouses. Sometimes these last were privately re-endowed, but where guilds effectively acted as the local government for communities, the dissolution did damage that could not so readily be repaired. The numbers of clergy serving in many parishes was necessarily reduced and the sources of revenue available to parishioners curtailed. For the Crown, however, as with the earlier dissolution, the suppression of the chantries was a major injection for the Treasury, amounting to some quarter of a million pounds by 1550. In 1549 minor religious orders were abolished and clerical celibacy was no longer required.

Our period concludes with the 1549 Act of Uniformity. This imposed a new English *Book of Common Prayer* as the required form of service throughout the English Church, replacing all earlier uses and, most radically, finally displacing the Latin mass with an English holy communion. The new prayer book precipitated, though it did not of itself cause, a major regional revolt focused on Devon and Cornwall. Somerset's fall from power was in part a consequence. The imposition of an English form of service in Cornish-speaking Cornwall was provocative enough, but it followed the suppression of numbers of distinctively Cornish holy days and the local pilgrimages that were integral to Cornish identity. Trouble had already flared at Helston the year previous. Similar sentiment prevailed in neighbouring Devon. Eamon Duffy's recent study of Morebath has shown how the parish was effectively without funds, its church denuded of so many of its treasures, which had been variously confiscated, sold or secretly hidden in private hands.[1] The very fears that prompted the risings of 1536–37 were now being realized. The actual rebellion was not difficult to suppress since it was almost entirely a peasant protest; the rebels found no common cause with the local gentry and gained no magnate patronage, but it was symptomatic of deep-seated popular opposition to radical religious reform that characterized some parts of the country.

It is unfortunate that the term 'Reformation' implies an event rather than a process. Some Continental European cities did attempt a swift and radical 'reformation' as a consequence of city governments adopting reformed ideology. The same cannot generally be said of Tudor England, though the beginning of Edward VI's reign is the exception to that rule. Henry VIII's initial breach with Rome is symbolically highly significant, but it was not a response to the teachings of Martin Luther or other early Protestant thinkers. Its purpose, as we have just seen, was twofold. It provided the means by which Henry was able to annul his marriage to Catherine of Aragon and so legitimize his union with Anne Boleyn, ensuring the legitimacy of the children this union promised. It also consolidated Henry's regalian authority by creating him pope

---

1. E. Duffy, *The Voices of Morebath: Reformation and Rebellion in an English Village* (New Haven and London, 2001).

in his own realm. From the perspective of ordinary parishioners the old devotion to the mass, the cult of saints, the emphasis on good works and the commemoration of the dead remained essentially unaltered. Only with the advent of Edward VI, at the very end of our period, was a more thoroughgoing Protestant Reformation policy adopted. This, too, was brought to an abrupt (if temporary) halt with Edward's death and the accession of his staunchly Catholic half-sister Mary. The third and fourth decades of the sixteenth century were not, however, untouched by religious controversy. The purpose of this present chapter, therefore, is to make some sense of the ongoing tensions and conflicts that characterized religious life at this time and that constituted the Henrician Reformation.

Just as the Henrician Reformation cannot be seen as a single event, it is questionable whether it can even be seen as a single process. That would imply a clear direction, but this was at best only true for the period of Cromwell's ascendancy. Rather it was a piecemeal series of acts and events, some of which provoked active opposition, most seriously in the Pilgrimage of Grace, but which on the whole fell some way short of either a fundamental attack on Catholic doctrine or a coherent Protestant programme. People could go along with it, not out of any particular enthusiasm or religious zeal, but rather from a sense of inertia. The dissolution, moreover, served to bind the aristocracy, particularly the lesser aristocracy who had most to gain materially from the sudden availability of land, into the process. This was indeed a step that even Mary found well nigh impossible to reverse despite her own ideological commitment to undoing the work of her father and half-brother. Opposition thus came more from what contemporaries would dub the commons than from the ranks of the aristocracy who effectively constituted the political classes.

Late medieval Catholicism seems to have been comparatively vibrant. A recent edition of Lincolnshire wills in the period 1532–34, the very eve of the break with Rome and the royal supremacy, only reinforces that perspective. There may well have been an underclass of persons largely untouched by the faith and in some communities there was an established minority tradition of Lollardy deeply hostile to many aspects of later medieval Catholic belief and practice. Neither unbelief nor Lollardy, however, can explain the events of the last two decades of our period. Rather we must explore the changing perspective of orthodox believers.

The previous chapter attempted to provide a picture of devotional life up until the 1530s, but this is not a static picture. Interest in Lollardy revived by the early years of the sixteenth century, although it is not always easy to distinguish between increased clerical vigilance and a real increase in activity. By the 1520s knowledge of reformed ideology was being brought into the country as a consequence of close trading connections with 'Germany'. As a consequence it becomes difficult to distinguish Lollard survival and revival from early Protestantism. An increasingly informed and articulate laity was more likely to voice criticism of clerical shortcomings, though we should not necessarily equate this anticlericalism to sympathy for Lollardy or early Protestantism. The appeal of Protestantism was not to those who were alienated by traditional Catholicism, but rather to those who previously had been devout Catholics. In the early 1530s Protestants were still a very small minority.

The archetypically Catholic fashion for perpetual chantries had been waning even from about the time of the Black Death because in real terms they were becoming more and more costly; during the fifteenth century the value of property had tended to fall precisely as wage costs rose, a trend only exacerbated in an inflationary period. Numbers of established chantries were amalgamated or allowed to lapse simply because the original 'perpetual' endowment had become insufficient. In 1478 three chantries managed by the mayor and burgesses at Appleby were given over to a single chaplain, who was also required to run a grammar school. There is little, however, to indicate that underlying concern for post-mortem remembrance expressed in the endowment of prayers and masses had lessened. Ordinary parishioners still left money to parish lights, images or the fabric. Parish guilds thrived and, in some parts of the country, proliferated. Wills still commenced with a dedication to God, the Virgin Mary and all the saints. Interest in pilgrimages appears to have been waning by the early years of the sixteenth century, but shrines and relics, many of which were monastic, still attracted devotees and gifts.

To judge by the volume of ordinations in the earlier sixteenth century, the appeal of a clerical career was also buoyant, even if this only mirrors wider demographic trends. Monasteries, however, were finding it harder to attract recruits and some would probably have failed in time if Henry VIII had not first dissolved them. At the same time, the scale of landed benefaction to religious houses became little more than a trickle. Enormous quantities of land had, however, been accumulated by the religious houses, which, as perpetual institutions, they had no interest in selling.

More generally there was a long established, though invariably subversive tradition that the Church should be disendowed. Such ideas had briefly flourished at the court of the boy king Richard II, had been voiced during the Peasants' Revolt, and were a much repeated Lollard objective. Because such views were subversive, they did not translate into political pressure for action, but they are symptomatic of a broader feeling of disquiet at the tension between the obvious material wealth of the Church and the emphasis in later medieval Catholicism on Christ's self-identification with the poor. There were thus material reasons for dissolving chantries, monasteries and even a more radical disendowment of the Church, but these were checked by the strength of belief in purgatory, the spiritual value of monasteries as quasi-chantries, as guardians of relics and places of pilgrimage, as (for the aristocracy) ancestral burial places and testaments to family piety, and of course by the weight of inertia.

The Henrician Reformation directly addressed only the landed and material wealth tied up in the nation's innumerable religious houses. The Church was nationalized rather than disendowed, becoming more emphatically than ever before an arm of the state. The numbers of holy days – that is, religious feast days on which people were to abstain from work – was pruned radically in 1536, but supposedly to promote industry rather than to undermine the cult of saints. The problem of the chantries was ducked; a direct attack on the doctrine of Purgatory was unacceptable to a monarch whose personal sympathies tended towards a rather traditional form of Catholicism. Such a move had to await the much more radical reformist policies of the boy king Edward VI. The dissolution of religious houses, moreover, was not officially presented as a challenge to traditional doctrine or practice, though some were to use it to this end. The government's agenda was presented as reform, not Reformation.

The initial act of 1536, predicated on a national visitation of religious houses that purported to reveal widespread superstition and scandal, was ostensibly framed in terms of revitalizing monasticism by sweeping away only the smaller and less well-endowed houses (valued at under £200 per annum), which were held to be too far decayed to be reformed themselves. The lands and revenues thus confiscated were, according to the act, to be directed to good works. From the autumn of 1537 friaries, excluded from the 1536 act, came to be included. During that same year the process of coerced suppression began to encompass all religious houses regardless of wealth, prompted in some instances by acts of opposition known collectively as the Pilgrimage of Grace. The great Lancashire Cistercian abbey of Furness, for example, surrendered in April 1537, though new legislation formally extending the process was not enacted until 1539. The process of dissolution rumbled on until 1540, culminating in the suppression, among others, of the great cathedral priories of Worcester and Canterbury and, at the very heart of royal government, the abbey of Westminster.

The dissolution of the monasteries was not without precedent. Henry V had dissolved a number of 'alien' priories dependent on houses subject to the French Crown. Bishop Alcock of Ely had suppressed St Redegund's nunnery in Cambridge to found his Jesus College in 1496 and Bishop Oldham of Exeter had effectively dissolved the Devon hospitals of Clyst Gabriel and Totnes (Warland) in 1509 to further the endowment of the cathedral's vicars choral. Several smaller houses had likewise been suppressed to endow Wolsey's foundation of Cardinal College (later Christ Church) in Oxford in 1525 and his projected collegiate foundation at Ipswich three years later.

The fashion for monasticism was thus long passed. New institutions were in favour. Monasteries, moreover, had long since ceased to be primarily places of retreat for those wishing to devote their lives to the service of God in prayer, devotion and labour. Most contained relics of some sort or another, but several housed important images, such as the rood (crucifix) of Bromholm (Norfolk), or major shrines, and were the focus of pilgrimage and the revenue pilgrims brought. Communities such as Glastonbury (Somerset), associated with Joseph of Aramathea or Walsingham (Norfolk), associated with the Virgin Mary and the object hitherto of veneration by Henry VIII, were indeed heavily dependent on pilgrim traffic. By dismantling these shrines to realize the precious metal and jewels that they contained, the dissolution represented an attack on the practice of pilgrimage, but also on the very cult of saints. This attack was actually extended to all shrines, even those contained in secular colleges and cathedrals, and often shrines were dismantled before the actual dissolution of the religious house.

The deliberate and sometimes ostentatious burning of previously revered images and the scattering of the bones of major English saints served as powerful propaganda for the Protestant cause and was a far deeper attack on traditional Catholicism than was envisaged by the 1536 act. This was indeed the intention of some of those engaged in the destruction, though in part their concern was to deflect criticism that their work was motivated only by greed for the wealth invested in these shrines. Thomas Cromwell's agents wrote of their work at Winchester that

> we intend . . . to sweep away all the rotten bones that be called relics; which we may not omit, lest it should be thought we came more for the treasure than for avoiding [i.e. doing away with] the abomination of idolatry.

By the later Middle Ages nearly all monks were in holy orders and were thus able to celebrate mass for the benefit of lay benefactors. Some monasteries even had chantries established within them. The dissolution was consequently also an implicit attack on the doctrine of purgatory.

In material terms the aristocracy, and perhaps particularly the gentry, benefited from the sudden availability of land. Some wealthy Londoners, like John Gresham, the son of a mercer, who was granted the small Norfolk priory of Weybourne, were able to acquire for themselves instant estates and so present themselves as country squires. Those in the service of the Crown also benefited. Thus the priory of Bromholme was granted to Robert Southwell, who held the position of solicitor in the Court of Augmentations (and was thus directly implicated in the dissolution process). For the most part, however, established families were able to consolidate and extend existing lands. It follows that the political classes as a whole, together with and including wealthy merchants and government bureaucrats, were materially advantaged by the dissolution and had a strong vested interest in maintaining the new order. This is not say that the aristocracy, and perhaps particularly older established and more noble families, were not troubled by the process, particularly where family burial places and monuments were threatened. The duke of Norfolk, for example, petitioned that Thetford Priory, the burial place of his wife and father, and also Henry VIII's own natural son, be spared by being refounded as a college. The petition failed and the tombs were hastily removed to a parish church. Much the same process of removal of family monuments, as for example those of the lords Roos from Belvoir Priory to the parish church of Bottesford, can be widely documented. On balance it was a price to which the aristocracy was willing to acquiesce.

The impact of the dissolution on the fortunes of persons of lesser rank was more mixed. The dissolution of the many monastic hospitals, which had provided accommodation for the bedridden and outdoor relief particularly for the urban poor, had a material impact that has often been overlooked. Although it has been argued that their welfare role had been much diminished by the late Middle Ages, many in fact were still very active. Some of the London hospitals were spared and some others survived until the suppression of the chantries in 1547, but the loss of such hospitals as St Leonard's, York, St Sepulchre's, Lincoln or God's House, Portsmouth, would have been felt by the poorest in society. The provision of alms by other religious houses, which though comparatively modest were still significant, also ended abruptly.

Most of the ex-religious themselves were granted pensions. In the case of some heads of houses these were fairly generous, but for numbers of monks and canons of lesser houses and most nuns they fell well below what was needed to live. Many former monks, however, by virtue of being in holy orders, subsequently found employment as priests. Of the tenants of religious houses, some merely exchanged monastic lords for lay lords, but where a house had exercised not just lordship, but had been a major consumer and purchaser of goods and services, then there were marked economic repercussions. Even a comparatively small house like Drax Priory (Yorks., WR) employed 29 servants and boys at the time of its suppression. The effect of the dissolution on small towns, whose economy was largely directed towards supplying the needs of the great abbey or priory in their midst, was probably considerable, and towns such as Ramsey (Hunts.) or Bridlington (Yorks., ER) would have suffered immediate recession and hardship.

Bridlington Priory was one of a number of wealthy religious houses suppressed as early as 1537 because of its complicity in a series of related regional revolts known collectively as the Pilgrimage of Grace. Indeed William Wood, the last prior, together with the heads or former heads of a number of other rebel houses, was tried and executed for treason. During the course of October 1536 groups of rebels joined together in Lincolnshire (the Lincolnshire Rising) and throughout the northern counties in response to the dissolution. Their purpose was to oppose government policy, to defend religious houses from suppression and to restore those religious houses already dissolved.

The revolt has a number of parallels with the Peasants' Revolt a century and a half previously. It was a regional rising made up of a number of smaller, local revolts, each with their own identities, grievances and leadership, though the Yorkshire gentleman, Robert Aske, swiftly emerged as the overall leader. It was a popular revolt in that most of the rebels and some of the leaders were below the rank of gentry, although there was much more gentry participation than was true of the earlier revolt. Letters were used to call for a wider participation in the revolt and some of these spoke in allegorical terms of Captain Poverty. The rebels were provoked by the disruptive intrusion of royal government. Taxation was an issue, as was the threat posed by an enemy power (in this instance the Scots), though unlike 1381, the particular fear was that Henry VIII would plunder parish churches in much the way he had started to plunder religious houses. The rebels drew up schedules of demands and it was their objective to present these to the king. The revolt collapsed when the king appeared to yield to the rebels' demands.

Resistance to government policy was, of course, also resistance to government. One of the effects of the royal supremacy and of the acts and injunctions that followed was to begin to impose a high degree of central control over what went on in parishes across the country, although this was most marked after 1547. That the major revolts of the early Reformation era – the Lincolnshire Rising and Pilgrimage of Grace (1536–37), the 1549 rebellions in Devon and Cornwall (the Western Rebellion), Kett's Rebellion (East Anglia) and lesser risings in Hampshire, Oxfordshire and Yorkshire – were all regional revolts is not accidental, though Kett's rebellion was not so clearly driven by religious conservatism (or religion at all), more radical sympathies being found alongside traditionalist gestures.

On balance it would be hard to argue for a popular groundswell of opinion in favour of either a break with Rome or the wholesale adoption of reformed ideology at the beginning of the 1530s. Within two decades that picture had changed. Some of the responses (or apparent lack of response) to government policy from the 1530s are to be explained by the 'magisterial' nature of the reformation process, but we should also note the piecemeal nature of the legislation. The Pilgrimage of Grace was potentially a major setback, but the Tudor dynasty was by now too well entrenched and most of the magnates had too much to lose to risk lending their active support to this popular uprising. The spoils of the dissolution in the form of land, moreover, ensured that there was a whole raft of political society below the level of the greater aristocracy who now had a vested interest in the break with Rome and the royal supremacy. Support for reformed ideology, which was at times stimulated and at others frustrated by Henrician policy, tended only to grow. This was especially true of the capital and the south-east. Conformity, however, should not always be read as evidence for enthusiasm, and Protestantism was still a minority position even by the end of our period.

The break with Rome and the royal supremacy created one or two high-profile martyrs, but they did little to impact on popular religious practice. The dissolution had a bigger impact, but it hardly impinged on parish worship. Despite the (rather patchy) growth in support of more radical reform, and despite the intentions of the

1538 Injunctions, it was still possible in many parishes to worship in the old way, but for the burning of lights, right up to 1547. Furthermore we must recognize the strength of popular sentiment in support of traditional Catholicism up until that date and beyond. As was reflected in the Pilgrimage of Grace, Lincolnshire and much of the north, especially the north-west, tended to be conservative in their sympathies. In the larger towns of this region the traditional Corpus Christi drama continued to be performed right up until Edward's reign (and was revived again immediately after). The south-west of the country likewise adhered firmly to traditional Catholicism and this underlies the rebellion of 1549. Deeply rooted beliefs and traditions were not to be changed in the matter of a single generation.

18 THE SEARCH FOR ORDER

In 1409 the jurors presented one Margery Welshwoman before the Justices of the Peace claiming that she had set fire to Sir Hugh Burnell's barns at Acton Pigot (Shropshire). Both were full of grain after the recent harvest and so would have burned easily. In one sense this incident is a small historical footnote and it is not the intention of the following discussion to determine Margery's guilt or otherwise, let alone something so intangible as motivation. Rather our concern is to locate this incident in the broader context of medieval justice, how the law was administered and what its purpose was. Margery's charge was a serious one. Arson, alongside such crimes as homicide (murder), robbery, grand larceny – the theft of goods valued in excess of a shilling (5 pence) – and (for most of our period) rape, was classified as a felony. As such it had necessarily to be tried by royal justices rather than any seigneurial or local court. This had become the norm by the beginning of our period. If found guilty, the penalty was invariably death by hanging. Arson was considered such a serious offence as to merit a capital sentence because it was an attack on property. The law was thus working here to protect the interests of the propertied in society. Sir Hugh Burnell certainly falls into that category.

To take this analysis a little further, we may notice three particular attributes of Margery. First, she was (presumably) a peasant, whereas the person she had allegedly wronged was a lord. Second, Margery's byname – Welshwoman – implies that she was Welsh or at least held to be Welsh in this border county with a long history of animosity to a traditional enemy. Third, and again as her byname forcefully reminds us, Margery was a woman. On three counts, therefore, Margery was an outsider, or 'the other', from the perspective of those who made and administered the law, in this case the jurors and Justices of the Peace and hence the upper levels of county society. A peasant, a foreigner – an alien in contemporary usage – and a female, Margery would surely have been thought guilty even without any judicial process. This is perhaps an extreme example, but the point stands: the law often functioned not according to modern (and hence anachronistic) notions of equal-handed justice, but as an instrument of authority and a vehicle whereby 'the other' was identified and controlled. It would be dangerous, however, to conclude that this was invariably the case.

The law was not solely an instrument of social control. Often it functioned as a mechanism for the resolution of disputes. Indeed the mere initiation of legal proceedings seems sometimes to have been sufficient to persuade another party to settle. Certainly this is the implication of very many actions begun, but subsequently abandoned. The picture differs according to what area of the law we look at. Medieval England was characterized by a range of different, overlapping and sometimes competing jurisdictions, each of which functioned according to its own legal conventions.

Broadly speaking, we need to distinguish between three different legal traditions – that is, the common law, customary law and canon law.

The common law – 'common' in the sense that it applied throughout the realm – was administered by royal justices whether centrally – usually at Westminster – or more locally. The palatinates of Chester, Durham, where the bishop exercised a princely jurisdiction, and (from 1351) Lancaster, though administered separately, were subject to the same legal discipline. This body of law was described in a treatise entitled *On the Laws and Customs of England*, traditionally ascribed to Henry of Bratton (and hence known as 'Bracton'), compiled during the 1230s and completed at the very beginning of our period, but was added to and revised continually thereafter in the form of parliamentary statute (statute law). As has already been noted, all felonies were subject to the common law and dealt with by royal justices. A number of lesser offences, known as trespasses, were also dealt with by royal justices. These included assault and, from 1349, the labour legislation relating to wages, prices and contracts. Private individuals could also initiate actions, but normally only if they were of free legal status. The serf or villein was deemed to be subject to the legal jurisdiction of the lord of the manor to which he or she was attached and so could only seek justice within the manorial court. The only exception was in respect of felonies since these automatically belonged to the Crown. Married women, who were deemed to be legally subject to a husband, likewise were debarred from initiating actions in their own right before royal justices other than for rape, for the murder of a husband (and then only if he died in her arms), for the destruction of a child still in the womb and, in special circumstances, for theft. In practice it seems that courts tended not to interpret these conventions rigidly and would, for example, allow appeals from women in respect of the murder of other close male kin.

The enforcement of common law and access to royal justice operated on a variety of levels that changed over our period. The two highest courts in the land, which had emerged by the earlier thirteenth century, came to be known as common pleas (or 'the bench') and king's bench (otherwise *coram rege*) respectively. Common pleas was normally based at Westminster, though in the earlier fourteenth century it was several times removed to York, whereas king's bench was supposed to follow the king. In practice king's bench, though comparatively peripatetic especially in the earlier fourteenth century, was from the mid-1360s almost invariably fixed in Westminster. Much of the business of common pleas concerned property disputes. Business was initiated by an aggrieved party obtaining a writ – in effect an order issued in the king's name requiring the defendant to answer a specific complaint – but the actual pleading was done on behalf of the litigants by attorneys. Distance from the court was thus no bar to persons initiating business there, though there was a cost involved in obtaining the initial writ and in maintaining an attorney. The court of king's bench was a court of appeal from the lesser courts, but more importantly it had jurisdiction over felony and during the course of the fourteenth century it became normal for all such cases to be referred to this forum.

At the beginning of our period, justices 'in eyre' were periodically sent from royal courts into the various counties in order to hear a wide variety of cases, both Crown, notably felony and the abuse of royal rights, and civil. Eyres took place only every several years – ideally every seven years – but the system was effectively disbanded in 1294. Their function was assumed both by the work of assize justices and commissions of oyer and terminer. The assizes came to operate on a regular basis – from 1330 at least triannually – within circuits of groups of counties. From 1299 the assize justices also took responsibility for gaol delivery, which involved trying prisoners held against the visitation of the justices. The later years of the thirteenth century and the early part of the century following also saw numbers of commissions of oyer and terminer. These commissions were designed to mete out a comparatively swift and robust form of justice to counter disorder and the abuse of office that was manifest during the troubled years towards the end of Edward I's reign to the earlier part of that of his grandson Edward III.

By the early fourteenth century large numbers of such commissions were being issued, together with similar commissions of Trailbaston targeted at armed gangs. These centrally appointed commissions seem to have provoked much adverse comment and it is likely that the justice they meted out was at times arbitrary and corrupt. A third stand of justice that grew up during the later thirteenth century was that administered by the 'keeper of the peace', although initially this role was primarily policing rather than judicial. These keepers of the peace evolved by the later fourteenth century into the better-known Justices of the Peace, or JPs, with responsibility from 1362 to hold sessions at least four times a year. At the same time assize justices came to be attached to peace commissions alongside locally appointed knights, usually backed by one or two men of higher rank. This last had the twin advantages both of using local men to administer justice within their own locality, but also, from the Crown's perspective, of appointing men whose political clout owed more to their royal appointment than their personal rank. Such men were more likely to prove reliable servants of the Crown, though during the second half of the fifteenth century regional magnates were often successful in ensuring the appointment of their own retainers.

Customary law is the term used to describe, as the name suggests, law based on local custom and hence a whole variety of codes that differed from place to place. The courts that operated according to customary law included, on the one hand, the county court and the courts of the various subdivisions of the county known as hundreds or wapentakes, both of which to a greater or lesser degree could be regarded as an extension of the Crown's judicial administration, and, on the other, the various seigneurial courts of which the manorial courts are the best known. In an urban context in particular, courts that were historically the prerogative of a lord could become communal, the prerogative of the burgesses or citizens, but the laws they administered were specific to the particular community. In practice there are many similarities between the customs of one borough and another, or between those of one manor and another, but though we can offer generalizations, we cannot say dogmatically that the law was such and such.

The manor courts have attracted particular scholarly interest both because they have generated a great deal of evidence in the form of court rolls and because, as we saw in Chapter 7, they offer one particular window on peasant society. The courts invariably met every three weeks and all servile tenants were bound to attend. Free tenants could, of course, bring actions within other jurisdictions and even, in theory, the royal courts, but in practice free and servile peasants alike found the customary court a useful forum for the resolution of private disputes. Land transfers associated with inheritance and transactions involving the alienation (sale) of peasant land had to go through the court since the lord had ultimate title to all manorial lands, but because such transactions were duly recorded – in writing from at least the later thirteenth century – the scope for subsequent dispute was limited and the court could provide a remedy. The courts, moreover, enforced the customary law on inheritance, variously partible (where the property was divided among all sons) or impartible inheritance, primogeniture or ultimogeniture (inheritance by the youngest son). The courts also had a policing function and served as the forum for the enforcement of various seigneurial rights – such as marriage and heriot fines – and the punishment of those who transgressed by, for example, failing to perform their labour services or marrying without the lord's consent.

Much of the business of the manor courts was generated from within the peasant community itself and had little to do with the lord or his seigneurial rights. The court rolls, for example, could also be, and were, used to register details of maintenance agreements whereby elderly tenants exchanged land for material support. Some of the recent historiography of the manor court has, moreover, stressed the degree to which the peasantry themselves were able to use the courts to their own advantage and to address their own needs, particularly as landholders or employers of labour. Private litigation is a common feature of most extant court rolls. To cite one example, in 1331 Thomas de Totehille successfully brought an action against William de la Leegh for the death of six of his pigs when chased by William's two dogs. The courts were thus not simply a vehicle for lords to assert their authority. No doubt this was yet more true of the period from the later fourteenth century when demesnes and even manors were increasingly leased out and villeinage became more and more an anachronistic irrelevance.

Though lords may increasingly have seen the customary courts primarily as a source of income rather than an extension of their power, we should not imagine the manor court as either democratic or egalitarian in its constitution. In many ways the courts functioned to the benefit of the better-off males within the peasant community. It is they who are found from the later thirteenth century as jurors of presentment, responsible for presenting (or implicitly concealing) transgressions against customary law to the court, and it is they who constitute the majority of litigants. Labourers, the landless and women, particularly married women, are rather less conspicuous and more likely to be defendants than litigants. There is some evidence to suggest that prejudices against women meant they were less likely to be successful where they did bring actions, and certainly numbers of women were presented for 'falsely' raising the hue and cry if attacked or fined for a 'false' plea if their action failed. On the other hand, the evidence is not conclusive and the manorial courts could serve, for example, to protect the dower rights of widows.

Canon law was the law of the Church. It derived from a different, Roman-law legal tradition and was universal to the whole of Latin Christendom, essentially western Europe. Much canon law was concerned with the conduct of the clergy. All clergy were exempt from the jurisdiction of the civil courts even in respect of felonies and were subject only to the church courts. This privilege was open to abuse since 'benefit' of clergy was theoretically available to any who could read out a Latin text, which, by the late Middle Ages effectively included numbers of laity possessing basic reading skills. This abuse was partly plugged by a statute of 1489 that allowed laity to claim benefit on only one occasion, though some abuse remained possible for nearly a century after. Canon law, however, was not merely concerned with clergy and their conduct. It also encompassed various aspects of the laity's responsibilities to the Church, notably in respect of the payment of tithes, and the moral and spiritual conduct of the laity. In particular, the church courts exercised jurisdiction over sexual behaviour, the validity of marriages, disputes concerning wills, defamation, the casting of spells and heresy. To a more limited degree the church courts entertained what was in effect debt litigation in the form of actions for breach of promise.

We can distinguish between actions initiated by the church courts in a sort of policing capacity (ex officio actions) and private litigation (instance actions). Large numbers of individuals, both male and female, were presented for committing adultery or simple fornication (sexual relations between people who are unmarried). Although public whippings were a common enough sanction in the earlier part of our period, by the later Middle Ages public penance, which entailed appearing in one's undergarments bearing a candle in the marketplace or, more frequently, in the parish church, was more normal. In practice numbers of those presented before the church courts for fornication or adultery managed to clear their name by bringing friends and neighbours who would vouch for them or were permitted to forgo public penance by paying a fine. (Interestingly this trend provoked a 1413 petition to Parliament demanding corporal punishment for such sins.) Most private litigation concerned marriage disputes, though this kind of action was in decline over the latter part of our period. Most actions were brought because one party, almost invariably the woman, claimed that a valid marriage had been contracted, but this was denied by the other. Rather fewer cases were designed to annul an established marriage and the notion that the church courts allowed or could be cynically exploited to engineer de facto divorces is largely untrue.

As the observation just made implies, women could bring actions under canon law regardless of their marital status. In the eyes of the Church, women and men enjoyed a spiritual equality and the civil law's understanding that the married woman had no voice did not apply, though canon law shared the common law's prejudice against the servile. Women could also appear as witnesses in the church courts, although, unlike the civic courts, oral testimony was never used, rather witnesses were examined separately and written versions of their responses (depositions) compiled. (In cases where annulment was sought on the grounds of the man's impotence, the church courts even appear to have employed women prostitutes as expert witnesses.) Because some of these depositions have survived, we actually have a clearer picture of how the canon-legal courts worked and were used than is usually true of the civil courts. This can sometimes prove revealing. Thus though a study of matrimonial litigation in the York consistory – that is, the court for the diocese – during the fourteenth and fifteenth centuries, shows no evidence of the court being prejudiced against women or the testimony of women in its judgements, it is apparent that the lay community (particularly well-to-do peasants) saw women as inferior and less trustworthy, preferring to produce male witnesses wherever possible.

It is sometimes apparent that people turned to the church courts as an alternative to the civil courts where they had failed to achieve through these other courts the resolution they had desired. To take a few examples from the York consistory, in 1363 Master John de Rissheton brought a breach of promise action against one Isabel in order to secure her service, but it is apparent from the case that John had earlier lost a civil action under the Statute of Labourers. Three years later John Marrays brought an action for restitution of conjugal rights against the abducted child heiress Alice de Rouclif. Again it becomes apparent from the surviving depositions that Alice's mother had also been pursuing an action under feudal law presumably to obtain wardship over her daughter and hence legal control over Alice, whose marriage to John Marrays she had promoted. Both actions, very different though they were in law, were intended to secure John Marrays' marriage; at least in the action before the church court we known John succeeded. A third case concerns an action for breach of promise by Robert Lascelles, a York merchant, against the chandler, Margaret Harman, which clearly arose out of a breakdown in a long-standing business partnership. Lascelles claimed to be owed a large sum of money that Harman had promised but had failed to pay. Again the depositions tell us that Harman already had an action in the borough courts for debt against Lascelles. Although the borough court was the normal forum for debt litigation, Lascelles clearly saw the canon law court as offering a means to get his own back on Harman.

Such ploys warn us that the reasons that motivated medieval people to turn to the law are often not straightforward. Obtaining a verdict and punishment for the wrong-doer were not necessarily the primary motivations. One telling illustration of this point is provided by evidence from rape cases, for here legal proceedings were often abandoned at an early stage. The medieval law on rape placed considerable burdens on the woman in terms of reporting the rape and initiating proceedings; many rapes must consequently have gone unreported. There was, moreover, a strong disincentive from pursuing actions. Apart from a brief interval between 1275 (the first statute of Westminster) and 1285 (the second statute), rape was deemed to be a felony and liable to a capital sentence. The underlying concern seems to have been to protect the chastity and marriages of aristocratic daughters and wives, rape being seen as a variety of property crime of which the victim was at least in part the woman's father or husband, but male juries were loath to sanction such a penalty and so regularly acquitted the alleged rapist. The plaintiff, consequently, was invariably unsuccessful, but, to add insult to injury, was liable to be punished for making a false plea. This begs the question of why women made such pleas at all. One possible reading would suggest that the concern was not to achieve justice, since that was illusory, but rather to assert publicly the victim's lack of consent. Later medieval law, in fact, made little distinction between rape and abduction, without or even with the woman's consent and there are some hints that men sometimes used force to try to effect marriages opposed as much by the woman's family as by the woman herself.

Within peasant society resort to the customary court to resolve disputes was probably very much a last resort, not least because litigation cost money. Even where they brought actions in the courts, peasants did not necessarily prosecute them to a conclusion, but rather settled out of court. This was common, for example, in debt cases. The implication is that initiating the action was sufficient to demonstrate the litigant's seriousness and to prompt the other party to come to some sort of settlement. Much the same was true of debt litigation within the borough courts. Over a third of debt cases in the Exeter courts during the period 1378–88 were not prosecuted and in a further sixth of all cases the parties formally agreed out of court. Less than half of all debt cases were pursued to a conclusion, though where this happened the creditor usually won.

In both the manor and the borough courts, we find certain highly litigious persons who were adept at using legal actions to enforce contracts and debts. Some even used the law to harass and intimidate those less experienced or able to use the law themselves. For example, later fifteenth- and early sixteenth-century Chancery petitions drawn up on behalf of female servants sometimes allege that their employers harassed them with false allegations of debt in order to retain their services beyond their period of contract, even without payment. Cases in the consistory courts occasionally suggest that couples manipulated the law to obtain de facto divorces, but any notion that the canon-legal courts were regularly abused or readily granted annulments are demonstrably wrong.

Much litigation in the royal courts concerned land and property disputes, although it is often implicit that litigation went alongside or was prompted by extra-judicial actions involving intimidation and actual violence. We see this clearly in the Paston letters of the mid-fifteenth century, most dramatically in respect of the disputed manor of Gresham, though here the wider context of civil war (the 'Wars of the Roses') tended to encourage the extra-judicial violence. Religious houses appear to have been particularly litigious, probably because individual abbots were merely custodians of the house and its rights. This is reflected, for example, in the chronicle compiled *c.*1400 by Abbot Burton of Meaux (near Hull) where the abbey's protracted legal disputes with local landowners constitute much of the writing, pushing more important events to the status of afterthought. The later Middle Ages do seem, however, to have witnessed a growing volume of litigation. Certainly by the fifteenth century the lesser aristocracy saw knowledge of the law as of considerable importance, even to the extent of having their sons spend time at the Inns of Court as part of their education.

Although it was primarily the landed classes that turned to the royal courts, it is apparent that there were individuals within peasant society who were aware of the law beyond the level of the manorial courts and customary jurisdiction, and who were prepared to use it so far as their legal status allowed. We see something of this in the proliferation of requests from various peasant communities in Wiltshire, Hampshire and neighbouring regions to the exchequer during 1377 for legal copies of Domesday Book entries for their manors in the hope that this would show that they were entitled to enhanced legal status. The Meaux chronicle tells of the Cellarer family of well-to-do peasants who were engaged in a long-running dispute with the abbey. On one occasion a Cellarer tried to bring an action against the abbot for a clear violation of the Statute of Labourers (discussed below) but was denied justice because of his alleged villein status. That royal justice was effectively stacked in favour of the landed classes and specifically excluded actions by those of servile status and, as we have seen, heavily circumscribed actions by women, only provoked further resort to extra-judicial actions. The Peasant's Revolt of 1381 was to a degree a revolt against the inequities of the judicial system in which the rebels meted out their own justice in the form of arson and targeted killings against those they thought had abused their authority. The 1406 indictment of Isabel, the wife of Ieuan Gronowessone, her sister and her daughter for the ambush and castration of Roger de Pulesdon at Ightfield (Shropshire) tells its own story.

The later years of the thirteenth century and the earlier part of the fourteenth, encompassing the lean years of the Agrarian Crisis, saw high levels of petty crime, particularly thieving, as numbers of people living at the margins tried to stay afloat. In particular, Barbara Hanawalt has shown a direct correlation between the theft of foodstuffs and clothing by poor women and years of poor harvest.[1] Although, to modern eyes, such transgressions would seem both comparatively trivial and excusable, the theft of goods worth more than a shilling was a felony and regularly resulted in the alleged culprit being hung. More serious crimes, involving a high degree of organized violence, were sometimes associated with members of the lesser aristocracy. In particular the political instability that particularly characterized the reign of Edward II and the earlier years of Edward III allowed a number of gentry-led gangs to flourish, of which the Coterel and Folville gangs are perhaps the best known. The Folvilles were a group of younger brothers from a Leicestershire gentry family who for about a decade committed murder, assault, robbery, rape and kidnap with relative impunity within the county and neighbouring parts. Their most audacious action was the forcible kidnap of Sir Richard Willoughby, a senior justice, a reflection of the comparative ineffectiveness of the law to combat such organized crime despite a growing sense that action was needed. The problem was compounded by the ease with which jurors could be intimidated and, at times, the willingness of justices and sheriffs to offer protection or otherwise abuse their authority. Willoughby was himself accused in 1341 of selling the laws 'as if they had been oxen or cattle'.

The high-profile cases of organized gangs probably tell us something of the limitations and priorities of medieval justice. Persons of lesser rank, lacking connections or patrons, were easy targets, and property crime was perhaps especially rigorously (in other words brutally) enforced. The law was also comparatively effective at protecting the rights and titles of property owners. It was less effective in tackling crimes of violence against the person (and completely ineffective in respect of the crime of rape) especially where the perpetrators were themselves well connected. The legacy of the earlier system of general eyres and the effect of the proliferation of first commissions of oyer and terminer, and subsequently commissions of the peace was both to extend the provision of royal justice throughout the realm and to stimulate use of the courts by the non-servile population. Indeed, more substantial free peasants and burgesses – that is, persons lacking the power or connections to resolve disputes or gain redress other than by recourse to the law – are easily the statistically most conspicuous group amongst those initiating litigation at a local level. It is also apparent that demand for legal remedies and the provision of justice grew significantly during the second half of the fourteenth century. This is reflected in the numbers of different kinds of writ available to initiate legal proceedings, which grew from some 900 in the earlier fourteenth century to some 2500 by the earlier sixteenth century.

The social and economic consequences of the advent of plague prompted a number of legal responses, the most significant of these being the new labour laws. We need to distinguish between some short-term legislative responses, particularly in the capital, and the broader picture prevailing in the century following. London seems to have faced a more substantial influx of immigrants in the aftermath of the Black Death than the city could readily accommodate. In 1359, indeed, the civic authorities conflated unemployment with an unwillingness to work in requiring all beggars to leave the city. This was but one facet of a wider policy of restoring order, which saw

1. B.A. Hanawalt, 'The female felon in fourteenth-century England', in S.M. Stuard, ed., *Women in Medieval Society* (Philadelphia, 1977).

regulations for prostitutes to wear distinctive dress (1351, 1382), injunctions against strangers bearing arms, illicit assemblies and the enforcement of the curfew (1354, 1357), and various orders for cleaning the streets (1357). Some of these concerns are reiterated in parliamentary legislation that was probably much influenced by the London experience and anticipated like concerns that surfaced again during the later fifteenth century.

The wider legislative response included the Statute of Labourers (1351), which built upon the earlier Ordinance of Labourers of 1349, but which itself may have been influenced by a longer history of regulation of wages and contracts in London. The statute was designed not only to peg wages and prices, ostensibly at pre-plague levels, but also to regulate the mobility of labour. In a culture searching for stability, mobile labour came to be regarded with suspicion. This perspective is forcefully articulated in a Commons petition of 1376 against vagrants, but one of a number of similar petitions from the 1370s. (It should be noted that this was precisely the period in which grain prices started to fall consistently and numbers of agriculturalists consequently shed labour in the retreat from arable production.) This and the experience of the Peasants' Revolt (1381) helps explain the 1383 statute against vagrancy, which required vagrants to find sureties for their conduct, and the radical reworking of the Statute of Labourers in 1388, dubbed the Statute of Cambridge. The new statute provided for the forcible return of migrant workers to their places of origin and required such migrants to resume their former employment as agricultural labour. By the early fifteenth century, the underlying concern had shifted from the need to impose order in the face of profound instability, a concern that was as much moral as economic, to a more straightforward desire to maximize the potential of the available labour force.

The labour legislation continued to be enforced through the fifteenth century and the legislation was repeatedly revised. Further statutes in 1414 and 1446 likewise returned to the vexed question of vagrants, but no longer with the same panicked urgency of the 1370s. In the context of an economy starved of labour, vagrancy was effectively understood in terms of those who would not be bound by the labour laws. This, however, changed during the later decades of the fifteenth century and the early decades of the sixteenth century. In the broader context of an economy that was either faltering or failing to keep pace with demographic recovery, there was a growth in unemployment. People were used to those who experienced poverty by reason of physical or mental incapacity or due to the frailty of age, but not for want of employment. The phenomenon of numbers of men and women alike who were physically fit to work, but who were instead (involuntarily) idle was both alien and shocking. As in much more recent periods of high unemployment, the perennial myth that their poverty was caused by laziness and a certain moral turpitude took root. The poor were seen as idle, preferring to spend their time at the alehouse, gaming and whoring than in honest toil. It followed that such new categories of poor – as opposed to the halt, the lame, the blind, the elderly, the widowed, categories that on biblical precedent could be counted 'deserving' – demanded discipline, even punishment. In due course the problem of unemployment and the subculture of petty crime associated with it and consequent upon it demanded new legislation.

From around the middle to later years of the fifteenth century the fear of vagrancy, sexual immorality and associated disorder was growing apace. Local courts throughout the realm saw a much higher proportion of presentments relating to disorderly alehouses, gaming and sexual immorality. This trend continued into the early six-teenth century and remained a feature for the rest of our period in a way that was largely untrue of the first century after the Black Death. People who 'entertained' ser-vants and apprentices – whether at illicit gaming, receiving stolen goods or for illicit sex – were particular targets since this represented a threat to the good governance of servant-keeping households. Thus Simon Jacob of Little Downham (Cambs.) was presented in 1491–92 for receiving servants at his alehouse and so encouraging them to 'subtract their service from their masters'. Alehouses were seen as particularly liable to promote disorderly conduct. In 1523 Robert Wasyll of Clare (Suffolk) was accused of giving 'hospitality in his inn to vagabonds and suspect persons who are of bad con-versation, to the harm of his neighbours'. Alehouses were also equated with sexual immorality and, more specifically, commercial sex.

Males, whether householders or alehouse keepers, may have been conspicuous among those charged with receiving suspect persons and the like, but women became more conspicuous over this same period as suspect persons associated with the kinds of disorderly conduct just noted. Agnes Robson of Northallerton (Yorks., NR), for example, was presented in 1497 for quarrelling with her neighbours and was conse-quently expelled. She was expelled again the year following as a suspected prostitute. Women were, of course, particularly identified with commercial sex and hers was but one of a number of such expulsions there during the last decades of the fifteenth century and early decades of the sixteenth. Thus 'Janet of the friars' was made to leave town in 1507 for being ill-governed of both body and tongue. This perception that women in particular required proper – that is, male – government is further reflected in actual legislation.

One of the earliest pieces of legislation is from London in 1475, but the most star-tling, because most ambitious, legislative programme was that set out at Coventry in 1492. This radical programme, which may reflect Lollard sympathies, was designed to reform the whole of society from civic governor – to be stripped of office if thought to have committed adultery – to the 'tapster' or barmaid – here equated with prosti-tute. (The same equation was made at Sherborne (Dorset) four years later.) A partic-ular target of the legislators, however, were women living on their own and hence not subject to male authority. The fear was that such women encouraged gaming, petty crime and sexual immorality. For the sake of the good order of other households and the creation of a godly (and hence prosperous) community, the leet jurats ordained that no 'singlewoman' below the age of 50 and capable of working should live by herself, but should 'go to service till they be married'. In the same set of ordinances was a ban on the keeping of pigsties. Contemporaries would have understood the symbolism of this, for the pig was representative of lust. The pig wandering through the streets was a nuisance in the same way as the prostitute soliciting in the street, hence to eradicate pigsties, and thus pig-keeping, was akin to eradicating immorality by preventing women from living on their own. It is unlikely that such a radical pro-gramme could in fact be enforced, but it is symptomatic of the way some town governors were thinking.

The 1500 ordinances of the Gloucester frankpledge jurors reflect something of the spirit of the earlier Coventry ordinances. Prostitutes were to be conveyed around the town in a cart and then shown in the marketplace together with their clients. All beggars were to be registered with the town clerk. Four years later, all beggars were expelled save for 36, mostly women, who were duly registered and sported a badge to prove their authorization. York adopted a like policy of distinguishing 'deserving' beggars, who wore shoulder badges, from 'sturdy' beggars in 1515. Such hostility to outsiders and the dispossessed was not an urban prerogative. On the manor of Ombersley (Worcs.) in 1496, for example, the constables were instructed 'to see that outside and suspicious wandering beggars are not permitted to remain here'. In some places hostility to the homeless and the unemployed took on an additional xenophobic dimension. Thus in the North Riding town of Northallerton two men were presented in the borough court in 1476 for harbouring Scots. Such presentments became much more common there by the 1490s. A like grouping of Scots, vagrants and other undesirables is found unsurprisingly at Durham at much the same period. The civic authorities in early sixteenth-century Chester similarly outlawed Welsh weddings, no doubt because they were associated with disorderly behaviour.

The legislative response at the local level was echoed by parliamentary legislation. The Vagrancy Act of 1495 required that vagrants be arrested, placed in the stocks for three days and then sent back to their supposed place of residence. A new statute of 1531 drew upon the response already adopted in a number of towns whereby 'deserving' beggars were licensed, as we have seen, but others punished. This now became the responsibility of justices of the peace nationally, but numbers of towns that had not previously used badges now began to adopt them. More radical legislation was attempted, however, in 1536, the very year the dissolution of religious houses commenced (and with it the suppression of a significant proportion of almshouses and hospitals, which provided both accommodation and outdoor relief, albeit primarily for the 'deserving' poor). The 1536 legislation proposed to outlaw all begging and all almsgiving save to a specially regulated parish fund, based on a London precedent of 1533, to aid the 'deserving' poor, whereas vagrants were to be set to work and their children put into service. The act that actually passed was much watered down, for almsgiving was still too central to popular devotion at this date and it is no coincidence that the next wave of legislation occurred only with the accession of Edward VI.

The Vagrancy Act of 1547 anticipated the temporary enslavement of vagrants as a way of obliging the supposedly work-shy to contribute to society and reiterated much of what had been intended in the 1536 act, but like the Coventry ordinances of 1492, ideology ran far ahead of what could in fact be enforced. The act was subsequently repealed, but a new act of 1552 more successfully attempted to do the work of the 1536 legislation without condemning voluntary almsgiving. In pragmatic terms, however, it was once more the towns that led the way. Compulsory levies to support the 'deserving' poor were instituted, for example, in Norwich in 1549 and York the year following. The York scheme, which involved weekly parochial collections by the constables and churchwardens, was itself the culmination of several years of increasingly rigorous constraints on public begging and 'voluntary' collections. At much the same time, some other towns were experimenting with compulsory work schemes. Thus Oxford attempted to establish in effect a textile factory employing some 2000 persons at the dissolved abbey of Oseney in 1546. This last illustrates both the shift in thinking over time and the extent of poverty and unemployment by this date.

As we have just seen, the regulation of prostitution represented another facet of the broader magisterial concern to reform society during the last 100 years of our period.

Broadly speaking, the century following the Black Death saw a fairly laissez-faire attitude to commercial sex. The church courts in their policing function regularly required individuals to appear before them on charges of fornication or adultery, but rarely designated any of the women so appearing as *meretrix* (prostitute). It is only from the repeated appearance of particular women's names associated with a number of different men that we can surmise that we are here dealing with women selling their bodies. Interestingly, certain male names also appear repeatedly, sometimes in connection with several different women. Clergy are conspicuous among those males. Civic authorities generally outlawed prostitution within the town walls, but appear not to have generally enforced this with any resolution. The London records suggest campaigns by individual mayors, but only in the immediate aftermath of the Black Death and the Peasants' Revolt was there anything approaching a sustained policy of suppression. The civic authorities in Hull even leased some land by the town walls and three arches of the walls to the town's prostitutes – common women in contemporary parlance. Others towns tacitly tolerated prostitution by levying regular fines in much the same way as commercial brewing or petty retailing was licensed. The presence of ecclesiastical liberties further limited the scope of civic governors. York's Grape Lane, the heart of the city's red-light district, lay within the cathedral chapter's liberty. Prostitution may theoretically have been outlawed in the City of London, but it flourished in Westminster Abbey's vill of Westminster and the bishop of Winchester's liberty of Southwark.

To judge from byname evidence, most women drawn into prostitution did so to supplement precarious livelihoods as spinsters, embroideresses, laundresses and petty retailers. The sex trade was thus a product of poverty. Byname evidence shows that women identified as outsiders – Scots in York, Flemings in Southwark – were particularly vulnerable in the labour market and may thus have turned to prostitution of necessity. The effect was to reinforce stereotypes of the woman petty trader and the alien as untrustworthy, sexually promiscuous and a threat to order. The worsening of the economic climate, particularly for the single woman, from the second half of the fifteenth century can only have increased the numbers of women turning to commercial sex to make ends meet. Prostitution may thus have become in real terms more conspicuous and hence more of a concern.

From the later fifteenth century we find a new level of sustained interest in the regulation of prostitution on the part of civic authorities. Earlier injunctions against prostitution within the town walls were reiterated in Coventry in 1445 and in Leicester in 1467. Nottingham enacted ordinances relating to prostitutes, brothels and the regulation of alehouses in 1463, and so specifically made the connection between illicit sex and alehouses that was more fully developed in the Coventry ordinances of 1492. Borough court records and the like suggest that, for once, there was an attempt to enforce these ordinances. A more radical solution was adopted in 1475 at the port of Sandwich, which attracted much Florentine trade and hence numbers of Florentine sailors. Here a civic brothel was established in a building known as 'the galley', presumably after the Florentine merchant vessels. Strict regulation of prostitution involving the issuing of tokens is also found at much the same period in Southampton, another port associated with north Italian merchants and sailors.

The climate of hostility to the trade in illicit sex became still more marked by the early sixteenth century, and the focus of civic concern seems to have been as much on the prostitutes themselves whereas previously it was brothel keepers that were targeted. In this respect borough courts were often effectively displacing the ecclesiastical courts, though without the latter's concern for the wrongdoing of the clients of prostitutes as well as the women themselves. Even in Westminster and Southwark a marked shift in attitude becomes apparent. In 1506 the 'stews' (brothels) of Southwark were temporarily closed, and Westminster expelled 31 suspected prostitutes in 1508. In some ways this policy seems to reflect a more puritanical attitude to sex on the part of well-to-do townsfolk, which saw a new intolerance of pre-marital sex and criticism of clergy who failed to honour their vows of chastity. Such sentiments seem to have blossomed in post-Reformation London. The 1540s witnessed a sustained campaign against commercial sex in both London and neighbouring Southwark and in 1546 the Southwark stews were permanently closed. The effect, of course, was not to eliminate prostitution, merely to criminalize it and drive it underground.

As has already been remarked, it is hardly possible to disentangle the hardening of magisterial attitudes to prostitution from wider concerns about order and stability. They must, moreover, be seen as part of the broader economic, political and religious climate. The early fourteenth century in particular had witnessed both economic and political dislocation, culminating in the Agrarian Crisis and the deposition of Edward II. The resulting disorder and high levels of crime prompted firm action in terms of law enforcement and encouraged high levels of litigation, particularly immediately following the deposition, but the response was essentially reactive rather than revolutionary. In the aftermath of the Black Death a concern to uphold a supposedly divinely sanctioned order and stability was predicated on a profound sense that the plague was God's punishment for sin. Here a more radical legislative response was attempted, notably in respect of the labour laws and the abortive sumptuary legislation, but such legislation remained essentially reactive and comparatively ineffective. What we see emerging by the end of our period is a willingness of governors and governments to enforce conservative ideologies of gender and hierarchy both through strict enforcement of the law and through radical legislation culminating in the various vagrancy acts, while at the same time strengthening the authority of the monarch through a raft of legislation attacking the ability of magnates, in effect, to maintain private armies, curbing private jurisdictions or liberties and culminating in the Henrician Treason Act and the Act of Supremacy.

19
LEARNING AND LITERACY

Formal education – the provision of tutors, the endowment of grammar schools, the establishment of colleges – leaves records. Formal training, so far as we should or can distinguish between the two, likewise leaves records in the form of guild ordinances, apprenticeship indentures, even litigation. The ownership of books and practice of writing also leaves records. Informal modes of education and training, the dissemination of more ephemeral writings than books, and levels of literacy in the sense of capacity to read or to write documents that were themselves ephemeral are, however, much more difficult to discern. The picture is further complicated by the observation that at the beginning of our period, England was a trilingual culture (English, French and Latin) and only really became essentially monolingual by the end of our period. Thus we find scholarly monographs on medieval universities and schooling, on books and book production both before and after the advent of print, even, though one has to look harder, a literature on apprentices (as part of a literature on youth). There is, however, only a modest article literature that tries to look beyond or behind the formal structures of education and training. Estimates of levels of literacy are few and vary profoundly.

The most common medieval paradigm for learning was that of the apprenticeship, an extended period of practical, 'on the job' instruction leading to a formally recognized qualification. The model applied not only to youthful would-be artisans learning in workshops, but even to university students who, on graduation, might adopt the courtesy title *magister*, or master. Similarly it was common for well-to-do youngsters to spend time in the households of persons other than their own immediate family to learn how to run a household themselves. When the 11-year-old Alice de Rouclif of Rawcliffe (near York) contracted to marry John Marrays she was sent to live with his married sister until she was of sufficient age to set up home with her new husband. At much the same date, Geoffrey Chaucer was first socialized in the manners of the nobility as a page in the household of the earl and countess of Ulster, from which he progressed into the royal household. Young men wanting a successful career in the Church appear similarly to have spent time in the households of senior churchmen. Thomas More, although part of a new generation of lay administrators, was trained as a child in the household of Archbishop Morton.

Learning, of course, started from a much earlier age. That children were expected to play is reflected both in literary and visual sources, and also in evidence for the commercial manufacture of toys at least from *c*.1400. Small boys might play with model knights or toy swords just as dolls and toy cooking utensils would have been intended for small girls. It is likely, however, that play activity merged with work activity and the learning of various household, craft or agricultural skills. Girls were probably taught to spin from an early age. Children were also regularly used to tend animals in the fields, scare birds from crops, and collect nuts, berries, firewood and the like. In aristocratic and, at least from the later fourteenth century, more well-to-do urban households, children may also have been exposed to writing and the learning of letters. Books of hours (otherwise known as primers), a devotional aid for lay use in the home and at church, were commonly owned in such homes. It is evident that these books were used to instruct the young in some of the most commonly used prayers, but also to teach basic literacy.

The prayers contained within the book of hours were normally Latin, the common language of devotion before the Reformation. Although such prayers could be memorized verbatim without any engagement with the form and sounds of letters, the user could be taught to recognize individual letters and to make the sounds they signified, and so work from the familiar and rote learned prayers of the Paternoster (Lord's Prayer) and Ave (Hail Mary) to 'reading' other, less familiar, prayers. Numbers of books of hours indeed include an alphabet immediately before these common prayers. It would not follow that such 'readers' actually understood the Latin text, though from a contemporary perspective the ability to articulate a Latin text was evidence that a person was *literatus*. However, the person who had learned their alphabet from the family book of hours might apply that knowledge to a vernacular text and move from the articulation of an alien language to the reading of a familiar one.

Such instruction in the household would normally have preceded any formal schooling – and in the case of girls would generally have constituted the only instruction in literacy provided. Grammar schools, essentially an urban phenomenon of the period from the later fourteenth century, were primarily intended to offer instruction in Latin grammar. Implicitly boys coming to them would already have some basic foundation in letter recognition and reading; this is indeed explicit in the 1527 foundation ordinances of Faversham school (Kent). In fact, some schools also catered for 'petty' scholars who came with no prior skills. This is documented at Hull in 1454 and at Ipswich in 1477.

Parochial clergy may sometimes have constituted an alternative source of basic instruction and one that was open to boys from peasant backgrounds. The provision of elementary education was sometimes tied to chantry foundations, though we tend only to know this from complaints at the dissolution of the chantries in 1547, and the nature of the schooling provided is a little enigmatic. At Enford (Wilts.), for example, the priest was partly occupied 'in teaching of children'. Numbers of clergy seem to have operated song schools that may have provided initial instruction in reading. Others specifically saw the teaching of reading skills as their main function. For example, we know that the priest at Rothwell (Yorks., WR), who was probably an Augustinian canon, was running a school in 1408, and in 1414 there is notice of Rothwell boys saying the psalter. At Sibthorpe (Notts.) provision is documented from 1342 for a clerk, for a fee, to teach small children their letters. The likelihood is that boys attended such schools at ages not unlike those for primary schooling today. Nunneries may sometimes have provided some elementary literacy training for young boys as well as girls. Some 18 girls were being taught at Stixwould Priory (Lincs.) in 1440, but only 2 at the much more modest Oxfordshire priory of Littlemore 5 years later.

Though clergy enjoyed a considerable hold over education, they by no means occupied a monopoly position. In late medieval London we find tantalizing evidence for informal schools, tantamount to what would later be called dame schools, offering elementary instruction. It may be that such informal schools were actually a little more common and even a little more widespread than the documentary evidence can allow. The main areas where the laity participated in formal educational provision, however, were in respect of grammar schools, where we see the emergence of a new profession of grammar master or schoolmaster, and the law, specifically the London Inns of Court. Grammar schools can be documented pretty much throughout our period, but most establishments before the late fourteenth century – and numbers after – were connected in some way with cathedrals, colleges and religious houses. Alongside these, however, can be found growing numbers of schools established as part of a private chantry foundation and even some, as at Hull, under the aegis of town governments.

Elementary schools – the providers of 'petty' education – tended to be small, housing fewer than 20 pupils and often only a handful. Grammar schools, on the other hand, varied considerably in size, but were invariably larger. The smallest probably provided for about 20 scholars. (Chipping) Campden school (Glos.), founded towards the middle of the fifteenth century by John Fereby, who had made his fortune in royal service, provided for 60–80 pupils. Skipton school (Yorks., WR), founded late the same century as a chantry school by Peter Toller, dean of Craven, had 120 pupils when the chantry was suppressed in 1548. It is unlikely that many other schools were this large, though often we have no evidence.

Most schools were found in an urban location. This reflects the demand for literate laymen as administrators, businessmen and traders. We know very little about numbers of pre-plague foundations, many of which are documented by chance. Implicitly they were almost as much a facet of urban identity as the possession of a leper hospital or a friary, but it is probable that they were often poorly endowed and essentially dependent on parents paying fees. More substantial endowments, in some cases refoundations, were common in the post-plague era. Some founders of schools were themselves townsmen. William Sevenoke, a London grocer and lord mayor in 1418, founded Sevenoaks school and an associated almshouse to provide for the education of boys in the town of his birth. Sir John Percival, another migrant who made his fortune in the capital as a merchant tailor, likewise endowed a chantry-cum-grammar school in his native Macclesfield in 1502, so as to address the needs of 'copious plenty of children to whose learning, bringing forth in cunning [knowledge] and virtue' there had hitherto been 'right few teachers and schoolmasters . . . whereby many children for lack of that teaching . . . fall to idleness and consequently live dissolutely all their days'.

The growing demand for schooled and literate employees and traders is reflected in evidence relating especially to high-status London crafts from the later fifteenth century. The goldsmiths' guild ordinances, for example, required apprentices to be already literate and apprenticeship indentures made by the haberdasher, Robert Chirche, provided for the youngsters to be schooled during the first two years of their term. The draper Simon Eyre's plan to found a school at Leadenhall in the City in 1459, whose syllabus would extend beyond the traditional grammar to embrace conveyancing and drafting is atypical, but symptomatic of the very pragmatic concerns underlying educational provision. Archbishop Rotherham's 1483 endowment of the grammar school at his native town provided for training in writing and accounts in specific recognition of the fact that schools were no longer solely to train aspirant priests. More traditional syllabuses, however, were the norm with Latin grammar and the speaking, writing and comprehension of Latin as the focus. Lancaster grammar school taught grammar, logic and rhetoric through a school day that began and ended at six, with long breaks in the morning and at noon.

Formal education beyond grammar school meant either time at one of the two universities of Oxford or Cambridge or, particularly by the fifteenth century, one of the Inns of Court that provided a training in law. Though both universities were established by the beginning of our period, they were still embryonic. A chancellor is first recorded for Oxford in 1214 and at Cambridge in 1225. Though this implies a recognition of the need to exercise some degree of regulation over a body of students, they were as yet officials of their respective diocesans (bishops). The friars dominated the scene for at least the first part of our period. The Oxford Dominican friary was designated a house of general study from 1261 and by 1277 housed 70 friars. The Franciscan community there likewise numbered 84 in 1317. The Cambridge Franciscans numbered 75 as early as 1289. At Oxford the presence of members of the enclosed orders should also be noted, notably Benedictines at Gloucester College (founded 1283) and subsequently also at Canterbury and Durham colleges. Cistercian and Augustinian colleges were only established in the middle of the fifteenth century.

Significant numbers of other students were drawn from the ranks of young men aspiring to clerical careers and, following the papal decree *Cum ex eo* of 1296, more established clergy seeking to improve their learning by spending time at one of the universities. (This is considered more fully in Chapter 10.) Most of these students probably lodged privately and in due course in halls, essentially private lodgings allowing groups of students to live communally and hence allowing the university to enforce some level of discipline and defuse the sometimes violent conflicts between students and townsfolk. Colleges, comprising bodies of teaching fellows supported by an endowment and ordinances, tended only to be of any significance in terms of providing for students from the later fourteenth century. Cambridge seems to have attracted a plethora of foundations around the time of the Black Death, namely Pembroke (1347), Gonville (1349–51), Trinity Hall (1350), Corpus Christi (1352) and Clare (1326, but substantially augmented 1359), but the major foundations tended to be later. At Oxford these were New College (1379), All Souls (1438), Magdalene (1448) and Cardinal College (1525), subsequently refounded as Christ Church (1546). The equivalent Cambridge foundations were King's Hall (1337), which was absorbed into the new foundation of Trinity (1546), King's (1441), Queens' (1448) and St John's (1511).

Bishop of Winchester William of Wykeham's foundation of New College is particularly important since it was specifically founded to provide for undergraduates, some of whom would have first attended his twin foundation of Winchester College. Nearly two-thirds of New College students prior to 1500 were from peasant backgrounds, mostly husbandmen and the like, the rest being made up of townsfolk and gentry, though it is hard to know how representative this was of the student body more generally. Such students were often younger than their modern counterparts – various Paston sons attended university in the mid-fifteenth century while still in their mid-teens – and it seems to have been acceptable for masters to beat their students if their work was unsatisfactory just as if they were still schoolboys.

Most students followed the arts degree comprising the *trivium* (grammar, rhetoric and dialectic) and *quadrivium* (arithmetic, music, geometry and astronomy). This was the essential diet of most students, who tended to be taught on an ad hoc basis by individual masters licensed by the university. Many students stayed only briefly and only a fraction of the four to six years normally required to complete a bachelor's degree. Only a minority of students – about a third in fifteenth-century Oxford – actually followed a course of study through to graduating. Instruction in theology, medicine and both canon and civil law was available through the pertinent higher faculties, though medicine in particular attracted few students. Those with ambition of senior administrative office in either episcopal or royal service would have chosen to study law. For much of our period, indeed, a significant proportion of the clerks and office holders in royal service were graduates in civil or canon law, a tradition epitomized by John Thoresby, whose career in royal service took him from clerk to chancery notary, master of the rolls, keeper of the privy seal and, finally, lord chancellor by 1349. His reward was high ecclesiastical office, culminating in his appointment as archbishop of York in 1352, where his obvious administrative talents were not wasted.

For those wanting a practical knowledge of the common law, as opposed to the canon and civil law taught at the universities primarily to ambitious clerics, training came to be given at the Inns of Court. These probably have a history not unlike that of the universities, with informal teaching being provided to students by lawyers associated with the royal courts from at least the later thirteenth century. A particular concentration of such lawyers grew up, for example, in the area of the Temple following the suppression of the order in the early fourteenth century. Only at a much later date do we see formal teaching establishments following the standard later medieval paradigm of the college with common hall and chapel. Lincoln's Inn is well documented from 1422. The Inner and New Temples and Gray's Inn are somewhat older, but may not have functioned as teaching establishments any sooner. In addition to these Inns of Court, training in chancery procedure came to be provided at the Inns of Chancery. These came in time to be seen as the junior establishments that provided a foundation for students to progress to the Inns of Court. Thus Davy's Inn, Furnival's Inn and Staple Inn were associated with Lincoln's Inn.

Instruction was through the form of readings, effectively we may surmise lecture series designed to explain particular points of law based on law texts, and moots, mock trials in which students participated alongside established lawyers. These last must have been akin to disputations that were used for similar didactic purposes in the universities. In addition to providing a forum for instruction, the Inns tried to impose some control over their students and their conduct. Lincoln's Inn forbade its students from carrying bows and arrows in order to shoot at the rabbits that were to be found on part of the Inn's property, but regulations seem to have been much more rigid in the more puritanical climate prevailing from the later fifteenth century. In 1475, for example, John Bradshaw was made to confess to playing cards and in 1481 William Elys was expelled from Lincoln's Inn for repeatedly consorting with a certain Grace, initially in his room and latterly at a dubious address in Newgate. It may be that law students were a little older than many university undergraduates, but the evidence is slight. This is what evidence from the legally minded Paston family would suggest. Edmund Paston, for example, was at Clifford's Inn of Chancery when already 20 or more, and his brother John only started at the Inner Temple after several years in Cambridge.

The example of the Pastons is demonstrative of gentry interest in their sons gaining some legal knowledge, but it may not be entirely representative of the social origins of those who went on to practise law professionally. William Paston, the founder of the family's fortunes and whose legal career culminated in his appointment as a justice in 1429, was only the son of a Norfolk husbandman. An analysis of the social origins of sergeants-at-law, in effect senior professional lawyers and part-time justices, in the period 1463–1521 demonstrates that William was hardly atypical and that rather fewer than half could be described as being of gentry origin. The law, then, like the Church, was open to talent and could sometimes be a building block to a successful career for the clever village boy lucky enough to get a grammar schooling. On the other hand, it should be remembered that most boys (let alone girls) never had this opportunity.

At the beginning of our period, England, as mentioned above, enjoyed a trilingual culture. Latin was the language of the Church and the educated, French the language of the aristocracy and the law, and English the spoken language of the ordinary people. French, which comprised both the indigenous Anglo-Norman that was the vernacular of the descendants of the Conqueror and the French of the Isle de France, was thus the language of authority, Latin that of learning and truth. English was associated with persons of low status and, to some extent, with women as the mother tongue, the language children learned from their mothers. Latin, in contrast, was gendered male; it was primarily, though not exclusively, a written language that was taught to boys intended for a clerical career. During the course of the fourteenth century French likewise shifted from being the vernacular of the aristocracy to a language children were trained in. English, however, never ceased to exist as a written language. A number of romances, such as *Havelok the Dane* and *Sir Orfeo*, pre-date the plague as does Robert of Gloucester's rhyming chronicle. The readership of these works may well have been essentially bourgeois.

The significance of the establishment of English as a written and literary language, and the preferred language of the court and the aristocracy by the earlier fifteenth century, a process already going on apace during the previous half century, cannot be underestimated. The effects are many, but one was to greatly increase the numbers who had access to the written word. Prior to this period most literature was in Latin or French. Although numbers of people probably knew such Latin prayers as the Paternoster (Lord's Prayer) and the Ave (Hail Mary) by rote, a working knowledge of Latin demanded a grammar education. On the other hand, English was the vernacular of all those below the level of the aristocracy. Once texts written in English began to circulate, the aspirant reader was presented with but one obstacle – the translation of letters into sounds – whereas previously they were confronted with two – the comprehension of a foreign tongue alongside the basics of letter recognition.

English was very much a living and developing language. It was also a language characterized by marked regional variations, and this becomes manifest in Middle English writings. It follows that Middle English texts can be located both spatially and chronologically. The English of the first part of our period, represented, for example, by *Ancrene Wisse*, a guidance text for anchoresses, is now almost incomprehensible other than to the specialist, whereas the London English of Chaucer, at the end of the fourteenth century, is quite recognizable and that of Skelton or Cranmer, writing in the first half of the sixteenth century, still more so. William Langland, Geoffrey Chaucer and the anonymous Gawain poet, who writes in a Cheshire dialect, all required great skill and imagination to convert a spoken language into a literary language. Chaucer in particular, writing for a court audience, used a vocabulary that employed a number of words with French roots given that French had hitherto been the vernacular of the ruling classes. From much the same period numbers of writings that had hitherto circulated in French start to be translated into English. By the fifteenth century English thus became the dominant written language and displaced French as the spoken language even of the aristocracy.

The prominence of Chaucer in the literary canon tends, however, to obscure the vitality of English as the spoken language of the majority of the population long before the age of Richard II; it is just that we have almost no direct record of that spoken language. It may equally obscure the fact that Chaucer was hardly typical of the moralizing tones of most of his contemporaries or that the *Canterbury Tales* are perhaps better known today than in Chaucer's own age. Langland's *Piers Plowman* was the more popular text, and it is indeed the very large number of devotional texts that constitute perhaps the major corpus of writings in English.

Although French bibles and bible extracts in English had circulated in aristocratic circles, it was in a sense an unfortunate historical accident that the first complete translation of the Bible into English, dating to the last years of the fourteenth century, was associated with Wyclif's followers – hence the epithet 'Lollard'. But there was perhaps also an underlying sense that English was an inappropriate language into which to render the scriptures since it lacked authority and was too much the prerogative of the common people. It followed that vernacular scriptures, and by extension all devotional literature in English, became suspect and subject under Archbishop Arundel's constitutions (1407) to careful monitoring and even proscription. This did not prevent, however, the profusion of English devotional writings. Nicholas Love's *Mirror of the Blessed Life of Jesus Christ*, for example, is almost contemporary with Arundel's constitutions, but was a popular and thoroughly orthodox text. Another is the devotional poem *The Prick of Conscience*, extant in over 100 manuscripts and the medieval equivalent of the bestseller. Major devotional writing in the vernacular can also be associated with the fourteenth-century mystics Richard Rolle and Walter Hilton. At least some devotional texts appear to have been aimed at and were indeed used by a female readership. This was true, for example, of *The Abbey of the Holy Ghost*, a text that invites the lay reader to recreate the devotional life of an abbey in her imagination.

Estimates of levels of literacy are hazardous for a number of reasons. We tend to understand literacy in terms of both reading and writing, but reading and writing were taught separately within medieval culture, the latter being regarded as the more difficult and in any case a skill only really necessary for those intended for clerical careers of one form or another. It follows that many more would have had some ability to read than to write. Unfortunately reading of itself does not generate direct evidence; the ownership of books is not itself a conclusive indication of the owner's literacy, though we may note the growing proliferation of books during the latter part of our period stimulated both from the later fourteenth century by the advent of paper as a cheap substitute for parchment or vellum and, from the late fifteenth century, of printed books both imported and produced locally. Some books were also made available as a consequence of the pious provision of books in churches or even the circulation of so-called 'common profit' books, which were designed to be passed from reader to reader without any claim of ownership.

Writing was not, however, confined to books. Much literary material circulated in the form of pamphlets and we also know of writings distributed in the form of single leaves of parchment or paper such as bills pinned to the doors of churches. Access to and awareness of written material was thus probably fairly widespread by the last two centuries of our period, particularly in urban and aristocratic society. Certainly it was not confined to those who could afford books of their own. The transmission of these various writings clearly depended on there being persons who were able to read, but may also have relied on and indeed expected that some of those readers would verbalize these texts for a wider audience. Indeed, reading for much of the medieval era seems often to have been a social activity and not a solitary or silent pursuit. The idea of silent reading was still fairly novel in our period. Attention has been focused on this social dimension to reading by the evidence for Lollard reading groups whereby Lollard writings were transmitted to a wider audience by individual Lollard literates. In early fifteenth-century Norwich, for example, Margery Baxter urged a female friend to come to her house to hear her husband 'read the law of Christ'. Such reading parties were not, however, a Lollard prerogative. The proliferation of so-called household manuscripts, comprising a miscellany of texts assembled by the owner and associated with mercantile and gentry households, suggests precisely parallel practices in orthodox homes.

Just as access to texts did not depend on the ability to read, so the ability to read need not be the only way we need understand literacy. Many people must have gained a familiarity with different kinds of written text and would necessarily have had knowledge of the nature and function of such texts without necessarily being able to read them in the modern sense. The picture is complicated further by the observation that different kinds of text were invariably written in different languages – English, French or Latin – and in different kinds of hand, some more highly abbreviated than others. Thus the distinctive form of the will, commencing with the Latin words '*in dei nomine amen*', would have been recognizable even to those unable to make out more than the testator's name, if that. Similarly the form of a title deed, an account roll or an inventory would have been readily recognizable and such documents would have been usable with only very modest reading skills. This is what scholars have dubbed 'pragmatic literacy'. In talking about literacy, therefore, we need to recognize a continuum from complete illiteracy, through a modest recognition of certain kinds of writings, to a moderate degree of competence in reading some vernacular texts, and lastly varying levels of reading and scribal ability both in the vernacular and in Latin.

Medievals described someone who could read a Latin text aloud, but not necessarily with understanding, as a 'literate'. We need to adopt more nuanced criteria. At the same time we can and should be shy of offering statistical data we simply do not possess. The likelihood is that at the beginning of our period relatively few outside those who used the skills of literacy for professional purposes had any literacy skills. The proliferation of documents through the period, whether manor court records from the later thirteenth century, wills, civic records or books of hours from the later fourteenth century, or as a consequence of the advent first of paper and subsequently of print, can only have produced significant growth in the numbers and proportion of the population who were consumers of documentary material and thus enjoyed varying levels of pragmatic literacy or were indeed producers of such materials. In urban society especially, the inexorable growth in the use of writing goes hand in hand with the increasing provision of schools already discussed. It is likely that by the end of our period relatively few adult males living in towns could actually be described as illiterate, though still only a minority would have been confident readers or capable of producing written text.

As this last observation implies, there is a gender dimension to the issue of literacy. Whereas it was thought appropriate for girls at least from the upper echelons of society to learn to read so, as the late fourteenth-century didactic text *The Knight of the Tour Landry* encouraged, they might occupy themselves with suitable devotional literature. From much the same period, however, boys from mercantile backgrounds may have been taught some basic writing skills as necessary to their trade. Extant letter collections from the fifteenth century indeed relate primarily to mercantile, including civic, or aristocratic, particularly gentry authors, though the aristocratic writers were particularly likely to employ professional scribes. Throughout our period youngsters intended for a clerical career were also trained in literacy, but specifically a Latin literacy. Such youngsters were of course exclusively male, though from the later fourteenth century especially, the clerical career that followed did not necessarily mean ordination and the priesthood, but could imply bureaucratic employment in an official or private capacity. The author and poet John Gower is a particularly well-known example of this.

Certain observations follow. We have a lot of evidence for aristocratic, mercantile and even a few townswomen of slightly lower status as owners or at least users of devotional and paraliturgical literature, most notably books of hours. These last are primarily Latin texts and may have been used to provide or prompt certain Latin prayers and devotions rather than to be read in the modern sense. Males of like status can also be associated with books, including histories and books used professionally. We have letters written by members of the aristocracy and by merchants at least for the fifteenth and early sixteenth centuries. Many of these – and nearly all in the case of women – were in fact written by a scribe. The same is normally true of wills, although occasionally autograph wills are to be found. We can sometimes find apparently non-professional hands associated with some of the materials included in so-called household books. The bulk of manuscript material, whether accounts, deeds, indentures or memoranda, was the work of professional writers including scriveners who specialized in producing legal documents and were thus probably akin to the modern solicitor. Different kinds of text were written in different kinds of hand. Book hands were intended for the general reader, but the script of the professional writer of legal texts and the like (often further complicated by the extensive use of contractions) was intended for fellow professionals and need not have been comprehensible to the uninitiated.

20 CULTURAL PRODUCTION

From street theatre to the interludes (plays) performed in great households, from popular song to complex polyphonic (many sounds) masses, from small chapels to great cathedrals, or from crude ceramic figurines to elaborate alabaster and polychrome (many colours) reredos (altar decorations), we can glimpse something of the rich diversity of material, visual and aural cultures of the later Middle Ages. It is hardly possible to offer within the confines of a single chapter a comprehensive account of the range of activities that can be labelled collectively as 'cultural production'. Rather than attempt a superficial catalogue, therefore, this chapter will offer a discussion of the broader context of production and consumption in which we may understand cultural production. Particular attention will be paid to the impact of the Black Death and its possible ramifications, both directly and indirectly, on cultural expression, with particular reference to ecclesiastical patronage. It will give more detailed consideration of only a few specific categories of production, namely books, drama, dress and sepulchral monuments including brasses, with a view to illustrating broader themes.

As scholars of the later medieval era we must confront certain problems relating to evidence. The material culture that has come down to us represents but a fraction of what was produced. So much has been lost. In some instances this represents deliberate destruction. Thus the dissolution of the monasteries, the iconoclasm associated with the Edwardian Reformation and the civil war era, not to mention the well-intentioned, but sometimes highly destructive church restorations of the Victorian era, have resulted in the all but total loss of religious art, whether sculpture, panel paintings, glass or metalwork. Rood screens, being made of wood and supporting prominent images of the crucified Christ flanked by the sorrowing Virgin Mary and St John, were obvious and vulnerable targets. Some of the best extant examples of *opus Anglicanum*, the elaborate embroidery used in vestments such as copes, survive from Continental Europe. The same is true of the devotional alabaster carvings, whose manufacture centred on Nottingham in the later fourteenth and fifteenth centuries. Some glass survives, notably in the cathedral churches of York and Canterbury, but we rarely have complete glazing schemes surviving from parish churches. Some wall paintings likewise survive, mostly because obliterated by a covering of whitewash rather than more radical excision, but nowhere do we have a church fitted out as it might have been at some moment prior to the Reformation era, complete with the smell of guttering candles, the sounds of the liturgy, the clutter (at least towards the end of our period) of screens and partitions, or the arbitrary juxtaposition of fine craftsmanship and the seemingly homemade, or of the ancient and the contemporary.

At least as much has been lost through the simple ravages of time. Reliquaries and liturgical plate may have been deliberately destroyed, but surprisingly little secular plate survives, almost no secular embroidery, and the painted hangings and various furnishings laboriously itemized in extant inventories are likewise largely lost. Obviously some media are more ephemeral than others. We have substantial evidence for choristers serving in great households and of minstrels employed by both lords and civic authorities. We know something of the form of many medieval instruments and we even have various extant musical manuscripts with various forms of notation. We know something of the evolution of musical traditions, whether the plainsong (unaccompanied singing) of the monastic tradition or the polyphony written for great secular churches and various aristocratic collegiate foundations at the end of the Middle Ages, but the actual sound of medieval music is something we can only guess at. The music of the streets, the alehouse or the home is almost completely gone.

This last alerts us to another problem. Our mental image of later medieval culture is coloured, literally and metaphorically, by our knowledge of the high status, the costly or the artistically exquisite. Two major exhibitions in recent years – 'The Age of Chivalry' and 'Gothic' – have tended to reinforce this perspective. The more mundane fragments found in excavations tend to end up in storage and are only illustrated in the finds' appendices to archaeological reports. The material, visual, let alone the aural, cultures of persons of lesser rank are either lost to us or partly hidden through a lack of scholarly interest. Only very recently, for example, have scholars investigated a culture of childhood and so have started to find evidence for medieval toys. We need, moreover, to pay more attention to regional cultures as vibrant and distinctive in their own right rather than as pale imitations of court or metropolitan (London) culture.

In thinking about cultural production, there are a number of different elements that need to be considered. On one level we might describe a broader cultural context, which determines the particular kinds of artefact produced. Thus within an ecclesiastical context there is need for vestments, liturgical books and vessels, or for altar furnishings and the like. The understanding that what was made in the service of God should reflect the beauty of the holy, a sort of foretaste of heaven itself, explains elaborate workmanship, bright colours and, so far as possible, expensive materials. It is, however, the patron that determines just how much money might be expended on any particular item. To give one example, the sumptuous gold, enamel, pearl and jewel-encrusted Reliquary of the Order of St-Esprit (c.1400), speaks volumes of the wealth of the patron who commissioned it and we know that early in its history it was served as a gift from a queen. The actual form taken depends on the interplay of a number of factors, that is to say the specifications of the patron (or his or her agents and advisers), the role of the artist or craftsman, the technical possibilities of the medium, convention and fashion.

The Luttrell Psalter, a particularly splendid illuminated manuscript of the psalms produced in East Anglia in the decade or so before the Black Death, may be used to explore these points. The Psalter must have been an expensive commission even for a man of the rank of Sir Geoffrey Luttrell of Irnham (Lincs.). It shows the hand not of one, but several artists, each working in a recognizably distinctive style, which tends to be associated with different aspects of the larger (and never completed) decorative scheme. Thus one artist is responsible for some of the more exuberant grotesque images that are a distinctive feature of the manuscript. Another hand is responsible for many of the more conventional representations of saints and scriptural narrative. Because significant parts of the decorative scheme are unique to this manuscript, notably the marginal representations of peasants labouring in the fields or the depiction of Sir Geoffrey on his war horse, it is evident that this was a very specific commission and we may surmise that its precise form was negotiated, perhaps at times face to face between Sir Geoffrey and one or more of the artists. Such a process of negotiation allows considerable input from the craftsmen who may be able to suggest models – the labouring scenes owe something to a tradition of illuminations of the labours of the months – but would also work within established iconographic conventions. Thus it may or may not have been Sir Geoffrey's decision to include a depiction of the Last Supper, but the way it is represented, indeed how we are able to identify this scene, is determined by long established iconographic conventions. The conscious reiteration of that iconography to represent Sir Geoffrey, Christ-like, at high table cannot simply be explained in terms of the one providing a convenient model for the other, but whether it was Sir Geoffrey, an adviser (for example, a cleric) or the artist that had this inspiration, we cannot say. Perhaps the artist realized that this was a visually appropriate way of realizing the broader ideological intentions of his patron, but equally the artist may have been following more specific direction. Even where we do have extant contracts, such as is sometimes the case in respect of buildings or glazing schemes, they tend to outline only the broad parameters, such as the approximate scale and main features of the building or the choice of the saints to be depicted.

That Sir Geoffrey Luttrell commissioned a psalter rather than an apocalypse, as might have been true of the later thirteenth century, or a book of hours, as might have been the case from the later fourteenth century, is, however, explained in terms of fashion. Similarly the rich foliate decoration and the striking invention of the numerous hybrid monsters or babewyns that fill the borders of parts of the manuscript, although recognizably the work of individual artists, are still broadly characteristic of the rather exuberant and inventive styles fashionable in the decades immediately prior to the Black Death, which we see, for example, elsewhere in the Percy tomb in Beverley Minster, with its elaborate canopy, or in the eastern parts of St Augustine's Abbey in Bristol. These exuberant fashions cannot be unconnected with the great material wealth enjoyed by the aristocracy at precisely this same time consequent upon high grain prices and rental values.

Developments in technology also played a role in determining the form of cultural production. Few examples are as dramatic as the advent of print, though it is striking that early printed books tended slavishly to imitate manuscript, even to the extent in some instances of printing on vellum and illuminating capitals by hand. The Reliquary of the Order of St-Esprit, noted earlier, was made possible by reason of a new enamelling technique. Stained glass design was altered by the introduction from the earlier fourteenth century of a process for painting a yellow stain on glass; individual colours had otherwise to be cut from separate pieces of coloured glass and held together with lead. Most technical change tended, however, to be more akin to an evolutionary process. This is perhaps best illustrated in terms of ecclesiastical architecture where improvements in buttressing (load-bearing supports adjoining walls) and vaulting (the arched roofing of internal spaces) allowed the weight of the roof increasingly to be deflected from the walls so allowing more and more of the wall space to be opened up with windows, a process that culminates in such structures as the great aisleless hall of King's College Chapel, Cambridge, or the parish church of Southwold (Suffolk).

THE IMPACT OF THE BLACK DEATH

The later years of the thirteenth century and perhaps more particularly the earlier years of the fourteenth had seen grain prices tending to rise, the value of land and rental income increase, but money wages fall (in real terms at least). It follows that the landed classes, both lay and ecclesiastical aristocracy, including religious houses and cathedral chapters, enjoyed high incomes at precisely the moment when the cost of labour was historically low. This meant that the capacity of this social elite to engage in cultural patronage was very marked and was manifested in such prestigious and labour-intensive commissions as the Percy tomb or the aforementioned Luttrell Psalter. Indeed, much patronage of buildings – at least in the form of stone structures designed for permanence and, to a lesser or greater degree, as statements of wealth and power – was aristocratic. This applies both to the castles, fortified houses and other residences they built for themselves, and to the religious houses and hospitals they endowed for their spiritual benefit. The celebrated angel choir of Lincoln, the cloisters at Norwich and Salisbury, the chapter house and nave of York, the scissor arches of Wells, the chapter house of Southwell, famed for its naturalistically carved foliage, the eastern parts of St Augustine's, Bristol, and extensive building work at Exeter all belong to this period, whose prevailing architectural style is appropriately termed 'the Decorated'. Revenue from pilgrimage should also be noted as a significant source of income in some instances, though not one confined to the pre-plague era. The sublime thirteenth- and earlier fourteenth-century rebuilding of the collegiate church of St John at Beverley (Yorks., ER) was funded by pilgrims to the shrine of the Anglo-Saxon bishop to whom the church was dedicated, and whose patronage had helped give protection against the Scots and subsequently gave Henry V victory at Agincourt. The new radical restructuring of Gloucester Abbey was predicated on income from the tomb of Edward II, whose brutal death turned him into a martyr and candidate for sainthood.

The impact of the Black Death on cultural production has been much debated and also the subject of much unsubstantiated supposition. Numerous popular church guidebooks and the like will state emphatically that building work stopped as a consequence of the Black Death and was not restarted for many years, or that the work was only completed in debased form by inferior craftsmen. On the other hand the flowering of vernacular literature (in the sense of English rather than French, the earlier vernacular of the aristocracy) seen in Langland, Chaucer and the Gawain poet follows within a generation of the plague. New kinds of illuminated manuscript, notably the primer or book of hours, became popular after the plague. The sometimes austere forms of the Perpendicular style of architecture displaced the earlier Decorated. It would be foolish, then, to insist that the plague had no impact. Its impact may, however, have been as much indirect and to stimulate already existing trends as it was direct and immediate.

So far as the very considerable mortality associated with the Black Death did have an immediate impact, it was in terms of killing off a large number of heads of workshops and individual artists and craftsmen at a single moment. It is likely, for example, that the master masons Henry de Snelleston, who had worked on, among other buildings, Conwy Castle, and William Joy, who was responsible for the highly imaginative scissor arches supporting the central tower of Wells cathedral, both died in the plague.

The same is probably true of the unknown craftsman who created the Elsing (Norfolk) brass to Sir Hugh Hastings. The immediate consequence of such deaths is that new masters came to the fore, whose training and inspiration might well differ from their predecessors. To offer a fuller account, however, we need to look at the indirect consequences of the Black Death.

The dramatic fall in population had an immediate impact on the cost of labour. It also had a less immediate, but no less significant, impact on the distribution of wealth. Labour was an important cost element in all artistic production. Patrons could only accommodate a sudden upward hike in the wages demanded by the craftsmen they engaged either by paying substantially more overall, by looking to find ways of econ-omizing or by abandoning projects altogether. We can certainly find evidence of the two last as responses. The sculptural programme on Exeter cathedral's west front, for example, was suspended for a generation or more, and major building works at Cley next the Sea (Norfolk) was interrupted and never subsequently entirely finished. Economies could be achieved by preferring less labour-intensive craftsmanship. Thus the new glazing in the Lady Chapel at Ely was much plainer than that which had been completed before the plague.

The shift from the Decorated to the Perpendicular architectural style fits this model. The Decorated style derives its name from the elaborateness of the freestone carving that is its hallmark, but such carving required not just skilled masons, but also much expenditure of time. It was as a consequence very expensive because labour-intensive. After the Black Death, aristocratic and institutional patrons found their incomes were tending to shrink, but their expenditure was rising. Their previous appetite for lavish cultural patronage was dampened, but by no means extinguished. New patrons were to emerge, but rarely on the grand scale of the previous era.

The Perpendicular was developed before the advent of plague. The earliest substan-tial work extant is the remodelled south transept of Gloucester Abbey, dating to the early 1330s, which represented in many ways the cutting edge of architectural design of the day. It is striking, however, that the Perpendicular became increasingly popular after the plague, as seen in the magnificent new cloisters at Gloucester, Bishop Edington of Winchester's collegiate church in his birthplace village of Edington (Wilts.) or the parish church of Yeovil (Somerset). The initial attraction of the Perpendicular was, therefore, primarily fashion, but it may have commanded growing interest both because its clean lines required less expenditure on well-paid craftsmen, and also because its somewhat angular austerity was felt to be more appropriate to a society that saw plague as divine punishment for sin. The popularity of the Perpendicular was not, however, immediate or universal. The Decorated remained in vogue in East Anglia and parts of the north and west of the country through the second half of the fourteenth century. This is the style used for the great east window of Carlisle cathedral, but it is also found in a number of East Anglian churches, as at Sutton (Cambs.) and Attleborough (Norfolk).

The new economic conditions fostered by the Black Death, and continued demo-graphic recession through the later fourteenth and earlier fifteenth centuries, impacted more on some regions than others. Just as there were those who lost out, moreover, there were numbers who gained. It is in the arable heartlands of Midland England that economic distress was most immediately and acutely felt. Areas that had tradi-tionally been more reliant on pastoral agriculture – the very regions indeed that adhered longest to the Decorated – were in a much stronger position to adapt. In all regions, however, those who sold their labour, peasant agriculturalists who found land both cheaper and more plentiful, and artisans and traders who serviced the demand for more mundane and inexpensive goods and services, all tended to benefit. Much the same was probably true of those merchants whose businesses did not specialize solely in providing luxury goods for aristocratic and institutional clients.

These wider structural changes and the associated redistribution of wealth have already been discussed at length. Our concern here is that they had an impact on cultural patronage. Whereas institutional and aristocratic patrons had to dig deeper to achieve the same impact as before the plague, persons of lesser rank, both as individuals and collectivities, were now in a stronger position to become cultural consumers. The building of guildhalls and town halls, such as the Holy Trinity guildhall in King's Lynn, are essentially post-plague phenomena. Demand for manuscript books, particularly the newly fashionable book of hours, began to extend beyond the clergy and aristocracy to merchants and even artisans. Parishioners can be seen to be actively involved in raising funds to support building projects or to provide new fittings and furnishings – images, vestments, altar cloths, glass, screens, pews, wall paintings, candelabra, font canopies, pulpits – for their parish churches. The fashion for monumental brasses, which extended beyond the aristocracy to more substantial townsfolk, was dictated both by cost and by the need not to obstruct too much of the fabric of parish churches with memorials to the dead; monumental effigies were more costly, but they also caused obstruction. (The broader context is that a higher proportion of people were probably opting to be buried within the church rather than in the churchyard.)

We also see changes in the focus of patronage. These have as much to do, so far as the two can be divorced, with developments in the wider devotional climate as the impact of the Black Death. Whereas aristocratic patronage of the monastic orders and hospitals was common in the twelfth century, and of the mendicant orders in the thirteenth and earlier fourteenth centuries, so patronage of collegiate and chantry foundations and of almshouses became more common by the late Middle Ages. We have already noted Bishop Edington's college at Edington. Similarly, the royal College of St George at Windsor was founded in 1348 and, ten years later John, Lord Cobham founded his college of Cobham (Kent). These were essentially rather grand chantry foundations. The university colleges performed a like function, but were also devoted to educating the clergy. Several new colleges were founded in the wake of the Black Death with the objective of providing clergy of a high calibre to satisfy the need created by plague mortality. This was specifically stated in the 1359 charter for Elizabeth de Burgh's refoundation of Clare College, Cambridge, and in William de Wykeham's statutes for his New College in Oxford, founded in 1379. Bishop Bateman's 1350 foundation of Trinity Hall, Cambridge, for teaching canon and civil law had the needs of government and diocesan administration in mind. We should be careful, however, before concluding that the impetus was entirely driven by the experience of plague. Marie de St Pol's foundation of Pembroke College dates to 1347 and Gonville (later Gonville and Caius) College was begun in January 1348 – before the advent of plague. This last was sounded by Edmund Gonville, a wealthy priest, who had acted for Marie de St Pol, was the founder of Rushford College (Norfolk) in 1342 and was also associated with Henry, duke of Lancaster, who was himself involved in the founding of Corpus Christi College in 1352. After Gonville's death in 1351, his foundation was furthered by his executor, Bishop Bateman.

Another type of foundation with chantry functions that gained in popularity after the Black Death was the almshouse or maisons-dieu (God's house). Some, like the de la Poles' multiple foundations of Charterhouse and the hospital at Hull in 1378, and of God's House, school and chantry at Ewelme (Oxon.) in 1437, were aristocratic in origin, but a number of urban foundations were mercantile. Several such foundations are recorded at, for example, London, Exeter, Hull and York, though plenty of examples can be found for smaller towns as at Burford (Oxon.) or Sherborne (Dorset).

What these new colleges, hospitals and chantry foundations allowed their patrons and founders was a degree of personal control, extending long after their own demise, that simply had not been possible with earlier conventual (monastic) foundations, including hospitals, which followed established rules and allowed their heads a high degree of autonomy. We also see a more imaginative understanding of what the founders could achieve. Thus when in 1360 the Newcastle burgess William de Acton established a house there for the small Trinitarian order, it was also to serve as a hospital and a school. On a grander scale, Ralph, Lord Cromwell's college of Tattershall (Lincs.) (founded 1439), like the de la Poles' foundation at Ewelme, was associated with an almshouse and provided a grammar school for the choristers. It follows that patrons were not looking solely for chantry functions, but also wanted to endow good works. This is explicitly stated, for example, in the statutes of God's House, Ewelme. We also have here concrete manifestations of good lordship. Similarly, Henry VII's chantry in Westminster Abbey makes a very clear statement about the authority of the new Tudor dynasty. Its function was thus as much political as devotional. (Much the same is true of the completion of Henry VI's great chapel at King's College, Cambridge, which bristles with the Tudor badges of the portcullis, the Tudor rose and the Tudor arms.)

The fashion for founding grammar schools followed much the same pattern as for colleges and, as we have just seen, these were sometimes part of a common foundation. This was true of Cobham College and also of Bishop Grandisson's 1338 foundation at Ottery St Mary. Chantry foundations sometimes required the priest (or one of the priests) also to teach grammar. It was only in the early sixteenth century that we begin to find schools founded in their own right, as at Nottingham (founded 1513) or Manchester (1525). As with almshouses, however, we find patronage extending to merchants and substantial artisans, and numbers of towns came to employ schoolmasters. The London goldsmith Edmund Shaw, for example, founded a grammar school in his native Stockport in 1487. Bristol Grammar School was founded by the merchant brothers Nicholas and Robert Thorne. Other urban grammar schools were established by churchmen with family roots in the town. For example, Bishop Alcock, then bishop of Worcester, endowed Hull's existing grammar school in 1479 – he also founded Jesus College, Cambridge (1496) – and Bishop Vesey of Exeter established a grammar school in his native Sutton Coldfield in 1527.

BOOKS

The production of books before the advent of print was inevitably a labour-intensive and hence relatively costly activity, though our perception of the medieval book is undoubtedly coloured by the sorts of prestigious and highly illuminated psalters and books of hours displayed in museums. Most books were largely or entirely unilluminated and written for use, not display. Often these are comparatively small and densely written, because parchment, which was made from the skin of sheep, was quite costly. Literary texts frequently circulated as unbound pamphlets and might only be bound together at a later date so as to create unique compilations of materials, often in different hands, and reflective of the interests of a particular owner or family. In focusing on books specifically created as works of art, whether for the glory of God or as objects of conspicuous consumption to reflect the status of the patron, we are looking only at one part of a wider whole. Immediately prior to our period, such production was located primarily in monastic scriptoria (writing workshops), but through our period much production, even for religious houses, was associated with secular craftsmen located in a number of urban centres, notably London/Westminster, Bury St Edmunds, Oxford and York. By the later fourteenth century most high-status manuscripts were the work of London workshops. Production by religious continued, however. The Tickhill Psalter of the early fourteenth century, for example, was the work of John Tickhill, prior of Worksop, and the early fifteenth-century Sherborne Missal was the work of a Benedictine scribe, John Whas, and a Dominican illuminator, John Sifewas.

Liturgical or service books feature prominently among the texts that were in demand from lay aristocratic patrons and ecclesiastical lords alike. At the very beginning of our period there was a fashion for lavishly illuminated apocalypses accompanied, significantly, by French texts, possibly for aristocratic female patrons. The lay aristocracy in particular were consumers of illuminated psalters, of which perhaps the most famous is the Luttrell Psalter, with its depictions of peasants labouring in the fields, produced as we have seen for the Lincolnshire knight Geoffrey Luttrell perhaps only a few years before his death in 1345. Thereafter lay aristocratic demand shifted to the books of hours, which lent themselves to private devotional use, especially on the part of aristocratic women. The early fourteenth-century Grey-FitzPayn Hours, for example, was commissioned by her husband, Sir Richard de Grey, as a wedding present for Joan FitzPayn. As is usual with aristocratic texts, heraldry is used as a visible mark of ownership, but Joan is also depicted kneeling in devotion before her God in the historiated (illustrated) capital letter commencing the psalm text 'Lord, open thou my lips and my mouth shall show forth thy praise.' The so-called Bolton Hours, noted for its voluminous collection of full-page illuminations of saints, can be shown to have been made just over a century later for Margaret Blackburn, the wife of a prosperous York merchant. Here representations of Margaret, her husband, a son and a daughter are depicted kneeling in devotion before the Trinity. There is no display of heraldry because of the mercantile rather than aristocratic status of the patron.

The above examples demonstrate one of the particular advantages of manuscript book production, namely that texts could be written and illuminated according to the particular requirements of the individual patron. Book artisans produced to commission rather than speculatively. It is apparent, however, that by the fifteenth century, demand for books of hours was sufficiently great to sustain speculative production, including manuscripts imported from Flanders for the English market. Such books could then be 'customized' if required; alternatively, some were custom-made such as that made in Bruges for the Stamford wool merchant John Browne and his wife. This pattern continued with the advent of print. Most of the early printed books of hours were produced for the English market by French printers acting through agents working in England. Manuscript production also facilitated the creation of books where text and image are intimately interrelated, as for example in the Luttrell Psalter, or where images are actually more important than the accompanying text, as in the early fourteenth-century *Holkham Bible Picture Book*.

At the beginning of our period, manuscript books are overwhelmingly academic, liturgical, theological or devotional. During the course of our period, however, we see a much greater diversity of illuminated texts being produced. Thus we find romances and other literary works, including the Ellesmere Chaucer, an illuminated edition of the *Canterbury Tales* produced in London at the beginning of the fifteenth century, or illuminated editions of Gower's *Confessio Amantis*. We find illuminated chronicles, girdle-books for medieval doctors, rolls of arms and other heraldic compilations. By the later fifteenth century we find aristocratic genealogical pedigrees such as the Rous Roll and the related illustrated history of Richard Beauchamp, earl of Warwick, known as the Beauchamp Pageant, but also civic manuscripts such as guild books, play texts or collections of civic customs and records such as Ricart's *Calendar*, produced in Bristol around 1480.

The cost of book production was substantially reduced by the advent of paper during the fourteenth century, though the kinds of books discussed above were produced exclusively on animal skin, either parchment from sheep or the higher quality, and hence still more expensive, vellum from calves. The advent of print from the second half of the fifteenth century further reduced costs and made it possible to circulate texts to a wider readership than had previously been possible, though this was also predicated on the growth in literacy consequent upon the proliferation of grammar schools during the fifteenth century. Many printed books were imported, but from 1476, when William Caxton set up his press in the precinct of Westminster Abbey, a small number of mostly French, Low Countries and German printers established presses at various locations, mostly in London (including Westminster and Southwark). The highest-quality early printed books might be printed on vellum and consciously attempted to mimic illuminated manuscripts by the extensive use of wood blocks and rubrication (printing text in red). This was true, for example, of Richard Pynson's editions of the Sarum Missal.

The early English printers focused on the kinds of text that were not available from Continental presses. This meant primarily texts in English. As such, English incunabula (early printed books) are a good guide to popular vernacular reading at the end of the fifteenth century and the early years of the sixteenth. These largely comprised histories, chronicles and devotional literature, plus a few school books. Thus Caxton published his translation of the *Golden Legend* in 1483 and Nicholas Love's *The Mirror of the Blessed Life of Jesus c.*1490. He also published Higden's *Polychronicon* and a version of the *Brut* history. Wynkyn de Worde likewise published Hilton's *Scale of Perfection*, a Latin pastoral manual, the *Manipulus Curatorum*, but also an edition of parliamentary statutes. By the early 1530s printers were furthering the religious controversy of the day by publishing works such as the debate between More and Tyndale, variously supportive and hostile to Lutheran teaching. It was of course the English printers Richard Grafton and Edward Whitchurch who were commissioned to produce Henry VIII's Great Bible of 1539 and print alone allowed the injunction that all parishes be provided with the new bible to be swiftly realized.

Print technology was not confined to moveable type. Woodblock engraving actually pre-dated moveable type and was used from the first to illustrate printed books. Indeed some of the earliest printed books used coloured woodblocks consciously to imitate the illuminated manuscript. Thereafter woodblocks were commonly used to enhance printed books, but also to furnish individual prints, particularly of devotional images such as of St Christopher. These last, by their nature, were essentially ephemeral and have not survived well, but it may be that, alongside painted canvas hangings, these became a common form of devotional image found in people's homes.

BRASSES AND SEPULCHRAL MONUMENTS

Monumental brasses depicting variously members of the aristocracy in full armour, priests in their vestments or merchants in civilian dress were produced in enormous quantity over the course of the later Middle Ages and continued in use well after our period. They were especially popular in the prosperous eastern and south-eastern counties. The earliest extant brasses date from the latter years of the thirteenth century. Their popularity over three-dimensional sepulchral monuments was latterly a product of their comparatively low cost and the fact that they did not take up space. These cannot always have been considerations. Numbers of brasses produced before the fifteenth century are of very high quality and were no doubt quite costly. This was true of some of the large imported Flemish brasses, such as those of Thomas de la Mare, abbot of St Albans, or the later fourteenth-century merchants' brasses in St Margaret's, King's Lynn. It was also true of the best English brasses made in the first part of the fourteenth century, notably the stunning brass of Sir Hugh Hastings (d. 1347) at Elsing (Norfolk), which featured enamelled details, and the stylistically similar brass of Sir John and Lady Ellen de Wautone, also of 1347, at Wimbish (Essex). Such brasses would have been visually quite stunning. Other than in cases of brasses mounted on tomb chests, they may also have had the advantage that they could be walked on. This was perhaps particularly true of cathedral and conventual churches where there were processional routes, but clergy and the religious may also have seen such memorials as being suitably modest. Numbers of medieval testators asked to be buried in locations such as doorways, which would allow the faithful to walk over their remains. The priest celebrating mass would have stood upon those buried in the chancels of their parish churches. In monastic churches it not unusual to find brasses (or at least their indents) in the cloister walks or within the chapter house, no doubt for similar reason. Brasses thus had a devotional advantage over conventional monuments.

During the fourteenth century, brass workshops were established in London, Norwich and York. By the fifteenth century brasses were effectively being mass produced and the quality of design of many fifteenth- and early sixteenth-century brasses is actually relatively crude. Such brasses were customized solely by means of the inscription, though numbers of brasses consisted only of a memorial plaque. The cost of such brasses was to no small extent determined by the cost of the stone in which the brass was set. As such they suited the pockets not just of the gentry, but of large numbers of merchants and even artisans. As is seen in the brasses of Henry Bourchier, earl of Essex, and his wife, or of Sir Thomas Bullen, father of Anne Boleyn, it remained possible to commission work of a very high quality, but by and large from the earlier fifteenth century those of knightly rank or above preferred effigies of alabaster.

Three-dimensional sepulchral monuments, often supporting lifelike effigies are almost exclusively an aristocratic phenomenon, in which we may include a clerical aristocracy of bishops and abbots. (The wooden effigy of Walter Helyon, franklin, at Much Marcle (Herefordshire), who is dressed in civilian clothes and dates to *c.*1360 probably represents the lowest level of gentility.) As such, these monuments are part of the culture of conspicuous consumption that was so much an attribute of the aristocracy. Mostly they are of stone – invariably limestone or, from the earlier fourteenth century, alabaster – but a few earlier effigies are of wood. Originally they were painted. A few very high-status effigies, such as that of Richard Beauchamp, earl of Warwick, were of brass. The effigy might stand on a tomb chest, be contained within a wall niche, or lie beneath a canopy.

As with monumental brasses, whose designs imitated these three-dimensional sepulchral effigies, the lay aristocracy are depicted, in the case of men, in full armour and, in the case of women, in fashionable robes. Bishops are represented with mitre and pastoral staff. Often the figures rest their feet on small animals, usually lions (symbolic of martial valour) or, in the case of ladies, dogs (symbolic of fidelity). Some earlier figures are comparatively animated, as for example Sir Roger de Kerdeston (d. 1337) at Reepham (Norfolk) or the figures of cross-legged knights found in the later thirteenth and early years of the fourteenth century. Thereafter they lie stiffly, their hands held in prayer, though a few husbands and wives are shown holding hands, a gesture rather more common in monumental brasses and one that offers a consciously positive representation of marriage as a lay ideal.

These were intended to be conspicuous images. The status of the dead would have been obvious from the dress and, in the case of the lay aristocracy, their family identity from their heraldry. Sometimes their ladies also wear heraldic dress. Above the tomb might be displayed the knight's helm and gauntlets in much the same way as wax votive offerings were hung above the shrines of saints. This may still be seen, albeit now in facsimile, over the tomb of the Black Prince. The more elaborate tombs often had mourning figures, known as weepers, arranged around the tomb chest, though some, as is true of the tomb of Sir Walter Griffith (d. 1481) and his wife at Burton Agnes (Yorks., ER), had representations of saints reflective of the particular devotions of the person represented. This would again have been visually reminiscent of shrines, which had niches round the sides where pilgrims could pray. The analogy can be taken further in the case of canopied tombs. Indeed the sumptuous canopied tomb of (perhaps) Lady Eleanor Percy in Beverley Minster, dating to the decade before the Black Death, is popularly known as the Percy shrine. The tomb of Edward II, made only a few years before, was indeed constructed as a shrine as part of an attempt by Gloucester Abbey to promote his cult.

The most dramatic way in which the greater aristocracy associated themselves in death with the heavenly company is found in a series of tombs that were associated with or doubled as Easter sepulchres – that is, the special receptacle for the reserved host during Easter Week. At Hawton (Notts.), the tomb of Sir Richard de Compton is placed next to, and is architecturally of a piece with, the Easter sepulchre, which was presumably of his gift. The Percy tomb in Beverley Minster, which is surmounted by angels bearing the instruments of the Passion and, at the centre, a large figure of the resurrected Christ holding the miniature soul of a lady in a napkin, is located just at the north side of the high altar. The tomb chest, which originally supported a brass, is flat. These observations suggest this is no mere tomb, but that it also served as an Easter sepulchre. Much the same argument may be made of the unusual and elaborate tomb, likewise without effigy, of Sir Geoffrey Luttrell and his wife at Irnham (Lincs.) that must be contemporary with the Percy tomb. Read together with the Luttrell Psalter, which, as noted earlier, represents Sir Geoffrey as a Christlike figure in a dining scene laden with Eucharistic symbolism, there is a real sense in which a lay lord was alluding to divine lordship to valorize his earthly authority and to win his due place in the next life.

This particular fashion may have been largely curtailed by the Black Death, though we do find a couple of much later examples, as at Long Melford (Suffolk) where the tomb recess of the Clopton chantry standing to the north of the high altar supported a wooden sepulchre in Easter week. A new fashion from the earlier fifteenth century was for the clothed effigy to be raised above a representation of the same person as a naked and decaying corpse (known as a transi tomb), or simply for the sole effigy to be in the form of a cadaver. This is reflective of the tone of disparagement used in respect of mortal remains in some contemporary wills that has sometimes been read as evidence for Lollard sympathy, but is probably an orthodox manifestation of the same devotional trend. These seem to have been especially popular with greater ecclesiastics as seen, for example, in the tombs of Bishop Fleming of Lincoln (d. 1431), Bishop Beckington of Wells (d. 1465) or, at the far end of our period, John Wakeman, the last abbot of Tewkesbury, but the fashion spread to some particularly devout laity. The cadaver tomb of John Baret of Bury St Edmunds is accompanied by a long inscription that concludes, 'he that will sadly [solemnly] behold me with his eye / may see his own mirror [and] learn for to die'. The tomb of Alice, duchess of Suffolk, who founded the God's House at Ewelme (Oxon.), is a particularly splendid alabaster cadaver tomb of the transi type. Such tombs remained popular through the rest of our period as seen, for example, in the elaborate wooden tomb of Sir Roger Rockley (d. 1522) at Worsborough (Yorks., WR) or the Wakeman monument already noted.

DRESS

Dress must be regarded as an aspect of cultural production. Certainly it was an integral and important part of the aristocratic convention of conspicuous consumption. The royal family set the trend; providing regular changes of wardrobe for the young Edward III and his queen against different feasts and seasons, for example, employed a veritable army of seamstresses, embroiderers, skinners (furriers) and tailors. Expenditure on fabrics and furs alone could represent a significant portion of aristocratic income. Thomas de Berkeley was spending some £142 a year on clothes in 1345–46, rather more than a tenth of his total outgoings. In the case of great lords a substantial amount of money was accounted for by the liberal provision of clothes or cloth to servants and retainers in the form of liveries.

Our knowledge of costume is largely confined to visual representations, to references in wills and inventories, and to expense accounts. With the exception of leather shoes preserved in waterlogged sites, very little by way of actual articles of dress survive from the period. Although we know the names of many cloths, we do not know what they were like, though it is clear that some were more highly regarded and more expensive than others. The visual evidence from tomb effigies, monumental brasses and portraits is heavily biased towards the upper levels of society and often represents ideals of dress – and certainly 'best' dress – rather than reflecting everyday usage. What is represented, therefore, may be more akin to the modern fashion plate than an informal snapshot. It is actually very hard to reconstruct the dress of the lower orders of society. Some general points may, nevertheless, be made.

Dress was an important marker of social rank, a point recognized in contemporary sumptuary legislation and notably the short-lived act of 1363. In particular, what fabrics and furs were considered appropriate was determined by status; more costly imported furs and silks were reserved to the greater aristocracy. An inventory of clothes belonging to a middle-ranking knight, Sir Osbert de Spaldington, in 1297 includes three cloths of gold and garments lined variously with red deer skin, miniver, squirrel and badger or trimmed with silk. Servants might be given their employers' cast-off clothing – their status would be reflected in the slightly old-fashioned appearance of their dress – but it is also apparent that much clothing was recycled either by being restitched to accommodate new ownership or changing fashions, or by having worn parts replaced. There was a very active market in second-hand clothing and this no doubt extended the possibilities for people to dress 'beyond their station'. Well-to-do testators would provide for cheap cloth – russet or Welsh frieze – to be purchased to dress poor persons attending their funerals precisely because their own cast-off clothing would be inappropriate.

Before the earlier fourteenth century, status was marked primarily by the quantity and quality of cloth worn. From the 1320s – furthered by the development of buttons from the middle of the same century – more close-fitting garments became fashionable, and a greater distinction between male and female dress followed. Thereafter fashions developed more quickly, and increasing emphasis was placed on cut and styling (and hence on labour cost precisely at the moment labour became more expensive as a consequence of the Black Death). At the same time, the upper echelons of society looked to a greater range of imported fabrics, including silks and velvets, and to a much wider range of colours. The use of fur trimmings and embroidery is likewise found through the remainder of our period. Fashionability became a marker of status. This was particularly pronounced in respect of women's head-dresses, which had reached an apex of elaborateness by the second decade of the fifteenth century. Thus the tomb of William Canyng (d. 1460), a Bristol merchant and mayor, and his wife Joan show them, as bourgeoisie, albeit very wealthy bourgeoisie, unfashionably dressed. Joan's head is veiled and there is but the simplest and most modest of supporting frames.

For those below the aristocratic and mercantile elites we are much more dependent on manuscript illuminations, though maintenance agreements concerning the material provision made to peasants in return for surrendering their land often specifies clothing. The domestic cloth industry grew again rapidly after the Black Death, having been moribund earlier, but the emphasis shifted to cheaper cloths for a new mass market. This market was driven by these middling and lower echelons of society, who, because relatively better off, were almost certainly better dressed after the plague. Even before the plague woollen tunics and linen undergarments were normal peasant dress. After

1348 they were probably more likely to wear tailored garments and to possess more than a single set of clothes. Even labourers may well have worn garments made from dyed cloth. The wearing of hose, hoods and cloaks, together with use of linings, belts, buckles and inexpensive jewellery, also became much more common.

DRAMA

A rich folk tradition of summer games, of hocking and other seasonal festivities are known to us almost by chance and no doubt form but part of a larger, hidden cultural heritage. Part of the problem is that oral, 'folk' traditions tend not to leave record beyond the odd disparaging comment or clerical censure. Part also is that the study of folklore has never entered the academic mainstream in this country and as such has been unjustifiably marginalized. It is likely, for example, that there was a vibrant tradition of mumming that may have its roots in pre-Christian times. Recently Michael Camille has intriguingly suggested that such traditions are reflected in some of the illuminations for the Luttrell Psalter. Some of these rural traditions were no doubt imported into urban culture. Hocking, for example, is noticed in London by the early fifteenth century, but after initial disapproval it soon became sanitized as a fundraising vehicle for parish churches. What we also find in towns, however, is a self-conscious projection of a distinctively urban culture, and deployment of drama and ceremonial as a form of civic advertisement. This was especially true of the so-called mystery plays or Corpus Christi plays.

The major urban play cycles associated with the feast of Corpus Christi, or Whitsun, have received much scholarly attention, though primarily from theatre historians (a branch of literature) rather than cultural historians. Theatre historians have, of course, been most interested in drama for which texts are extant, so only some of the major Corpus Christi cycles, notably York, Wakefield and Chester, but not Beverley or Durham, have attracted much scholarly interest. Also less well known consequently are the multiplicity of other dramatic productions that went on in the streets of most towns and even some villages through the year. Of particular interest are the many saints' plays that are mostly recorded during the last century before the break with Rome. This in part must be an accident of survival, but it may also be that such plays became genuinely popular in this era. They were performed to teach about particular saints, either by a guild dedicated to that saint or by other groups within the community. Thus we know of plays of St James and of St Denys in fifteenth-century York, the latter associated with the parish church of the same dedication, but we do not know who performed them. Canterbury had an early sixteenth-century pageant of the martyrdom of St Thomas à Becket replete with a bag of blood to add effect to the staging of his death. Plays of St Katherine are particularly widespread and some of these were no doubt guild productions.

It would appear that the staging and performance of the pageants that made up the Corpus Christi play cycles evolved markedly over the era. The earliest evidence for cycles comes from Beverley and York in the 1370s, though there is nothing to suggest that they had yet acquired texts or had evolved to the full-scale dramatic productions documented about a century later. They appear initially to have been an enterprise involving all the members of the collectivity or guild that came together for that purpose. By the later fifteenth century, it became one where non-guild members might be paid to act particular parts and any sense of ownership passed from guilds to civic government; players performed because they were required to rather than because they necessarily wanted to. These changes had profound implications. Among these were the way women participated in the drama and the way in which women were represented in the drama.

Whereas before the mid-fifteenth century women probably played female parts, by the end of the following century men filled these roles. Our most telling evidence that women played women's parts in guild drama comes from the York cycle. Here those pageants that contain parts for women tend to be associated with crafts in which women appear to have been most visible. Since the York pageants were recorded from the guilds' own scripts sometime around the 1470s, they probably represent texts created some decade or more previous, and hence to a period before any process of exclusion of female actors. This last is only apparent from evidence at the very end of the century. The Coventry smiths' accounts for 1496 refer to 'Ryngolds man Thomas that playtt pylatts wyff' and those for 1499 likewise account for payments made 'to dame Percula for his wages' and 'to pylatts wyffe for his wages'. We can know little about the way female roles were presented before the later fifteenth century due to the way texts have survived. It is striking that in the early sixteenth-century Chester cycle, we can observe, alongside the Virgin Mary, roles such as Noah's wife and the dishonest alewife (played by men in drag) that are the butt of a humour constructed from a misogynistic (and magisterial) discourse.

The major play cycles were primarily an urban phenomenon, though the survival of a later fifteenth-century text of the East Anglian 'N-Town' cycle suggests a distinctive regional pattern of peripatetic performance not focused on any specific urban centre. In northern England, where a distinctive tradition of Corpus Christi drama emerged in the later fourteenth century, even comparatively modest urban centres such as Durham and Doncaster staged their own cycles by some point in the fifteenth century. In the case of Wakefield the creation of a cycle partly borrowed from York sometime towards the end of the century may be read as an assertion of urban identity for a seigneurial borough made newly prosperous on the back of its textile industry. Cornwall likewise enjoyed its own vernacular tradition reflected in the *Ordinalia*, a culturally distinct religious drama cycle written in Cornish with textual interventions in English, French and Latin, and saints' plays relating to local cults. Here the cultural links are more obviously with Brittany than beyond the Tamar.

Though the fashion for elaborate cycle drama was probably at its height in the later fifteenth century, these highly traditional devotional productions seem regularly to have continued into the Reformation era and were halted only at the very end of our period with the advent of Edward VI's more radical policies. (In several instances the cycles were to be revived under Mary and continued well into Elizabeth's reign.) The same would be true of the rather less common cycles focused not on a Creation-to-Doomsday narrative or Christ's Passion, but rather on the exposition of the Creed and of the Lord's Prayer.

A different secular dramatic tradition developed within an aristocratic context culminating, or more precisely substantively documented, in the later fifteenth and sixteenth century in so-called interludes. These were dramatic productions staged not in the street, but within the lord's great hall. Their purpose was twofold. In the first instance they served to educate the young gentlemen serving in the household by providing contrasting exemplars of model and inappropriate conduct. By setting an example of how an orderly household should be managed, however, the interludes also served to project the authority of the lord in whose hall the interlude was performed and even to offer tacit political comment on the nature of good government.

Unlike the guild drama discussed earlier, we know the authors of a number of extant texts. These include Henry Medwall, author of *Fulgens and Lucrece* and of *Nature*, who wrote for Cardinal Moreton at the very end of the fifteenth century, and John Heywood, whose work includes the comic *The Four Ps* of *c*.1530. Heywood's near contemporary John Bale used Thomas Cromwell's protection to write drama highly critical of traditional Catholicism. His best-known work, *King John*, however, is a history play and as such represents an evolutionary link between later medieval drama and the Shakespearean stage.

GLOSSARY

Ale Staple drink of the Middle Ages in the absence of a safe water supply. Beer, brewed with hops, was initially imported from northern Europe and only came to displace ale from the later fifteenth century. An 'ale' was a social event at which ale was sold for the purposes of fundraising.

Alien Person from outside the realm (in modern parlance, a foreigner). At times such persons were treated with suspicion, even hostility: Flemish merchants were attacked in London during the Peasants' Revolt of 1381, and Scots and Welsh were commonly victims of prejudice in northern England and the Welsh border region respectively.

Anchorite, anchoress Man or woman recluse committed to a devout life and confined to a cell, which, by the later Middle Ages, was usually attached to a church, often in an urban location. Earlier recluses tended to occupy cells located away from settlement.

Boon work Additional labour service, invariably associated with the busiest moments in the agricultural year, notably harvest, rendered by servile tenants to their lords supposedly as a favour.

Borough Community granted certain privileges, particularly in respect of property rights, by its lord through a charter.

Burgage A (moderately substantial) strip of land within a *borough*, invariably running backwards from a narrow street frontage on which a house might be built. Historically, holders of burgages enjoyed burgess status, though during the course of the later Middle Ages individual plots were sometimes subdivided, and the link between tenure and status was broken.

Burgess Privileged member of a *borough* enjoying the rights granted to that borough by charters of its lord. Originally the holders of specific and distinctively shaped holdings (*burgages*). Where a *guild merchant* was established, the guild attempted to limit the rights of a burgess to those who were members of the guild. By the later Middle Ages burgesses came to be admitted on the basis of being the son of a burgess, having served an apprenticeship, or by making a payment.

Canon Priest living within a community. Secular canons were attached to collegiate churches or minsters, including some cathedral churches. Regular canons were enclosed and followed a monastic rule. There were two main orders of canons: the Augustinians and the Premonstratensians.

Canon law Law of the Church.

Cathedral Church that houses the seat (Latin = *cathedra*) of a bishop and hence the centre of a diocese.

Chancel (Ritual) eastern parts of a church, invariably demarcated by an arch or screen, containing the high altar; that part of a church that was the responsibility of the priest.

Citizen Same as a *burgess* except in relation to a *city*.

City Urban community that was recognized as of particular importance because the seat of a bishop or, as was true from the late Middle Ages, because created a city by the Crown.

Custom Established convention or practice that has legal force within a particular locality. The manor court operated according to customary law, the body of conventions traditional on that particular *manor*. Originally transmitted orally and remembered within the community, by the later Middle Ages invariably to be written down.

Danelaw Region broadly comprising the counties of Derbyshire, Leicestershire, Lincolnshire, Northamptonshire, Nottinghamshire and Yorkshire, under Danish rule prior to the Conquest.

Demesne Part of a *manor* retained by the lord and not leased out to tenants. Our knowledge of the manorial economy is largely limited to the demesne.

Fair Annual gathering of merchants and traders at a specific location permitted by royal licence. Most were small scale, but some, such as Stourbridge Fair in Cambridge, had their own specific site, lasted several days, and drew traders and customers over a wide distance. Numbers of more important towns had more than one fair. The era of the great fairs was supposedly over by the time of the Black Death, but many operated throughout our period.

Famulus Latin term used to describe servants generally, but also more specifically members of a manorial lord's permanent staff of *demesne* workers, usually comprising ploughmen, shepherds and dairymaids.

Farm Property leased for a fixed (Latin = *firma*) annual rent was said to be 'at farm', hence the leaseholder was a 'farmer'. Only in more recent times has farmer come to mean agriculturalist per se.

Felony More serious crime reserved to the royal courts and punishable by death, normally hanging. Alleged felons (those who commit felony) could be outlawed if they fled from justice ('waived' in the case of females). Included homicide, rape, wounding and theft of goods worth more than a shilling (equivalent to 5 pence). Lesser offences were *trespasses*.

Feudal Technically, refers to military society and the obligations of a knight to his suzerain (lord). The knight owed military service in return for the land, that is the feoff (Latin = *feudum*), held of the lord. In more general sense, used by Marxist historians to describe a society characterized not by the money nexus (capitalism), but by the obligation of servile peasants to their lords.

Forest Historically an area of woodland used for hunting purposes. There were over 70 forests in the earlier fourteenth century, with particular concentrations in Hampshire and Wiltshire. In the case of 'royal' forests, an area of the forest subject to the jurisdiction of forest law, regulations designed to preserve game – hence forest is essentially a legal category. Royal forests decreased in extent over our period; forests were 'disafforested' (removed from the jurisdiction of forest law), often to allow revenue to be raised from the sale of timber.

Franchise Area of distinct and separate legal jurisdiction usually associated with a religious house or cathedral. Also used in the term 'urban franchise' to indicate the community of burgesses or citizens.

Frankpledge, see *tithing*.

Friar Member of one of the mendicant orders, that is religious (those following a rule) ministering within the community and looking to the laity for alms. There were four main orders of friars: Dominicans or Black Friars; Franciscans or Grey Friars; Carmelites or White Friars; and Austins.

Gentry Term used to designate the lower ranks of the aristocracy, conventionally comprising knights, esquires and 'mere' or 'parish' gentry (gentlemen).

Guild merchant Collectivity of traders and craftsmen that exercised influence over both the economic and the political structure of a number of larger towns before the later Middle Ages.

Hall Principal space in a secular building. In grander buildings with separate living and sleeping accommodation, hall used for eating. Head of household and immediate family might dine separately at a table raised up on a dais at one end visible to all others using or entering hall, a pattern imitated in some guildhalls.

Heriot Payment, usually of best beast, but money sum in the absence of livestock, made from the holding of tenant to lord when tenant dies or otherwise surrenders tenancy. Since surrender was often occasioned by the tenant's death, heriot is sometimes rendered as 'death duty', but numbers of heriots were also paid as a consequence of tenants selling their holdings.

Hocking Annual custom whereby women captured and 'ransomed' men and vice versa on successive days. Often used as a parish fundraising activity from the fifteenth century.

Hundred Administrative subdivision of a county. In *Danelaw* region, tended to be known as wapentake.

Journeyman Term, derived from the French, for a craftworker employed on a daily wage.

Lay subsidy Regular system of taxation imposed on the population other than clergy (taxed separately). Before 1334 persons individually assessed according to means, but from 1334 until the Henrician subsidies communities assigned a specific tax obligation, actual distribution being decided locally. Unlike the *poll taxes*, only asked tax of a more prosperous minority of the population.

Lollardy Term given to heretical movement originating with the teachings of John Wyclif, an Oxford academic, at end of the fourteenth century. In practice came to represent a heterogeneous group of persons hostile to certain facets of contemporary Catholicism, notably the mass, images, pilgrimage and ecclesiastical hierarchy.

Manor Administrative unit of land of variable size subject to the authority of a lord.

Merchet Fine paid in respect of villein women to secure lord's consent to their marriages. May represent tax on dowry; wealthier families did pay higher merchets.

Marriages off the *manor* appear also to have attracted larger fines. Paid either by the woman or on her behalf. Used as a mark of servility.

Monk Male member of enclosed religious community. Monks, unlike canons, were not necessarily in holy orders (priests), but by the end of the Middle Ages, invariably were. There were two main orders: the Benedictines and the Cistercians.

Nave Main body of a church regarded as the responsibility of the parishioners, represented by sidesmen or churchwardens.

Nuclear family Co-resident group of close kin comprising no more than husband, wife and children. May also encompass live-in servants, but rarely includes more distant kin or more than two generations.

Poll tax Head tax (poll = head). Experimental form of taxation levied in 1377, 1379 and 1380–81, but abandoned after the Peasants' Revolt.

Probate inventory Document drawn up by suitably experienced persons after death of the will maker, providing a valuation of possessions. Sometimes goods recorded room by room so allowing some insight into the furnishing of a medieval house.

Serf, see *villein*.

Subsidy Usual term for a tax levied by the Crown, mostly assessed on property or wealth.

Tithing Group of males over 12 ordinarily resident within community. Members of tithing vouched for each other's conduct, and reported misdemeanours to local court or tourn.

Trespass Lesser crime. See *felony*.

Vicar Someone who deputizes for another, usually on a fixed stipend. Many parishes were served by a vicar because the actual incumbent was non-resident or because the parish had been appropriated (taken over) by a local religious house.

Villein Peasant of semi-free or servile legal status, legally bound to the *manor*. May only seek justice in the court of the manorial lord. Villeinage was hereditary through the male line. Villeins holding land of lord legally obliged to work on lord's demesne. In practice labour services were often 'commuted' to simple money payment.

Will Document drawn up in the lifetime of maker providing for distribution of money and possessions, primarily for the benefit of soul. Often drawn up when maker believed him or herself close to death. Much detail concerned with provision for benefit of maker's soul. Mostly survive as registered copies.

FURTHER READING

Where not otherwise specified, place of publication is London.

GENERAL

C. Dyer, *Making a Living in the Middle Ages: The People of Britain 850–1520* (New Haven, 2002) impresses with its chronological range and clarity. R.H. Britnell, *The Commercialisation of English Society, 1000–1500* (Cambridge, 1993) is an important economic analysis. A thoughtful and accessible set of essays is contained in R. Horrox, ed., *Fifteenth Century Attitudes: Perceptions of Society in Late Medieval England* (Cambridge, 1994). R.H. Britnell, ed., *Daily Life in the late Middle Ages* (Stroud, 1998) is more popular in touch. More specialized are: M.M. Postan, *Essays on Medieval Agriculture and General Problems of the Medieval Economy* (Cambridge, 1973); C.H. Clough, ed., *Profession, Vocation and Culture in Later Medieval England* (Liverpool, 1982); and R. Britnell and J. Hatcher, *Progress and Problems in Medieval England* (Cambridge, 1996). For housing see J. Grenville, *Medieval Housing* (1997).

GENDER AND HIERARCHY

J. Cadden, *Meanings of Sex Difference in the Middle Ages: Medicine, Science, and Culture* (Cambridge, 1993) discusses medieval understandings. D. Hadley, ed., *Masculinity in the Middle Ages* (1999) is a useful collection on masculinity, but only some of the essays are specific to England. For ideas about women see: A. Blamires, *The Case for Women in Medieval Culture* (Oxford, 1997); K.M. Phillips, *Medieval Maidens: Young Women and Gender in England, 1270–1540* (Manchester, 2003).

FAMILY AND HOUSEHOLD

A sensible introduction is P. Fleming, *Family and Household in Medieval England* (Basingstoke, 2001). Essays offering a wider European perspective are M. Carlier and T. Soens, eds, *The Household in Late Medieval Cities: Italy and Northwestern Europe Compared* (Leuven, 2001).

MANOR AND BOROUGH

For rural society a good starting point is G. Astill and A. Grant, eds, *The Countryside of Medieval England* (Oxford, 1988). For the manor court see Z. Razi and R. Smith, eds, *Medieval Society and the Manor Court* (Oxford, 1996). A good exploration of one particular manor is P.D.A. Harvey, *A Medieval Oxfordshire Village: Cuxham, 1240–1400* (Oxford, 1965). There are many good local studies. Three examples are B. Harvey, *Westminster Abbey and its Estates in the Middle Ages* (Oxford, 1977); M.K. McIntosh, *Autonomy and Community: The Royal Manor of Havering, 1200–1500* (Cambridge, 1986); and M. Bailey, *A Marginal Economy?: East Anglian Breckland in the Later Middle Ages* (Cambridge, 1989).

For town society C. Platt, *The English Medieval Town* (1976) remains an accessible introduction, though R. Holt and G. Rosser, eds, *The Medieval Town: A Reader in English Urban History* (1990) is invaluable. For the earlier period see E. Miller and J. Hatcher, *Medieval England: Towns, Commerce and Crafts* (1995). For the later period see A. Dyer, *Decline and Growth in English Towns 1400–1640* (1991). The best work is contained in studies of individual towns. Outstanding are: C. Phythian-Adams, *Desolation of a City: Coventry and the Urban Crisis of the Late Middle Ages* (Cambridge, 1979); R.H. Britnell, *Growth and Decline in Colchester 1300–1525* (Cambridge, 1986); and M. Kowaleski, *Local Markets and Regional Trade in Medieval Exeter* (Cambridge, 1995).

CHURCH AND PARISH

A recent essay collection is K.L. French, G.G. Gibbs and B.A. Kümin, eds, *The Parish in English Life 1400–1600* (Manchester, 1997). A good recent study of the diocese of Bath and Wells is K.L. French, *The People of the Parish: Community Life in a Late Medieval English Diocese* (Philadelphia, 2001). J.A.F. Thomson, *The Early Tudor Church and Society, 1485–1529* (1993) is also useful.

GUILD AND FRATERNITY

There has been a flurry of local studies of 'religious guilds' of late: V.R. Bainbridge, *Gilds in the Medieval Countryside: Social and Religious Change in Cambridgeshire, c.1350–1558*; D.J.F. Crouch, *Piety, Fraternity and Power: Religious Gilds in Late Medieval Yorkshire, 1389–1547* (York, 2000); K. Farnhill, *Guilds and the Parish Community in Late Medieval East Anglia c.1470–1550* (Woodbridge, 2001). A good study of medieval crafts is H. Swanson, *Medieval Artisans: An Urban Class in Late Medieval England* (Oxford, 1989). Numbers of individual town studies also have good material on craft guilds. A prosperous London company is the subject of P. Nightingale, *A Medieval Mercantile Community: The Grocers' Company and the Politics and Trade of London 1000–1485* (New Haven, 1995).

COUNTING HEADS

There is little monograph literature in this area. A useful introduction to the post-plague era is still J. Hatcher, *Plague, Population and the English Economy 1348–1530* (1977). L. Poos, *A Rural Society after the Black Death: Essex 1350–1525* (Cambridge, 1991) actually presents valuable regional demographic evidence back to the later thirteenth century. Important, though controversial, is another regional study: Z. Razi, *Life, Marriage and Death in a Medieval Parish: Economy, Society and Demography in Halesowen 1270–1400* (Cambridge, 1980). Also to be noted is B. Harvey, *Living and Dying in England 1100–1540: The Monastic Experience* (Oxford, 1993) about the monks of Westminster.

HUSBANDMEN AND LABOURERS

The best introduction to peasant society is R.H. Hilton, *The English Peasantry in the Later Middle Ages* (Oxford, 1975). B.A. Hanawalt, *The Ties that Bound: Peasant*

Families in Medieval England (New York, 1986) is not always as sound. Still useful for the pre-plague era is E. Miller and J. Hatcher, *Medieval England: Rural Society and Economic Change 1086–1348* (1978).

MERCHANTS, ARTISANS AND LABOURERS

The classic work is S. Thrupp, *The Merchant Class of Medieval London* (Chicago, 1948). A more recent study of merchants is J. Kermode, *Medieval Merchants: York, Beverley and Hull in the Later Middle Ages* (Cambridge, 1998). For artisans see H. Swanson, *Medieval Artisans: An Urban Class in Late Medieval England* (Oxford, 1989). There is invaluable material in C. Dyer, *Standards of Living in the Later Middle Ages: Social Change in England, c.1200–1520* (Cambridge, 1989). For women in towns see P.J.P. Goldberg, *Women, Work, and Life Cycle: Women in York and Yorkshire c.1300–1520* (Oxford, 1992).

LORDS, KNIGHTS, ESQUIRES AND GENTLEMEN

A readable introduction is C. Given-Wilson, *The English Nobility in the Late Middle Ages: The Fourteenth-Century Political Community* (1987). For aspects of (greater) aristocratic culture see: N. Orme, *From Childhood to Chivalry: The Education of the English Kings and Aristocracy, 1066–1530* (1984); K. Mertes, *The English Noble Household, 1250–1600: Good Governance and Politic Rule* (Oxford, 1988); and C. Woolgar, *The Great Household in Late Medieval England* (New Haven, 1999), an attractively presented and informed study. For women of the aristocracy see J. Ward, *English Noblewomen in the Later Middle Ages* (1992); and B.J. Harris, *English Aristocratic Women, 1450–1550: Marriage and Family, Property and Careers* (New York, 2002). There are a number of regional gentry studies. Particularly good are N. Saul, *Knights and Esquires: The Gloucestershire Gentry in the Fourteenth Century* (Oxford, 1981); and N. Saul, *Scenes from Provincial Life: Knightly Families in Sussex, 1280–1400*.

CLERKS, CLERICS, ECCLESIASTICS AND THE RELIGIOUS

A good introduction is J.C. Dickinson, *An Ecclesiastical History of England: The Later Middle Ages* (1979). Clergy have been somewhat neglected in terms of monographs, but see: P. Heath, *English Parish Clergy on the Eve of the Reformation* (1969); and P. Marshall, *The Catholic Priesthood and the English Reformation* (Oxford, 1994). For the religious see: D. Knowles, *The Religious Orders in England*, 3 vols. (Cambridge, 1948–59), old, but still essential; and R. Gilchrist, *Gender and Material Culture: The Archaeology of Religious Women* (1997), a very different perspective; M. Oliva, *The Convent and Community in Late Medieval England* (Woodbridge, 1998).

THE YEARS OF HUNGER, 1250–1348

Useful are: S. Raban, *England under Edward I and Edward II, 1259–1327* (Oxford, 2000); B.M.S. Campbell, ed., *Before the Black Death: Studies in the 'Crisis' of the Early*

Fourteenth Century (Manchester, 1991); and J. Masschaele, *Peasants, Merchants, and Markets: Inland Trade in Medieval England, 1150–1350* (Basingstoke, 1997).

THE BLACK DEATH AND ITS AFTERMATH, 1348–1381

A useful collection of essays is M. Ormrod and P. Lindley, eds, *The Black Death in England* (Stamford, 1996). A first-rate collection of Western European sources and introduction is R. Horrox, ed., *The Black Death* (Manchester, 1994). A good survey is S.L. Waugh, *England in the Reign of Edward III* (Cambridge, 1991). For issues relating to labour and the labour laws see J. Bothwell, P.J.P. Goldberg and W.M. Ormrod, eds, *The Problem of Labour in Fourteenth-Century England* (York, 2000).

THE PEASANTS' REVOLT, 1381

An excellent essay collection is R.H. Hilton and T.H. Aston, eds, *The English Rising of 1381* (Cambridge, 1984). R.B. Dobson, ed., *The Peasants' Revolt of 1381* (2nd edn, 1983) contains useful introductions as well as an excellent selection of primary sources. For a solid Marxist perspective see R.H. Hilton, *Bond Men Made Free: Medieval Peasant Movements and the English Rising of 1381* (1973). A recent synthesis is A. Dunn, *The Great Rising of 1381* (Stroud, 2002), though this misses modern work on the poll taxes.

DIVERSITY AND ADAPTATION, 1382–1450

J. Day, *The Medieval Market Economy* (Oxford, 1987) is good on the bullion crises. For Cade's revolt and its social context see I.M.W. Harvey, *Jack Cade's Rebellion of 1450* (Oxford, 1991).

STAGNATION AND INFLATION, 1450–1550

Useful overviews are provided by W.G. Hoskins, *The Age of Plunder: The England of Henry VIII 1500–1547* (1976); and more recently R.H. Britnell, *The Closing of the Middle Ages?: England, 1471–1529* (Oxford, 1997). Rural society is well served by J. Whittle, *The Development of Agrarian Capitalism: Land and Labour in Norfolk 1440–1580* (Oxford, 2000). Also useful is J.C.K. Cornwall, *Wealth and Society in Early Sixteenth Century England* (1988). For the Pilgrimage of Grace see M. Bush, *The Pilgrimage of Grace: A Study of the Rebel Armies of October 1536* (Manchester, 1996); and R. Hoyle, *The Pilgrimage of Grace and the Politics of the 1530s* (Oxford, 2001).

DEVOTION BEFORE THE BREAK WITH ROME

A brilliant introduction from a broader European perspective is still J. Bossy, *Christianity in the West, 1400–1700* (Oxford, 1985). A more traditional study with excellent bibliography is R.N. Swanson, *Church and Society in Late Medieval England* (Oxford, 1989). A useful collection of primary sources is R.N. Swanson, *Catholic England* (Manchester, 1993). There are a number of good regional studies, e.g. N.

Tanner, *The Church in Late Medieval Norwich, 1370–1532* (Toronto, 1984); A.D. Brown, *Popular Piety in Late Medieval England: The Diocese of Salisbury 1250–1550* (Oxford, 1995); K.L. French, *The People of the Parish: Community Life in a Late Medieval English Diocese* (Philadelphia, 2001). For Lollardy see: R. Rex, *The Lollards* (Basingstoke, 2002); and S. McSheffrey, *Gender and Heresy: Women and Men in Lollard Communities, 1420–1530* (Philadelphia, 1995).

DEVOTION UNDER THE HENRICIAN REFORMATION

There is a large and growing literature in this area. An easy introduction is W.J. Sheils, *The English Reformation 1530–1570* (1989). A fascinating local study is E. Duffy, *The Voices of Morebach: Reformation and Rebellion in an English Village* (New Haven, 2001). Some other regional studies include: M. Bowker, *The Henrician Reformation: The Diocese of Lincoln under John Longland 1521–1547* (Cambridge, 1981); S. Brigden, *London and the Reformation* (Oxford, 1989); R. Whiting, *The Blind Devotion of the People: Popular Religion and the English Reformation* (Cambridge, 1989). A useful collection of essays is C. Haigh, ed., *The English Reformation Revised* (Cambridge, 1987). Other studies include: J.J. Scarisbrick, *The Reformation and the English People* (Oxford, 1984); C. Haigh, *English Reformations: Religion, Politics, and Society under the Tudors* (Oxford, 1993).

THE SEARCH FOR ORDER

An essential work is M.K. McIntosh, *Controlling Misbehaviour in England, 1370–1600* (Cambridge, 1998). An accessible account of the law is A. Musson and W.M. Ormrod, *The Evolution of English Justice* (Basingstoke, 1999). For the regulation of prostitution see R.M. Karras, *Common Women: Prostitution and Sexuality in Medieval England* (New York, 1996), a study with a particular focus on London evidence. For attitudes to the poor see: M. Rubin, *Charity and Community in Medieval Cambridge* (Cambridge, 1987), an influential, but not necessarily convincing study; and P. Slack, *Poverty and Policy in Tudor and Stuart England* (1988).

LEARNING AND LITERACY

For schools see: N. Orme, *English Schools in the Middle Ages* (1973); and J.A.H. Moran, *The Growth of English Schooling 1340–1548* (Princeton, 1985). For women and literacy see: C.M. Meale, ed., *Women and Literature in Britain, 1150–1500* (Cambridge, 1993); and M.C. Erler, *Women, Reading, and Piety in Late Medieval England* (Cambridge, 2002).

CULTURAL PRODUCTION

Invaluable are the two major Gothic art catalogues: J. Alexander and P. Binski, eds., *The Age of Chivalry: Art in Plantagenet England, 1200–1400* (1987); and R. Marks and P. Williamson, eds., *Gothic: Art for England, 1400–1547* (2003). An excellent introduction to medieval drama is R. Beadle, ed., *The Cambridge Companion to*

Medieval English Theatre (Cambridge, 1994). For glass see R. Marks, *Stained Glass in England during the Middle Ages* (1993). For a stimulating cultural study of a single manuscript see M. Camille, *Mirror in Parchment: The Luttrell Psalter and the Making of Medieval England* (1998).

INDEX